MOSSAD

MOSSAD

THE GREATEST MISSIONS OF THE ISRAELI SECRET SERVICE

MICHAEL BAR-ZOHAR AND NISSIM MISHAL

ecco

An Imprint of HarperCollins *Publishers*

HarperCollins books may be purchased for educational, business, or sales promotional use. For information please write: Special Markets Department, HarperCollins Publishers, 10 East 53rd Street, New York, NY 10022.

FIRST EDITION

Library of Congress Cataloging-in-Publication Data has been applied for.

ISBN 978-0-06-212340-4

12 13 14 15 16   OV/RRD   10 9 8 7 6 5 4 3 2 1

Dedications

For heroes unsung

For battles untold

For books unwritten

For secrets unspoken

And for a dream of peace

never abandoned, never forgotten

—Michael Bar-Zohar

To Amy Korman

For her advice,

her inspiration,

and her being my pillar of support

—Nissim Mishal

CONTENTS

INTRODUCTION

ALONE, IN THE LION'S DEN

On November 12, 2011, a tremendous explosion destroyed a secret missile base close to Tehran, killing seventeen Revolutionary Guards and reducing dozens of missiles to a heap of charred iron. General Hassan Tehrani Moghaddam, the "father" of the Shehab long-range missiles, and the man in charge of Iran's missile program, was killed in the explosion. But the secret target of the bombing was not Moghaddam. It was a solid-fuel rocket engine, able to carry a nuclear missile more than six thousand miles across the globe, from Iran's underground silos to the U.S. mainland.

The new missile planned by Iran's leaders was to bring America's major cities to their knees and transform Iran into a dominant world power. The November explosion delayed the project by several months.

Even though the target of the new long-range missile was America, the explosions that destroyed the Iranian base were probably set by the Israeli Secret Service, the Mossad. Since its inception more than sixty years ago, the Mossad has served fearlessly and secretly against the dangers threatening Israel and the West. And more so than ever before, the Mossad's intelligence gathering and operations affect American security abroad and at home.

Right now, according to foreign sources, the Mossad is challenging the blunt, explicit promise of the Iranian leadership to obliterate Israel from the map. Waging a stubborn shadow war against Iran by sabotaging nuclear facilities, assassinating scientists, supplying plants with faulty equipment and raw materials via bogus companies, organizing desertions of high-ranking military officers and major figures in nuclear research, introducing ferocious viruses into Iran's computer systems, the Mossad allegedly is fighting the threat of a nuclear-armed Iran, and what that would mean for the United States and the rest of the world. While the Mossad has delayed the Iranian nuclear bomb by several years, their covert battle is reaching its peak, before last-resort measures—a military strike—are employed.

In the fight against terrorism, the Mossad has been capturing and eliminating scores of major terrorists in their strongholds in Beirut, Damascus, Baghdad, and Tunis, and in their battle stations in Paris, Rome, Athens, and Cyprus since the 1970s. On February 12, 2008, according to the Western media, Mossad agents ambushed and killed Imad Mughniyeh, the military leader of the Hezbollah, in Damascus. Mughniyeh was a sworn enemy of Israel, but he was also number one on the FBI's Most Wanted list. He had planned and executed the massacre of 241 U.S. Marines in Beirut. He had left behind a bloody trail strewn with hundreds of Americans, Israelis, French, and Argentineans. Right now, Islamic Jihad and Al Qaeda leaders are being hunted throughout the Middle East.

And yet, when the Mossad warned the West that the Arab Spring could turn into an Arab Winter, no one seemed to listen. Throughout 2011, the West celebrated what they believed was the dawning of a new era of democracy, freedom, and human rights in the Middle East. Hoping to obtain the approval of the Egyptians, the West pressured President Mubarak, its best ally in the Arab world, to step down. But the first crowds that swept Tahrir Square in Cairo burned the American flag; then they stormed the Israeli embassy, demanded the end of the peace treaty with Israel, and arrested American NGO activists. Free elections in Egypt have brought the Muslim Brotherhood to power, and today, Egypt wavers on the brink of anarchy and economic catastrophe. A fundamentalist Islamic regime is taking root in Tunisia, with Libya likely to follow. Yemen is in turmoil. In Syria, President Assad is massacring his own people. The moderate nations like Morocco, Jordan, Saudi Arabia, and the Emirates of the Persian Gulf feel betrayed by their Western allies. And the hopes for human rights, women's rights, and democratic laws and rule that inspired these landmark revolutions have been swept away by fanatic religious parties, better organized and better connected with the masses.

This Arab Winter has turned the Middle East into a time bomb, threatening the Israeli people and its allies in the Western world. As history unfolds, the Mossad's tasks will become riskier but also more vital to the West. The Mossad appears to be the best defense against the Iranian nuclear threat, against terrorism, against whatever may evolve from the mayhem in the Middle East. Most important, the Mossad is the last salvo short of open war.

The unnamed warriors of the Mossad are its lifeblood, men and women who risk their lives, live away from their families under assumed identities, carry out daring operations in enemy countries where the slightest mistake can bring their arrest, torture, or death. During the Cold War, the worst fate for a secret agent captured in the West or the Communist bloc was to be exchanged for another agent on some cold, foggy bridge in Berlin. Russian or American, British or East German, the agent always knew he was not alone, there was always someone who would bring him back from the cold. But for the lonely warriors of the Mossad, there are no exchanges and foggy bridges; they pay with their lives for their audacity.

In this book, we bring to light the greatest missions and the most courageous heroes of the Mossad, as well as the mistakes and failures that more than once tarnished the agency's image and shook its very foundations. These missions shaped Israel's fate and, in many ways, the fate of the world. And yet, for the Mossad agents, what they all share is a deep, idealistic love of their country, a total devotion to its existence and survival, a readiness to assume the most dramatic risks and face the ultimate dangers. For the sake of Israel.

CHAPTER ONE

KING OF SHADOWS

In the late summer of 1971, a fierce storm was lashing the Mediterranean coast, and tall waves battered the shores of Gaza. The local Arab fishermen prudently stayed ashore; this was not a day to brave the treacherous sea. They watched with astonishment as a ramshackle boat suddenly emerged from the roaring waves and landed heavily on the wet sand. A few Palestinians, their clothes and *keffiyehs* rumpled and soaked, jumped out and waded ashore. Their unshaven faces showed the fatigue of a long journey at sea; but they had no time to rest, they were running for their lives. From the angry seas, an Israeli torpedo boat emerged, pursuing them at full speed, carrying soldiers in full battle attire. As it approached the shore, the soldiers jumped into the shallow waters and opened fire on the fleeing Palestinians. A couple of Gazan youngsters, playing on the beach, ran toward the Palestinians and led them to the safety of a nearby orchard; the Israeli soldiers lost track of them but continued to search the beach.

Late that night, a young Palestinian man carrying a Kalashnikov snuck into the orchard to investigate. He found the fugitives huddled together in a remote corner. "Who are you, brothers?" he asked.

"Members of the Popular Front for the Liberation of Palestine," came the answer. "From the Tyre refugee camp, in Lebanon."

"*Marhaba*, welcome," the youth said.

"You know of Abu-Seif, our commander? He sent us to meet with the Popular Front commanders in Beth Lahia (a terrorist stronghold in the south of the Gaza strip). We have money and weapons, and we want to coordinate our operations."

"I'll help you with that," the young man said.

The following morning, several armed terrorists escorted the newcomers to an isolated house inside the Jabalia refugee camp. They were led into a large room and invited to sit at a table. Soon after, the Popular Front commanders they hoped to meet walked in. They exchanged warm greetings with their Lebanese brothers, and sat, facing them.

"Can we start?" asked a stocky, balding young man wearing a red *keffiyeh*, apparently the leader of the Lebanese group. "Is everybody here?"

"Everybody."

The Lebanese raised his hand and looked at his watch. It was a prearranged signal. Suddenly, the "Lebanese envoys" drew their handguns and opened fire. In less than a minute, the Beth Lahia terrorists were dead. The "Lebanese" ran out of the house, made their way through the crooked alleys of the Jabalia camp and Gaza's crowded streets and soon crossed into Israeli territory. That evening, the man with the red *keffiyeh*, Captain Meir Dagan, commander of the Israeli Defense Forces' (IDF) secret Rimon commando unit, reported to General Ariel (Arik) Sharon that Operation Chameleon had been a success. All the leaders of the Popular Front in Beth Lahia, a lethal terrorist group, had been killed.

Dagan was only twenty-six, but already a legendary fighter. He had planned the entire operation: posing as Lebanese terrorists; sailing in an old vessel from Ashdod, a port in Israel; the long night of hiding; the meeting with the terrorist leaders; and the escape route after the hit. He had even organized the fake pursuit by the Israeli torpedo boat. Dagan was the ultimate guerrilla, bold and creative, not someone who stuck to the rules of engagement. Yitzhak Rabin once said: "Meir has the unique capacity to invent antiterrorist operations that look like movie thrillers."

Future Mossad chief Danny Yatom remembered Dagan as a stocky youngster with a mane of brown hair, who had applied to join the most prestigious Israeli commando unit, Sayeret Matkal, and amazed everybody with his knife-throwing skills. With his huge commando knife, he could hit dead-on any target he chose. Although he was an excellent marksman, he failed the Sayeret Matkal tests and initially had to content himself with the silver wings of a paratrooper.

In the early seventies, he was sent to the Gaza strip, which had been conquered by Israel in the 1967 Six-Day War and had since become a hornet's nest of deadly terrorist activity. The Palestinian terrorists murdered Israelis daily in the Gaza strip and in Israel with bombs, explosives, and firearms; the IDF had all but lost their control over the violent refugee camps. On January 2, 1971, when the sweet Arroyo children, the five-year-old Avigail and the eight-year-old Mark, were blown to pieces when a terrorist threw a hand grenade into their car, General Ariel (Arik) Sharon decided he had to put an end to the bloody massacre. He recruited a few old friends from his battle-scarred youth, along with several talented younger soldiers. Dagan was one, a round-faced, short, sturdy officer who walked with a limp—he stepped on a land mine in the Six-Day War. While recuperating in the Soroka Hospital in Beer-Sheva, he had fallen in love with his nurse, Bina. They married when he recovered.

Sharon's unit officially did not exist. Its mission was to destroy the terrorist organizations in Gaza using risky and unconventional methods. Dagan used to wander occupied Gaza with a cane, a Doberman, several pistols, revolvers, and submachine guns. Some claimed to have seen him disguised as an Arab, leisurely riding a donkey in the treacherous Gaza alleys. His infirmity didn't cool his determination to carry out the most dangerous operations. His views were simple. There are enemies, bad Arabs who want to kill us, so we have to kill them first.

Within the unit, Dagan created "Rimon," the first undercover Israeli commando unit, which operated in Arab disguise deep in enemy strong-holds. In order to move freely in Arab crowds and reach their targets un-detected, they had to operate in disguise. They quickly became known as "Arik's hit team" and rumors had it that they often killed captured terror-ists in cold blood. Sometimes, it was said, they escorted a terrorist to a dark alley, and told him: "You've got two minutes to escape"; when he tried, they shot him dead. Sometimes they would leave behind a dagger or a gun, and when the terrorist reached for it, he would be killed on the spot. Journal-ists wrote that, every morning, Dagan would go out to the fields, use one hand for peeing and the other for shooting at an empty Coke can. Dagan dismissed such reports. "There are myths that stick to all of us," he said, "but some of what's written is simply false."

The tiny unit of Israeli commandos were fighting a tough, cruel war, risking their lives daily. Almost every night Dagan's people donned wom-en's or fishermen's disguises and went in search of known terrorists. In mid-January 1971, posing as Arab terrorists in the north of the Strip, they lured Fatah members into an ambush, and in the gunfight that erupted, the Fatah terrorists were killed. On January 29, 1971, this time in uniform, Dagan and his men traveled in two jeeps to the outskirts of the Jabalia camp (a Palestinian refugee camp). Their paths crossed with a taxi, and Dagan recognized, among its passengers, a notorious terrorist, Abu Nimer. He ordered the jeeps to stop and his soldiers surrounded the cab. Dagan ap-proached, and at that moment Abu Nimer stepped out, brandishing a hand grenade. Staring at Dagan, he pulled its pin. "Grenade!" Dagan shouted, but instead of scrambling for cover, he jumped on the man, pinned him, and tore the grenade from his hand. For that action he was awarded the Medal of Courage. It's been claimed that after tossing away the grenade, Dagan killed Abu Nimer with his bare hands.

Years later, in a rare interview with Israeli journalist Ron Leshem, Dagan said: "Rimon wasn't a hit team . . . It was not the Wild West, where everybody was trigger-happy. We never harmed women and children . . . We attacked people who were violent murderers. We hit them and deterred others. To protect civilians, the state needs sometimes to do things that are contrary to democratic behavior. It is true that in units like ours the outer limits can become blurred. That's why you must be sure that your people are of the best quality. The dirtiest actions should be carried out by the most honest men.

emocratic or not—Sharon, Dagan, and their colleagues largely annihilated terrorism in Gaza, and for years the area became quiet and peaceful. But some maintain that Sharon half-jokingly said of his loyal aide: "Meir's specialty is to separate the head of an Arab from his body."

Yet very few knew the real Dagan. He was born Meir Huberman in 1945 in a train car, on the outskirts of Herson, in the Ukraine, while his family was escaping from Siberia to Poland. Most of his family had perished in the Holocaust. Meir immigrated to Israel with his parents and grew up in a poor neighborhood in Lod, an old Arab town about fifteen miles south of Tel Aviv. Many knew him as an indomitable fighter; few were aware of his secret passions: an avid reader of history books, a vegetarian, he loved classical music and pursued painting and sculpting as hobbies.

He was a man haunted from an early age by the terrible suffering of his family and the Jews during the Holocaust. He dedicated his life to the defense of the newborn State of Israel. As he climbed the army hierarchy, the first thing he did in every new office he was assigned to was to hang on the wall a large photo of an old Jew, wrapped in his prayer shawl, kneeling in front of two SS officers, one holding a bat and the other a gun. "This old man is my grandfather," Dagan would tell visitors. "I look at the picture, and I know that we must be strong and defend ourselves so that the Holocaust never happens again."

The old man, indeed, was Dagan's grandfather, Ber Ehrlich Slushni, who was murdered in Lukov a few seconds after the photograph was taken.

During the Yom Kippur War, in 1973, Dagan was among the first Israelis to cross the Suez Canal in a reconnaissance unit. In the 1982 Lebanon War, he entered Beirut at the head of his armored brigade. He soon became the commander of the South Lebanon security zone, and there the adventurous guerrilla fighter reemerged from the starched colonel's uniform. He resurrected the principles of secrecy, camouflage, and deception of his Gaza days. His soldiers came up with a new name for their secretive chief. They called him "King of Shadows." Life in Lebanon, with its secret alliances, betrayals, cruelty, phantom wars, was a place after his own heart. "Even before my tank brigade entered Beirut," he said, "I knew this city well." And after the Lebanon war ended, he did not give up his secret adventures. In 1984 he was officially reprimanded by Chief of Staff Moshe Levy for hanging out, dressed as an Arab, by the Bahamdoun terrorist headquarters.

During the Intifada (the Palestinian rebellion of 1987–1993), when he was transferred to the West Bank as an adviser to Chief of Staff Ehud Barak, Dagan resumed his old habits and even convinced Barak to join him. The two of them donned sweat suits, as befit true Palestinians, found a baby-blue Mercedes with local plates, and went for a ride in the treacherous Nablus Kasbah. On their return, they scared and then astonished the Military Headquarters sentries, once the latter recognized who was sitting in the front seat.

In 1995, Dagan, now a major general, left the army and joined his buddy Yossi Ben-Hanan on an eighteen-month motorcycle journey across the Asian plains. Their trip was cut short by the news of Yitzhak Rabin's assassination. Back in Israel, Dagan spent some time at the head of the antiterrorist authority, made a halfhearted attempt to join the business world, and helped Sharon in his Likud electoral campaign. Then, in 2002, he retired to his country home in Galilee, to his books, his records, his palette, and his sculptor's chisel.

Thirty years after Gaza, a retired general, he was now getting acquainted with his family—"I suddenly woke up and my kids were grown-ups already"—when he got a phone call from his old buddy, now prime minister, Arik Sharon. "I want you at the head of the Mossad," Sharon said to his fifty-seven-year-old friend. "I need a Mossad chief with a dagger between his teeth."

It was 2002 and the Mossad was losing steam. Several failures in the preceding years had dealt severe blows to its prestige; the much-publicized failure to assassinate a major Hamas leader in Amman and the capture of

Israeli agents in Switzerland, Cyprus, and New Zealand had seriously damaged the Mossad's reputation. The last head of the Mossad, Efraim Halevy, didn't live up to expectations. A former ambassador to the European Union in Brussels, he was a good diplomat and a good analyst, but not a leader and not a fighter. Sharon wanted to have at the head of the Mossad a bold, creative leader who would be a formidable weapon against Islamic terrorism and the Iranian reactor.

Dagan was not welcomed at the Mossad. An outsider, focused mostly on operations, he didn't care very much about learned intelligence analyses or secret diplomatic exchanges. Several top Mossad officers resigned in protest, but Dagan didn't much care. He rebuilt the operational units, established close working relations with foreign secret services, and busied himself with the Iranian threat. When the second, disastrous Lebanon War erupted in 2006, he was the only Israeli leader who objected to the strategy based on massive bombardments by the air force. He believed in a land offensive, doubted the air force could win the war, and came out of the war unblemished.

Still, he was much criticized by the press for his tough attitude toward his subordinates. Frustrated Mossad officers, who were retired, ran to the media with their gripes, and Dagan was under constant fire. "Dagan Who?" scribbled one popular columnist.

And then, one day, the headlines changed. Flattering articles loaded with superlatives filled the daily papers, lauding "the man who restored honor to the Mossad."

Under Dagan's control, the Mossad had accomplished the heretofore unimaginable: the assassination of Hezbollah's mad killer Imad Mughniyeh in Damascus, the destruction of the Syrian nuclear reactor, the liquidation of key terrorist leaders in Lebanon and Syria, and, most remarkable of all, a relentless, ruthless, and successful campaign against Iran's secret nuclear weapons program.

CHAPTER TWO

FUNERALS IN TEHRAN

On July 23, 2011, at four thirty P.M., two gunmen on motorcycles emerged on Bani Hashem Street in South Tehran, drew automatic weapons out of their leather jackets, and shot a man who was about to enter his home. They vanished after the killing, long before the arrival of the police. The victim was Darioush Rezaei Najad, a thirty-five-year-old physics professor and a major figure in Iran's secret nuclear weapons program. He had been in charge of developing the electronic switches necessary for activating a nuclear warhead.

Rezaei Najad was not the first Iranian scientist who had recently met a violent end. Officially, Iran was developing nuclear technology for peaceful purposes, and they claimed that the Bushehr reactor, an important source of energy built with Russian help, was proof of their good intentions. But in addition to the Bushehr reactor, other clandestine nuclear facilities had been discovered, all heavily guarded and virtually inaccessible. Over time, Iran had to admit the existence of some of these centers, though they denied allegations of developing weapons. But by then, Western secret services and local underground organizations had exposed several major scientists in Iran's universities who had been tapped to build Iran's first nuclear bomb. In Iran, what could only be identified as "unknown parties" waged a brutal war to stop the secret nuclear weapons program.

On November 29, 2010, at seven forty-five A.M., in North Tehran, a motorcycle emerged from behind the car of Dr. Majid Shahriyari, the scientific head of Iran's nuclear project. As he passed the car, the helmeted motorcyclist attached a device to the car's rear windshield. Seconds later, the device exploded, killing the forty-five-year-old physicist and wounding his wife. Simultaneously, in Atashi Street in South Tehran, another motorcyclist did the same to the Peugeot 206 of Dr. Fereydoun Abassi-Davani, another major nuclear scientist. The explosion wounded Abassi-Davani and his wife.

The Iranian government immediately pointed its finger at the Mossad. The roles these two scientists played in Iran's atomic weapons project were veiled in secrecy, but Ali Akbar Salehi, the head of the project, declared that the attack had made a martyr of Shahriyari and deprived his team of its "dearest flower."

President Ahmadinejad, too, expressed his appreciation of the two victims, in an ingenious way: as soon as Abassi-Davani recovered from his wounds, Ahmadinejad appointed him Iran's vice president.

The men who attacked the scientists were not found.

On January 12, 2010, at seven fifty A.M., Professor Masoud Ali Mohammadi came out of his home at Shariati Street, in the Gheytarihe neighborhood in North Tehran. He was on his way to his lab at the Sharif University of Technology.

When he tried to unlock his car, a huge explosion rocked the quiet neighborhood. The security forces that rushed to the scene found Mohammadi's car shattered by the blast and his body blown to pieces. He had been killed by an explosive charge, concealed in a motorcycle that was parked by his car. The Iranian media claimed that the assassination had been carried out by Mossad agents. President Ahmadinejad declared that "the assassination reminds us of the Zionist methods."

Fifty-year-old Professor Mohammadi was an expert in quantum physics and an adviser to the Iranian nuclear weapons program. European media reported he had been a member of the Revolutionary Guards, the pro-government parallel army. But Mohammadi's life, like his death, was shrouded in mystery. Several of his friends maintained that he was involved only in theoretical research, never with military projects; some also claimed that he supported the dissident movements and had participated in antigovernment protests.

Yet it turned out that about half of those present at his funeral were Revolutionary Guards. His coffin was carried by Revolutionary Guard officers. Subsequent investigations ultimately confirmed that Mohammadi, indeed, had been deeply involved in advancing Iran's nuclear ambitions.

In January 2007, Dr. Ardashir Hosseinpour was allegedly killed by Mossad agents with radioactive poison. News of the assassination ran in the *Sunday Times* in London, citing information from the Texas-based Stratfor strategy and intelligence think tank. Iranian officials ridiculed the report, claiming that the Mossad could never carry out such an operation inside Iran, and that "Professor Hosseinpour suffocated by inhaling fumes during a fire in his home." They also insisted that the forty-four-year-old professor was only a renowned electromagnetic expert and not involved with Iran's nuclear endeavors in any way.

But it turned out that Hosseinpour worked at an Isfahan secret installation where raw uranium was converted into gas. This gas was then used for uranium enrichment by a series ("cascades") of centrifuges in Natanz, a faraway, fortified underground installation. In 2006, Hosseinpour was awarded the highest Iranian prize for science and technology; two years earlier, he had been awarded his country's highest distinction for military research.

The assassinations of Iranian nuclear scientists were just one front in a much larger war. According to the *Daily Telegraph* in London, Dagan's Mossad had rolled out an assault force of double agents, hit teams, saboteurs, and front companies and brought their strength to bear over years and years of covert operations against Iran's nuclear weapons program.

Stratfor's director of analysis, Reva Bhalla, was quoted as saying: "With cooperation from the United States, Israeli covert operations have focused both on eliminating key human assets involved in the nuclear program and in sabotaging the Iranian supply chain." Israel, she claimed, had used similar tactics in Iraq in the early eighties, when the Mossad killed three Iraqi nuclear scientists, thus hampering the completion of the Osiraq atomic reactor, near Baghdad.

In its purported war against the Iranian nuclear program, Dagan's Mossad was effectively delaying the development of an Iranian nuclear bomb for as long as possible, and thereby thwarting the worst danger to Israel's existence since its creation: Ahmadinejad's threats that Israel should be annihilated.

Yet these small victories cannot atone for the worst mishap in Mossad's history—its failure to expose Iran's secret nuclear project at its outset. For several years now Iran had been building its nuclear might—and Israel had no clue. Iran invested huge sums of money, recruited scientists, built secret bases, carried out sophisticated tests—and Israel had no idea. From the moment Khomeini's Iran decided to become a nuclear power, it used deception, ruses, and stratagems that made fools out of the Western secret services, the Mossad included.

Iran's shah, Reza Pahlavi, started building two nuclear reactors, both for peaceful and military purposes. The shah's project, begun in the 1970s, didn't cause any alarm in Israel; at the time, Israel was Iran's close ally. In 1977, General Ezer Weizman, Israel's defense minister, hosted General Hasan Toufanian, who was in charge of modernizing Iran's army, in the Ministry of Defense in Tel Aviv—as allies, Israel supplied Iran with modern military equipment. According to the minutes of their confidential meeting, Weizman offered to supply Iran with state-of-the-art surface-to-surface missiles, while the director general of the ministry, Dr. Pinhas Zusman, impressed Toufanian by saying that the Israeli missiles could be adapted to carry nuclear warheads. But before the officials could act on their plans, the Iranian revolution transformed Israeli-Iranian relations. The revolutionary Islamic government massacred the shah's supporters and turned against

Israel. The ailing shah escaped from his country as it fell under Ayatollah Khomeini's control and into the hands of his loyal mullahs.

Khomeini put an immediate end to the nuclear project, which he considered "anti-Islamic." The building of the reactors was stopped and their equipment dismantled. But in the 1980s, a bloody war erupted between Iraq and Iran. Saddam Hussein used poison gas against the Iranians. The use of nonconventional weapons by their vilest enemy made the ayatollahs rethink their policy. Even before Khomeini's death, his heir apparent, Ali Khamenei, instructed his military to develop new weapons—biological, chemical, and nuclear—to fight back against the weapons of mass destruction that Iraq had unleashed on Iran. Soon after, complacent religious leaders called from their pulpits to discard the ban on "anti-Islamic" weapons.

Fragmentary news about Iran's efforts started spreading in the mid-eighties. With the collapse of the Soviet Union in 1989, Europe was inundated by rumors about Iran's attempts to buy nuclear bombs and warheads from unemployed officers or famished scientists in the former Soviet military establishment. The Western press described, in dramatic detail, the disappearance of Russian scientists and generals from their homes, apparently recruited by the Iranians. Reporters with fertile imaginations wrote about sealed trucks rushing eastward from Europe, bypassing border controls to reach the Middle East. Sources in Tehran, Moscow, and Beijing revealed that Iran had signed an agreement with Russia for building an atomic reactor in Bushehr, on the Persian Gulf coast, and another agreement with China, for building two smaller reactors.

Alarmed, the United States and Israel spread teams of special agents through Europe on the hunt for the Soviet bombs sold to Iran and the recruited scientists. They came up with nothing. The United States put great pressure on Russia and China to cancel their agreements with Iran. China backed off, and canceled its Iranian deal. Russia decided to go ahead but kept delaying it. The reactor took more than twenty years to build and was limited in its use by strict Russian and international controls.

But Israel and the United States should have expanded their search when the leads went cold. The heads of both the Mossad and the CIA failed to realize that the Russian and Chinese reactors were just diversions, a smoke screen for "the world's best secret services." Iran had surreptitiously launched a mammoth project intended to make it a nuclear power.

In the fall of 1987, a secret meeting was held in Dubai. Eight men met in a small, dusty office: three Iranians, two Pakistanis, and three European experts (two of them German) who were working for Iran.

The representatives of Iran and Pakistan signed a confidential agreement. A large sum of money was transferred to the Pakistanis, or—more precisely—to Dr. Abdul Qadeer Khan, the head of Pakistan's official nuclear weapons program.

A few years before, Pakistan had launched its own nuclear project, to achieve military equality with its archenemy, India. Dr. Khan badly needed the fissile substances necessary for assembling a nuclear bomb. Yet he chose not to make use of plutonium, which is harvested in the classic nuclear reactors, but to utilize enriched uranium. Mined uranium ore contains only 1 percent of uranium-235, which is vital for the production of nuclear weapons, and 99 percent uranium-238, which is useless. Dr. Khan developed a method for converting the natural uranium into gas, and feeding this gas into a line of centrifuges connected in a chain, called a cascade. With the centrifuges churning the uranium gas at a mind-boggling rate of 100,000 spins a minute, the lighter uranium-235 separates from the heavier uranium-238. By repeating that process thousands of times, the centrifuges produce an enriched uranium-235. This gas, when converted into solid matter, becomes the substance needed for a nuclear bomb.

Khan had stolen the centrifuges' blueprints from Eurenco, a European company where he worked in the early 1970s, and then started manufacturing his own in Pakistan. Khan soon turned into a "merchant of death," selling his methods, formulas, and centrifuges. Iran became his major client. Libya and North Korea were also clients.

The Iranians bought centrifuges elsewhere, too, and then learned how to make them locally. Huge shipments of uranium, centrifuges, electronic materials, and spare parts arrived in Iran now and then. Large facilities were built for the treatment of raw uranium, for storing the centrifuges, and for converting the gas back to solid matter; Iranian scientists traveled to Pakistan and Pakistani experts arrived in Iran—and nobody knew.

The Iranians were careful not to put all their eggs in one basket. They dispersed the nuclear project among places spread throughout their country, in military bases, disguised laboratories, and remote facilities. Some were built deep underground, and surrounded with batteries of surface-to-air missiles. One plant was erected in Isfahan, another in Arak; the most important—the centrifuge facility—was established in Natanz, and a fourth center in the holy city of Qom. At even a hint that a location might be exposed, the Iranians would move the nuclear installations elsewhere, even removing layers of earth that could have been irradiated by radioactive substances. They also skillfully misled and deceived the inspectors of the International Atomic Energy Agency. Its chairman, the Egyptian Dr. Mohamed El-Baradei, behaved as if he believed every false statement of the Iranians, and published complacent reports that enabled Iran to continue with its deadly scheme.

On June 1, 1998, the American authorities saw the true extent of the Iranians' work for the first time. A Pakistani defector appeared before FBI investigators in New York, asking for political asylum. He introduced himself as Dr. Iftikhar Khan Chaudhry and revealed the full extent of the secret cooperation between Iran and Pakistan. He exposed Dr. Khan, described meetings in which he had participated, and named Pakistani experts who had taken part in the Iranian project.

The facts and figures of Chaudhry's testimony were checked by the FBI and found to be accurate. The FBI indeed recommended that Chaudhry be allowed to stay in the United States as a political refugee—but his amazing testimony was never given any follow-up. Perhaps out of sheer negligence, American higher-ups buried Chaudhry's transcripts, initiated no action, and did not warn Israel. Four more years had to pass until the truth about Iran would come to light.

Suddenly, in August 2002, the Iranian dissident underground, Mujahedeen el Khalq (MEK), revealed the existence of two nuclear facilities in Arak and Natanz to the world media. In the following years, MEK kept disclosing more facts about the Iranian nuclear project, which aroused some suspicion that its information came from outside sources. The CIA was still skeptical and assumed that the Israelis and the British were trying to involve the United States in hazardous operations. Specifically, the CIA appeared to believe that the Mossad and the British MI6 were feeding MEK intelligence they had obtained, using the Iranian opposition as a hopefully credible source. According to Israeli sources, it was, in fact, a watchful Mossad officer who had discovered the mammoth centrifuge installation at Natanz, deep in the desert. That same year, 2002, the Iranian underground handed over to the CIA a laptop loaded with documents. The dissidents wouldn't say how they had got hold of the laptop; the skeptical Americans suspected that the documents had been only recently scanned into the computer; they accused the Mossad of having slipped in some information obtained from their own sources—and then passing it to the MEK leaders for delivery to the West.

But other evidence now was piling up on the desks of the Americans and the Europeans, who finally had to open their eyes. The rumors about Dr. Khan's lucrative and deadly trade spread all over the world. Finally, on February 4, 2004, a tearful Dr. Khan appeared on Pakistani TV and confessed that he indeed had sold know-how, expertise, and centrifuges to Libya, North Korea, and Iran, making millions in the process. The Pakistani government hastened to grant full pardon to "Dr. Death," the father of their nuclear bomb.

Israel now became a major source of information about Iran. Meir Dagan and his Mossad provided U.S. intelligence with fresh data about the secret facility the Iranians had built at Qom; Israel allegedly was also involved in the defection of several senior officers from the Revolutionary Guards and the atomic project; the Mossad provided several countries with up-to-date facts, prompting them to seize ships carrying nuclear equipment to Iran from their ports.

But merely obtaining such intelligence would not suffice for Israel. While a fanatic Iran threatened it openly with annihilation, the rest of the world recoiled from any vigorous action. Israel was left with no choice but to launch an all-out undercover war against the Iranian nuclear program.

After sixteen years of colossal ignorance by his predecessors, Dagan decided to act.

In January 2006, a plane crashed in central Iran. All its passengers perished. Among them were senior officers in the Revolutionary Guards, including Ahmed Kazami, one of their commanders. The Iranians maintained that the crash was due to bad weather, but the Stratfor group hinted that the aircraft had been sabotaged by Western agents.

Only a month before, a military cargo plane had crashed into an apartment building in Tehran. All ninety-four passengers died. Many were also officers in the Revolutionary Guards and influential pro-regime journalists. In November 2006, another military aircraft crashed during takeoff from Tehran—and thirty-six Revolutionary Guards were killed. On national radio, the Iranian minister of defense declared, "According to material from intelligence sources, we can say that American, British, and Israeli agents are responsible for these plane crashes."

Meanwhile, quietly, without any overt mention, Dagan had become the main strategist on Israel's policy toward Iran. He believed that Israel perhaps might have no choice but to finally launch a full-scale, all-out attack on Iran. But such an action, Dagan thought, should only be a last resort.

The sabotage began in February 2005. The international press reported an explosion in a nuclear facility at Dialem that had been hit by a missile fired from an unidentified plane. And that same month an explosion took place close to Bushehr, in a pipeline supplying gas to the Russian-built nuclear reactor.

Another facility to be attacked was the test site Parchin, close to Tehran. There, Iranian experts were developing "the explosive lens," the mechanism that would transform the bomb core into a critical mass and trigger the chain reaction for an atomic explosion. The Iranian underground claimed that the explosion at Parchin had caused major damage to the secret labs.

In April 2006, the Holy of Holies—the central installation in Natanz—was the scene of a festive assembly. A large crowd of scientists, technicians, and the heads of the nuclear project gathered underground, where thousands of centrifuges were churning around the clock. In a celebratory mood, they came to watch the first test of activating a new centrifuge cascade. Everyone waited for the dramatic moment when the centrifuges would be started. The chief engineer pressed the activation button—and a powerful explosion shook the huge chamber. The pipes blew up in a deafening blast, and the entire cascade shattered.

Furious, the heads of the nuclear project ordered a thorough investigation. "Unknown persons" apparently had planted faulty parts in the equipment. CBS reported that the centrifuges had been destroyed by tiny explosive charges attached to them shortly before the test. It also claimed that Israeli intelligence had assisted American agents in causing the Natanz explosion.

In January 2007, again, the centrifuges became the target of a sophisticated sabotage. The Western secret services had established Eastern European front companies that manufactured insulation material used in the ducts between the centrifuges. The Iranians couldn't buy theirs on the open market, because of the limitations imposed on them by the UN; so they turned to bogus Eastern European companies run by Russian and Iranian exiles, who were secretly working for the Western intelligence agencies. Only after the insulation was installed did the Iranians find that it was defective and couldn't be used.

By May 2007, President George W. Bush had signed a secret presidential order authorizing the CIA to initiate covert operations to delay Iran's nuclear project. Soon after, a decision was made by some Western secret services to sabotage the supply chain of parts, equipment, and raw materials for the project. In August, Dagan met with U.S. Undersecretary of State Nicolas Burns to discuss his strategy toward Iran.

Mishaps, sabotage, explosions have kept occurring in installations throughout Iran during the last seven years. One mysterious hitch caused problems in the cooling system of the Bushehr reactor, which delayed its completion by two years; in May 2008, an explosion in a cosmetics plant in Arak caused significant damage to the adjacent nuclear facility; another explosion devastated a high-security compound in Isfahan, where uranium was being converted to gas.

In 2008 and in 2010, the *New York Times* revealed that the Tinners, a Swiss family of engineers, had helped the CIA in exposing the nuclear programs of Libya and Iran, and were paid $10 million by the agency. The CIA also helped protect them from prosecution by the Swiss authorities for illegal traffic with nuclear components. The father, Frederic Tinner, and his two sons, Urs and Marco, had sold the Iranians a faulty installation for electric supply to the Natanz facility, which destroyed fifty centrifuges. The Tinners purchased pressure pumps from the Pfeiffer Vacuum Company in Germany, had them doctored in New Mexico, and then sold them to the Iranians.

Time magazine asserted that the Mossad was involved in the hijacking of the ship *Arctic Sea*, which had sailed from Finland to Algeria with a Russian crew and under a Maltese flag, carrying "a cargo of wood." On July 24, 2009, two days after setting out on her voyage, the vessel was seized by eight hijackers. Only after a month did the Russian authorities declare that a Russian commando unit had taken over the ship. The London *Times* and the *Daily Telegraph* maintained that the Mossad had sounded the alarm. Dagan's men, they said, had informed the Russians that the ship was carrying a cargo of uranium, sold to the Iranians by a former Russian officer. But Admiral Kouts, who leads the fight against piracy in the European Union, offered *Time* magazine his own version. The only plausible explanation, he said, was that the ship had been hijacked by the Mossad to intercept the uranium.

But in spite of these continuous attacks, the Iranians did not remain idle. Between 2005 and 2008, in total secrecy, they built a new installation close to Qom. They planned to install three thousand centrifuges in the new underground halls. However, in mid-2009, the Iranians realized that the intelligence organizations of the United States, Britain, and Israel had full knowledge of the Qom plant. Iran reacted right away. In September 2009, Tehran surprised the world by hurriedly informing the IAEA about the existence of the Qom installation. Some sources claimed that the Iranians had caught a Western spy (possibly a British MI6 agent), who had gathered reliable information about Qom; so they disclosed its existence to diminish their embarrassment.

A month later, CIA director Leon Panetta told *Time* that his organization had known of Qom for three years and that Israel was involved in its detection.

The Qom discovery permitted a glimpse into the secret alliance that had been forged between three groups engaged in the battle against Iran: the CIA, MI6, and the Mossad. According to French sources, the three services were acting together, with the Mossad carrying out the operations inside Iran, and the CIA and MI6 helping the Israelis. The Mossad was responsible for several explosions in October 2010, in which eighteen Iranian technicians were killed at a plant in the Zagros Mountains that assembled Shehab missiles. With the help of its British and American allies, the Mossad had also eliminated five nuclear scientists.

This alliance had been established largely by the efforts of Meir Dagan. From the moment he became the director of Mossad, he had been pressuring his men to establish close cooperation with foreign secret services. His aides advised him against revealing the Mossad secrets to foreigners, but he brushed off their arguments. "Stop this nonsense," he grumbled, "and go, work with them!"

Beside the British and the Americans, Dagan had another important ally who brought precious information from inside Iran: the leaders of the Iranian resistance. In unusual press conferences held outside of Iran, leaders of the Iranian National Council of Resistance revealed the name of the leading scientist in the Iranian project. His identity had so far been kept secret. Mohsen Fakhri Zadeh, forty-nine years old, was a physics professor at the Tehran University. He was said to be a mysterious, elusive man. The resistance disclosed many details about him, including his member-

ship in the Revolutionary Guards since the age of eighteen, his address—
Shahid Mahallalti Street, Tehran—his passport numbers—0009228 and
4229533—and even his home phone number—021-2448413. Fakhri
Zadeh specialized in the complex process of creating a critical mass inside
the atomic device to trigger the chain reaction and the nuclear explosion.
His team was also working on the miniaturization of the bomb, to fit it in
the warhead of the Shehab missile.

Following these revelations, Zadeh was denied entry into the United
States and the EU, and his bank accounts in the West were frozen. The resistance described in detail all his functions, disclosed the names of the scientists working with him and even the location of his secret laboratories. This
abundance of detail and means of transmission leads one to believe that,
again, "a certain secret service" ever suspected by the West of pursuing its
own agenda, painstakingly collected these facts and figures about the Iranian scientist and passed them to the Iranian resistance, which conveyed
them to the West. His exposure was meant to warn him that he might be
"the next in line" for assassination and inspire him to either scramble for
cover or choose the better solution: to defect to the West.

General Ali Reza Asgari, a former Iranian deputy minister of defense,
vanished in February 2007 while traveling to Istanbul. He had been
deeply involved in the nuclear project. The Iranian services searched for
him all over the world but couldn't find him. Almost four years later, in
January 2011, Iran's foreign minister, Ali Akbar Salehi, turned to the UN
secretary general and accused the Mossad of abducting him and jailing
him in Israel.

But according to the *Sunday Telegraph* in London, Asgari had defected
to the West; the Mossad had planned his defection and had taken care of
his protection in Turkey. Other sources maintain that he had been later
debriefed by the CIA and supplied them with valuable information about
Iran's nuclear program.

A month after Asgari's disappearance—in March 2007—another senior
Iranian officer vanished. Amir Shirazi served in the "Al Quds" unit, the

elite force of the Revolutionary Guards, charged with secret operations be-yond Iran's border. An Iranian source revealed to the London *Times* that besides the disappearances of Asgari and Shirazi, another high-ranking of-ficer had vanished: the Revolutionary Guards commander in the Persian Gulf, Mohammad Soltani.

In July 2009, the nuclear scientist Shahram Amiri joined the list of de-fectors. Amiri, who was employed at Qom, disappeared in Saudi Arabia during a pilgrimage to Mecca. The Iranians demanded that the Saudis find out what had happened to him. Amiri surfaced a few months later in the United States, was thoroughly debriefed, got $5 million, a new identity, and a new home in Arizona. CIA sources disclosed he had been an informer to Western intelligence for years and had supplied them with "original and substantive" intelligence. Amiri revealed that the Malek-Ashtar University of Technology, where he had taught, served as an academic cover for a research unit designing the warheads for the Iranian long-range missiles; Fakhri Zadeh headed that university.

After a year in America, Amiri changed his mind and decided to go back to Iran. He supposedly couldn't cope with the stress of his new life. In a homemade video, shown on the Internet, he claimed he had been ab-ducted by the CIA; a few hours later, he posted another video, disclaiming the first, and then produced a third video, disclaiming the second. He got in touch with the Pakistani embassy, which represented Iranian interests in the United States, and asked to be sent back to Iran. The Pakistanis helped; in July 2010, Amiri landed in Tehran. He appeared at a press conference, accused the CIA of kidnapping and mistreating him—and disappeared. Observers accused the CIA of failure, but a CIA spokesman cracked: "We got important information and the Iranians got Amiri; well, who got a bet-ter deal?"

But the Iranians were not without resources against the Mossad. In December 2004, Iran had arrested ten suspects for spying for Israel and the United States; three worked inside the nuclear installations. In 2008, the Iranians announced that they had dismantled another Mossad cell:

three Iranian citizens who had been trained by the Mossad to use so-phisticated communications equipment, weapons, and explosives. In November 2008, they hanged forty-three-year-old Ali Ashtari, who was found guilty of spying for Israel. In the course of his trial, he admitted meeting three Mossad agents in Europe. They were said to have given him money and electronic equipment. "The Mossad people wanted me to sell earmarked shipments of computers and electronic equipment to the Iranian intelligence services and to plant listening devices in com-munications instruments that I sold," Ashtari testified.

On December 28, 2010, in the grim courtyard of Evin prison in Teh-ran, Iranian officers hanged another spy, Ali-Akbar Siadat, who had been found guilty of working for the Mossad and supplying it with information about Iran's military capabilities and the missile program operated by the Revolutionary Guards. For the previous six years, Siadat had been meeting with Israeli agents in Turkey, Thailand, and the Netherlands, and receiving payments of $3,000 to $7,000 for each meeting. Iranian officials promised that more arrests and executions would follow.

But 2010 was the year of the greatest setback for the Iranian nuclear project. Was it because of the lack of high-quality spare parts for the Iranian equipment? Because of the faulty parts and metals that Mossad's bogus companies sold to the Iranians? Because of planes crashing, laboratories set on fire, explosions in the missile and nuclear installations, defection of senior officials, deaths of top scientists, revolts and upheaval among the minorities' groups—all those events and phenomena that Iran (correctly and incorrectly) attributed to Dagan's people?

Or was it because of Dagan's last "major coup," according to the Eu-ropean press? In the summer of 2010, thousands of computers control-ling the Iranian nuclear project were infected with the perfidious Stuxnet virus. Labeled one of the most sophisticated in the world, Stuxnet struck computers controlling the Natanz centrifuges and wreaked havoc. Its com-plexity left no doubt that it was the product of a large team of experts and considerable funds. One of the virus's distinctive features was that it could be targeted to a specific system, causing no harm to others en route. Its presence in a computer was also difficult to detect. Once in the Iranian system, it could modify the speed of rotation of a centrifuge, making its product useless, without anyone being aware of it. Observers spoke of two countries as having the ability to carry out such cyberattacks: the United States and Israel.

President Ahmadinejad tried to downplay the effect Stuxnet had had, and declared that Iran had the situation well in hand. The truth, though, was that at the beginning of 2011, about half of Iran's centrifuges were immobilized.

Dagan's people allegedly delayed Iran's nuclear weapons program with their incessant attacks on so many fronts over so many years: diplomatic pressure and sanctions imposed by the UN Security Council; counter-proliferation—keeping the Iranians from getting the materials needed to produce a bomb; economical warfare—prohibiting the banks in the free world from doing business with Iran; regime change, by supporting and fomenting political unrest and by fanning the ethnic divisions inside Iran, where Kurds, Azeris, Beloshis, Arabs, and Turkmen constitute 50 percent of the population; and most immediately, covert measures, black and special operations against the Iranian project.

But they couldn't permanently stop it, no matter how good they were, nor how much cooperation they had. "Dagan is the ultimate James Bond," a high-placed Israeli analyst said, but even James Bond couldn't save the world in this case. At best, he could slow down the Iranians. Only an Iranian government decision or a massive attack from abroad can put an end to the Iranian dream of creating a formidable nuclear giant where the Persian Empire once stood.

And yet, when Dagan was appointed *ramsad* (the abbreviation for *rosh hamossad*—head of the Mossad), experts predicted that Iran would reach nuclear capacity in 2005; the date was later moved ahead to 2007, 2009, 2011. And when Dagan left office on January 6, 2011, he had a message for his country: Iran's project has been delayed at least until 2015. He therefore recommended a continuation of the same actions, so effective in the last eight years, and a freeze of any military attack on Iran. Only when the dagger blade starts cutting into our flesh, he said, should we attack; that dagger blade remains four years away.

Dagan served as *ramsad* eight and a half years—more than most Mossad directors. He was replaced by Tamir Pardo, a veteran Mossad officer who started his operational career as a close aide to Yoni Netanyahu, the hero of the 1976 Israeli raid in Entebbe, and later distinguished himself as a daring agent, an expert in new technologies, and a creative planner of unusual operations.

When passing the torch to Pardo, Dagan spoke of the terrible solitude of the Mossad agents operating in enemy countries, when they have no one to turn to, no one to rescue them in case of need. He also candidly admitted some of his failures; the most important being lack of success in finding the place where Hamas was hiding the Israeli soldier Gilad Shalit, kidnapped five years ago. (Shalit was later released in exchange for hundreds of Palestinian terrorists.) Yet, despite such failings, Dagan's achievements honor him as the best *ramsad* so far. Prime Minister Benjamin Netanyahu thanked him "in the name of the Jewish people" and hugged him warmly. In an unprecedented, spontaneous reaction, the Israeli cabinet ministers stood up and applauded the sixty-five-year-old *ramsad*. George W. Bush saluted him in a personal letter.

But the most important tribute to Dagan came a year before, from a foreign source, the Egyptian daily *Al-Ahram*, a newspaper known for its virulent and hostile criticism of Israel. On January 16, 2010, it published an article by the well-known writer Ashraf Abu Al-Haul. "Without Dagan," Al-Haul wrote, "the Iranian nuclear project would have been completed years ago . . . The Iranians know who was behind the death of the nuclear scientist Masud Ali Mohammadi. Every senior Iranian leader knows that the key word is 'Dagan.' Only few people are familiar with the name of the director of the Israeli Mossad. He works quietly, far from the media attention. But in the last seven years he has landed painful blows on the Iranian nuclear project and stopped its advance.

"The Mossad is responsible for several daring operations in the Middle East," Al-Haul added, and mentioned some of Dagan's feats against Syria, the Hezbollah, the Hamas, and the Islamic Jihad.

"All this," he concluded, "has turned Dagan into the Superman of the State of Israel."

There were no supermen around the crib of the Israeli Secret Service when it was born in May 1948, just a handful of veterans of the "Shai," who had already acquired much experience in espionage and covert operations as the intelligence service of the Haganah, the major military underground of the Jewish community in Palestine. And in their first year, these modest and devoted undercover fighters, the nascent military secret service, were shaken by violence, internal strife, cruelty, and murder in what became known as the Be'eri Affair.

CHAPTER THREE

A HANGING IN BAGHDAD

sser Be'eri, also known as "Big Isser," was a tall, gangly man with sparse graying hair. His bushy eyebrows shielded dark, cavernous eye sockets, and a sardonic smile often hovered over his thin lips. Born in Poland, he was reputed to be an ascetic, a modest man of flawless integrity; but his rivals claimed he was a dangerous and fierce megalomaniac. A longtime member of the Haganah, Big Isser was the director of a private construction company in Haifa. He was a loner, silent and unsociable, and lived with his wife and son in a small, windswept house in the coastal village of Bat Galim.

Shortly before the creation of Israel, Be'eri had been appointed head of the Shai by the commanders of the Haganah. When independence was declared, on May 14, 1948, Israel was attacked from all sides by its neighbors, and Be'eri became the head of the newborn military secret service. Be'eri was active in the left wing of the Labor movement and had excellent political connections. His friends and colleagues praised his devotion to the defense of Israel. The Independence War would go on until April 1949.

Yet, soon after Be'eri became head of the secret service, strange, blood-curdling events—seemingly unrelated—started to happen.

A couple of hikers on Mount Carmel made a grisly discovery. In a deep gully at the foot of the mountain they found a half-burned body riddled with bullets. It was identified as a well-known Arab informant of the service, Ali Kassem. His assassins had shot him, and then tried to burn his body.

Some weeks later, at a secret meeting with Prime Minister Ben-Gurion, Big Isser accused Abba Hushi, an influential leader of Mapai—Ben-Gurion's party—of being a traitor and a British agent. Ben-Gurion was stunned. Great Britain had been the ruling power in Palestine before the establishment of the State of Israel; the Haganah carried an underground struggle against its restrictions on the Jewish community. British intelligence had frequently tried to plant their spies inside the Jewish leadership. But Abba Hushi, a pillar of the Jewish community and the charismatic leader of Haifa's workers—a traitor? It seemed impossible. At first, Israel's leaders who were in the know indignantly dismissed Be'eri's accusation. But Be'eri had found two confidential telegrams sent by British intelligence from Haifa's post office in May 1948. He laid them on Ben-Gurion's desk—irrefutable evidence of Hushi's treachery.

At the same time, Be'eri ordered the arrest of a friend of Hushi's, Jules Amster. Be'eri had Amster brought to a salt deposit in Atlit, outside Haifa, had him beaten and tortured for seventy-six days, and pressured him to admit that Hushi was a despicable traitor. Amster refused to yield, and was finally released, a broken man. His teeth were gone, his legs were covered with wounds and scars, and he was haunted for years by fear.

On June 30, 1948, while shopping at a Tel Aviv market, army captain Meir Tubiansky was arrested and brought to Beth Giz, a recently occupied Arab village. It was suspected by military intelligence that Tubiansky, while in Jerusalem, had disclosed top-secret information to a British national, who, in his turn, had passed it to the Arab Legion, Jordan's army. The Jordanian artillery, acting on that information, had heavily shelled several strategic targets throughout Jerusalem. In a summary court-martial that lasted less than an hour, Tubiansky was accused of being a spy for the Arabs, found guilty, and sentenced to death. A hastily assembled firing squad executed him in front of a group of stunned Israeli soldiers. (Tubiansky would be the only person ever executed in Israel, beside Adolf Eichmann.)

Inquiries into the deaths and torture led investigators to the perpetrator: Big Isser.

He had suspected Ali Kassem of being a double agent and had ordered his assassination.

He framed Abba Hushi. According to several investigators, Big Isser had a personal score to settle with Hushi. He might have succeeded if the main forger in the employ of the service, besieged by guilt, hadn't confessed to his superiors that he had falsified the telegrams implicating Abba Hushi, under Be'eri's direct orders.

And Be'eri had also been the one who had ordered the hasty arrest and the execution of Captain Tubiansky.

Prime Minister Ben-Gurion acted immediately. Be'eri was tried in a military court, then in a civil one, stripped of his rank, dishonorably discharged from the IDF, and found guilty in the deaths of Ali Kassem and Meir Tubiansky.

Israel's leaders were flabbergasted. Be'eri's methods seemed taken straight from the infamous KGB; his sinister personality, his orders to forge, torture, and murder were a stain on the moral and humane principles on which Israel had been founded.

The Be'eri affair left a gruesome scar on the secret service and had a profound impact on its evolution. If, in wartime, the civil leaders had recoiled from condemning Be'eri, Israel's secret service might have assumed a totally different character. It might well have become a KGB-like organization for whom framing, forgery, torture, and murder were routine practices. Instead, in the future, Be'eri's methods would be forbidden. The secret service placed limits on its own power and based its future operations on legal and moral principles that would guarantee the rights of individuals.

With the removal of Be'eri, another man stepped onto the center stage of Israel's shadow world, Be'eri's polar opposite: Reuven Shiloah.

* * *

euven Shiloah, forty, soft-spoken, secretive, was a man of mystery. He had come from a rich culture, possessed a sharp, analytical mind, an in-depth knowledge of the Arab Middle East, its tribal traditions, ruling clans, fleeting alliances, and blood feuds. One of his admirers called him "the queen in Ben-Gurion's chess game" while he served as political adviser to David Ben-Gurion. Some compared him to the wily Cardinal Richelieu of France; others saw him as a subtle manipulator, a master puppeteer, a man who knew how to pull strings behind the scenes. Shiloah had been active, all his life, in secret missions and undercover work.

The suave, urbane son of a rabbi, Shiloah had been born in Old Jerusalem. Always formally dressed, the trim, balding young man had set out on a mission to Baghdad, long before the creation of Israel. He had spent three years in Iraq, posing as a journalist and a teacher and studying that country's politics. During World War II, he negotiated with the British to set up a Jewish Commando Corps to sabotage operations in Nazi-occupied Europe. He helped create two such special Jewish commando units: one was a German battalion equipped with German weapons and uniforms, which undertook daring missions behind enemy lines in Europe; the other was an Arab battalion whose members spoke Arabic, dressed like Arabs, and were trained for missions deep in Arab territory. He also convinced the British to parachute Jewish volunteers from Palestine into occupied Europe, to organize local Jewish resistance to the Nazis. Shiloah was the first to establish contacts with the OSS (Office of Strategic Services), precursor to the CIA. On the eve of Israel's Independence War, he traveled to the neighboring Arab capitals in secret and brought back a priceless trophy: the Arab armies' invasion plans.

Shiloah's compulsive need to act under a thick cloak of secrecy became a source of myriad legends. His friends used to joke that once he hailed a taxi. "Where to?" the driver asked. Shiloah answered: "It's a state secret."

During the Independence War, Shiloah headed the external political information service. It was one of several quasi-independent intelligence groups created before the birth of Israel. But on December 13, 1949, Ben-Gurion issued an order to establish "an institute (in Hebrew, *mossad*) to coordinate state intelligence agencies," to be headed by Reuven Shiloah.

Yet it took two more years of delays and disputes before the Mossad could be created. One intelligence unit, called the political department, whose members had been gathering intelligence abroad, enjoying generous expense accounts and a glamorous lifestyle, revolted and refused to continue spying for Israel when they heard of the plan to disband their unit and incorporate it into the Mossad. Only after they were reprimanded—and most of them fired—could Shiloah create the Mossad.

Its title would eventually be changed to the Institute for Intelligence and Special Operations, and its motto chosen from Proverbs 11:14: "Without stratagems would a people fall, and deliverance is in a wise counsel."

But neither the new title nor the motto made the Mossad unique. Shiloah was determined to confer upon it an exceptional feature. The Mossad would not only be the long arm of Israel, but also the long arm of the entire Jewish people. At a meeting of his first recruits, the *ramsad* declared: "Beside all the functions of a secret service, we have another major task: to protect the Jewish people, wherever they are, and to organize their immigration to Israel." And indeed, in the years following, the Mossad would secretly help create self-defense units in places where the Jewish communities were in peril: Cairo, Alexandria, Damascus, Baghdad, and some South American cities. Young militant Jews were surreptitiously brought to Israel and trained by the army and Mossad, weapons were smuggled into unstable or enemy countries and hidden, local Jews were organized into defense units to create forces able to defend the Jewish community from attacks by a mob or by irregular armed groups—at least until help came from government forces or international organizations.

In the fifties, the Mossad brought to Israel tens of thousands of imperiled Jews from the Arab countries in the Middle East and Morocco; and years later, in the eighties, it was again the Mossad that organized the rescue of Jews trapped in Khomeini's Iran and carried out the mass exodus of Ethiopia's Jews to Israel. But during its first undercover operation in Iraq, disaster struck.

* * *

In the large Baghdad department store Orosdi Bak, on Rashid Street, a young man named Assad was manning a necktie counter. A Palestinian refugee, he had left his home in Acre after the Israeli army had captured that city. Shortly before leaving Israel, he had done a favor for his cousin who had fallen ill, by taking his place as a waiter in a café near the military governor's compound. For a week, Assad had walked the corridors of the military governor's building, carrying an ornate brass tray and serving tiny cups of strong Turkish coffee to Israeli army officers. The faces of some of those young officers stayed with him.

On that day, May 22, 1951, he was observing the customers walking through the store, when he noticed a familiar face. It can't be, he thought at first; it's impossible! But he did remember the man he saw—not in summer shirt and pants, like today, but in a khaki uniform. Assad urgently alerted the police. "I've seen an Israeli army officer! Right here in Baghdad!"

The police promptly arrested the European-looking man, who was accompanied by a thin, nondescript, bespectacled Iraqi Jew. His name was Nissim Moshe, and he told the police that he was a mere civil servant at the Jewish Community Center. "I met this tourist yesterday at a concert," he explained, "and he asked me to show him around the stores." When they reached headquarters, the two men were separated. The Iraqi detectives brutally interrogated Moshe about the man who had been identified as Israeli. Moshe stuck to his story: he had met the tourist only yesterday, and didn't know him. In the dark cellars of police headquarters, the interrogators strung up Moshe by his feet and then by his hands, beat him, and threatened to kill him. But their seedy prisoner seemed to know nothing. After a week of torture, the Iraqis decided that Nissim Moshe was a nobody and released him.

The other prisoner kept repeating he was Iranian, named Ismail Salhun, and he showed his captors his Iranian passport; but they continued torturing him. He didn't look Iranian, and he didn't speak a word of Persian. Finally, they set up a confrontation between him and Assad, the Palestinian who had identified him. "My blood froze in my veins when I saw him," the prisoner said later. He broke down and confessed: he was

Yehuda Taggar (Yudke Tadjer), an Israeli, a captain in the IDF. The detectives dragged him to his apartment, broke the furniture, probed the walls, and then discovered a cache of documents—a voluminous file taped to the bottom of a drawer in his desk.

And the nightmare began. Not only for Taggar, but for the entire Baghdad Jewish community.

Several clandestine Jewish and Israeli organizations operated in Baghdad, including an illegal emigration unit, a self-defense group, and a few Zionist and youth movements. Some had been created even before the birth of the State of Israel. Around Baghdad, in several caches, weapons and documents were stocked, some within the central Mas'uda Shemtov synagogue. The recent additions to these groups were a few espionage networks, hastily established prior to the creation of the Mossad; compartmentalization was almost nonexistent, and the fall of one could easily bring down all the others. The Iraqi Jews sat on a powder keg: Iraq was the vilest enemy of the young State of Israel, and the only one that had refused to sign an armistice agreement with it. Every member of the secret Jewish networks knew that the Iraqis would show no mercy, and his life would hang on a thread.

For that reason, Yehuda Taggar had been sent there to detach the espionage network from all the others. A former officer in the Palmach elite forces, Taggar was twenty-seven and sported a rebel forelock and a ready smile. This was his first mission abroad, and prior to his capture he had done his best to isolate the network he led from the other groups, but some of his own men nonetheless still took part in other secret activities; another Israeli with a genuine British passport, Peter Yaniv (Rodney the Hindu), ran a separate network but remained in contact with Taggar.

Taggar's communications to Tel Aviv passed through the top commander of all the groups operating in Baghdad: a secretive man whose identity was known to few. His cover name was Zaki Haviv, but he was really Mordechai Ben-Porat, an Iraqi-born Israeli, a former officer during Israel's Independence War. He had been loath to go back to Baghdad and was on the verge of getting married to a girl he had met in the army, but finally yielded to the pressure of the intelligence community and undertook this perilous mission.

In the days following Taggar's arrest, the entire secret organization crumbled. Iraqi special police units arrested scores of Jews. Some broke down under interrogation and led their captors to their hideouts. The Iraqis discovered documents that linked certain Jews to espionage. Under the flagstones of the Shemtov synagogue, the police uncovered a huge cache of weapons, built up over the years, starting after a bloody pogrom in 1941 in which 179 Jews had been slaughtered, 2,118 wounded, and hundreds of women raped. The number of weapons found amazed the Iraqis: 436 grenades, 33 machine pistols, 186 revolvers, 97 machine-gun chargers, 32 commando daggers, and 25,000 cartridges.

During the ferocious Iraqi interrogation, a name popped up more and more frequently: Zaki Haviv, the mysterious top man of the underground. But who was he? And where? Finally, a smart young detective made the connection: Zaki Haviv had to be none other than Nissim Moshe, the self-effacing fellow who had been arrested with Taggar and then released. Scores of agents raided Moshe's house—but found nobody. A manhunt of epic proportions was conducted throughout Baghdad, but Zaki Haviv had vanished.

Actually, he was in the one place the police hadn't dreamt of searching. He was . . . in jail.

A couple of days after his release from the initial arrest with Taggar, Ben-Porat was awakened by a loud pounding on his door. "Open, police!" the agents were shouting. Ben-Porat thought that was his end. The house had no back exit, and there was no one in Baghdad who could save him now. And he knew, for a man in his position, there could be only one verdict in the Iraqi courts: the gallows. He resigned himself and unlocked the door. Two police officers were outside. "You are under arrest," one said.

Ben-Porat feigned surprise. "But what have I done?"

"Oh, nothing serious," the cop said, "just an automobile accident. Now, get dressed."

Ben-Porat couldn't believe his ears. He had forgotten all about the accident in which he had been involved some months earlier. He had ignored the court summons, and now was going to face Iraqi justice. The trial was swift, barely an hour. The judge sentenced him to two weeks in jail. And so, while an army of Iraqi agents were on full alert, searching for him, Zaki Haviv was paying his debt to society in a Baghdad jail.

Prior to his release two weeks later, he was being taken to headquarters to be fingerprinted and photographed. He knew that if that were to happen, he was doomed. They would then be able to identify him as Zaki Haviv, and this time it would not be a two-week sentence. He walked with his two guards along Baghdad's streets to the headquarters, at some distance. En route they passed through the crowded Shurja souk, an exotic market crammed with tiny dark shops, merchants screaming the praise of their wares, and narrow, crooked alleys. At what he hoped was the right moment, Ben-Porat pushed his guards aside, dove into the crowd, and vanished. The cops didn't even try to chase him. After all, he was due to be released in less than an hour, so why bother?

But when they reported the incident, all hell broke loose. They had let Zaki Haviv, the most wanted man in Iraq, go! The opposition press found out and attacked the government's ineptitude with screaming headlines. "Where is Haviv?" asked a newspaper, and answered: "Haviv—in Tel Aviv!"

Back in Tel Aviv, Ben-Porat's superiors meticulously prepared his escape from Iraq. While he hid at a friend's house, the daring plan was put into action. At that time, a mammoth airlift was under way, bringing the entire Jewish community from Iraq to Israel, via Cyprus. About 100,000 Jews were fleeing Iraq, with big planes taking off almost every night.

On the night of June 12, Ben-Porat put on his best clothes and hailed a cab. His friends had drenched him with arrack—the local liquor—and, reeking of alcohol, he collapsed on the backseat of the taxi and feigned sleep. The driver helped his drunken fare out and into a back street near Baghdad airport, and left. Once alone, Ben-Porat hurried to the airport fence—he knew exactly where it had been cut—and slipped inside. On the tarmac, a plane had just finished loading its emigrants and was taxiing on the runway. Suddenly the pilot aimed his lights at the control tower, momentarily blinding the air controllers. The plane gathered speed, its rear door slid back, ten feet aboveground, and a dangling rope appeared. Coming out of the dark, Ben-Porat darted toward the plane, grabbed the rope, and was hauled into the aircraft, which immediately took off. Neither ground crews nor passengers noticed this escape, which seemed taken straight from an action movie.

As the plane passed over the city, its lights flashed on and off three times. "God be praised," murmured a few men gathered on a rooftop. Their friend was safe and on his way.

A few hours later, Haviv, indeed, was in Tel Aviv.

He married his sweetheart, and in the years that followed turned to politics, became a member of parliament, a cabinet minister, and today is a venerated leader of the Iraqi Jews in Israel.

Those left behind were not so fortunate. Scores of Jews were arrested, beaten, and tortured. Taggar and twenty-one others were tried for subversion. Two prominent Baghdad Jews, Shalom Salach and Joseph Batzri, were accused of possessing explosives and weapons and sentenced to death.

Shortly before his trial was to start, Taggar was awakened in the middle of the night, his cell full of policemen. "You are going to be hanged tonight," the chief investigator announced.

"But you can't hang a man without trial!" Taggar protested.

"Can't we? We know all about you already, you're an Israeli officer, you're a spy—we don't need anything more."

A bearded rabbi entered and sat beside Taggar, reading him Psalms. At three thirty in the morning, the officers took Taggar to the execution chamber. He walked between them, stunned. Only weeks ago he had been visiting his family in Jerusalem, then on his way here he had enjoyed the pleasures of Paris and Rome. And now he was going to dangle from the end of a rope.

The Iraqis made him sign several forms—bureaucracy at work, even at such a time—then the hangman took away his rings and watch. Taggar demanded that his body be sent to Israel. The hangman made him stand over a trapdoor and tied sandbags to his feet. He was forced to turn his back to the hangman, who placed the noose on his neck and grabbed the handle controlling the trapdoor. Taggar rejected the black hood that they tried to pull over his head. The hangman now looked at his commanding officer, standing with several others in front of the man who was going to die. Taggar thought of his family, of his native Jerusalem, of the life he could have had. Will my neck be broken? he wondered, and felt an all-consuming dread taking hold of his entire being.

And then, all of a sudden, the officers left. Taggar was pulled back from the trapdoor. The scowling hangman removed the sandbags from his feet and the noose from his neck, muttering that he had lost his pay for to-night. Taggar realized, amazed, that he was not going to die! Everything, down to the smallest detail, had been a ruse. They had hoped to break him and make him reveal more details about his accomplices. But now, as he trudged back to his cell, still alive, Taggar was certain he wouldn't die in an Iraqi prison. His friends would get him out of there.

When the trial ended, he was sentenced to death, but his sentence was immediately commuted to life in prison. Batzri and Salach were hanged. They spent their last night on earth with Taggar, who tried to cheer them up.

Then began for "Yudke" a Via Dolorosa that he somehow managed to survive. In the company of murderers, political prisoners, and sadistic jail-ers in several Iraqi prisons, he nevertheless believed that he wouldn't die in captivity. One day he would be free!

He had to wait nine years. In 1958, General Abdul Karim Kassem seized power in a coup and murdered the Iraqi prime minister and the royal family. Two years later, though, some of his closest aides concocted a plot to murder him (which they would do a few years later). The Mossad learned of the plot, and the *ramsad* immediately established contact with Kassem's loyalists, and struck a deal: he would give them the names of the conspirators—for the freedom of Yehuda Taggar.

Taggar was in his dark, gloomy cell, when his jailers came with a change of khaki clothes. "Put that on!" they ordered. "You are going to Baghdad."

A police car took the stupefied Taggar to the royal palace. Several soldiers escorted him to a huge office. Behind an ornate desk sat a familiar figure—President Kassem himself. Taggar suddenly realized: they were setting him free! Kassem took his time studying the face of the Israeli. "Tell me," he finally said, "if war were declared between Iraq and Israel, would you fight against us?"

"When I am back in my own country," Taggar answered, "I will do all I can to bring about understanding and peace between Israel and the Arab States. But if war should break out, I will fight for Israel, just as you have fought many times for your country."

Kassem must have liked this answer. He stood up. "When you get home," he said, "tell your people that Iraq is an independent state now. We are not the lackeys of imperialism anymore."

From the palace, a car took Taggar to the airport. He still couldn't believe what was happening. They put him on a plane to Beirut, then a flight to Nicosia, Cyprus, and finally he landed in Israel. At the airport, his friends and colleagues were waiting. They expected to meet a broken man, a human wreck—but the man who descended from the plane was the same vigorous, extroverted, smiling fellow whom they had last seen more than nine years ago. How did you make it, they asked. How did you hang on to your sanity, your optimism? "I knew you'd get me out of there," Yudke said simply.

By bringing Taggar home, the heads of the Mossad had adhered to another of the principles forged at its inception: spare no effort, no means, and no sacrifices, to bring our people back home.

In Israel, Taggar married, started a family, and after a brilliant diplomatic career abroad became a university professor.

Reuven Shiloah was in no way involved in the Baghdad tragedy. And yet, at the end of 1952, he resigned. He was replaced by a star, newly emerged in the shadow world of Israel's secret services.

Little Isser.

CHAPTER FOUR

A SOVIET MOLE
AND A BODY AT SEA

Ze'ev Avni yearned to become a Mossad agent.

As he arrived, one rainy day in April 1956, at Mossad headquarters, he was wishing with all his heart to come out of there as an employee of the Mossad. For years he had been trying to become one of the selected few, and this had been his most important goal in life.

Born Wolf Goldstein in Riga, Latvia, he had grown up in Switzerland, served in the Swiss Army during World War II, and immigrated to Israel in 1948. He had changed his name to the Hebrew Ze'ev Avni, and after a couple of years of living and working at kibbutz Hazorea, he had joined the Ministry of Foreign Affairs and was posted in Brussels. Personable, well-read, fluent in several languages, he had charmed his superiors with his manners and diligence as well as with his willingness to volunteer for any chore, especially those connected with the Mossad. Whenever a diplomat was needed for a secret courier job, for an urgent trip to another city, for delivering classified documents to a Mossad undercover unit anywhere in Europe—Avni was the first to volunteer. His frequent cooperation with the Mossad informally made him one of their guys in

Europe; and that collaboration became more intense when he was transferred to Israel's embassy in Belgrade, Yugoslavia. In several letters to the *ramsad*, Isser Harel, Avni suggested establishing a Mossad station in Belgrade. Harel refused: the Mossad had no need for a station in Yugoslavia—but Avni didn't give up. In April 1956, he came back to Israel on a private visit and asked to see the *ramsad*. His demand was granted, and that day he was to meet Isser Harel for the first time.

Tense and nervous, he entered Harel's office in an old house in the former German colony in Tel Aviv. Harel had been appointed *ramsad* less than four years earlier, but was already a legend. People admired and feared this short, enigmatic man; true and false stories about him wafted through the dim Mossad corridors. Avni had heard bits and pieces about Harel, who had been nicknamed "Little Isser"—to tell him apart from the notorious "Big Isser." Avni feared this encounter, given the rumors about Little Isser's stubbornness, his brusque manners, and fantastic intuition.

But the short, lean, and balding man in khakis and a short-sleeved shirt who received Avni in his monastic office was soft-spoken and kind. He admitted to being impressed by Avni's demeanor and political savvy. He asked Avni for the reason of his visit to Israel right now, and Avni explained that his daughter from his first marriage had demanded that he come to see her.

"How old is your daughter?" Isser asked, smiling.

"Eight."

"Eight?" Isser looked surprised. He seemed to find it odd that a diplomat would rush home from abroad just because his little daughter had summoned him. Avni then went into a detailed explanation about his complex relationship with his first wife, his child, and his current wife. Isser grew impatient, cut him short, and told him that there would be no Mossad station in Belgrade. As for Avni's future, he said, "We'll see after you complete your tour of duty in Yugoslavia." Avni felt crushed.

However, before he left, Isser offered to meet with him again, in a couple of days, "but not in this building, too many people come in and out. You'll meet me in my secret downtown office, my driver will take you there."

There was still hope, Avni thought. If not—why would Isser want to see him again?

A few days later, Avni walked into a nondescript apartment in central Tel Aviv. He had no reason to fear Isser anymore; after all, he had been friendly at their first meeting.

Isser was waiting for him and led him into a big room: bare walls, a desk, a couple of chairs, shuttered windows. Avni sat down and Isser suddenly metamorphosed into a raging bull. His face contorted; he banged his fists on the desk and roared: "You are a Soviet agent! Confess! Confess!" And again: "Confess!" He kept hammering his clenched fists on his desk, and shouting: "I know the Soviets sent you! I know you're a spy! Confess!"

Avni, thunderstruck, froze. He felt unable to say a word.

"Confess! If you cooperate with me, I'll try to help you, but if not . . ."

Avni's heart pounded madly in his chest. He was covered in cold sweat and his tongue felt like lead. He was certain that his last moment had come and Isser would have him killed.

He finally gathered up the strength to utter a few words.

"I confess," he mumbled, "I work for the Russians."

Isser opened a concealed door, and in walked two of his best agents and a police officer. The officer arrested Avni, and he was taken away, to an interrogation facility. Then, step by step, he revealed his identity and his true aim. A fervent Communist since his teens, he had been recruited by the Soviet GRU (the Red Army espionage service) while still living in Switzerland, and had spied for the Soviet Union during World War II. Shortly after, he had been advised to immigrate to Israel and wait. He was to become a long-term mole. For many years, he had expected a message from Moscow, but the Russian master spies had waited to contact him only when he had been posted to Brussels. There, he delivered to them important information about Israel's deals with the F.N. arms industry in Belgium, had supplied them with the Israeli foreign ministry codes, and even revealed to them the names of two German ex-Nazis who were spying for Israel in Egypt. To the surprise of their handlers, the two Germans had been hastily expelled from Egypt. But that had not been enough for Avni's Russian case officers. They wanted their man to infiltrate the Mossad. And that's what Avni tried so hard to do, until the moment when Isser shouted: "Confess!"

And when he confessed, he didn't know what was most shocking: he could have walked out of Isser's trap a free man! The *ramsad* hadn't the slightest shred of evidence against him, only suspicions, not even a hint of proof that Avni was a spy. True, long ago, somebody had mentioned to Isser that Avni had been expelled from his kibbutz because of his Communist views. But a Soviet spy?

Isser had acted on intuition alone. Avni's relentless efforts to join the Mossad; the seemingly strange visit to his daughter; his attempts to convince Isser to establish a Mossad station in Belgrade . . . All these minor occurrences merged in Isser's sharp mind and led him to an unlikely conclusion: a mole, a traitor, had almost penetrated Israel's *sanctum sanctorum*.

At his trial, Avni made a full confession and was sentenced to fourteen years in prison. He was paroled after nine, became a model citizen and a psychologist. Isser told his biographer that Avni was the most dangerous spy ever caught in Israel but also "the most charming," and spoke warmly of him as "the gentleman spy."

Avni himself told us that over the years some of the high-ranking police officers and Shabak (rough equivalent of the American FBI) interrogators had become his good friends.

Operation Pygmalion, as the Avni affair was called, for many years was one of the closest-guarded secrets of the Mossad. But for the few who were in the know, it was one more proof of Isser's amazing instincts.

But who was Little Isser? Taciturn, shy, stubborn as a mule, he purportedly had been born in the ancient fortress town of Dvinsk, in Imperial Russia; it was said that when he immigrated to Israel at eighteen, he was carrying in his knapsack a loaf of bread, inside of which he had baked a revolver. Little Isser first settled in kibbutz Shefayim, where he married a joyful horsewoman, Rivka. Tough, stubborn, and assertive, he left the kibbutz for unknown reasons with a wife, a child, and only the shirt on his back. During World War II, he joined the Haganah and soon became head of the Shai's Jewish Department, which tracked traitors and dissidents. The "dissidents" were members of the Irgun and the Stern group—two clandestine right-wing organizations that contested the authority and the politics of David Ben-Gurion and of the organized Jewish community. After the demise of "Big Isser," Little Isser became head of the Internal Security Service, the Shabak.

The Mossad had barely started functioning when Ben-Gurion, in a sudden move, accepted Reuven Shiloah's resignation and appointed Isser head of the Mossad. The official reason for the change was a traffic accident that was said to have incapacitated Shiloah, but the Mossad gossip was that Isser had bullied Shiloah out, after convincing Ben-Gurion that the *ramsad* was erudite and a nice guy but unable to lead tough agents and carry out secret operations.

Under Isser, the intelligence community acquired what became its definitive shape. It was composed of five services: the Mossad, the Shabak, the Aman (military intelligence), the special branch of the police, and the research division of the foreign ministry. Of these, only Mossad, Aman, and Shabak were important; the other two were not as highly regarded. The directors of the five services and their deputies formed the "Heads of Services Committee." Isser was appointed its chairman. Ben-Gurion also created a special title for him: *memunneh*—chief executive in charge of the security services. When he first appointed Little Isser to this new position, Ben-Gurion remarked: "Of course you'll continue to direct the Shabak, even though you now have Mossad." Isser selected a new Shabak director, though the overall control of both Mossad and Shabak remained in his hands.

Thus, Little Isser became Israel's intelligence tsar.

The Pygmalion affair was but one of several key operations Isser directed in the first years of Israel's existence, mostly against Soviet spies, many of whom were captured, jailed, or expelled.

But not all spies worked for the Soviets—and not every spy story had a happy ending.

* * *

One afternoon in early December 1954, a lone cargo aircraft kept circling over the Eastern Mediterranean. When its pilots had made sure there were no seagoing vessels in the area, one of the aircraft doors opened and a big object was dropped into the sea—a body.

The plane turned back and, an hour later, landed in Israel, marking the end of Operation Engineer (not its real name), an operation that remained ultra-confidential for more than fifty years.

In 1949, three brothers from a Jewish family in Bulgaria arrived in Haifa. The oldest, Alexander Israel, had just graduated from the engineering school in Sofia. He enlisted in the army, was given the rank of captain, and was posted to the Israeli Navy. Captain Israel was a handsome and extremely charming young man. He was valued by his superiors and was assigned to top-secret research in electronic warfare and development of new weapons. Given a high security clearance, he had access to some of the most sensitive material. He changed his first name to the Hebrew Avner and in 1953 he married Matilda Arditi, a pretty, young woman of Turkish origin. The young couple settled in Haifa, close to Israel's major naval base. Matilda was very much in love with her charismatic husband, but unaware of the less delightful aspects of his personality.

She didn't know that he had a long and colorful police record. Avner Israel had been accused of simultaneously leasing the same apartment to more than one renter; of posing as a refrigerator company representative who collected down payments for refrigerators that were not delivered; and of other such dealings. One case came to court, and he was summoned to report for trial on November 8, 1954.

Matilda, heavy with child, knew nothing of her husband's fraud, nor of his affair with a pretty clerk at the Italian consulate in Haifa. Avner even proposed, and the Italian girl agreed on one condition: he must first convert to Catholicism.

For young Avner this posed no great problem. He already had converted once before, in Bulgaria, when he was forced to marry another Christian girl whom he had seduced. Her furious family had demanded—almost at gunpoint—that he convert and marry the young woman. Right after the wedding he fled from Sofia, his wife committed suicide, and then he returned to Sofia and to Judaism. Now he did it again. He traveled to Jerusalem with his paramour, was baptized in the Terra Santa convent, and changed his name to Ivor. Using documents provided by the Church, the charming captain registered with the Ministry of Interior and was issued a passport in his new name, Alexander Ivor.

He and his Italian girlfriend set November 7, 1954, as the date for their wedding. The trial in Haifa was set for November 8. Avner Israel, aka Alexander Ivor, had no intention of honoring any of those commitments. The time had come for him to vanish.

At the end of October, Captain Israel went on a two-week leave. He had no exit visa—but Alexander Ivor had one, and a full set of documents, some authentic, others fake. He bought a plane ticket to Rome, and on November 4 he left. Neither his wife nor his "fiancée" knew about his departure. Her fiancé gone, the Italian woman started an anxious search. Finally she turned to the Haifa police; with their help she discovered his address, where she was shocked to meet Mrs. Matilda Israel, in her seventh month of pregnancy.

In Rome Avner Israel vanished, but not for long. The Mossad resident agent there had good sources in the Arab diplomatic community in Italy. On November 17 an urgent cable reached Mossad headquarters in Tel Aviv: "An Israeli officer, Alexander Ivor or Ivon or Ivy is here, and is trying to sell military information to the Egyptian military attaché."

The *ramsad* and the new head of Shabak, Amos Manor, joined forces to find out who this was. In a few days they discovered his identity, and were dismayed to learn that he was an Israeli naval officer. Another telegram from Rome was even more troubling: the Mossad agent reported that Israel had sold the Egyptians the detailed plans of a large IDF base in Israel, and had been paid $1,500, which he had deposited in the Credit Suisse Bank. He was said to have promised the Egyptians more information, and agreed to fly to Egypt, to be debriefed there.

A few days later, another cable: "The Egyptian embassy has ordered two tickets to Cairo for the end of November, at the TWA agency. Apparently the two passengers will be the Egyptian military attaché and the Israeli officer."

Alarm bells rang at Mossad headquarters. To Isser, there was a huge difference between a debriefing of an informant by a military attaché in a foreign country—and the transfer of that same informant to Egypt's capital, where he would be interrogated by experts, who would obtain even more detailed and dangerous information from him. Isser was determined to prevent—at all costs—the flight of Avner Israel to Cairo.

He decided to dispatch his operational team to Rome. At these early days, the Mossad didn't have an operations department yet and used the operational unit of the Shabak. Its commander, one of the best agents Israel had, was a legend to his men—Rafi Eitan. Born on a kibbutz, he was a stubby, bespectacled, jolly little fellow but also daring, creative, and ruthless. A Palmach fighter in the years preceding independence, he had been deeply involved in Aliya Beth, the secret organization that smuggled Jews to Palestine despite the British restrictions. They had to escape from Europe on ramshackle boats, evade British warships cruising the shores of Palestine, land at deserted beaches, and then blend into the local Jewish population. Rafi's most famous exploit had been to blow up the British radar installation on Mount Carmel, near Haifa, which detected the approach of Aliya Beth vessels. To reach the radar, Rafi had crawled through repulsive sewers and got himself named "Rafi the Smelly." His future activities during the War of Independence confirmed his bravery and his wily intelligence. When Isser assembled his operational team, he recruited people with varying backgrounds: Holocaust survivors, Palmach and Haganah veterans, former members of the Irgun and the Stern group—right-wing militants whom he had hunted during the pre-state struggle. (One of the Mossad recruits was Yitzhak Shamir, a former leader of the Stern group and a future prime minister.)

Rafi was appointed head of the operational team.

He took off for Rome, together with agents Raphael Medan and Emmanuel (Emma) Talmor. Other agents joined them soon after. They immediately set up an ambush at Rome's Fiumicino Airport. At the last briefing before their departure, Isser had ordered them to stop Avner Israel at the airport. "He must never get on that plane. Fake a brawl, overpower him, and wound him if need be. And if all other moves fail—shoot and kill him!"

That was the first time ever that a license to kill was given to Israeli agents.

But the airport attack didn't happen. The information about the trip to Egypt appeared erroneous; Israel stayed on in Rome awhile, and then, suddenly, left and started traveling across Europe, with Eitan's team on his heels. As if trying to shake those who were chasing him, he went to Zurich, Geneva, Genoa, Paris, Vienna . . .

And then, all of a sudden, Captain Israel vanished. The Mossad agents looked for him everywhere, but failed. But then, Rafi Eitan's usual luck came through. In Vienna there was an Israeli envoy of a secret organization, Nativ, whose mission was to expedite the flight of Jews from Russia and the Eastern Bloc—and bring them to Israel. The Nativ man maintained close ties with the Mossad. One day in December, his Bulgarian-born wife had a surprise for him.

"You won't believe this," she said, beaming. "This morning I was walking on the street, and I bumped into a friend of mine from Sofia. I hadn't seen him for years. We went to school together, in the same class! What a coincidence, don't you think?"

"Really? What's his name?" the husband asked.

"Alexander Israel. We're meeting tomorrow for lunch."

The Nativ envoy knew of Eitan's search for a man who corresponded to his wife's description and alerted him right away. The following day two Mossad agents went for lunch to the same restaurant, and sat not far from where Alexander Israel and his childhood friend were reminiscing. When Israel left the Nativ man's wife, they clung to him like shadows.

A few days later, "Alexander Ivor" boarded an Austrian Airlines plane to Paris. In the seat next to his was a young and attractive woman. Ivor, a consummate womanizer, started a conversation with her, and she pleasantly responded. They decided to meet again in Paris for a night on the town. Just before landing, she turned to the officer: "Some friends of mine are meeting me at the airport. Would you like to join us? I'm sure there'll be room in the car."

Ivor was delighted. At the airport, two well-dressed gentlemen were waiting for the lady. The four of them got into a car and headed for Paris. Ivor sat beside the driver. Night had fallen; the driver noticed a man standing by a poorly illuminated crossroad and waving, as if trying to hitch a ride. "Let's take him," he said. He stopped the car, and suddenly the "hitchhiker" and a few other men, emerging from the darkness, converged on the vehicle, while another automobile stopped behind them.

"We are being abducted!" Ivor shouted. Suddenly the man behind him grabbed him by the throat. Ivor struggled frantically against the grip of his attacker. The car door opened and the man standing outside jumped on Ivor and overpowered him. He drew a gun and shouted in Hebrew: "Another move—and you're dead!"

Ivor froze. A hand, holding a chloroform-soaked pad, was slapped on his face, and Ivor sank into deep sleep.

He was surreptitiously brought to a safe house in Paris, where Rafi Eitan and his men interrogated him. He admitted that he had sold top-secret documents to the Egyptians, and that he had done it for the money. From Israel, Isser telegraphed an order to bring him back. Even the basest traitor, he believed, should stand trial, and his legal rights be respected. Eitan and his men drugged Avner, put him in a large crate, and loaded him on an Israeli Air Force Dakota cargo aircraft that used to fly once a week from Paris to Tel Aviv.

The road home was long and strenuous. The plane had to refuel in Rome and Athens. A well-known doctor—an anesthetist by the name of Yona Elian—flew with the group. Before each landing and takeoff, the doctor would inject their passenger with a soporific drug. After the Athens takeoff, however, disaster struck. Avner Israel, unconscious, suddenly started breathing heavily; his pulse accelerated and his heartbeat became irregular. Dr. Elian made feverish efforts to stabilize him and bring his fit under control, including trying to revive the convulsing man with artificial respiration, but to no avail. Long before the plane landed in Israel, the prisoner died.

Immediately after the landing, the Mossad agents called Isser and informed him of Israel's death. The *ramsad* ordered them to leave the body on the plane and told the pilot to take off again. Far from Israel's coast, the body was thrown from the aircraft.

This unexpected mishap led to a commotion at Mossad headquarters. Isser hurried to Prime Minister Moshe Sharett's office, and asked him to appoint a board of inquiry to investigate the officer's death. Sharett appointed a two-man board, which cleared the Mossad agents from all wrongdoing. All they had done, the board ruled, was to bring the man to trial; they were not to blame for his death. The main reason for the death, they concluded, was apparently an overdose of the soporific that the doctor had injected. When asked years later, the doctor maintained that the death had been caused by abrupt changes in air pressure within the aircraft. (In 1960 he participated, once again as anesthetist, in Eichmann's capture in Argentina.)

Isser's men checked Avner Israel's papers and discovered affidavits and letters of recommendation from the Catholic Church in Jerusalem; after selling his secrets to the Egyptians, he had planned to escape to South America. In his bags the agents found a ship ticket to Brazil.

The next problem Isser had to face was with Israel's family. He should have invited Matilda to come in and tell her the whole truth. But the Mossad heads, embarrassed by the sorry end of the affair, preferred to bury the story and got the full support of Prime Minister Sharett. The Mossad leaked fabricated stories about Captain Avner Israel to the newspapers. They hinted that he had escaped from Israel after becoming entangled in personal debts and romantic affairs. These stories made fat headlines in the papers.

For many years, Matilda, her husband's brothers, and her son, Moshe

Israel-Ivor, didn't know what had happened. They believed he was still living somewhere, maybe South America. That lie was unforgivable.

The first failure of this mission was the way they treated Israel, even though he was a traitor; the second was their conspiracy of silence, the expunging of Israel's name from military records, the Mossad's misleading of his wife and brothers. Rafi Eitan and several Mossad officers strongly objected to the *ramsad*'s decision to throw the body in the sea and deceive the family, but their hands were tied. "Little Isser was Mr. Security those days," Eitan told us. "He was the absolute ruler of the secret services, and the intelligence community never disputed his decisions."

The publication of this story, years later, demonstrates how difficult it is to obliterate the existence of a person. Even after they're dead, they sometimes talk to us from beyond the grave.

CHAPTER FIVE

"OH, THAT? IT'S KHRUSHCHEV'S SPEECH . . ."

I t all started with a love affair.

In the spring of 1956, Lucia Baranovski was head over heels in love with a handsome journalist, Victor Grayevski. Her marriage to the deputy prime minister of Communist Poland was on the rocks, and they hardly saw each other anymore. Lucia worked as a secretary to Edward Ochab, secretary general of the Polish Communist Party. The members of his staff had grown accustomed to charming Victor's frequent visits to his lovely girlfriend. There were no secrets about Lucia's feelings for this dashing young man.

Victor was a senior editor at the Polish News Agency (PAP), in charge of Soviet and Eastern European affairs. He was actually Jewish, and his real name was Victor Shpilman. But years ago, when he had joined the Communist Party, his friends had let him know that with a name like Shpilman he wouldn't get far. So he changed it to Grayevski, which sounded Polish.

When the German Army invaded Poland in World War II, he was a child. His family had managed to cross into Russia and narrowly escaped the Holocaust. After the war, they came back to Poland. In 1949, Victor's parents and younger sister emigrated to Israel. But he, a staunch and ardent Communist, stayed behind; Stalin's admirer, he longed to help create a workers' paradise.

But neither his friends and colleagues, nor even his beloved, knew that disenchantment had started gnawing at the young Communist's heart. In 1955 he visited his family in Israel, and saw another world—free, progressive, a Jewish democratic nation, a dream of sorts, utterly different from the Communist propaganda he had been exposed to. Back in Poland, thirty-year-old Victor began to consider emigrating to Israel.

That morning in early April 1956, Victor came, as usual, to visit his sweetheart at the party secretary's office. On a corner of her desk, he saw a brochure bound in a red cover, numbered, and stamped with the inscription TOP SECRET.

"What is this?" he asked her.

"Oh, that's just Khrushchev's speech," she answered casually.

Victor froze. He had heard about Khrushchev's speech, but had never met anybody who had heard or read a single sentence from it. It was one of the best-kept secrets of the Communist bloc.

Victor did know that Nikita Khrushchev, the almighty secretary general of the Soviet Communist Party, had delivered the speech at the party's Twentieth Congress that had taken place the previous February at the Kremlin. On February 25, shortly before midnight, all foreign guests and heads of foreign Communist parties were asked to leave the hall. At midnight, Khrushchev took the podium and spoke to the fourteen hundred Soviet delegates. His speech was said to be a surprise and a terrible shock for everyone present.

But what had he said? According to an American journalist who dispatched a first report to the West, the speech had lasted for four hours, and Khrushchev had described in detail the terrible crimes of the man worshipped by millions of Communists all over the world—Stalin. Khrushchev, rumor had it, had accused Stalin of the massacre of millions. Some whispered that while listening to the speech many delegates cried and pulled out their hair in despair; some fainted or suffered heart attacks; at least two committed suicide after that night.

But not a word about Khrushchev's revelations was published by the Soviet media. Rumors wafted about Moscow, and some passages of the speech were read in closed sessions of the party's supreme bodies. But the full text of the speech was guarded, as if it were a state secret. Foreign reporters had told Victor that the Western secret services were mounting an all-out effort to obtain the text. The CIA had even offered a $1 million award. It was estimated that the publication of the text, at the height of the Cold War between the West and the Soviet bloc, could generate a political earthquake in the Communist countries and trigger an unprecedented crisis. Hundreds of millions of Communists, inside and outside Russia, blindly worshipped Stalin. The exposure of his crimes could destroy their faith and perhaps even cause the collapse of the Soviet Union.

But all the efforts to get the speech failed. It remained an enigma.

Lately Victor had learned that Khrushchev had decided to send a few numbered copies to Communist Party leaders in Eastern Europe, which was how that brochure, bound in red, had reached Lucia's desk.

When Victor Grayevski spotted it, he had a crazy idea. He asked Lucia to lend it to him for a couple of hours, so he could read it at home, without all the hustle-bustle in this office. To his surprise, she agreed. She was happy to please him . . . "You can take it," she said, "but you must bring it back before four P.M., I have to lock it in the safe."

At home, Victor read the speech. It was indeed stunning. Khrushchev had shattered, boldly and mercilessly, the myth of Yosif Vissarionovich Stalin. Khrushchev had revealed that Stalin, during his years in power, had committed monstrous crimes and ordered the murder of millions. He'd reminded his audience that Lenin, the father of the Bolshevik Revolution, had warned the party against Stalin. Khrushchev condemned the cult of personality of the man who'd been hailed as the "Sun of the Nations." He told of the forced relocation of entire ethnic groups in the Soviet Union, which led to countless deaths; of the "great purges" (1936–1937), when 1.5

million Communists were arrested and 680,000 of them executed. Out of 1,966 delegates to the Seventeenth Congress of the party, on Stalin's orders 848 were executed, as well as 98 out of 138 candidates to the Central Committee. Khrushchev also spoke of the Doctors' Plot, the fabricated accusations against some Jewish doctors who allegedly had conspired to murder Stalin and other Soviet leaders. Khrushchev's words revealed Stalin as a mass murderer, who had massacred millions of Russians and other nationals, many of them loyal Communists. In four hours, the messiah had metamorphosed into a monster.

Khrushchev's speech shredded Victor's last illusions about Communism. And he realized that he held in his hands an explosive device that could shake the Soviet camp to its foundations. He decided to return the red brochure to Lucia. But on his way to her, he had second thoughts, and his feet carried him elsewhere—to the Israeli embassy. He walked in confidently, and the wall of Polish policemen and secret service agents parted and let him pass. A few minutes later, he was in the office of Yaacov Barmor, officially a first secretary of the embassy, but in reality, the Shabak representative in Poland.

Grayevski handed him the red brochure. The Israeli perused it and his jaw dropped. Will you wait a few minutes, he asked, grabbed the brochure, and left the room. He came back an hour later. Grayevski realized that Barmor had photocopied it, but asked no questions. He picked it up, concealed it under his coat, and left. He reached Lucia's office on time, and she put it in the safe. Nobody bothered him or asked him about his impromptu visit to the Israeli embassy.

On Friday, April 13, 1956, in the early afternoon, Zelig Katz entered the office of the director of Shabak, Amos Manor. Katz was Manor's personal assistant. Shabak headquarters were located in an old Arab building in Jaffa, not far from the picturesque flea market. Manor asked Katz the routine Friday question: "Any material from Eastern Europe?" Friday was the day when the diplomatic pouch brought reports from Shabak agents behind the Iron Curtain.

Zelig nonchalantly quipped that a few minutes ago he had received from Warsaw "some speech of Khrushchev at the Congress . . ." Manor jumped from his seat. "What?" he roared. "Bring it at once!"

Manor, a tall, handsome young man, had immigrated to Israel only a few years earlier. Born Arthur Mendelovitch in Romania, to a well-to-do family, he was sent to Auschwitz, where his entire family—parents, sister, and two brothers—were murdered. He survived, weighing barely eighty pounds when the camp was liberated. Back in Bucharest, he worked for Aliya Beth, helping smuggle Jewish refugees into British-controlled Palestine. He used the war name of Amos, and several other names, to cover his tracks. When his turn came to leave for Israel, in 1949, the Romanian authorities wouldn't let him go. He managed to escape with a forged Czech passport in the name of Otto Stanek. His friends started calling him "the man with the thousand names"; in Israel, he became Amos Manor.

He rose quickly in the secret services. Isser was fascinated by him. Manor was his opposite. Isser small, Manor big. Isser tough and gruff, Amos suave and urbane. Isser played no sport, while Manor was a swimmer, and played soccer, tennis, volleyball. Isser spoke Russian and Yiddish, Manor spoke seven languages. Isser was a devoted Labor Party member, Amos didn't care about politics. Isser dressed modestly, Amos was fashionable, European-looking. But besides all that, he was intelligent and resourceful. Isser recruited him to the Shabak in 1949; barely four years later, he was appointed director by Ben-Gurion on Isser's recommendation. He also was put in charge of the Israeli intelligence community's secret relations with the CIA.

On that rainy Friday, Manor threw himself into the sheaf of photocopied papers. He had no problems reading it—one of his seven languages was Russian. Reading the pages, he realized the huge importance of Khrushchev's speech. He jumped into his car and rushed to Ben-Gurion's house.

"You must read this," he told the prime minister. Ben-Gurion, who also knew Russian, read the speech. The following morning, a Sabbath, he summoned Manor urgently. "This is a historic document," he said, "and it all but proves that in the future Russia will become a democratic nation."

Isser got the speech on April 15, and right away saw that it could be a bonanza for Israel. In it was the means to upgrade the Mossad's ties with the CIA, first established in 1947. In 1951, when visiting the United States, Ben-Gurion had called on General Walter Bedell Smith, whom he had met in Europe at the end of World War II. Bedell Smith was the director of the CIA (and about to be replaced by Allen Dulles, an OSS veteran and brother of a future secretary of state). Bedell Smith agreed, hesitantly, to establish limited cooperation between the CIA and the Mossad. The main element of such cooperation was the debriefing by the Israelis of Soviet and Eastern bloc emigrants. Many were engineers, technicians, and even army officers who had worked in Soviet or Warsaw Pact installations and were able to supply detailed information about the capacities of the Communist bloc's armies. This information was regularly conveyed and it impressed the Americans; the CIA appointed as liaison with Israel a legendary figure— James Jesus Angleton, the head of CIA counterintelligence. Angleton visited Israel and came to know the heads of its services. He established a friendly rapport with Amos Manor and even spent a few nights in his tiny two-room apartment over bottles of scotch.

But this time Isser and Amos offered far more than emigrants' debriefings. They decided to hand over Khruschev's speech to the Americans—not via the CIA man in Tel Aviv, but directly, in Washington. Manor dispatched a copy of the speech with a special courier to Izzi Dorot, the Mossad representative in the United States, who rushed to Langley and handed it to Angleton. On April 17, Angleton brought the speech to Allen Dulles, and later that day it was on President Eisenhower's desk.

The American intelligence experts were stunned. Israel's tiny spy services had obtained what the giant, sophisticated services of the United States, Britain, and France couldn't get. Skeptical, CIA senior staff had the document examined by experts, who unanimously concluded it was genuine. Based on that, the CIA leaked it to the *New York Times*, which published it on its front page on June 5, 1956. Its publication caused an earthquake of sorts in the Communist world, and prompted millions to turn their backs on the Soviet Union. Some historians hold that the spontaneous uprisings against the Soviets in Poland and Hungary, in the fall of 1956, were motivated by Khrushchev's revelations.

The intelligence coup led to a major breakthrough in the Mossad's relations with its American counterpart, and the modest brochure that sweet Lucia had shown to her handsome Victor had surrounded the Israeli Mossad with a legendary aura.

Back in Warsaw, no one suspected Victor Grayevski of having smuggled Khrushchev's speech to the United States. In January 1957, Victor emigrated to Israel. Grateful Amos Manor helped him get a job in the East European Department at the Ministry of Foreign Affairs. Shortly afterward, he was also hired as an editor and reporter in the Polish section of Kol Israel, the state-owned radio network.

But soon he also got a third job. Shortly after coming to Israel, he'd met a few Soviet diplomats at an *ulpan,* a special school where immigrants and foreigners were taught the Hebrew language. One of the Russian diplomats happened to meet him in a foreign ministry's hallway, and was impressed by the important position held by this new immigrant. Soon afterward, a KGB agent popped up "by chance" at Grayevski's side on a Tel Aviv street. He conversed with Grayevski and reminded him of his past in Poland, as an anti-Nazi and a Communist. Then he made him an offer: become a KGB agent in Israel. Grayevski promised to think about it, then made a beeline for Mossad headquarters. "What should I do?" he asked.

The Mossad people were delighted. "Wonderful," they said, "go ahead and accept!" They would turn Grayevski into a double agent who would feed the Russians false information.

So began a new and long career for Victor. For many years he supplied the Russians with information concocted and doctored by the Mossad. His KGB handlers would meet him in the forests around Jerusalem and Ramleh, in Russian churches and monasteries in Jaffa, Jerusalem, and Tiberias, during "chance" encounters in crowded restaurants and at diplomatic receptions. Not once, in the fourteen years that Grayevski spent as a double agent, did the Soviets suspect that he was the one using them. They complimented him over and over for the excellent materials that he provided; in KGB headquarters in Moscow, rumor had it that the Soviet Union had an agent embedded deep in Israeli governing circles.

Through all those years, the Soviets trusted Grayevski and never questioned his credibility. The exception was in 1967, when they ignored him and his conclusions; ironically, this was the only time when he delivered fully accurate information. During the "waiting period" in 1967 before the Six-Day War, Egypt's president, Gamal Abdel Nasser, erroneously believed that Israel intended to attack Syria in May. So he massed his troops in Sinai, expelled the UN peacekeepers, closed the Red Sea straits to Israeli ships, and threatened Israel with annihilation. Israel had had no intention to attack and was eager to prevent a war with Egypt. Prime Minister Eshkol then asked the Mossad to inform the Soviets that if Egypt didn't cancel its aggressive measures, Israel would have to go to war; he hoped that the Soviet Union, which had a huge influence on Egypt, would stop Nasser. Grayevski conveyed to the KGB a document detailing Israel's true intentions. But the USSR made a wrong assessment of the situation; Moscow ignored Grayevski's report and encouraged Nasser in his belligerence.

The result was that Israel, in a preemptive attack, destroyed the armies of Egypt, Syria, and Jordan and conquered much of their territory. And the Soviet Union, too, was a great loser; its weapons were proved inferior, it reneged on its promises and failed to support its badly beaten allies.

Nevertheless, the long-lasting affair between Grayevski and the KGB reached its peak that year. He was summoned to a meeting with his Soviet handler in a forest in central Israel. The KGB agent solemnly informed him that the Soviet government wanted to thank him for his devoted services and had decided to award him its highest distinction, the Lenin Medal!

The Russian apologized for not being able to pin the medal on Grayevski's lapel in Israel, but assured him that the medal was being kept for him in Moscow, and he would receive it whenever he got there. Grayevski preferred to stay in Israel.

And in 1971 he retired from the spy game.

But he was not forgotten. In 2007, he was invited to Shabak headquarters, where he was welcomed by a select group that included present and past directors of Shabak and Mossad, as well as many of his friends, colleagues, and relatives. The Shabak director at the time, Yuval Diskin, presented him with a prestigious award for his distinguished service—and Grayevski became the only secret agent to be decorated twice: by his own country, which he had served with devotion all his life, and by his country's foe, whom he had misled and deceived, regardless of the risks.

A reporter called him "the man who began the end of the Soviet Empire," but Grayevski didn't feel that way. "I am not a hero, and I didn't make history," he said. "The one who made history was Khrushchev. I just met history for a couple of hours, and then our ways parted."

He died at the age of eighty-one. And somewhere in the Kremlin, in a little box padded with red velvet, his medal, engraved with the profile of Vladimir Ilyich Lenin, perhaps still awaits him.

CHAPTER SIX

"BRING EICHMANN DEAD OR ALIVE!"

"And what's your name?" the girl asked.

"Nicolas," the smiling suitor said. "But all my friends call me Nick. Nick Eichmann."

THE BLIND JEW'S DAUGHTER

In the late fall of 1957, Isser Harel received a strange message from Frankfurt, Germany. It said that Dr. Fritz Bauer, attorney general of Hesse, requests to convey some secret information to the Mossad. Isser knew of Bauer, a much-respected figure in Germany. A tall, charismatic man with a pugnacious jaw, he was known for aggressively pursuing Nazi criminals. His leonine mane of white hair gave him a vague resemblance to David Ben-Gurion. Bauer, too, was Jewish, and a born fighter. In 1933, with Hitler's ascension to power, he was thrown into a concentration camp. But the horrid experience did not break his spirit. He later escaped to Denmark and then to Sweden. At the end of the war he decided to devote his life to the pursuit and punishment of Nazi criminals. And he was outspoken about his disappointment with West Germany's authorities, who did little to uproot Nazism.

In November 1957, Isser sent Shaul Darom, an Israeli security officer, to meet with Bauer. He arrived in Frankfurt and had a long conversation with the attorney general. A few days later, Darom walked into Isser's office in Tel Aviv. "Dr. Bauer told me," Darom said, "that Eichmann is alive, and he is hiding in Argentina."

Isser started. Like millions of Jews, he knew SS Colonel Adolf Eichmann as the embodiment of Nazi horror. The Obersturmbannführer Eichmann had personally directed "the final solution"—the systematic annihilation of European Jewry. He had devoted his life to the meticulous massacre of 6 million Jews. He had disappeared after the war, and nobody knew where he was; he was said to be living in Syria, Egypt, Kuwait, South America . . .

Darom recounted in detail his conversation with Bauer. A few months earlier, Bauer had received a letter from Argentina, sent by a German émigré, half-Jewish, who had suffered under the Nazis during the war. He had read newspaper reports about Bauer's relentless pursuit of Nazi criminals and knew that on top of that list of wanted men was Adolf Eichmann. When his pretty daughter, Sylvia, told him she was dating a young man, Nick Eichmann, he was stunned. He thought that young Nick must be related to the missing mass murderer. He wrote to Bauer that he could lead his agents to Eichmann's hideout; Eichmann was said to live in Buenos Aires under a false identity.

Bauer already knew that Eichmann had escaped from Germany after the war. His wife, Vera, and his three sons had stayed on in Austria, but a few years later they vanished. Eventually, Bauer found out that they had emigrated to Argentina, where Vera had remarried. Bauer was convinced that she had joined Eichmann and her second marriage was fictitious. "Her second husband" had to be Eichmann himself, who had been waiting for her.

Bauer feared that if he asked the German government to request Eichmann's extradition from Argentina, he'd lose him. He didn't trust the German judicial branch, still full of former Nazis. He also suspected a few employees at the Buenos Aires German embassy. Bauer feared that even before an official extradition demand was handed to the Argentineans, somebody at the embassy or in Germany would warn Eichmann and he'd vanish again.

Bauer spoke frankly with Shaul Darom. He wanted the Mossad to find out if this man in Buenos Aires was indeed Eichmann; and, if so, Israel should demand his extradition or launch a covert operation and abduct Eichmann.

"I am speaking to you after many days and nights of soul-searching," Bauer admitted. "Only one man in Germany knows about my decision to give you this information, minister-president of Hesse Georg August Zinn (a Social-Democrat and a future president of Germany's federal council, the Bundesrat)."

Shaul Darom, now back in Israel, put on Isser's desk a single sheet of paper, revealing Eichmann's hideout. Isser's eyes focused on one sentence: "4261 Calle Chacabuco, Olivos, Buenos Aires."

In early January 1958, a young man strolled down Calle Chacabuco. This was Emmanuel (Emma) Talmor, a member of Mossad special operations. Isser had sent him to check the accuracy of Bauer's message. Emma didn't like what he saw. Olivos was a poor neighborhood, inhabited mostly by laborers. On both sides of the unpaved Calle Chacabuco stood decrepit shacks, including number 4261. In its tiny courtyard Talmor noticed a fat, shabby woman.

"I don't believe that that could be Eichmann's house," Talmor said to Isser in his Tel Aviv office a few days later. "I'm certain that Eichmann transferred a ton of money to Argentina, like all the Nazi big shots, who prepared their escapes long before the Reich fell. I can't believe he lives in such a hovel and such a slum. Nor can that fat woman in the courtyard be Vera Eichmann."

Talmor's objections didn't convince the *ramsad*. Isser wanted to continue investigating, but he needed to contact Bauer's source. He got in touch with Bauer, who immediately revealed the name and address of his informant: Lothar Hermann. He had now moved to another town, Coronel Suarez, about three hundred miles from Buenos Aires. Bauer sent Isser a letter of introduction, asking Hermann to do everything to assist the bearer of the letter.

And in February 1958, an overseas visitor came to Coronel Suarez—Efraim Hoffstetter, head of investigation of the Tel Aviv police; he happened to be in Argentina for an Interpol conference and agreed to cooperate with Isser. But, being cautious, when he knocked on the door at Libertad Avenue, he introduced himself as a German, Karl Huppert. In the living room he saw a blind man, plainly dressed, his hands resting on a massive wooden table. As Hoffstetter walked in, the blind man heard his footsteps and turned toward him, groping for his hand. This was Lothar Hermann.

"I am a friend of Fritz Bauer," Hoffstetter said. He hinted that he was connected with Germany's secret service.

Hermann told him he was Jewish and had been a policeman until the Nazis took power. His parents had been murdered and he had been sent to Dachau, where he had lost his sight; he later emigrated to Argentina with his German wife. When he stumbled upon the name of Eichmann, he had contacted Bauer. His only motive, he claimed, was to help punish the Nazi criminals who had massacred his family.

"You see," he said, touching the arm of his lovely daughter, Sylvia, who had entered. "She is the one who found Eichmann for you."

The girl blushed and hesitantly told Hoffstetter her story.

Until a year and a half ago, she said, her family had lived in the Olivos neighborhood in Buenos Aires. There she'd met Nick Eichmann, a nice young man with whom she had had a few dates. She didn't tell him that she was of Jewish origin, since the Hermanns were known as an Aryan family. But Nick didn't mince his words. He had once remarked to her that the Germans should have finished the job and annihilated all the Jews. And on another occasion he mentioned that his father had served as an officer in the Wehrmacht during World War II and had fulfilled his duty to the Fatherland.

Nick freely shared his views with Sylvia, but never invited her to his home. Even after her family left Buenos Aires and they exchanged letters, he withheld his home address, and had her write to him at a friend's address.

This odd behavior triggered Lothar Hermann's suspicions that Nick could be Eichmann's son. He traveled with his daughter to Buenos Aires and took a bus to Olivos. Sylvia, with the help of some friends, found Nick Eichmann's address, and even managed to enter the house on Calle Chacabuco. But Nick wasn't home. There she met a balding man who wore spectacles and sported a thin mustache; he told her he was Nick's father.

Hermann now told Hoffstetter that he would agree to go again to Buenos Aires with Sylvia, to help pursue this investigation. Sylvia was needed to accompany her blind father everywhere, and to write and read his correspondence. Hoffstetter gave him a list of items he needed for the definitive identification of Eichmann: his photograph, present name, workplace, official documents about him, and his fingerprints. Hoffstetter and Hermann then established a secure system for corresponding, and Hoffstetter gave Hermann some money for expenses. Finally, he took a postcard out of his pocket and tore it in two. He gave one half to Hermann. "If somebody brings to you the other half," he said, "you can tell him everything. He will be one of us."

Hoffstetter left them, returned to Israel, and reported to Isser.

A few months later, Hermann's report arrived at Mossad headquarters. He reported with enthusiasm that he had found out everything about Eichmann. The house on Calle Chacabuco had been built by an Austrian, Francisco Schmidt, ten years earlier. Schmidt had rented the house to two families: Daguto and Klement. Hermann emphatically claimed that Schmidt was Eichmann. He believed that Daguto and Klement only served as a cover for the real Eichmann.

Isser asked his agent in Argentina to verify Hermann's report. The man cabled back: "There is no doubt that Francisco Schmidt is not Eichmann. He does not live and has never lived in the house on Calle Chacabuco."

Isser concluded that Hermann was not reliable, and decided to end the investigation.

THE MISTAKE

Isser's decision was a huge mistake and it could have ruined Israel's opportunity to capture Eichmann. One couldn't help but wonder about the incompetence that plagued the early stages of the operation. How could a covert, complex investigation have been entrusted to an elderly, blind, and unskilled man? How could the Mossad have taken seriously his mistaken identification of Eichmann? How could Isser have ignored the fact that Sylvia had visited Calle Chacabuco and met Nick Eichmann's father? Instead of sending to Buenos Aires a professional investigator who could have checked the identities of the two tenants and the landlord, Isser simply walked away. This grave error, in particular, was unlike Isser.

A year and a half later, Fritz Bauer came to Israel. He didn't want to meet Isser Harel, whom he blamed for having failed to capture Eichmann. He went and met directly with Attorney General Haim Cohen, in Jerusalem. He let his anger explode when he described to Cohen the lame handling of this investigation by the Mossad.

Haim Cohen summoned Isser and Zvi Aharoni, the Shabak chief investigator, to Jerusalem. Bauer was waiting in his office and accused Harel of botching the investigation. He also threatened that if the Mossad was unable to carry out the mission, he would have no choice but ask the German authorities to take it on. But it was not his threat that persuaded Harel to reopen the case. It was a new piece of information that Bauer had brought with him: two words that appeared to solve the mystery. Eichmann's fictitious name in Argentina, Bauer revealed, was Ricardo Klement.

All at once, Isser realized where he had gone wrong, and where his men had erred. Eichmann actually was one of the tenants on Calle Chacabuco. Only not Schmidt—it was Klement.

Hermann's daughter had indeed dated Eichmann's son, and the Eichmann family did live on Calle Chacabuco. But Hermann didn't know that Eichmann had changed his name to Klement, and instead had mistakenly pointed him out as Francisco Schmidt. If Isser had done his job and sent skilled agents to investigate Hermann's story, he would long ago have discovered Eichmann's true identity.

Isser now suggested to Cohen and Bauer that Zvi Aharoni be put in charge of the investigation. Aharoni was a tall, lean man with a clear forehead, a square mustache, and a razor-sharp mind. A German Jew himself, he was personally close to Cohen—but less so with Isser. Aharoni was still angry that, in 1958, when he had come to Buenos Aires on another case, Isser hadn't tasked him with checking out the Hermann testimony. But that had to be forgotten. Today Isser badly needed Aharoni's expertise.

And so, in February 1960, Aharoni landed in Buenos Aires. He asked a friend, a local Jew, to have a look at the house on Calle Chacabuco. The man came back upset. The house was empty, he reported. A few painters and masons were refurbishing one of the two apartments—in fact, the former flat of the Klements. But they had left; destination unknown. Aharoni now had to devise a way to trace Klement without raising suspicion.

In early March, a young Argentinean in a bellboy's uniform came to the house on Calle Chacabuco. He was carrying a small, gift-wrapped package addressed to Nicholas Klement. It contained an expensive lighter and a perfumed card with a short inscription: "Dear Nick, greetings for your birthday." It looked like a birthday present sent by a woman who wanted to remain anonymous.

The messenger entered the flat, where a few painters were working, and asked for the Klement family, but most of the workers had no idea who the Klements were. One of the painters, though, told the bellboy he thought they had moved to the San Fernando neighborhood, on the other side of Buenos Aires. He then led the bellboy to a nearby workshop, where Nick Eichmann's brother worked. He was a blond man named Dieter; but though his manners were pleasant, he refused to disclose the Klements' new address. Nevertheless, the talkative Dieter told the bellboy that his father was temporarily working in the faraway city of Tucumán.

The bellboy returned to Calle Chacabuco and kept pestering the painters with incessant questions. Finally he got to a man who vaguely recalled a new address for the Klements. "You should take the train down to San Fernando station," he said. "Then you'll take bus 203 and get off at Avijenda. Across the street you'll see a kiosk. On its right, a bit apart from the other houses, you'll see a small brick house. That's the Klement home."

The delighted messenger hurried back and reported to Aharoni. The next day Aharoni took the train to San Fernando, followed the painter's instructions, and found the house at once. At the nearby kiosk he stopped and inquired about the name of the street.

"Calle Garibaldi," the old vendor told him.

The investigation was back on track.

CALLE GARIBALDI

In mid-March, Aharoni put on a business suit and headed to a house on Calle Garibaldi, across the street from the Klement home. "I represent an American company," he said to the woman who opened the door. "We manufacture sewing machines and we are looking to build a factory in this area. We would like to buy your house." And then he added, pointing at the Klement home: "And that house as well. Would you like to sell?"

While chatting with the woman, Aharoni kept pressing a button concealed in the handle of a small case he was carrying. It activated a hidden camera that took pictures of the Klement house from various angles.

The next day Aharoni checked the city archives, and found that the lot on which the Klement home sat belonged to Ms. Vera Liebl de Eichmann, proof that Vera hadn't married again, and, following Argentinean custom, she had registered the deed in both her maiden and married names. Ricardo Klement apparently chose not to be mentioned in official documents.

Aharoni returned to Calle Garibaldi several times, on foot, by private car or small truck, and took photos of the house, Vera, and of the little boy he saw playing in the yard. He did not see Klement, but he decided to wait for a special date: March 21. Aharoni's file indicated that this would be the twenty-fifth wedding anniversary of Adolf Eichmann and Vera Liebl. He expected Eichmann would return from Tucumán, to celebrate this with his family.

On March 21, Aharoni returned there with his camera. In the courtyard, he saw a thin, balding man of average height, with a thin mouth, a big nose, and a mustache; he was wearing spectacles. These features all matched the description in his intelligence file.

Eichmann.

In Israel, Isser drove to Ben-Gurion's house. "We have located Eichmann in Argentina," he said. "I think we can capture him and bring him to Israel."

Ben-Gurion immediately responded. "Bring him dead or alive," he said. He thought for a moment and added: "It would be better to bring him alive. This will be very important for our youth."

THE ADVANCE TEAM ARRIVES

Isser formed the operational team. All of its twelve members were volunteers. Some were Holocaust survivors, with concentration camp numbers tattooed on their forearms. The core of the team was the operational unit of the security services. At its head were the two top agents of the Shabak. Rafi Eitan was appointed commander. At his side was Zvi Malkin, whom Eitan described as "brave, physically strong, and endowed with tactical creativity." A balding man with bushy eyebrows, strong jaw, and deep, melancholy eyes, he was known as the best spy-catcher of the Shabak. He never carried a gun ("one may be tempted to use it"), he relied on "common sense, inventiveness, and improvisation" and had unmasked several top Soviet agents. He'd spent some of his childhood in Poland, and immigrated with his family to Israel after a bloody pogrom in the village of Grasnik Lubelski. Only his sister Fruma and her family had stayed behind; all of them and Zvi's other relatives perished in the Holocaust. He grew up in Haifa and fought in the Independence War. Among his many talents were painting, writing "compulsively," and acting. During a stay in New York he had become close with Lee Strasberg, founder of the Actors Studio, and had learned a lot from him about acting. "In many of the Mossad operations in which I participated," he later said, "I played as if I were on stage, using disguises and makeup. In other operations I felt as if I was directing a play. I wrote out my operational orders like screenplays."

Another team member was Vienna-born Avraham (Avrum) Shalom, a stocky, tight-lipped man who was Eitan's deputy, and a future Shabak director. Some of the others were Yaacov Gat, a discreet Paris-based field operative; Moshe Tavor, a former soldier in the British Army and a member of the secret "Avengers" group, which hunted Nazi criminals at the end of the war, some of whom he had personally killed; and quiet, self-effacing Shalom Danny, a talented painter and "a genius" in document forging. Some claimed that he had escaped a Nazi concentration camp by forging an authorization on toilet paper.

Most of the men were married, with families.

The team was also well-composed professionally. Efraim Ilani knew Argentina well and was familiar with the streets of Buenos Aires. He was a skilled locksmith, a man of great physical strength, and an agent with a very "honest" face who could inspire trust in anyone. Yehudith Nissiyahu, a religious woman and the best female agent in the Mossad, also volunteered. Yehudith was quiet, shy, unobtrusive, rather overweight and plain. She was married to a Labor Party activist, Mordechai Nissiyahu. She hosted one of the authors of this book several times, and there was nothing in her behavior that appeared out of the ordinary.

Dr. Yona Elian, a physician who had participated in several Mossad operations in the past, would be there to assist in bringing Eichmann back to Israel. Zvi Aharoni, the investigator, also joined. But the first volunteer to join the team was Isser himself. He loved to lead his men in dangerous operations abroad. But this time, he knew that in the course of taking action, immediate decisions at the top level would need to be made. And this could also have far-reaching political consequences. It was therefore crucial that the Israelis be led by someone who could make political decisions if necessary. Isser felt he had to assume command.

At the end of April, an advance team of four agents entered Argentina from different directions. They smuggled essential equipment into the country: walkie-talkies, electronic tools and instruments, medical supplies, and also a part of Shalom Danny's ambulant lab, equipped to produce passports, documents, and affidavits.

They rented an apartment in Buenos Aires (code-named "the Castle"), where several team members would live and work, and stocked it with food. The following day the four rented a car and drove to San Fernando, arriving there at seven forty P.M.

Darkness had fallen and they got a big surprise. While driving slowly on route 202, they suddenly saw, walking directly toward them, Ricardo Klement! He paid them no attention, simply turned and entered his house.

The agents concluded that Klement probably came home every evening at approximately this same time, and his capture could be carried out on the same deserted dark stretch between the bus station and his home.

That night, they wired Israel, in code: "Operation feasible."

A PLANE FOR ABBA EBAN

Isser felt he was in luck. He learned that on May 20 Argentina would celebrate the one hundred fiftieth anniversary of its independence. High-ranking delegations would be coming from all over the world to participate in the festivities. An Israeli delegation headed by Minister of Education Abba Eban would also come. Abba Eban was happy to learn that El Al would be putting at his disposal a special plane—a Britannia "Whispering Giant." Nobody told Eban that the real reason for El Al's generosity was Operation Eichmann.

Flight 601 to Buenos Aires had been scheduled for May 11. The plane crew was carefully selected and Isser had revealed the secret only to two of El Al's senior officials, Mordechai Ben-Ari and Efraim Ben-Artzi. The pilot, Zvi Tohar, was advised to take a qualified mechanic with him, in case the plane suddenly had to take off without the assistance of an Argentinean land crew.

On May 1, at dawn, Isser landed in Buenos Aires with a European passport. A freezing wind swept the airport runways. In Argentina, it was almost winter. Eight days later, on the evening of May 9, several Israelis slipped into a tall new apartment building in Buenos Aires. They went up to an apartment that had been rented a few days earlier (code-named

"Heights"). All members of the operational unit were present. Earlier, they had settled in various hotels around town. The last to enter was Isser; for the first time, "the twelve" were together.

Since coming to Argentina, Isser had established an ingenious mode of communication with his team: in his pocket, he carried a list of three hundred cafés in Buenos Aires, with their addresses and their hours of operation. Every morning he would set out on a walking tour, going between these cafés, following an itinerary and a timetable he had designated beforehand. This way his men knew exactly where he could be found at every moment of the day. The one big inconvenience in this system was the gallons of strong Argentinean coffee that the *ramsad* had to absorb in these daily circuits. From the cafés Isser directed the preparations for the abduction.

These were days of feverish activity: bringing and setting up equipment needed for keeping a prisoner; renting cars for surveillance and for the capture, renting additional apartments and secluded villas out of town, where Eichmann would be held. The most important villa ("The Base") was on the way to the airport. It was rented by two Mossad agents posing as tourists. One of them was Yaacov Meidad (Mio), a stocky, German-born man who had lost his parents in the Holocaust and fought in the British Army during the war. The woman who played the role of his companion was Yehudith Nissiyahu. Within the villa the agents built a hiding place for Eichmann and his guard, if the local police were ever to investigate. A second flat was prepared as an alternative.

The plan now was for Eichmann to be captured on May 10, the plane to arrive on May 11, and on May 12, to set off for Israel.

But a last-moment change screwed up the plan. Because of the great number of visitors coming for the anniversary celebrations, the Protocol Department of the Argentinean Ministry of Foreign Affairs informed the Israeli delegation that they would have to delay their arrival until May 19, at two P.M. For Isser that meant either delaying Eichmann's capture till May 19—or executing the plan on May 10 and then waiting in hiding with their captive for nine or ten days. That could be very risky, especially if, at his family's request, an intensive search was organized for the missing Eichmann. There was a real danger that Eichmann and his Israeli abductors might be found by the police.

Despite reservations, Isser decided to move ahead as originally planned; but because of his people's fatigue, he decided to push it back one day. D-day was set for May 11, and H-hour for 7:40 P.M.

The operational plan was now laid out and ready in minute detail: Eichmann returned from work every evening at seven forty P.M. He got off bus 203 at the kiosk and walked home along Calle Garibaldi. The street was dark, traffic was sparse. The operation would be carried out by agents in two cars: one team for the abduction, another for security and protection. The first car would be parked at the roadside with its hood raised, and the agents would appear to be repairing it. When Eichmann passed by them, they would jump him, overpower him, and throw him into the car. It would then at once dart forward, with the other car following. The doctor would travel in the second car, to be close by in case the captive needed to be drugged.

Isser, in a strict tone, gave precise orders. "If you run into any kind of trouble," he said, "you do not let go of Eichmann even if you're stopped. If the police arrest you, say that you are Israelis, acting on your own, to bring this Nazi criminal to justice." All those who escape arrest, he added, leave the country according to the current plan.

He also instructed Meidad and Yehudith Nissiyahu to move into the villa and act like a couple of tourists. "Every so often come out and make yourselves comfortable on the lawn with snacks and newspapers."

All the other agents were ordered to leave their hotels and move to the designated safe houses.

COUNTDOWN

May 11, morning.

The operational unit completed its preparations. Even before H-hour, the men had started covering their tracks. Most of the rented vehicles were returned. All members of the group had their disguises in place—makeup, false mustaches, beards, and wigs. Each got new documents that suited their new faces. The twelve who had arrived in Buenos Aires a few days back—who walked the streets, rented cars and apartments, checked into hotels, surveyed the house on Calle Garibaldi—vanished; twelve others, looking different, carrying different documents with different names, took their place.

Isser, too, left his hotel, checked his luggage at the railroad station, and returned to the city. Today, as every day, he would keep moving between the cafés. His movements today were in a business and entertainment area, where the cafés were at barely a five-minute walk from one to the next.

1:00 P.M.—Isser, Rafi Eitan, and a few of the lead operatives met for a final briefing in a big restaurant in the city center. All around them, merry Argentineans laughed, drank, and devoured local grilled meats. At 2:00 P.M., the team dispersed.

2:30 P.M.—In a large midtown parking garage, the agents took the capture car that had been there for a few days, and drove it to "the Base." The second car set off from another garage.

3:30 P.M.—The two cars were stationed by "the Base," ready to move.

4:30 P.M.—Last briefing in "the Base." The operational unit guys changed clothes, took their papers, and prepared to leave.

6:30 P.M.—The two cars departed. Four agents were in the capture car: Zvi Aharoni as the driver; Rafi Eitan, the commander; Moshe Tavor and Zvi Malkin. Three more agents were in the second car: Avraham Shalom, Yaacov Gat, and Dr. Elian, who carried a case with drugs, instruments, and sedatives.

The cars arrived separately and met at a crossroads, not far from the Klement house. The agents checked the area and established that there were no checkpoints or police forces nearby.

7:35 P.M.—The two cars parked on Calle Garibaldi. Thick darkness had settled over the place already. The capture car, a black Chevrolet sedan, was parked at the sidewalk, turned toward the Klement house. Two agents got out and raised the hood; Aharoni remained at the wheel, and the fourth man crouched inside the car, watching the spot where Eichmann was expected to emerge from the dark. One of the men put on thin gloves, in case he had to touch Eichmann; the very thought of touching him filled him with disgust. Across the street was the second car, a black Buick. Two agents got out and busied themselves around the car. The third remained in the driver's seat, ready to turn on his lights and blind Klement as he approached. The trap was set.

But Klement didn't show.

7:40 P.M.—Bus 203 stopped at the corner, but nobody got out.

7:50 P.M.—Two more buses came, one after the other. Klement was in neither. Anxiety swelled through the agents. What had happened? Had he changed his habits? Did he smell danger and flee?

8:00 P.M.—At an earlier briefing, Isser had told the group that if Klement didn't show by eight, they were to abort and leave. Rafi Eitan, though, decided to wait until eight thirty.

8:05 P.M.—Another bus stopped at the corner. At first the Israelis saw nothing. But Avrum Shalom, who was in the second team, suddenly discerned a silhouette coming along Calle Garibaldi. Klement! He turned on his lights, aiming a blinding beam at the approaching figure.

Ricardo Klement was walking toward his house. The dazzling lights struck him in the face and he averted his eyes. He kept walking. He noticed a car by the side of the road—probably engine trouble—and a few people beside it. At that moment, a man by the Chevrolet turned to him. *"Momentito, señor"* (Just a moment), he said. It was Zvi Malkin, using the only two words he knew in Spanish.

Klement reached for the flashlight in his pocket, one he often used in this dark part of the street. Then it all happened with lightning speed. Malkin feared Klement was drawing a gun. He leaped on Klement and threw him on the dirt at the roadside. Klement let out a loud, shrill shout. From the car, another man, and another, sprung on him. Strong arms took hold of his head and covered his mouth. They pulled him into the back of the car and laid him, stunned, on its floor. The driver started the car and it darted forward. Barely half a minute had passed between the moment Klement appeared and the car's departure.

Seconds later, the other car took off and followed.

Agile hands quickly tied Klement's hands and feet. And somebody stuck a rag in his mouth. His glasses were removed and replaced by opaque black spectacles. A voice barked in German, close to his ear: "One move and you're dead!" He obeyed; for the entire trip he didn't budge. Meanwhile, two hands slipped under his clothes and felt his skin. Rafi Eitan's hands were searching for his scars—one under the left armpit, one on the right side of his belly. Eitan looked at Malkin, and nodded. They shook hands. Eichmann was in their grasp.

Eitan thought he had his feelings under control. But then he suddenly realized that he was humming the song of the Jewish partisans in the war against the Nazis, and repeating the refrain: "We are here! We are here!"

The car was moving very fast, then suddenly stopped, its engine still running. Klement could not know that it was for a train barrier. The two capture cars had to wait long minutes while an endless freight train passed. This felt to the agents like the most critical moment in the entire operation. Their cars were surrounded by other cars, all waiting for the barrier to be raised. Outside voices could be heard, but Klement didn't dare move. None of the Argentineans alongside them noticed anything strange lying on the car's floor. Minutes later, the barrier was raised and the cars all smoothly moved forward.

20:55 P.M.—The two cars came to a stop in the driveway of "the Base." Klement, trudging like a blind man between his captors, was ushered into the house. He did not object when the men holding him started undressing him. They demanded in German that he open his mouth. He obeyed. They checked inside it, searching for a poison capsule perhaps lodged between his teeth. Still wearing opaque glasses, he didn't see a thing, but felt hands checking his body again and touching his scars. An expert hand slipped under his left armpit and touched the tiny scar that remained, when, a few years ago, he had tried to remove the small tattoo of his blood type, customary among SS officers.

Suddenly a voice rang out in German.

"The size of your hat . . . your shoes . . . date of birth . . . father's name . . . mother's name . . . "

Like a robot, he answered in German. Even when they asked, "What is the number of your Nazi Party card? Your number in the SS?" he couldn't stay silent.

45326. And another number, 63752.

"Your name?"

"Ricardo Klement."

"Your name?" the voice repeated.

He shivered. "Otto Heninger."

"Your name?"

"Adolf Eichmann."

A silence settled around him. He broke it. "I am Adolf Eichmann," he repeated. "I know that I am in the hands of the Israelis. I also know some Hebrew, I studied with a rabbi in Warsaw . . ."

He recalled some verses of the Bible and started reciting them, trying to speak the Hebrew words with the proper pronunciation.

No one else spoke.

The Israeli boys stared at him, stupefied.

A MESSENGER TO SDEH BOKER

Isser was moving from one café to another. It was late at night when he entered another café and slumped in a chair facing the door. Suddenly he saw two of his men at the entrance. He jumped up. "We got him," Aharoni said, beaming. "He's been definitely identified and he's confessed that he is Adolf Eichmann."

Isser shook their hands and they left. Now he had to go back to the railroad station, pick up his suitcase, and check into a new hotel under his new identity, as if he had just arrived in Buenos Aires. The night air was cool and crisp and he decided to walk. He had been running a slight fever and suffering from a cold, but now he felt wonderful. He walked, alone in the dark, enjoying the cool night air and feeling uplifted—the kind of intoxication he would never forget.

The next day a car stopped by a wooden cabin in kibbutz Sdeh Boker. A thin man, wearing glasses, came out of the car, showed his ID to the guards, and entered Ben-Gurion's study. This was Yaacov Caroz, Isser's close aide.

"Isser sent me," he said. "We got a cable from him. Eichmann is in our hands."

The Old Man was silent. Then he asked: "When is Isser coming back? I need him."

Looking at the distraught faces of his men, Isser realized how Eichmann's very presence in their company was depressing them. The German monster was next to them, now, separated by only a thin wall—and that unnerved these tough people and filled them with disgust. They couldn't get used to looking after a man who, in their eyes, was the symbol of Evil; who, for many of them, had been the murderer of their closest relatives—fathers, mothers, brothers and sisters, all vanished in the crematoriums. And taking care of Eichmann meant tending to his needs twenty-four hours a day. They couldn't give him a razor, so they shaved him; they couldn't leave him alone for a second, lest he commit suicide; they had to be with him even when he went to the toilet. Yehudith Nissiyahu cooked and served Eichmann's meals, but refused to wash the dishes from which he ate. Her repulsion for him overwhelmed her. Zvi Malkin, sitting in a corner, fought his disgust by drawing sketches of Eichmann on an old copy of *A Guide to South America*. The guards, who changed every twenty-four hours, were totally stressed out, and Isser felt he had to give each of them a day's leave. Let them walk about Buenos Aires, he thought, taste the bustling life of this big city, and for a few hours forget the obscene reality at "the Base."

These were becoming the ten longest days of their lives—hiding themselves in a foreign country, and living in fear of a tiny mistake that could trigger a police raid and an international scandal.

PLANNING THE ESCAPE

Eichmann sat in a bare room, with no windows, illuminated day and night by a lone bulb. He was obedient and readily fulfilled his guards' instructions. It seemed as if he had resigned himself to his fate. The only one who spoke with him was Aharoni, who interrogated him about his life prior to his capture. Eichmann answered all the questions. He told Aharoni that after Germany's defeat in May 1945, he had assumed the identity of a Luftwaffe private, Adolf Karl Barth. He later posed as a lieutenant in the Twenty-second Waffen-SS Cavalry Division, Otto Eckmann, and was incarcerated in a POW camp. At the end of that year, when his name was introduced in the Nuremberg trials of the top Nazis, he escaped from the camp. As Otto Heninger, he hid until 1950 in Zelle in Lower Saxony and that same year escaped to Argentina, via Italy, using one of the escape routes of Nazi criminals.

Nine years had passed since he disembarked in Argentina, dressed in a white shirt, bow tie, and winter coat, wearing sunglasses and sporting a pencil-thin mustache. He spent four months with friends in the Jurmann pension in a Buenos Aires suburb and four more months at the home of a German contact named Rippler. Only then did he risk moving around alone and left Buenos Aires for Tucumán, a small town about six hundred miles away. There he was employed by Capri, a little-known construction company, said to be a cover company whose mission was to supply fugitive Nazis with jobs.

On April 4, 1952, Eichmann received his Argentinean ID card in the name of Ricardo Klement, born in Bolzano, Italy, unmarried, mechanic by profession.

A year before, in early 1951, Eichmann, using a false name, had sent a letter to his wife in Austria. He informed her that "the uncle of her children, the man she believed dead, actually was alive and well." Vera Liebl immediately recognized his handwriting and told her sons that Uncle Ricardo, their dead father's cousin, had invited them to join him in Argentina.

She obtained a legal passport for herself and for her children. The secret Nazi machine kicked into feverish action and took care of blurring and erasing Vera's tracks. When Israeli secret agents finally got their hands on the "Vera Liebl" file in the Austrian archives, what they found was an empty folder the contents of which had seemingly evaporated.

In June 1952, Vera Liebl and her three sons, Horst, Dieter, and Klaus vanished from their home in Austria. In early July they surfaced briefly in Genoa, and on July 28 they came ashore in Buenos Aires. On August 15, they got off the train in the dusty Tucumán station.

"Vera Eichmann," Moshe Pearlman wrote in his book, "still carried in her memory the picture of the dashing Nazi officer, who looked so impressive in his dress uniform and shining boots. But the man who waited for her on the Tucumán platform was a middle-aged man, modestly dressed, his face pale and wrinkled, his expression depressed and his walk slow. This was her Adolf."

Eichmann the Terrible had become unrecognizable. He had gotten thin and was balding, his cheeks were sunken and his face had lost the air of arrogance that had been so characteristic of him. He appeared resigned and anxious; only his thin lips still suggested cruelty and malice.

In 1953, Capri went bankrupt and Eichmann had to search for a job. First he tried opening a laundry in Buenos Aires with two other Nazis, then worked on a rabbit farm, and later in a fruit-juice cannery. Finally, with the help of another secret Nazi organization, Ricardo Klement was appointed a foreman at the Mercedes-Benz assembly plant in Suárez. By then he had started believing that he would end his life peacefully. Until May 11, 1960.

Meanwhile, Eichmann's sons searched for him in hospitals, morgues, and police stations; they turned for help to the Fascist-Peronist youth organization Tacuara, which joined the search. But Eichmann's sons soon concluded that the Israelis must have captured their father. They then tried but failed to convince the pro-Nazi organizations to take some drastic action, perhaps kidnap the Israeli ambassador and hold him until their father was released; but the Argentineans refused.

Isser instructed his men about what to do if the hideout was located by the police. If they raid "the Base," Isser said, Eichmann should be rushed to the secret chamber that had been prepared inside the house. If the police set out to do a thorough search, Eichmann was to be whisked out of the house by a side exit that had been specifically set for such an emergency. Several agents were to escape with Eichmann, while the others were to do anything possible to hinder the search, despite the risks that might involve.

To whoever would be with Eichmann, Isser said, "If the police find the hideout and break in, handcuff yourself to him and throw away the keys, so they won't be able to tear you away from him. Tell them that you're Israeli, and together with your friends you have captured the world's most hated criminal, Adolf Eichmann, in order to bring him to trial. Then give the police my real name—Isser Harel—as well as my false identity, and the name of the hotel where I am staying. If they get hold of you and of Eichmann—I'm to be arrested as well."

A few days later, Eichmann agreed to sign a document, stipulating that he was willing to be taken to Israel and put on trial there. It read:

> I, the undersigned Adolf Eichmann, of my own free will hereby declare: now that my real identity has been discovered, I recognize that there is no further use in trying to evade the course of justice. I agree to be taken to Israel and stand trial before a qualified tribunal. It is understood that I shall be given the assistance of an advocate and that I shall be permitted to lay before the court, without travesty of the facts, an account of the last years of my service in Germany, so that a truthful description of those events may be passed on to the future generations. I am making this declaration of my own accord. Nothing has been promised to me and I have not been threatened. My desire is to find inner peace at last.
>
> As I am unable to remember all the details, and may become confused when stating the facts, I ask that the relevant documents and testimonies be placed at my disposal to help me in my efforts to establish the truth.
>
> Adolf Eichmann, Buenos Aires, May 1960.

This declaration, of course, had no legal validity.

THE PLANE ARRIVES

May 18, 1960, 11:00 A.M.

A formal ceremony took place at Lod International Airport near Tel Aviv. Many high-ranking personalities, including the chief of staff General Laskov, the director general of the Ministry of Foreign Affairs, and the Argentinean ambassador to Israel, came to see off the impressive delegation to Argentina, for the one hundred fiftieth anniversary celebration. The El Al "Whispering Giant" took off, also carrying some regular passengers, bound for stopovers along the way.

Few of the passengers noticed that in Rome three more civilians came aboard. After a couple of hours, these new passengers had become El Al crew members and were moving in the aisles in El Al uniforms. Actually, they were Mossad agents en route to assist their colleagues in Buenos Aires. One of them was Yehuda Carmel, a bald fellow with a prominent nose and a thin mustache. He was not very happy about this trip. He knew he had been chosen not because of his talents but because of his outward appearance. A few days earlier he had been called to his boss's office, where he saw two photos on the desk—his own and one of an unknown man. They looked very similar. When he was told that the unknown man was Adolf Eichmann, he shuddered. He was even more shocked when he was told that he had been chosen to serve as Eichmann's double. Isser's plan was to bring Carmel to Argentina as an El Al crew member, to take his uniform and documents, and then use these to get a drugged Eichmann on the plane. Carmel carried an Israeli passport in the name of Ze'ev Zichroni.

Isser had also prepared a backup plan. He summoned, with the help of a go-between, a young kibbutz member, Meir Bar-Hon, who was visiting relatives in Buenos Aires. Meir was asked to come to Bar Gloria on Bartolome Mitre Avenue, where two men were waiting for him: Isser and Dr. Elian. Isser instructed him: "When you return to your relatives' home, call a doctor and tell him that you were in a car accident, and that you suffer from dizziness, nausea, and general weakness. The doctor will likely conclude that you suffer from a concussion and will put you in a hospital. On May 19, in the morning, you'll tell him that you feel much better and you'll ask to go home. You'll be discharged and the hospital will provide you with a document certifying you have been treated for a concussion."

Dr. Elian then briefed Meir on the specific concussion symptoms that he should present.

Meir left Bar Gloria and followed Isser's instructions. He lay there and moaned for three days in a big Buenos Aires hospital. On May 19, he was discharged. An hour later, Isser held in his hands an official hospital document issued to Meir Bar-Hon, certifying that he had been discharged after being hurt in a car accident.

So, if the plan to smuggle Eichmann out of Argentina as an El Al crew member were to fail, Isser would have him put on a stretcher and carried to the plane as Meir Bar-Hon, a patient still suffering from a serious concussion.

May 19.

That afternoon the El Al plane landed in Buenos Aires. Protocol officials from the Ministry of Foreign Affairs, enthusiastic local Jews, and children carrying little blue-and-white flags stood on both sides of the red carpet laid by the gangway.

A couple of hours later, Isser conferred with the pilot, Zvi Tohar, and an El Al executive and fixed the takeoff time: May 20, at midnight.

Isser presented his plans. After a short discussion they agreed to go for plan A: Eichmann would be brought aboard as a crew member who had been taken ill. His double, Yehuda Carmel, had already turned over his uniform and documents in the name of Ze'ev Zichroni, an El Al navigator, to the Mossad team. Shalom Danny, the team's master forger, doctored the documents so as to fit Eichmann perfectly. Carmel was given new documents and told that he would leave Argentina sometime soon.

That evening a beehive of activity took over "the Base." After a week of strained waiting, the Mossad agents sprang back to life. Eichmann was drugged and fell asleep. The agents meticulously stripped the house. The various instruments and devices were all disassembled, the personal effects packed, and the house fully restored to its previous state. By the wee hours nothing remained that could even hint at the role the villa had played in the last eight days. And similar actions took place in all the other safe houses.

May 20.

Isser left his hotel for the last time, hailed a cab to the railroad station, and checked his luggage. Then he resumed his café routine of the previous days. The El Al people were the first to report to him, and together they prepared a detailed timetable.

At midday the last stage began. Isser paid his check at the final café he visited, picked up his luggage, and drove to the airport to oversee the escape operation. He walked through the terminal, looking for a place where he could best set up his command post. He wandered through the shopping and ticketing areas, and finally discovered the cafeteria for airport employees. Outside it was bitterly cold and the cafeteria teemed with clerks, ground crew, and flight personnel, who all came in for a hot drink or a light meal. Isser was delighted. This was ideal. Nobody would notice him or become aware of his hurried and hushed consultations with his men. Isser waited until a chair was vacated, and from it he now began to supervise the final moves on Argentinean soil.

"HI, EL AL!"

9:00 P.M.—In the safe house, all was ready. Eichmann was washed, shaved, dressed in an El Al uniform, and had in his pocket an ID in the name of Ze'ev Zichroni. His face was so well made up that even his own son wouldn't have recognized him. The doctor and two agents were also in El Al uniforms. The doctor injected Eichmann with a drug that didn't put him to sleep but only blurred his senses. He was able to hear and see and even walk, but he couldn't speak and didn't quite understand what was happening.

Aharoni, also wearing an El Al uniform, took the wheel of the car, and an agent sat beside him. Eichmann was put in the backseat, between the doctor and another Mossad agent. The car set out.

At the same time two other cars departed from a popular hotel in the city center. These cars carried the real El Al crew. Their trip to the airport was meticulously synchronized with the progress of the Mossad vehicles.

In his improvised command post, Isser received minute-by-minute updates. He ordered his men's baggage to be brought to the airport. He had prepared individual escape routes for each one, but if the main plan proceeded smoothly, they would all leave Argentina on the El Al aircraft. Not far from Isser, Shalom Danny was sipping from a steaming mug of black coffee. Passersby had no idea that this customer had a lot of cheek: he had set up his forgery lab under their very eyes, and was busy doctoring the passports of the Mossad agents, putting in all the necessary stamps and inscriptions to allow for their easy departure.

11:00 P.M.—A man materialized next to Isser. All the cars, Mossad, and El Al had arrived, he reported. Isser hurried to the parking lot and checked the El Al cars. The crew members were silent. They sensed that they were participating in something extraordinary, but had no idea what it was. They listened to Isser's instructions quietly and asked no questions. Isser peeked into the third car, where Eichmann was dozing between his escorts. "Go," he said. "Good luck!"

The three cars moved ahead, while Isser returned to the terminal. The little convoy reached the Argentinean Airlines barrier; the Israeli aircraft was parked in their lot. "Hi, El Al!"—one of the Israelis merrily called. The guards recognized him and were, in fact, used to the Israelis going in and out of their lot all day. They cast a weary look at the passengers in the three vehicles, all dressed in El Al uniforms. In two of the cars, the passengers were singing, laughing, and loudly chatting, while those in the third car were asleep in their seats.

The barrier was raised and all three cars drove toward the plane. Their doors opened and the dozen or so uniformed men moved in a cluster toward the gangway. Eichmann trudged in their middle, largely concealed by the others. Two men held him, helped him up the stairs, and placed him by a window in first class. The doctor and the security team spread out on the seats around him and pretended to be asleep. If Argentinean immigration officers were to come and check their papers, they were to be told that these are the men who work the second shift, and need to rest before the next leg of the flight.

11:15 P.M.—Isser, back in his seat at the cafeteria, heard the characteristic rumbling of the "Whispering Giant"'s engines. The plane taxied to the terminal and stopped at its departure gate. Isser walked swiftly to the Departure Hall and looked around. In odd corners he saw his men, standing beside their luggage. Isser walked around to them, and as he approached each of the agents, he whispered: "Get on the plane." They moved casually and joined the line to passport control. All had their passports ready. And Shalom Danny had done a fine job with them.

11:45 P.M.—Having passed immigration and customs without any problems, the group went through the departure gate and walked toward the plane. Isser was the last to pick up his luggage, go through the checkpoints, and get on the plane, which almost immediately moved out to the runway.

0:00 hours; the night between May 20 and 21. The plane stopped. A delay was ordered by the control tower. The agents were all tense with anxiety. Had something happened? Had a last-minute tip reached the Argentinean police? Would they be ordered to turn back? But after a few minutes of terrifying anxiety, the plane was finally cleared. The "Whispering Giant" took off over the silvery waters of Rio de la Plata. Isser breathed a sigh of relief.

"I HAVE TO INFORM THE KNESSET . . ."

May 22. The plane landed at Lod Airport early in the morning.

At nine fifty A.M. Isser came directly to Jerusalem. Ben-Gurion's secretary, Yitzhak Navon, immediately ushered him into the prime minister's office.

Ben-Gurion was surprised. "When did you arrive?"

"Two hours ago. We got Eichmann."

"Where is he?" the Old Man asked.

"Here, in Israel. Adolf Eichmann is in Israel, and if you agree, we'll deliver him to the police right away."

Ben-Gurion fell silent. He didn't burst into tears, as some journalists later reported, nor did he laugh triumphantly, as others wrote. He didn't hug Isser, or show any emotion.

"Are you sure that this is Eichmann?" he asked. "How did you identify him?"

Isser, surprised, answered yes. He detailed for Ben-Gurion all the criteria by which Eichmann had been identified, and stressed that the prisoner himself had admitted that he was Adolf Eichmann. But the Old Man was not entirely satisfied. Not enough, he said. Before he would authorize any further steps, he wanted one or two people who had known Eichmann to meet him and formally identify him. He needed to be one hundred percent sure, and he wouldn't say a word about this to his government until then.

Isser called his office and ordered his staff to find some people who could identify Eichmann personally. In no time, they located two Israelis who in the past had met Eichmann. They were brought to the cell where he was being held, spoke with him, and formally identified him.

At midday, an Israeli envoy burst into a restaurant in Frankfurt and rushed to one of the tables, where a white-haired man, visibly nervous and tense, sat alone. "Herr Bauer," he said, "Adolf Eichmann is now in our hands. Our men have captured him and brought him to Israel. At any moment we can expect a statement in the Knesset by the prime minister."

Bauer, pale and deeply moved, got up. His hands were trembling. The man who had given the Mossad Eichmann's address in Argentina, the man without whom Eichmann would likely have never been caught, couldn't restrain himself anymore. He burst into tears, grasped the Israeli's shoulder, hugged him, and kissed him.

4:00 P.M.—At the Knesset plenary session, Ben-Gurion got on the speaker's podium. In a firm, clear voice, he read a short statement: "I have to inform the Knesset that the security services of Israel have just recently laid hands on one of the greatest of Nazi criminals, Adolf Eichmann, who was responsible with other Nazi leaders for what they called 'the final solution,' that is to say the extermination of six million European Jews. Eichmann is at present under arrest here in Israel. He will soon be put on trial in Israel, in accordance with the law on the crimes of the Nazis and their collaborators."

Ben-Gurion's words were received with shock and wonder, which turned into huge, spontaneous applause. Amazement and admiration spread through the Knesset and throughout the world. At the end of the Knesset session, a man got up from his seat, behind the government bench. Few knew his face or his name. It was Isser Harel.

The trial of Adolf Eichmann opened in Jerusalem on April 11, 1961. One hundred and ten Holocaust survivors were the witnesses for the prosecution. Some had never before spoken of their past, and now told their horrendous stories. It was as if the entire State of Israel was glued to the radio and followed with great pain and horror the dreadful story that emerged from the testimonies. And it felt as if the entire Jewish people identified with the prosecutor, Gideon Hausner, who confronted the Nazi criminal as the representative of his 6 million victims.

On December 15, 1961, Eichmann was sentenced to death. His appeal was rejected by the Supreme Court, and pardon was refused by President Yitzhak Ben-Zvi. On May 31, 1962, Adolf Eichmann was informed that his end was imminent. In his cell, the condemned man wrote a few letters to his family and drank half a bottle of red Carmel wine. Toward midnight, the Reverend Hull, a Nonconformist minister, entered Eichmann's cell, as he had on previous occasions. "Tonight I shall not discuss the Bible with you," Eichmann said to him. "I have no time to lose."

The minister left, but then an unexpected visitor walked into Eichmann's cell. Rafi Eitan.

The abductor stood facing the condemned man, dressed in a prisoner's light brown uniform. Eitan said nothing. Eichmann looked at him, and said in German: "I hope that your turn will come after mine."

The guards led Eichmann to a tiny room that had been converted to an execution chamber. He was placed on a trapdoor and a noose was slipped over his neck. A small group of officials, journalists, and a doctor, all allowed to be present at the execution, heard his last words, spoken in the Nazi tradition: "We'll meet again . . . I have lived, believing in God . . . I obeyed the laws of war and was loyal to my flag . . ."

Two police officers behind a screen simultaneously pressed two buttons, only one of which worked the trapdoor. Neither knew who had the controlling button, so the name of Eichmann's executioner remains unknown. Eitan didn't see the actual execution, but heard the thud of the trapdoor.

Eichmann's body was incinerated in an aluminum oven in the prison courtyard. "Black smoke rose toward the sky," wrote an American reporter. "No one said a word, but it was impossible not to recall the crematoriums at Auschwitz . . ."

Shortly before dawn on June 1, 1962, a swift boat of Israel's coast guard passed beyond Israel's territorial waters. The engine was turned off, and while the boat drifted silently a police officer cast Eichmann's ashes into the Mediterranean.

The wind and the waves dispersed the remains of the man who twenty years earlier had merrily declared: "I'll jump laughing into the grave, happy at having exterminated 6 million Jews."

At the deathbed of his mother, Zvi Malkin thought of his massacred relatives, of his sister Fruma and her small children, perished in the Holocaust. He bent toward his mother and whispered to her: "Mother, I got Eichmann. Fruma is avenged."

"I knew you wouldn't forget your sister," the dying woman whispered.

CHAPTER SEVEN

WHERE IS YOSSELE?

While Isser, his agents, and the captive Eichmann were waiting in their Buenos Aires safe houses for the arrival of the Britannia "Whispering Giant" aircraft from Tel Aviv, the *ramsad* was busy with another project. Isser had decided to check the rumors that another Nazi criminal was hiding in the city: Dr. Josef Mengele, "the angel of death," the monstrous doctor who would receive the trainloads of Jews on the Auschwitz platform and indifferently send the healthy-looking ones to work and the weaker, the women, children, and old people to the gas chambers. Mengele had become a symbol of the Third Reich's cruelty and madness. After the war he vanished, quite possibly to Argentina.

Mengele came from a rich family. While he was in hiding, they continued to support him, funneling large sums of money to him. The money trail, followed by Mossad agents, led to Buenos Aires; yet so far they had failed in their efforts to find Mengele.

But this time they were lucky. In May 1960, shortly before the Britannia landed in Buenos Aires, Isser's agents found Mengele's address. The man was living in Buenos Aires under his real name! Apparently, he was sure he was well protected. Isser sent his best investigator, Zvi Aharoni, to check the address, but Mengele was not at home. His neighbors told Aharoni that the Mengele couple had left for a few days, but they would soon be back. Excited, Isser summoned Rafi Eitan. "Let's watch and follow," he said, "and when Mengele comes back, we'll kidnap him, too, and bring him to Israel together with Eichmann."

Rafi refused. The Eichmann operation is very complex, he said; we captured one man and we have a good chance of succeeding in getting him on the plane and bringing him to Israel. But another operation for the capture of a second man would increase the risks tremendously. It would be a serious mistake.

Isser gave in, and Rafi made him an alternative offer: "If you bring Eichmann to Israel and keep his capture secret for a week, I'll bring you Mengele."

"How will you do that?" Isser asked.

"We still have a few safe houses in Buenos Aires from the Eichmann operation, which nobody knows about. Let's keep them. When you take off with Eichmann, on your way to Israel, I'll fly with Zvi Malkin and Avraham Shalom to one of Argentina's neighboring countries. You'll arrive in Israel and keep Eichmann's capture secret; nobody will know we did it, and nobody will look for us. We'll return to Buenos Aires then, we'll take Mengele. We'll keep him in one of our safe houses and after a few days we'll bring him to Israel."

Isser agreed. When the Britannia, with Eichmann on board, took off for Israel, Eitan, Shalom, and Malkin flew to Santiago, the capital of neighboring Chile. They intended to return to Buenos Aires after a day or two, if Eichmann's capture was kept secret, and to launch Operation Mengele.

But the following morning all the world's media announced in their headlines the capture of Eichmann in Argentina by the Israelis. It was out of the question that some of the leading Mossad agents would return to Argentina and carry out another kidnapping. Rafi and his friends had to abandon their project and return to Israel.

Later, Isser Harel told Rafi that he had asked Ben-Gurion to keep Eichmann's capture secret for a week, but the Old Man had refused. "Too many people know already that Eichmann is in our hands," Ben-Gurion allegedly said to Isser. "We won't be able to keep the secret any longer. I've decided to inform the Knesset of his capture, this afternoon."

Eichmann's capture was announced—and Israel lost its chance to bring to trial one of the most sadistic criminals in history.

Shortly after the Eichmann capture, Mengele felt the ground was burning under his feet. He moved to Paraguay and vanished until his death of a heart attack almost twenty years later, in February 1979.

In early March 1962, Isser Harel was summoned by Ben-Gurion. The Old Man greeted him warmly, chatting with him for a while about various subjects. What does he want? Isser wondered. He knew Ben-Gurion well, and was sure that he hadn't invited Isser in for small talk. The two men liked each other, and were similar. They were both short, stubborn, and decisive, born leaders of men, dedicated to Israel's security; they both weren't ones to waste time and words. And since Eichmann's capture they had become much closer.

All of a sudden, in the middle of the conversation, Ben-Gurion turned to Isser. "Tell me, can you find the child?"

He didn't say what child he was talking about, but Isser understood right away. For the last two years, one question kept popping up all over Israel, screaming from newspaper headlines, shouted from the Knesset podium, and angrily thrown in the faces of ultra-Orthodox Jews by secular youth: "Where is Yossele?"

Yossele was Yossele Schuchmacher, an eight-year-old boy from the city of Holon, who had been kidnapped by ultra-Orthodox Jews, headed by his grandfather. The old Hassid wanted to raise Yossele in the ultra-Orthodox tradition, and had snatched the child from his parents. Since then, the boy had vanished without a trace. Each day he remained missing, the dispute over the child grew, from a family affair to a national scandal to an increasingly violent confrontation between secular and ultra-Orthodox Jews.

Some feared a civil war could erupt and tear the nation apart. As a last resort, Ben-Gurion turned to Isser.

"If you want me to, I'll try," Isser said. He drove back to his office and had an operational file opened. He called it Operation Tiger Cub.

Yossele was a good-looking, vivacious child. His only mistake, apparently, had been to choose the wrong parents. That was the opinion of his grandfather, Nahman Shtarkes. Old Shtarkes, skeletal, bearded, and bespectacled, was a fanatical Hassid, a man tough and stubborn. Nobody could break him, neither the KGB thugs, nor the Soviet labor camps in frozen Siberia, where he had spent a part of World War II. In Siberia he had lost an eye, and three toes from frostbite, but his morale had remained intact; his vicissitudes had only fueled his hatred for the Soviets, which peaked in 1951 when a gang of hoodlums stabbed his son to death. He consoled himself with his other two sons, Shalom and Ovadia, and his daughter, Ida, who was married to a tailor.

The young couple lived for a while in Shtarkeses' old home in Lvov, where they had settled after wandering through Russia and Poland. There, in 1953, the second child in the Schuchmacher family was born: Yossele.

The boy was four years old when he immigrated to Israel with his parents. Grandfather and Grandmother Shtarkes, and one of their sons, Shalom, had arrived in Israel a few months earlier. Nahman Shtarkes, who belonged to the Breslau Hassidim sect, settled in Mea Shearim, the ultra-Orthodox sector of Jerusalem. It was another world, of men wearing long black coats or silk caftans, black hats or fur hats, bushy beards and long side-locks; women in long, prim dresses, covering their hair with wigs or scarves; a world of yeshivas, synagogues, courts of famous rabbis. Shalom joined a yeshiva; his other brother, Ovadia, moved to England.

Ida and Alter Schuchmacher settled in Holon. Eventually, Alter got a job in a textile factory in the Tel Aviv area; Ida was hired by a photographer. They bought a small apartment and struggled to make a living. They went deeply into debt. To make ends meet, they sent their daughter, Zina, to a religious institution at K'far Habad, and entrusted Yossele to his grandparents.

Rocked by hard times, Ida and Alter Schuchmacher wrote to friends in Russia that perhaps they shouldn't have come to Israel. Some of the replies to the couple's complaints fell in the hands of old Nahman Shtarkes. He concluded that the Schuchmachers intended to go back to Russia with their children. Seething with fury, he decided not to give Yossele back to his parents.

By the end of 1959, though, the Schuchmachers' economic situation improved. They were better off now, and they decided to reunite their family. In December, Ida went to Jerusalem to pick up her child, but neither Yossele nor his grandfather was home. "Tomorrow your brother Shalom will bring the boy to you," Ida's mother said. "Right now he is with his grandfather at the synagogue, and you must not disturb them."

On the following day, though, Shalom arrived in Holon alone, and told his sister that their father had decided not to give back Yossele. The distraught Ida rushed to Jerusalem with her husband. They spent the weekend at the Shtarkes house, and that time Yossele was there. On Saturday evening, when they were about to leave with the child, Ida's mother objected. "It's very cold outside," she said. "Let the child sleep here, and tomorrow I'll bring him back to you." They agreed. Ida kissed her son, who curled up in his bed, and left with her husband. How could she know that years would pass before she saw her little boy again?

The following day, neither Yossele nor his grandmother showed up in Holon. Once again, Ida and Alter got on the road to Jerusalem. But to no avail. The child had vanished, and old Shtarkes bluntly refused to return him, despite Ida's tears. Her son was gone.

After a few more trips, Ida and Alter realized that the old man wouldn't give them back their child or disclose his whereabouts. In January 1960, they decided to turn to the courts. They lodged a complaint against Nahman Shtarkes at the Tel Aviv rabbinical court. Shtarkes didn't answer. And their nightmare began . . .

January 15—Israel's Supreme Court orders Nahman Shtarkes to return the child to his parents within thirty days and summons him to court. He replies two days later, "I cannot come because of my poor health."

February 17—The family lodges a complaint with the police, and asks that Nahman Shtarkes be arrested and held in custody until he returns their son. The Supreme Court orders the police to find the child. Ten days later, the police open a file for Yossele and the search begins.

April 7—The police cannot find any trace of the boy and ask the Supreme Court to be relieved of the search.

May 12—Indignant, the Supreme Court orders the police to continue with the search and finally orders the arrest of Nahman Shtarkes. He is taken into custody the next day.

But if anyone had thought that a stay in jail would break old Shtarkes's resolve, they were dead wrong. The tough old man didn't say a word.

It became immediately evident that Shtarkes hadn't hidden the child by himself, and had been helped by a network of ultra-Orthodox Jews who had deceived the police. They had all engaged in a sacrosanct mission: to thwart the devious plan of taking the child to Russia and converting him to Christianity—or so Shtarkes had told them. Even Rabbi Frank, chief rabbi of Jerusalem, published a ruling supporting old Shtarkes and urging the Orthodox community to help him in every way.

The question appeared on the Knesset agenda in May 1960 and the press had a field day. The first to realize the far-reaching implications of the affair were the representatives of the religious parties. Knesset member Shlomo Lorenz felt that the abduction of the child might ignite a religious war in Israel. He offered to Shtarkes and the Schuchmacher family his services as a go-between. He brought to Shtarkes, who was still in jail, a draft agreement saying that the parents promise to give the child an Orthodox education. Shtarkes agreed to sign the paper on one condition: that Rabbi Meizish, one of the most fanatical rabbis in Jerusalem, would order him to do so.

Lorenz hurried to Jerusalem and met with the rabbi. Meizish implied that he'd consent to the agreement only on condition that the abductors wouldn't be prosecuted.

Now Lorenz went to the chief of police, Joseph Nahmias. "I agree,"

Nahmias said. "Take my car and bring the child. You have parliamentary immunity, and no one would follow my car anyway, so the people involved will remain unknown."

Overjoyed, Lorenz returned to Rabbi Meizish, but the rabbi changed his mind. Lorenz was back at square one. He knew that the child was probably hidden in one of the religious communities, Talmudic schools, or Orthodox villages. But impeded by a wall of silence, finding the child there was an impossible mission.

On April 12, 1961, Nahman Shtarkes was released from jail "for reasons of health," after he had promised he'd try to find the little boy. But he didn't keep his word, and the Supreme Court had him arrested again, stating that the abduction was "a shocking and despicable crime." In August 1961, a National Committee for the Return of Yossele was created and it started distributing leaflets, organizing public meetings, alerting the media. Many thousands signed its petitions; the sinister shadow of a cultural war loomed on the horizon.

In August 1961, the police raided the Hassidic village Komemiut, only to find out that the bird had flown the coop. Yossele had been hidden in the village a year and a half before, in December 1959, when his uncle Shalom had brought him to the home of a Mr. Zalman Kot. The child was hidden under the name "Israel Hazak."

In the meantime, though, the child had been whisked away, and Shalom Shtarkes had left the country and settled in the Hassidic community Golders Green in London. On the demand of the Israeli police, Shtarkes was arrested by the British; when his first child, Kalman, was born, his family brought the baby to the prison where the circumcision ritual was performed.

But Yossele was gone, without a trace. Some believed that he had been smuggled out of the country, or even got sick and died. The police became a laughingstock. Violent clashes erupted between secular and Orthodox Jews. Yeshiva students were caught and beaten in the street by passersby. Secular youngsters taunted Orthodox youths with the cries "Where is Yossele?"

The fury of the Israeli public reached its boiling point. Stormy debates shook the Knesset.

That's when Ben-Gurion called Isser.

When Isser Harel agreed to assume the search for Yossele, he didn't realize that he was accepting the most difficult and complicated assignment of his career. He never used to discuss operational matters with his wife, Rivka. But this time he told her: "The authority of the government is at stake." One of his best agents, Avraham Shalom, had a different opinion: "Isser wanted to prove that he could succeed where the police had failed."

The police were only too happy to palm off their unwanted task. Joseph Nahmias, the chief of police, asked Isser: "Do you really believe it is possible to find the child?" Amos Manor, the head of the Shabak and Isser's close collaborator, was against the entire project. Many of the Mossad and the Shabak senior officers agreed. They all thought that this assignment was outside their duties; they were supposed to work for the security of Israel, and not chase a kid in Hassidic schools. Unlike Isser, they didn't believe the secret service served to preserve the reputation of the Jewish state. Yet, once Isser had made up his mind, they didn't contest his decision. His authority was absolute.

Isser and his assistants created a task force of about forty agents—the best Shabak investigators, members of the operational team, religious agents or people posing as such, and even civilians who volunteered for the operation. Most of the volunteers were members of the Orthodox community who realized the danger that Yossele's abduction posed for the nation. But their first operations ended in dismal failure. They crudely tried to penetrate the ultra-Orthodox bastions and were immediately recognized, mocked, and rejected. "I felt as if I had landed on Mars," said one of Isser's agents, "and had to blend in among a crowd of little green men without being noticed."

Isser patiently studied the file, reading and rereading each document. There was no trace of Yossele anywhere in Israel. Isser finally reached a conclusion: the child had been taken out of the country.

Out of the country, but where? A strange piece of news drew his attention. In mid-March 1962, a large group of Hassidic Jews had traveled to Israel from Switzerland. Scores of men, women, and children came to escort the coffin of their venerated rabbi and bury him in the Holy Land. Isser came to suspect that the funeral was just a cover story used to spirit Yossele out of the country when the group returned to Switzerland a few weeks later. Isser posted his men at the airport, and sent a small team of his men, headed by Avraham Shalom, to Zurich, to follow the Hassidim on their return. The Mossad agents even went to the children's boarding school and snuck in to its courtyard at night to peek in the windows and scrutinize every child. "We reached this yeshiva in the middle of the forest," Shalom recalled. "We stuck to the windows; we knew he might be disguised but we looked for a child that could be of the same age." After a week of nightly adventures, he had to report to Isser that Yossele definitely was not among the Swiss children.

Isser decided to assume command of the operation. He placed all pending matters into the hands of his aides, settled in an improvised headquarters in Paris, and sent his men all over the world. They carried out investigations in France, Italy, Switzerland, Belgium, England, South America, the United States, and North Africa. Using different covers, they tried to penetrate Orthodox yeshivas and communities, in order to list the centers where the child could be hidden. A young Orthodox Jew from Jerusalem arrived in the famous yeshiva of Rabbi Soloweichik in Switzerland, posing as a scholar who came to study the Torah with the renowned master. A modest religious woman, pious and devout, arrived in London, carrying warm letters of recommendation from Shalom Shtarkes's mother-in-law, whose trust she had won. She was invited by the Shtarkes family to stay with them as their houseguest. They didn't know that the good woman was Yehudith Nissiyahu, Isser's best female agent who had participated in Eichmann's abduction.

Yehudith wasn't the only Mossad agent operating in London these days. London was an important center of ultra-Orthodox Hassidim of the Satmar sect (named after the Romanian village Satu Mare, where the sect had originated). Isser sent another team of agents to the Hassidim residential neighborhoods in London. Another team rushed to Ireland. During the operations in England, Isser's men had stumbled upon a young religious couple who had suddenly rented an isolated house in Ireland. The Mossad agents believed that the couple would use the house as the new hideout for Yossele, and prepared a detailed plan for the capture of the child. Hurriedly, they rented apartments and cars, smuggled equipment, prepared false documents. The operation was planned to the smallest detail.

And then the failures came.

The first to return home frustrated was the Ireland team. It turned out that the "religious couple" was indeed a religious couple. They had just decided to go on vacation to Ireland. Yehudith Nissiyahu also failed to obtain any information from the Shtarkes family, and the young man who went to study the Holy Scriptures in Switzerland returned enlightened but empty-handed. From all over the world, negative answers poured into Isser's headquarters. The child had vanished.

The worst fate awaited the team that tried to penetrate the Satmar Hassidim in London. Some young, smart yeshiva students in the Stamford Hill neighborhood immediately made the uninvited guests and confronted them, shouting: "Here come the Zionists! Come, Yossele is here!" They even called the London police. Isser's assistants had to work hard to spring their colleagues from Her Majesty's jail.

One after another, Isser's most devout supporters lost hope. They told him: "Isser, it won't work. Call off the hunt. You're looking for a needle in a haystack. We won't find the child."

But he didn't give up. Stubborn as a bulldog, he waved off all the doubts and complaints, and continued, obsessed by the search and confident that even against all odds he would find the child.

In Paris, he summoned Yaacov Caroz, the head of the Mossad station. Caroz, born in Romania, had lost his parents in the Holocaust, and had been involved in espionage and security matters since his studies at Hebrew University in Jerusalem. Slim, with a clear forehead, delicate features, and eyeglasses, Caroz had the outward appearance of an intellectual. He was the former head of Tevel (Universe), the Mossad department in charge of covert relations with foreign secret services, and had forged some of Israel's most secret and unexpected alliances. He had helped build a "peripheral pact" between Israel and Iran, Ethiopia, Turkey, and even Sudan (all non-Arab countries on the periphery of the Middle East); he had established close cooperation with the heads of the French, British, and German secret services; he had struck an alliance with the formidable General Oufkir, Morocco's dreaded minister of interior, and secretly visited Morocco's King Hassan; he had even helped the Ethiopian emperor, Haile Selassie, crush an attempted coup by his closest aides. During an undercover mission in Algeria, he had fallen in love with a young woman, Juliette (Yael), who became his wife. Caroz, soft-spoken and deceptively polite, was a master spy in a suit and tie who had never acted as a field agent; yet he was a man of the world who spoke fluent French and English, which made him a valuable asset for Isser.

Isser worked around the clock. He had rented a hotel room, but spent most of his days and nights in the apartment that he had turned into his operational headquarters. His assistants bought him a folding cot (they called it "Yossele's bed"), and once in a while he would collapse on it for a short nap. That lasted for months. Most of the time he was busy checking reports, writing telegrams, and talking to his men, who were dispersed all over Europe. At dawn he would leave his office and go to his hotel, where he showered, freshened up, and returned to work. On the first night, as he returned to the hotel in the wee hours, the porter flashed him an appreciative smile. This little gentleman apparently enjoyed Paris's nightlife to the full. The second night, the porter allowed himself to address a friendly wink to the gentleman. But when the nightly adventures continued in the third, and fourth, and fifth nights, the porter couldn't keep his cool anymore. When Isser returned at dawn, his eyes red from lack of sleep, his face covered with stubble, his clothes ruffled, the porter theatrically removed his hat, bowed, and declared: "My respects, *monsieur!*"

Then, one April morning, a curious report reached the Mossad agents.

It had been dispatched by a young Orthodox Jew named Meir, who had been sent to Antwerp, Belgium. There he had become acquainted with a group of religious diamond merchants who followed old Rabbi Itzikel and considered him to be a holy man. When they wanted to solve their business disputes, they didn't seek help from the state courts, instead asked the rabbi to be the mediator and the judge—often for deals worth many millions. His word was law. Even in modern-day Europe, this particular group of merchants observed the customs of ancient times.

Meir succeeded in penetrating the circle of the rabbi's followers and learned that during World War II they had acted as an anti-Nazi underground, and had saved many Jews from the Gestapo. After the war, the group continued using the same methods and experience they had acquired as an underground organization, to engage in business ventures throughout the world. The diamond merchants told Meir an extraordinary story about a blond, blue-eyed Frenchwoman, a Catholic, who had been part of their organization during the war, helping them to rescue Jews from Hitler's grasp. The woman had been profoundly influenced by the rabbi's charisma; she converted to Judaism and became devoutly Orthodox, and more so, a priceless asset for the group. Her years in the underground had taught her a lot; she was bright, daring, she knew how to cover her tracks, change disguises, and use her charm as a weapon. Besides, she had an instinct for business and a keen natural intelligence. She had traveled the world on missions for the Antwerp group with her French passport. "She's a holy woman," the Antwerp Jews told Meir. They also told him that she had visited Israel; her son from her first marriage, Claude, had also converted, and after studying in yeshivas in Switzerland and Aix-les-Bains, was now a student at a Talmudic school in Jerusalem. But even the Antwerp people didn't know where the fabulous holy woman was now.

That story fired up Isser's imagination. On the face of it, there was nothing in the report to connect the Frenchwoman to Yossele. But in Isser's eyes, she appeared as a person with enormous potential, a woman with a thousand faces. She could be a real godsend for the Orthodox leaders, if they needed somebody to set out on secret missions concerning Yossele.

Isser decided to follow his intuition, abandon all other leads, and concentrate on the mysterious convert. He cabled to Israel all the details he knew, and instructed his service to find the son and his mother.

A few days later, the answer came. The son's name was now Ariel and he was in Israel indeed. Yet nobody knew where his mother was. Her name was originally Madeleine Ferraille; in Israel, she was called Ruth Ben-David.

The reports streaming to Isser's headquarters painted a more accurate picture of Madeleine Ferraille. The pretty young woman had studied history and geography at the Toulouse University and the Sorbonne in Paris. She had married her college sweetheart, Henri, and their son was born shortly after the outbreak of World War II. Madeleine had joined the Maquis Resistance during the war, and her underground activities had brought her into contact with French and Belgian Jews, among them the Antwerp group. At the war's end, she even initiated joint import-export ventures with some of them.

In 1951 she divorced Henri, after falling in love with a young rabbi in a small Alsatian town. The rabbi, a fervent Zionist, wanted to emigrate to Israel, and the two lovers decided to marry there. Her conversion to Judaism, therefore, was not so much for love of the religion itself as for love of one of its adherents. The recently converted Ruth Ben-David tied a scarf on her blond hair, changed her elegant clothes for the shapeless vestments of an Orthodox Jewess, and followed her fiancé to the Holy Land. But in Israel the affair turned sour; the rabbi left her, and she remained alone, depressed and frustrated. Her personal crisis apparently motivated her to approach the most extremist circles in Jerusalem and their leader, Rabbi Meizish. She gained a lot of respect in the religious circles after using her French passport to cross into the Jordanian sector of Jerusalem and pray at the Wailing Wall.

In the early fifties, Ruth returned to France and started traveling extensively again. The Mossad agents found out that she often stayed in Aix-les-Bains, or in a religious women's institution close to Paris. But she had no permanent address.

The immigration authorities informed Isser's men that in the last few years Ruth had visited Israel twice. The second time, on June 21, 1960, she had left Israel with a little girl, who was recorded in her passport as her daughter. She had departed on an Alitalia flight, and her final destination was Zurich. But who was the small girl? Ben-David had no daughter. Isser felt that he was on the right track. "Find her!" he said to Yaacov Caroz.

Armed with a detailed description of the woman, Caroz and another agent set out for Aix-les-Bains. But as they drove into the small town, they saw something amazing: Ruth Ben-David—or, in this case, Madeleine Ferraille—elegantly dressed, stood by the road hitchhiking! They were startled. Elegant, refined Frenchwomen trying to thumb a ride on the roads of France were not a common sight, to say the least. The driver immediately made a U-turn and darted toward the lady, but another car stopped ahead of him and departed with the pretty woman.

The agents returned from Aix-les-Bains empty-handed; but from another source, they learned that Ruth Ben-David kept close ties with Joseph Domb, a rich London jewel merchant. She had been sighted sitting alone with Domb in an automobile, which was inappropriate for a Hassidic man. Isser knew of Domb; he was a staunch enemy of the State of Israel. He belonged to the Satmar Hassidic sect, was a close confidant of the Satmar rabbi in New York, and knew the major Satmar leaders in various communities in Europe. "If the Satmar rabbi in New York is the pope," one expert told Isser, "then Domb is his archbishop."

Isser realized that all the roads led to London. Here lived the two sons of old Shtarkes. Here was based an active community of the Satmar sect, led by Domb. Here he was seen with Ruth Ben-David, who might have smuggled Yossele out of Israel. Isser had no more doubts: it had to be the Satmar Hassidim in Israel and Europe who had orchestrated the kidnapping of the child. Domb had been in charge of the operation. Ruth Ben-David had been instrumental in the abduction, because of her talents, her experience, and her French passport; she might know where the child was hidden.

His suspicions were confirmed by a Shabak agent who intercepted several letters Ruth Ben-David had written to her son; they contained some veiled hints about Yossele Schuchmacher.

Yet Isser needed more information; he decided to penetrate the Satmar Hassidim. His men in London identified a *mohel*—a rabbi who specialized in the circumcision of newborn Jewish boys—named Freyer (not his real name). He was a chatterbox, a man with a taste for life's pleasures under a cloak of righteousness, and—last but not least—a man who was close to Domb and claimed that he knew where Yossele was.

Isser launched a complicated operation, intended to bring Freyer to Paris: one of his men, posing as a Moroccan prince, came secretly to Freyer and told him he had fallen in love with a Jewish girl. They had married in secret, and kept the Jewish faith at home, in Morocco. Now his wife had given birth to a baby boy and he wanted him circumcised, but couldn't do it in Morocco; his family would murder him if they only knew . . . His wife and child were in Paris, would Rabbi Freyer come to circumcise the baby? He would be handsomely rewarded.

Freyer readily agreed, and a few days later arrived in Paris. The moment he stepped into the apartment of "the Moroccan prince," he was apprehended by Mossad agents. They escorted him to a bare room, where he was interrogated for hours by Victor Cohen, the head of the Shabak investigation department. The *mohel* was scared to death, offered no resistance, and was ready to talk. But when asked about Yossele, he raised his hands. "I am dreadfully sorry," he said, "but I don't know a thing."

It turned out, indeed, that Freyer knew nothing about the abducted child, and all his braggadocio was just intended to impress his friends. Once again, Isser's efforts hit a wall.

Surprisingly, another team of his men had struck gold. With the help of the French Secret Service, they had succeeded in intercepting several letters sent to Madeleine Ferraille, and in one of them they found the opportunity they were looking for. It was a reply to a newspaper ad offering for sale her country house in Orleans, a lovely city in "the Garden of France"—the Loire Valley. They dispatched a letter to the post office box given in the advertisement and offered Ferraille more than she was asking for her house; they claimed they were Austrian businessmen looking for a location for their vacations. Madeleine Ferraille answered, giving the address of her house; soon after, they wrote to her again, saying they had visited it and it suited their needs. They fixed an appointment for closing the deal on June 21, 1962, in the lobby of a big hotel in Paris.

A few days before the appointment, Isser's men arrived in Paris one by one and engaged in feverish activity. They rented cars and safe houses in Paris and its suburbs, established escape routes, prepared documents and equipment, and brought from Israel experts in surveillance and interrogation.

Isser also decided that the best means to make Ruth Ben-David spill her secrets was through her son. Ariel studied in a yeshiva in Israel and apparently knew a lot about Yossele. Isser decided to arrest him simultaneously with his mother's abduction in France. Ariel was Orthodox, but less fanatical than his mother. Isser established a system of communication that would enable the Mossad agents to synchronize the questioning of Ruth with that of her son in Israel, so they could use the answers of the son for the questioning of the mother.

And indeed, on the morning of June 21, a tall, elegant, strikingly beautiful woman walked into the hotel lobby. This was Madeleine Ferraille.

The charming Frenchwoman introduced herself to the two Austrians who were waiting for her. One of them was Herr Furber, the other Herr Schmidt. She spoke excellent English, and also had a good command of German. She never suspected the identity of her two buyers. They quickly reached an agreement about the sale of the house, but their lawyer was late. Furber called him from one of the hotel phone booths; when he came back, he said that the lawyer had profusely apologized. He had been detained at home, he said, by several urgent matters. He had asked if they could come to his house in the town of Chantilly, close to the city, and gave Furber the address and detailed directions. He would receive them immediately and they would sign all the papers on the spot.

"Shall we go?" Furber asked

Madeleine agreed. They got into the two Austrians' rental car and drove to the lawyer's villa. But the Frenchwoman's charm almost caused the failure of the entire operation. Furber, the agent at the wheel, was so entranced by Madeleine that he went through a red light. The strident shriek of a whistle brought him back to reality. A fat, angry police officer was running toward him, blowing his whistle and pointing to the red light.

Furber stopped the car, fraught by ominous premonitions. What should he do? He was in a foreign country, with phony papers, driving a rented car with a woman who was about to disappear. He would get a traffic ticket, a procedure against him would be initiated by the police, and . . . But Madeleine Ferraille, who had caused all his troubles, was also the one who came to his rescue. She stuck her head out of the window, and flashed a charming smile at the police officer. *"Monsieur l'agent,"* she said sweetly, "this man is a tourist. He is in a foreign country, travels with a woman, and tries to amuse her with his stories . . . You certainly can understand that. Please forgive him . . ." The police officer, too, was entranced by the lady's charm, and let the panic-stricken agents off without even writing a ticket.

Presently the car entered the beautiful town of Chantilly, where the "lawyer" lived. They entered the villa's driveway and stopped before the main entrance. The two businessmen politely helped their guest out of the car, escorted her to the house, the door opened, and she walked in.

She was led to the "lawyer's office."

The part of the lawyer was played by Yaacov Caroz. "Madame," he said in French, "you are not here to discuss your house in Orleans but another matter."

"What? What's going on?"

"I want to talk to you about the child Yossele Schuchmacher."

At that moment, two other men materialized at her side. When she turned back, she realized that the two "businessmen" had vanished without a trace. She was struck with fear.

"I've fallen into a trap!" she hoarsely whispered in French.

"You've fallen in the hands of the Israeli services, Madame," Caroz said.

At that very moment, police officers arrested Ariel Ben-David, the Frenchwoman's son, in the town of Be'er Yaacov, in Israel.

In Chantilly, Caroz turned to Ruth Ben-David. "Madame, you are involved in the abduction of Yossele Schuchmacher. We want the child!"

"I know nothing and I'll say nothing," she answered firmly. After the initial shock, she had recovered quickly. Caroz had brought over his sister-in-law, a trained nurse, to stand by in case of emergency.

The Israelis understood that Ruth was their last hope. But they also assumed that this iron lady would not break easily, and that might take quite a while. She was handed over to Yehudith Nissiyahu, who had arrived from London. Nissiyahu treated her well, and took care of her needs as a religious woman. She provided her with prayer books and candles for the Sabbath; she cooked kosher food for her. The wing where she was kept was out of bounds for men. The nurse occupied the room next to hers.

The interrogation started. The convert spent hours facing the agents, mostly Yaacov Caroz and Victor Cohen, who addressed her in French. She was amazed to discover that the Israelis knew all about her; but she stubbornly refused to reveal any information about Yossele. "I'll say nothing," she kept repeating. She called Victor Cohen *"flic,"* which in French slang means "cop." She stubbornly denied any connection with the abduction. "So I started to talk to her about all kinds of subjects," Victor Cohen recalled later, "just to soften her. I wanted to understand how a Christian girl had become a fanatical Orthodox. These are two different worlds. At first, when we spoke, she insisted that there had to be another woman in the room with us. Later she agreed to sit alone with me, but the door had to remain open."

One of her interrogators was charged with the unpleasant duty of throwing insulting accusations in her face, in order to make her lose her calm. The Mossad men hoped that she would react impulsively, and blurt out things she didn't mean to say; they could be used in the simultaneous interrogation of her son in Israel.

And indeed, the interrogation of Ariel Ben-David started bearing fruit.

The chief investigator in Israel was Avraham Hadar, a tough guy incongru-
ously code-named "Pashosh" (Thrush). He told the young man that his
mother had capitulated. "Your mother has confessed to everything," he
said. "Your lies will get you nowhere. Tell the truth!"

And after a while Ariel broke down. He said he knew what had happened to the child, and would talk "only if my mother and I get immunity."

Pashosh told him, "You got it!" He immediately brought Ariel to Amos
Manor, the head of the Shabak. As they entered, Manor yelled at Ariel:
"Whatever Pashosh promised you—I agree. Now, where is the child?!" Ariel
was shaken. He finally admitted that his mother had smuggled Yossele out
of Israel, disguised as a little girl. She had forged her passport, where he had
been registered under his former name, Claude. She had changed the name
to Claudine, and also changed the birth date, so it could fit Yossele's age.
He knew that the child had been taken to Switzerland.

Ariel's confession was rushed to Chantilly, and Ruth Ben-David's interrogators confronted her with the new facts. "Ariel is in our hands," Victor
Cohen told her. "He is facing stiff punishment. He has confessed everything. Don't you care what will happen to your son?"

"He is not my son anymore," she muttered. She remained unbreakable.
The interrogators couldn't help admiring the tremendous strength of that
woman.

Gradually, the situation became untenable. The solution seemed so
close, and yet the interrogators felt that everything might end in total failure.

Finally, Isser decided, the time had come for him to take over.

In the bare, dark room, Isser Harel and Ruth Ben-David faced each other
across the table. Some Mossad agents stood behind them; Cohen and
Caroz served as interpreters.

Isser firmly believed that this fiercely determined woman would not
yield to any threats. The only way, he thought, was to convince her with
moral arguments. She was religious, indeed, but she would listen to logic.
After all, she had not been an ultra-Orthodox Jewess all her life, and the fa-

naticism of former generations didn't flow in her veins since her birth. She was an intelligent, shrewd woman, and she should be addressed as such.

"I represent the Israeli government," Isser said, weighing every word. "Your son has told us everything, and we have a lot of other information about you. Most of your secrets are known to us. We are sorry that we had to bring you here by force. You converted to Judaism, and Judaism means Israel. Without Israel, Judaism would not survive. The abduction of Yossele has dealt a terrible blow to the religious community in Israel. It stirred feelings of fury against the Orthodox. You could be the cause of bloodshed and a civil war. If you don't return the child, a blood libel may result. Just think what might happen to that child! He could get sick, even die. How could you and your accomplices face his parents then? That would haunt you for the rest of your lives. And you'll never be absolved!

"You are a woman and a mother. If someone disapproved of the way you're bringing up your son and took him away from you, how would you feel? Could you sleep at night?

"We are not fighting against religion. Our only purpose is to find the child. As soon as we have him in our hands, you'll go free, your son will go free—and Israel will be united again."

Isser watched as Ruth's face began to show her inner conflict. She seemed torn by contradictory feelings. Ruth was in a state of high tension, fighting against herself as only a strong person can before an uncompromising dilemma.

The Mossad agents were motionless like statues. They, too, believed that the moment of truth had arrived.

Ruth raised her head. "How do I know that you are a genuine representative of the State of Israel? How can I trust you?"

Without a blink, Isser pulled out his diplomatic passport, issued in his real name, and handed it to Ruth Ben-David.

His men were dumbfounded. Has he gone mad? To give her his name and passport—that was a tremendous risk! Isser, however, felt that only if he showed her he was sincere and had confidence in her did he have a chance of success.

For a long moment Ruth gazed at the seal of Israel embossed on the passport. She bit her lips till drops of blood popped on her mouth. "I can't take it anymore," she murmured. "I am going to break down . . ."

Then, suddenly, she raised her head. "The child is with the Gertner family, one twenty-six Penn Street, Brooklyn, New York. They call him Yankele."

Isser jumped to his feet. "As soon as we get the child, you'll be free."

He left the room.

A feverish exchange of telegrams alerted Jerusalem, then New York and Washington. Isser called Israel Gur-Arie, the security officer of the Israeli diplomatic missions in North America. Gur-Arie, who was based in New York, checked the Brooklyn address; he cabled back that the address was correct and that the Gertner family lived in a district largely populated by Satmar Hassidim. Jerusalem dispatched a cable to Avraham Harman, Israel's ambassador in Washington, instructing him to contact the FBI and ask them to find the child and deliver him to Israel.

Gur-Arie himself called his counterpart at the FBI and gave him all the details—"what the child eats, what he wears," et cetera. The FBI agent answered: "If you know so much about him, go get him yourself." Gur-Arie replied: "Give me the authorization." The FBI agent refused.

Disquieting telegrams began pouring into Isser's headquarters. The Americans are hesitating, Gur-Arie and the Israeli ambassador reported. They ask, are you absolutely certain that the child is at that address? What would happen if we raided that house and didn't find the child? The FBI hinted that their reticence was due to the upcoming congressional elections. The Satmar sect controlled almost one hundred thousand votes, and the administration didn't want to risk alienating them.

In Chantilly, Isser was losing patience. At midnight, he picked up the phone. "Get me Harman in Washington," he ordered.

When the connection was established, he was blunt. "Harman," he said, "this is Isser Harel. I want you to get in touch with Attorney General Robert Kennedy, immediately, and tell him in my name that the FBI should get the boy at once."

Harman was stunned. "Isser, how can you talk like that?" He hinted that the American services might be monitoring their conversation.

"So much the better," Isser said. "I am not talking only to you." He hoped that the Americans were listening in, and his firm stand would rouse them to action.

Harman kept hesitating and tried to warn Isser about possible diplomatic complications.

"I didn't ask your opinion," Isser snapped. "Tell them that if they don't act immediately, they will be held responsible for anything that happens."

A few hours later, Isser was called to the telephone. It was New York. The consulate officials informed him that Robert Kennedy had taken immediate action. A team of FBI agents, accompanied by the Israeli security officer, had gone to Brooklyn. The child was indeed found and taken to a safe place. It was Yossele.

A young reporter named Elie Wiesel (the future Nobel Prize winner) called Gur-Arie. "I heard that you found the child." Gur-Arie, who had been sworn to secrecy, firmly denied. Wiesel didn't forgive him for years.

The Fourth of July 1962 was a national holiday in Israel as well, as on that day the plane carrying Yossele home landed at Lod Airport. The press enthusiastically praised the dedicated efficiency of the secret service. Israel was fast becoming the only country in the world where that shadow organization was loved and admired by the whole nation. A well-known Israeli lawyer, Shlomo Cohen Zidon, wrote a letter of thanks to Ben-Gurion for finding the child. Ben-Gurion wrote back: "You should thank our secret services and mostly their head, who spent days and nights on that mission, and didn't rest, even when his assistants almost gave up, till he found the child and pulled him out of his hideout, which was not easy either."

While all of Israel was celebrating Yossele's rescue, Isser was in Paris, where his men threw a modest party for him. One of the agents raised his glass "to the child returned to his fatherland, to the iron-willed man who found him, to the state that knows so well to protect its citizens." Another agent presented Isser with a stuffed toy tiger cub as a souvenir of the operation; his colleagues shipped to his home in Tel Aviv "Yossele's bed," on which he had passed so many sleepless nights.

N ow that the boy had been found, the whole truth came to light.
     It had all started with a telegram.

In the spring of 1960, while Yossele was being clandestinely shuttled from one yeshiva to another in Israel, Ruth Ben-David received a telegram from her friend Rabbi Meizish: "Come immediately to Jerusalem, I have a good match for you." When Ruth arrived, she found out that the "match" was actually a secret mission: to smuggle Yossele out of Israel.

Ruth returned to France, altered her passport, changing the name of her son from Claude to Claudine and his date of birth from 1945 to 1953. She then changed her clothes and her name, becoming Madeleine Ferraille. She flew to Genoa and bought a passage on a ship that sailed to Israel carrying passengers and new immigrants.

On Genoa's dock she began to play, as if by chance, with the eight-year-old daughter of a family of immigrants. When the boarding begun and the immigrants were struggling with their packages and suitcases, the charming Madeleine took the little girl by the hand and led her up to the ship's deck. The Italian immigration officers checked her passport and noted that she had got on board with her little girl. In Israel she repeated the same procedure and the Israeli immigration duly noted that she had come out of the boat with her little daughter.

A few days later, Madeleine Ferraille boarded a plane at Lod Airport with her "daughter Claudine," who was none other than Yossele Schuchmacher, wearing a neat girl's dress and patent-leather pumps.

Yossele spent almost two years in ultra-Orthodox boarding schools in Switzerland and France. But when the search for Yossele in Israel reached a larger scale, Madeleine showed up at the boarding school in Meaux, where the child was hidden now under the guise of "Menachem, an orphan of Swiss parentage."

She dressed him in girl's clothes once again and flew with him to America. There she was helped by the head of the Satmar sect, Rabbi Joel Teitelbaum, who directed a milkman named Gertner to take "Yankele" to his home and pass him off as a cousin from Argentina who had come for a long visit.

The Mossad experts realized that the ultra-Orthodox clandestine network spread all over America and Europe was comparable to the secret organizations of the world's best intelligence services. And, most of all, they were amazed by Ruth Ben-David. She stuck to the rules of conspiracy: she never had a permanent address, carried all her important papers in her handbag, changed identities as easily as one changes one's clothes. The lovely Frenchwoman was the Mata Hari of the Orthodox world.

But while all of Israel was rejoicing over the return of Yossele to his parents, Ruth Ben-David felt broken and vanquished. "I am guilty," she said to her friends, sobbing. "I betrayed our cause. I can never forgive myself. I had a precious treasure entrusted to me, and I could not keep it."

Yet Madeleine Ferraille/Ruth Ben-David—had so admirably demonstrated all the qualities necessary for a secret agent that Isser Harel decided to offer her a job at the Mossad. But he was too late. Ruth returned to Jerusalem and vanished in the ultra-Orthodox world; three years later, she married Rabbi Amram Blau, the seventy-two-year-old head of the most fanatical of all sects, Neturei Karta.

Isser Harel and Yossele Schuchmacher met only nine years later, when one of the authors of this book threw a party in Isser's honor and invited Yossele. Yossele—now a private first class in a tank division—shook hands with Isser and declared: "I am deeply touched. Isser Harel has been the most important person in my life. Without him I would not be here among you."

CHAPTER EIGHT

A NAZI HERO AT THE SERVICE OF THE MOSSAD

O n a stifling hot day in August 1963, two men entered the offices of an engineering company in Madrid and asked to meet the owner, an Austrian by the name of Otto Skorzeny. They introduced themselves to Skorzeny as NATO intelligence officers and told him they had come on the recommendation of his estranged wife. They had for him an offer he couldn't refuse . . .

Very soon, the respectable businessman realized that his visitors knew all about him and his past. During World War II, SS officer Skorzeny had been one of the great heroes—if not the greatest—of Nazi Germany. A tall, charismatic athlete, his face scarred in a fencing duel, he had become a daredevil commando officer who carried out spectacular operations. On September 12, 1943, he had landed, with a paratrooper battalion carried by gliders, on top of the Gran Sasso, the highest peak in the Italian Apennines, and stormed the Campo Imperator Hotel, where former Fascist dictator Benito Mussolini had been jailed by a new, anti-Nazi Italian government. SS Captain Skorzeny rescued Mussolini and brought him to a grateful Hitler, who showered Skorzeny with medals and promotions. In the Battle of the Bulge, in late 1944, Skorzeny—now a Waffen SS colonel—snuck through the front lines with two dozen of his men, dressed as American soldiers, and caused disorder and confusion in the Allied ranks. His operations earned him the reputation of "the most dangerous man in Europe." Found not guilty at the Dachau trials after the war, he moved to Spain where he enjoyed the protection of Fascist dictator Franco, and established his company.

His visitors that day in 1963 didn't waste time on small talk. "We are not exactly from NATO," one of them admitted in perfect German. "Actually, we belong to the Israeli secret services." The two men were Rafi Eitan and the head of the Mossad station in Germany, Avraham Ahituv.

Skorzeny paled. Barely a year ago, the Israelis had hanged Adolf Eichmann. Were they after him now? He had been cleared at the war trials, but some claimed that he had taken part in burning Jewish synagogues during Kristallnacht, in November 1938.

But the short man sitting in front of him dispelled his fears. "We need your help," he said. "We know you have good connections in Egypt." He then proceeded to tell the SS colonel why the Jewish state needed his assistance.

On July 21, 1962, only two weeks after the triumphant return of Yossele to Israel, Egypt amazed the world by launching four missiles. Two were of the Al-Zafir (The Victor) type, with a range of 175 miles, and two of the Al-Qahir (The Conqueror) type, with a range of 350 miles. The huge missiles, draped in Egypt's flags, were proudly paraded in the streets of Cairo on Revolution Day, July 23. President Gamal Abdel Nasser boasted to an ecstatic crowd that his missiles were capable of hitting any target "south of Beirut."

South of Beirut, Israel's leaders were seized with astonishment and anxiety. Nasser's missiles could indeed hit any target in Israel. That came as a complete surprise to Israel, and in the corridors of power angry words were addressed to Isser Harel. While Nasser was building his deadly rockets, the critics said, Little Isser was busy chasing Yossele. While terrible dangers threatened the very existence of the Jewish state, Isser's best agents were running from one yeshiva to another, disguised as ultra-Orthodox Jews. A worried Ben-Gurion summoned Isser Harel, who promised to get all the information about the Egyptian project as soon as possible. Back at his headquarters, Isser sent his best men on a mission, and activated his moles and informants in Egypt. And indeed, on August 16, less than a month after the launching of the four missiles, he came back to Ben-Gurion with a detailed report.

The missiles were being built by German scientists, Isser reported.

In 1959, Nasser had decided to establish a secret arsenal of unconventional weapons. He had appointed General Mahmoud Khalil, a former Air Force Intelligence commander, head of the Bureau for Special Military Programs, to develop these ultrasecret modern weapons—jet fighters, rockets, and missiles, as well as chemical and radioactive substances. The bureau was allotted a huge budget.

Khalil's first task was to find the men to make these weapons a reality. And he knew where to look.

His agents started to recruit hundreds of German experts and scientists, most of whom had been employed in the rocket and aviation research institutes and testing grounds of Nazi Germany. More than three hundred Germans, tempted by high salaries, bonuses, and myriad privileges, clandestinely trickled into Egypt, and helped Nasser build three secret installations.

The first was Factory 36, where genius aircraft builder Willy Messerschmitt was assembling an Egyptian jet fighter. Messerschmitt was the father of the deadly fighter planes of the Luftwaffe, the Nazi air force, during World War II. Mahmoud Khalil had signed a contract with him on November 29, 1959.

In the second plant, known by the code 135, an engineer named Ferdinand Brandner was building jet engines for Messerschmitt's aircraft. Brandner had spent several years in Russia; after his return to Germany, Khalil had got in touch with him with the help of Dr. Eckart, a director of Daimler-Benz.

But the most secret was Factory 333, hidden in a remote area in the desert. There, Hitler's former wunderkinds now built Nasser's wonder weapons, the intermediate-range missiles.

According to Isser's sources, the Egyptian project had shifted to high gear in December 1960. That month, an American U-2 reconnaissance aircraft had photographed a huge building site in Dimona, Israel, that seemed to be a nuclear reactor. The world press announced the discovery with banner headlines; nobody believed Israel's stilted statements that the structure was a textile factory. Egypt and several other Arab nations issued furious threats against Israel. But threats were not enough, and Egypt hoped to neutralize Israel's secret nuclear project by developing its own unconventional weapons.

The head of the German rocket scientists in Egypt was Professor Eugen Sänger, the director of the Institute of Research on Jet Propulsion in Stuttgart. After the war, Sänger had spent a few years in France, where he built the Veronique rocket, a mediocre replica of the German V-2 rocket. He came to Egypt with his assistants—Professor Paul Goerke, an electronics and guidance expert, and Wolfgang Pilz, formerly an engineer at the Peenemünde installation, where the brilliant Wernher von Braun had developed Nazi Germany's V-2 rockets. Another guidance and control expert closely collaborating with his colleagues in Egypt was Dr. Hans Kleinwachter, whose lab for developing missile guidance systems was in the picturesque German city of Lorrach, close to the Swiss border. The chemistry department was headed by Dr. Ermin Dadieu, a former SS officer. The Germans and the Egyptians established several front companies—"Intra," "Intra-Handel," "Patwag," and "Linda"—that purchased parts and materials for the missile project. The administrative director of "Intra-Handel" was Dr. Heinz Krug, who also managed the Institute for Jet Propulsion in Stuttgart. Hassan Kamil, an Egyptian millionaire living in Switzerland, was also enlisted as a façade and liaison man. With his help, the Egyptians established two dummy companies in Switzerland, MECO (Mechanical Corporation) and MTP (Motors, Turbines, and Pumps), whose task was to acquire basic materials, electrical apparatuses, and precision tools; they also recruited specialists and experts. The three directors of these companies were Messerschmitt, Brandner, and Kamil.

In 1961, Sänger and many hundreds of engineers, technicians, and local Egyptian employees had started building the Egyptian missiles. But at the end of that year, the German government discovered the secret connection between the Egyptian project and the Institute for Jet Propulsion in Stuttgart. The German authorities forced Sänger to resign, return to Germany, and cease all activity. Professor Pilz succeeded him as head of the Egyptian project.

By July 1962, Factory 333 produced thirty missiles. Four of them were launched with great fanfare before a select crowd of government guests and journalists; twenty others (some of them dummies), draped with the Egyptian flag, were paraded through Cairo's streets.

When Isser Harel came to Ben-Gurion in August, he produced a letter from Pilz to Kamil Azzab, the Egyptian director of 333, which Rafi Eitan and his men had succeeded in copying. It was a request for 3,700,000 Swiss francs for machine parts and other equipment needed for building five hundred missiles of Type 2 and four hundred missiles of Type 5.

Nine hundred missiles! Isser's report caused deep anxiety in the defense community. The Israeli experts were certain that the Egyptians had no intention of loading the missiles' warheads with conventional explosives; they wouldn't have spent millions of dollars building them merely for the missiles to carry a half-ton of dynamite. A bomber could do that with more precision. It was clear that Egypt would load the warheads with atomic bombs or some other substance forbidden by international law, such as poison gas, bacterial cultures, or deadly radioactive waste.

According to Isser, the German scientists were working on a devious plan to destroy Israel: they were developing doomsday weapons, huge missiles, radioactive warheads that could "kill any living thing" and poison the air in Israel for many years; they were even working on death rays and other kinds of hellish contraptions.

"We took them too seriously," General Zvi Zur, the chief of staff at the time, admitted later. "Our scientists were amateurs and didn't know how to handle the information." Still, the Israelis discovered the Achilles' heel of the Egyptian project—the Germans hadn't succeeded yet in developing a proper guidance system to direct the missiles to their targets. As long as that obstacle wasn't overcome, the missiles couldn't be used.

Isser Harel was no longer the same man his people knew and admired. Since Eichmann's capture, he had undergone a profound change. This coolheaded man, who was known for his nerves of steel, now regarded Germany as the eternal enemy of Israel and the Jewish people. He staunchly believed that the current German government was supporting the scientists in Egypt and secretly helping them in their efforts to destroy Israel. The *ramsad* asked Ben-Gurion to alert Germany's chancellor Konrad Adenauer and demand that he act immediately to stop the scientists' activities. Ben-Gurion refused. Quite recently, Germany had given Israel a huge loan of $500 million to develop the Negev desert; Ben-Gurion and Adenauer had established personal relations of trust and mutual respect; Adenauer and his minister of defense Franz Josef Strauss supplied Israel with huge quantities of modern weapons worth hundreds of millions of dollars—tanks, cannons, helicopters, aircraft—all of this for free, in a secret effort to atone for the Holocaust and Germany's crimes against the Jewish people. Ben-Gurion trusted the current German government, and didn't want to jeopardize Israel's relations with it by hurling accusations and demands to intervene in the Egyptian crisis. He instructed Deputy Minister of Defense Shimon Peres to write a personal letter to Strauss and discreetly ask for his help.

But this wasn't enough for Isser, who decided to launch his own all-out campaign to disrupt the Germans' activities in Egypt.

On September 11, 1962, at ten thirty A.M., a swarthy stranger with a Middle Eastern cast to his features entered the Intra offices on Munich's Schillerstrasse. The clerk who ushered him into the office of the company director, Dr. Heinz Krug, heard him say he had been sent by Colonel Nadim, an Egyptian officer who maintained close contacts with Krug. Half an hour later, the Egyptian left the building with Krug. A United Arab Airlines stewardess saw the two men go by the airline ticket office. She was the last person to see Krug.

The following morning, Mrs. Krug informed the police that her husband was missing. Two days later, the police found Krug's white Mercedes abandoned on the outskirts of Munich. The car was covered with mud, and its tank was bone-dry. An anonymous phone call to the police announced: "Dr. Krug is dead." But some information from other sources made the police believe that Krug had been abducted by Mossad agents and taken to Israel. Today, there is no more doubt that Krug is dead.

On November 27, Hannelore Wende, Pilz's secretary at Factory 333, saw a thick envelope in the morning mail; the sender was a well-known Hamburg lawyer. Hannelore opened the package. A deafening explosion shook the office. Gravely wounded, Pilz's secretary was taken to the hospital, where she was to spend a few months before leaving blind, deaf, her face badly scarred.

The next day, a big package marked BOOKS arrived at Factory 333; when an Egyptian clerk opened it, the package exploded, killing five people. The sender's address, a Stuttgart publisher, turned out to be false.

The explosive packages kept arriving the following days. Some of them had been sent from Germany, others from inside Egypt. Some blew up, causing casualties, others were defused by Egyptian army experts alerted by 333 officials. The identity of the senders wasn't officially established, but the Egyptians and the journalists were certain that the bombs were prepared and sent to Cairo by the Israeli Mossad. Much later, it was established that several of the letter bombs had been mailed by the "Champagne Spy." This was an Israeli agent, Ze'ev Gur-Arie, who operated in Egypt under the cover of "Wolfgang Lutz," a German owner of a horse farm near Cairo. Posing as a former SS officer, he had settled in Cairo with his German wife and established close relations with Egypt's high society and its military leaders.

The letter bombs deeply disturbed the German scientists, who now felt their lives were in danger. Many of them got anonymous phone calls threatening them or their families if they kept working on Nasser's project. Strict security measures were applied at the three "factories" in Egypt and at the sister companies in Europe. When visiting Europe, the scientists had to move in large groups, accompanied by German security officers. This practice probably saved Professor Pilz on his trip to Europe in late 1962. A group of strangers followed him in Germany and Italy but didn't get the opportunity to come near him.

Isser spent the fall and winter of 1962 in Europe, directing several Mossad operations intended to obtain more accurate and updated information. Rafi Eitan succeeded in penetrating a diplomatic mission that handled the German scientists' mail. Such operations were his favorite. "That's much better than recruiting agents," he said. "When you recruit an agent you have to train him, build him a foolproof cover, put him in place, and give him time to establish contacts . . . But reading your enemy's mail is much better—you get immediate results and first-class material."

For his unconventional operations, Eitan needed some very sophisticated electronic equipment, but did not know where to get it. The equipment, used by the CIA and other intelligence agencies, could not be found in stores. While reading his newspaper in his Paris office, Eitan noticed a short item about the notorious Jewish mobster Meyer Lansky, who was the mob boss of Miami. In his scheming mind, that seemed like an opportunity. He called the operator: "Find Meyer Lansky in Miami!"

Three minutes later, Lansky was on the line. "*Shalom*, Meyer," Eitan said. "I am an Israeli, operating in Paris, and I need your help for the Zionist state."

"No problem," Lansky answered. "In a month I shall be in Lausanne, in Switzerland. Let's meet there."

Eitan met with Lansky in Lausanne, and told him what he needed. Lansky gave him the address of a certain man in Chicago. "He'll get you what you want," he said. A week later, Eitan landed in Chicago and headed for the man's address. "The electronic equipment we got from this guy served us well all through our operations against the German scientists," Eitan summed up.

One of these operations brought a new name to Isser Harel: Dr. Otto

Joklik. According to the source material, Joklik was an Austrian scientist specializing in nuclear radiation. Dr. Joklik was allegedly employed by a top-secret Egyptian project to obtain nuclear weapons in record time. The Egyptians intended to establish a front company, Austra, for Joklik in Austria, which would purchase radioactive materials for Joklik's project and ship them to Egypt. Austra would be separate from Intra, to avoid being investigated by the German authorities. Joklik was to carry out two nuclear tests for Egypt and produce several atom bombs that would be fitted into the missiles' warheads.

All this indicated that Joklik was a very dangerous man, perhaps the most dangerous of the German scientists. An urgent order was sent to all the Mossad stations in Europe: Find Joklik!

But Isser was in for a stunning surprise. On October 23, 1962, a stranger rang the door of an Israeli embassy in Europe and asked to see the security officer: "My name is Otto Joklik. I am ready to give you a full report about my activity for the Egyptian war effort."

Two weeks later, in utter secrecy, Joklik landed in Israel.

Many months later, when the Joklik defection came to light, European reporters wrote that Joklik probably contacted the Israelis because of the disappearance of Intra director Heinz Krug. Joklik had maintained close contact with Krug, who was among the few in the know of Joklik's role in Egypt's "special military programs." When Krug disappeared, Joklik panicked. What if Krug had been abducted by the Israelis? He might talk and reveal Joklik's secret tasks. And then, Joklik knew, he was as good as dead. Therefore, he decided to cross the lines and surrender to the Israelis; that way, he hoped, he at least would save his life.

Joklik spent four days in Israel. He was kept in strict isolation, in a top-security facility of the Mossad. Isser decided to use him for two main tasks: as a source of intelligence about the Egyptian project and as a double agent who would return to Egypt and work there for the Mossad.

Otto Joklik told the Israelis that he had been recruited by a senior German clerk in the United Arab Airlines who introduced him to General Mahmoud Khalil, nicknamed by the German scientists "Herr Doktor Mahmoud." His meeting with the Herr Doktor resulted in two projects: Ibis and Cleopatra. The secret of those projects was shared only with Professor Pilz and Dr. Krug.

Operation Ibis was to provide Egypt with a radiological weapon that could spread dangerous nuclear radiation. Joklik took it upon himself to obtain large quantities of radioactive isotope cobalt-60 and to experiment with it in Egypt. If the experiments succeeded, Joklik would try getting more cobalt, which would be placed in the missiles' warheads and spread deadly radiation on impact.

The goal of the second project, Cleopatra, was to produce two atomic bombs. Joklik suggested an ingenious method for manufacturing the bombs: buying uranium enriched to 20 percent in the United States or in Europe; enriching it up to 90 percent by special centrifuges developed in Germany and Holland by the scientists Dr. Wilhelm Groth, Dr. Jacob Kistemaker, and Dr. Gernot Zippe; and building the bomb with the enriched uranium.

Joklik flew to the United States and tried to get the enriched uranium there; he also met with several German scientists and invited them to build centrifuges in Egypt. Simultaneously, he purchased some cobalt-60 in Europe and dispatched it to a gynecologist in Cairo, whose name was Dr. Khalil—the sister of Herr Doktor Mahmoud . . .

When Joklik's debriefing in Israel was over, his testimony was sent to several experts for review and assessment. For some reason, their reports didn't get the proper attention. Concerning the Cleopatra Project, the experts said there were almost no chances that Joklik would get 20 percent enriched uranium. Even if he did, Egypt would need at least one hundred of the best centrifuges in order to harvest the necessary uranium for assembling one bomb within two to three years. And even if they managed to build a bomb, it wouldn't go off, for Joklik's formulas were incorrect. The experts dismissed Ibis and the radiological weapons, whose impact, they said, would cause no more damage than an ordinary bomb.

The soothing tone of the reports didn't calm the nation's leadership. They were even more alarmed by the reports that the Egyptians were also developing chemical weapons. On January 11, 1963, their fears were justified when the Egyptians used poison gas in their war in Yemen. Israeli Minister of Foreign Affairs Golda Meir met with President John F. Kennedy and talked to him about the danger that the Egyptians would arm their missiles with unconventional warheads; she asked him to intervene, but Kennedy did not.

The unconventional warheads were indeed very dangerous, but the first priority was given to disrupting the development of the missiles' guidance systems.

In the winter of 1963, the Factory 333 guidance expert, Dr. Kleinwachter, was spending some weeks in Germany. On the evening of February 20, he left his lab in Lorrach, and drove his car to the narrow lane leading to his home. The lane was dark and deserted, covered with deep snow. Suddenly, in a shrieking of tires, a car emerged from a cross street and blocked the way. A man got out of the car and walked toward Kleinwachter. The scientist glimpsed a third man in the car.

"Where does Dr. Shenker live?" the man demanded. Without waiting for a reply, he drew a revolver equipped with a silencer and fired. The bullet shattered the windshield and lodged in the scientist's woolen muffler. Kleinwachter groped in the glove compartment for his own revolver, but his assailant ran back to a second car, which darted out of sight.

The police found the first car abandoned about one hundred yards from the scene of the attack. The three men had made their escape with another car. They had left behind a passport in the name of Ali Samir, one of the heads of the Egyptian secret service. It turned out, however, that this was a red herring; on the day of the attack Samir was in Cairo and had been photographed with a German journalist.

The men who had attacked Kleinwachter were never found. Yet the unanimous opinion of the press was that the assassination attempt had been carried out by the Israelis, and had ended in failure.

A few weeks later, the Mossad tried again—this time going after German-born Dr. Paul Goerke in Switzerland.

Goerke, like Kleinwachter, was working on a guidance system for the

Egyptian missiles in his lab at Factory 333. He was deemed very important by the Egyptians—and by the Mossad as well. His daughter Heidi lived in Freiburg, a German town close to the Swiss border. Shortly after the attempt on Kleinwachter's life, Dr. Joklik called Heidi and told her that he had met her father in Egypt, where he was working on the development of terrible weapons intended to destroy Israel. Joklik hinted that if Goerke didn't cease his activities, he would be exposing himself to frightful risks. If, on the other hand, he were to leave Egypt, he would not be harmed.

"If you love your father," Joklik concluded, "come on Saturday, March 2, at four P.M., to the Three Kings Hotel in Basel, and I will introduce you to one of my friends."

Heidi, scared, immediately contacted H. Mann, a former Nazi officer who had been charged by the Egyptians with the scientists' security. Mann alerted the Freiburg police, who notified the Swiss authorities. And so, when Joklik and his friend entered the Three Kings Hotel, several police cars were waiting behind the building, detectives were stationed in the lobby, and tape recorders were installed close to the table where Heidi Goerke was sitting.

Joklik and his friend—Mossad agent Joseph Ben-Gal—walked right into the trap. They suspected nothing, and talked with Heidi Goerke for an hour, careful not to make any direct threats but alluding to the danger for her father if he kept building his terrible weapons. They offered Heidi a plane ticket to Cairo so that she could persuade her father to return to Germany where he and his family would be safe.

The meeting over, the two men left the hotel and took the six o'clock train to Zurich, where they went their separate ways. But while Joklik was waiting for another train on the platform, he was arrested by plainclothes policemen. Ben-Gal was apprehended near the Israeli consulate.

That evening the German police asked the Swiss to extradite the two men who were suspected of threatening Heidi Goerke and also of having participated in the attack on Dr. Kleinwachter.

From his headquarters in Europe, Isser activated his contacts and tried to persuade the Swiss to release Ben-Gal and Joklik, but they refused because of the German extradition request. Isser then flew back to Israel and met with Minister of Foreign Affairs Golda Meir. Lately, they had become very close and shared the same hostility and suspicions toward Germany. Golda suggested that Israel approach Chancellor Adenauer and demand that West Germany withdraw the extradition request.

Isser immediately drove to Tiberias, where Prime Minister Ben-Gurion was vacationing. He urged Ben-Gurion to send a special envoy to Bonn, West Germany's capital. The envoy would present Adenauer with proof of the atrocious activities of the German scientists in Egypt, and demand the withdrawal of the extradition request.

Ben-Gurion refused.

Isser didn't let go. "You have to decide what to do if the arrest is made public. Then the entire affair will blow up."

"What do you mean, blow up?" Ben-Gurion asked.

"As soon as Ben-Gal's arrest becomes known, the entire affair of the German scientists in Egypt will also come to light. Israel will have to explain why Ben-Gal acted as he did. We shall also have to disclose that the Egyptians have been buying equipment for their rockets and other military projects from Germany."

Ben-Gurion thought a moment and finally said: "So be it."

That was the beginning of the rift between the two men.

In the evening of Thursday, March 15, 1963, United Press International announced the arrest of Joklik and Ben-Gal "on suspicion of having threatened the daughter of a German scientist in the employ of Egypt." Isser Harel called a secret meeting with the editors in chief of the daily newspapers; at the meeting he described the background to Ben-Gal's arrest. He particularly stressed Joklik's part in the affair, the kind of work he had been doing for the Egyptian project, and the fact that he changed sides voluntarily and was trying to repair the damage.

During the next few days, Isser's aides secretly briefed three Israeli journalists: Naftali Lavi of *Haaretz*, Shmuel Segev of *Ma'ariv*, and Yeshayahu Ben-Porat of *Yedioth Ahronoth*. They were given all the facts, and the addresses of Intra, Patwag, and the Stuttgart Institute. The three men then left for Europe to gather data on the German scientists and cable it to their papers in Israel. News about the German scientists' project would be more credible coming from Europe, Isser thought. Other Mossad men were sent abroad to brief pro-Israeli journalists.

Isser Harel didn't realize that the German issue was one of the most sensitive topics in Israel. His unbridled attack on Germany started an avalanche that couldn't be stopped, a deluge of accusations against the scientists that provoked real panic in Israel.

By March 17, the Israeli and foreign press were floundering in a sea of sensational headlines: German scientists, most of them former Nazis, were producing deadly weapons in Egypt. They were preparing biological, chemical, nuclear, and radioactive weapons. They were developing poison gas, terrible germs, death rays, warheads equipped with atomic bombs or radioactive waste that would spread lethal radiation. The newspapers competed with one another by publishing reports that seemed plagiarized from the Flash Gordon comics: the death ray, hissing and scorching everything in its path . . . the air over Israel that would be poisoned for ninety years at least . . . the germs spreading atrocious plagues, et cetera. The campaign also accused the government of the Federal Republic of Germany of refraining from putting an end to the devilish activities of its subjects working for Egypt, and actually following in Hitler's footsteps. The reporters sent to Europe added more fat to the fire, by "discovering" every day new details about the scientists' diabolical plot.

Ben-Gal and Joklik's trial in Basel ended with light sentences for the two men—two months in jail, with time served. But it had a secondary result with enormous implications.

During the trial, the judge suddenly noticed that one of the spectators was carrying a gun.

"How dare you carry a gun in my court?" he indignantly asked.

The man answered: "I have a permit to carry a weapon at all times. I am the security officer of the German scientists in Egypt."

He identified himself as H. Mann—the man who has been contacted by Heidi Goerke after Joklik's phone call, and who actually had alerted the German police.

An undercover Mossad informant left the courtroom at once and reported the incident to his superiors. As he heard the report, veteran Mossad agent Raphi Medan jumped aboard the first train to Vienna and hurried to the home of the famous Nazi hunter, Simon Wiesenthal. Wiesenthal immediately agreed to help the Mossad.

"Do you know anything about a German named H. Mann?" Medan asked.

Wiesenthal went to work in his overflowing archives. After a few hours, he returned to Medan with a file in his hands. "He was an SS officer during the war," he said. "He served in a commando unit under Colonel Otto Skorzeny."

Medan brought the information to the omnipresent Rafi Eitan and to Avraham Ahituv.

A balding, sunburned man with mustache and glasses, Ahituv was born in Germany as Avraham Gotfried and immigrated with his religious parents to Israel at the age of five. At sixteen, he already was a member of the Haganah; and at eighteen, one of the founders of the Shabak. Extremely intelligent, he had completed his studies during his service, and graduated from law school summa cum laude. In 1955, he had caught the most important Egyptian spy in Israel, Rif'at El Gamal, who operated under the Israeli identity of Jack Bitton. Ahituv turned El Gamal, making him one of the Mossad's best double agents, who fed the Egyptians expertly doctored information for more than twelve years. In 1967, on the eve of the Six-Day War, El Gamal would inform the Egyptians that Israel would launch a ground attack before sending its aircraft into battle; the resulting laxity of the Egyptian Air Force facilitated its destruction on the ground by the Israeli jets. In the future, Ahituv would become one of the best Shabak directors, mostly appreciated for his efforts to integrate Israeli Arabs into the mainstream of Israel's society.

On this evening in May 1963, Ahituv listened to Medan's report about

Mann and Skorzeny, then turned to Eitan: "Why don't we try to recruit Skorzeny?"

The idea seemed bizarre at first, but it had its inner logic: if Skorzeny turned on Mann, he had a chance to obtain highly classified material from his former subordinate. Now the question was how to contact Skorzeny. A quick check revealed that Skorzeny's estranged wife had stayed very close to him; she was now managing a company that specialized in metal trading. The Mossad agents found an Israeli businessman, Shlomo Zablodovitch, who was in the same line of business, and contacted him. Yes, he said, he knew Ms. Skorzeny. He introduced them to the lady, who told them all they needed to know.

That was how Eitan and Ahituv showed up in Skorzeny's office in Madrid. They now asked the former Third Reich hero to become their agent and provide the Mossad with information about the activities of the German scientists in Egypt. Besides H. Mann, Skorzeny knew quite a few leaders of the German community in Egypt, many of whom were his former fellow officers.

"How can I trust you?" Skorzeny asked. "How can I be sure that you won't go after me later?" He feared that Israeli avengers would find him as they found Eichmann, and his fate would be the same.

Rafi Eitan found the solution right away. "We are authorized to offer you freedom from fear," he said. He took a sheet of paper and wrote Skorzeny a letter, in the name of the State of Israel, which guaranteed him "freedom from fear" and assured him that he would not be subject to any kind of persecution or violence.

Skorzeny perused the document, then fell silent. He got up and paced back and forth, immersed in thought.

He finally turned to the Israelis. "I agree," he said.

In the following months, Skorzeny brought to his Mossad handlers priceless intelligence about the activities of the German scientists in Egypt. With the help of H. Mann and his other former cohorts, he obtained detailed lists of the German scientists and their addresses, reports about the progress of their projects, plans, and blueprints of the missiles, correspondence about the failures to assemble a guidance system for the missiles.

But Isser Harel wasn't there anymore to read Skorzeny's reports.

In the meantime, the Israeli media had been set loose. Shrieking headlines, editorials, cartoons, and even poems announced that Germany of 1963 was the same as Germany of 1933; and the same Germany that had massacred 6 million Jews was now helping Egypt prepare a new Holocaust. In the Knesset, opposition leader Menahem Begin shouted at Ben-Gurion in an inflammatory tirade: "You are selling Uzis to the Germans, and they are sending germs to our enemies." In a speech, Isser's ally Golda Meir accused the Germans in Egypt of producing weapons "whose aim is to destroy all living things."

These accusations were exaggerated, almost totally detached from reality. Amos Manor, head of the Shabak and a close friend of Isser, would tell us later: "During this period, when Isser directed the campaign against the German scientists, he was an unbalanced man. It was much deeper than obsession. You couldn't have a normal conversation on this subject with him."

Deputy Minister of Defense Shimon Peres, who returned to Israel on March 24 from a trip to Africa, immediately perceived the tremendous danger that could arise from Isser Harel's crusade. He also realized that the stories about the weapons "that kill any living thing" were simply ludicrous. Aman, the IDF's intelligence branch, presented him with a totally different estimate. "We gathered all that we could collect," said the IDF intelligence chief, General Meir Amit, "and slowly a picture emerged: this story had been blown out of any proportion . . . Our people said that this couldn't be true; it couldn't be something serious."

Amit's people didn't find any indication that the German scientists were developing chemical or bacteriological weapons; the stories about doomsday weapons seemed borrowed from science fiction; the quantities of cobalt brought to Egypt were infinitesimal. It was also established that Dr. Otto Joklik, whose testimony had played a major part in the whole business, was no more than an opportunist who could not be trusted.

The Aman report reached Ben-Gurion's desk on March 24. He immediately summoned Isser Harel and questioned him about his sources. He demanded full and accurate answers. Isser admitted having sent reporters to Europe, after a thorough briefing; he also admitted that he had no information about poison gas, radiology, or cobalt bombs.

The next day Ben-Gurion met with Shimon Peres, who came with the chief of staff and General Amit. The Aman chief made a detailed report that painted a clear picture: the scientists working in Egypt were mediocre, and they were building obsolete missiles. Their activities were dangerous indeed, but the panic that had spread in the governing circles in Israel, including the Ministry of Defense and the IDF, was utterly out of proportion.

Ben-Gurion summoned Isser again. Their conversation was tense, and Ben-Gurion expressed doubts as to the accuracy of Isser's reports and assessments. The total trust that characterized the relations between the two men was replaced by an angry debate that also touched upon the other aspects of German-Israeli relations. Isser, furious, returned to his office and dispatched a letter of resignation to Ben-Gurion.

Ben-Gurion tried to talk him out of leaving, but Isser was adamant. I resign, he said, and that's final.

This was the end of an era.

Ben-Gurion then asked Isser to stay until a replacement was found. Isser refused. "Tell Ben-Gurion to send somebody right away and take the keys," he said to Ben-Gurion's secretary. The prime minister had to find a replacement for the legendary *ramsad* right away. "Get me Amos Manor at once," he said to his secretary, who rushed to the telephone.

But the head of the Shabak was unreachable; he was on his way to kibbutz Maagan in the Jordan Valley to visit relatives, and cell phones had yet to be invented.

"Then get me Meir," Ben-Gurion said impatiently. General Meir Amit was on a tour of inspection in the Negev, but was reached by radio and summoned to Tel-Aviv. On his arrival, he learned that he was being appointed acting Mossad director until a new chief took charge of the organization. A few weeks later, Amit's appointment became final.

* * *

Following Peres's discreet letter to Franz Josef Strauss, Germany charged a respected expert, Professor Boehm, to devise the means of bringing back the scientists from Egypt. Germany indeed succeeded in tempting many of the scientists by offering them employment in research institutions on its territory. The others gradually left Egypt. They didn't finish building missiles, their navigation systems failed, the missile warheads were not filled with radioactive materials, and even Messerschmitt's plane never took off.

One of the authors of this book traveled to Huntsville, Alabama, and met there with NASA's blue-eyed boy, Dr. Wernher von Braun. Von Braun went over the lists of German scientists in Egypt and their alleged projects and concluded that there were very slim chances that these second-rate scientists would have ever been able to build effective missiles.

Herr Doktor Mahmoud's Egyptian endeavor ended in complete failure.

The affair of the German scientists brought about the fall of Isser Harel and the rise of Meir Amit. Harel developed a deep loathing toward his successor, and bitterly fought him during his years as *ramsad*. The affair of the German scientists also undermined Ben-Gurion's political power, and he resigned from office a few months later.

In Cairo, the Egyptian secret services unmasked Wolfgang Lutz, the "Champagne Spy," and arrested him in 1965. Yet they failed to crack his German cover; he was sentenced only to jail and released after two and a half years.

The end of the affair was also the end of the Mossad's work with Otto Skorzeny, the most improbable agent who ever spied for the Jewish state.

CHAPTER NINE

OUR MAN IN DAMASCUS

My dear Nadia, my dear family,

I am writing to you these last words, hoping that you'll remain united forever. I ask my wife to forgive me, to take care of herself and give a good education to our children . . . My dearest Nadia, you may remarry, so that our children will have a father. You are absolutely free in that respect. I ask you not to mourn the past but turn to the future. I am sending you my last kisses.

Please pray for my soul.

Yours, Elie.

This letter reached the desk of the new *ramsad*, Meir Amit, in May 1965. Elie Cohen, one of the boldest spies in the history of espionage, had written it with a trembling hand, just a few minutes before his life came to an abrupt end on the gallows of Damascus.

The secret life of Elie Cohen had begun more than twenty years before. A young, handsome Egyptian Jew, Cohen was on his way home one humid afternoon in mid-July 1954. He was thirty, of medium height, sporting a neat black mustache and a disarming smile. On a Cairo street he bumped into an old friend, a police officer. "Tonight we'll arrest some Israeli terrorists," the officer confided. "One of them is called Shmuel Azar." Elie faked awe and admiration, but as soon as he parted with his friend, he ran to his rented apartment and removed the handgun, the explosives, and the documents he kept there. Elie was deeply involved in clandestine activities. He planned escape routes and prepared false documents for Jewish families that wanted to emigrate to Israel. He also was a member of the Jewish underground responsible for an ambitious operation known as the Lavon Affair.

In early 1954, Israel's leaders learned that the British government had decided to pull out of Egypt completely. Egypt was the strongest of the Arab countries and a sworn enemy of Israel. As long as the British Army was present in Egypt and maintained scores of army bases and military airfields along the Suez Canal, Israel could count on its moderating influence over the military junta that governed the country. With the decision to evacuate Egypt that influence would evaporate at once; besides, modern bases, airfields, and huge stores of equipment and war materials would fall in the hands of the Egyptian Army. Israel, then only six years old, could be the target of an aggressive attack by a larger, better equipped Egyptian Army that wanted to avenge its shameful defeat in the 1948 Israel Independence War.

Could the British decision be revoked? Ben-Gurion was not at the helm of Israel anymore; he had retired to kibbutz Sdeh Boker. He had been replaced by a moderate but weak leader, Moshe Sharett. Minister of Defense Pinhas Lavon openly disputed Sharett's authority. Without Sharett's knowledge, and without informing the Mossad, Lavon and Colonel Benyamin Gibli, the head of military intelligence (Aman), concocted a dangerous and foolish plan. They found a clause in the British-Egyptian agreement that allowed Great Britain to return to its former bases in case of a grave crisis, and naively concluded that if several terrorist bombings were to sweep

Egypt, Britain would conclude that Egypt's leaders couldn't maintain law and order. Therefore the British would cancel their decision to pull out of the country. Lavon and Gibli decided to carry out several bombings in Cairo and Alexandria, targeting American and British libraries and cultural centers, cinemas, post offices, and other public buildings. Aman's secret agents in Egypt recruited some young local Jews, fervent Zionists, who were ready to give their lives for Israel. By doing that, Aman broke a sacrosanct rule of Israel's intelligence community: never use local Jews in hostile operations, as that could cost them their lives and place the entire Jewish community in grave danger. In addition, the young men and women had no preliminary training for such operations.

The bombs were rudimentary, made out of eyeglass cases in which a chemical substance had been placed. Another substance was poured into a condom introduced into the case; highly corrosive, the chemical would burn its way through the condom and come into contact with the other substance inside the case, producing a minor burst of fire. The condom was used as a timing tool, to allow the person placing the incendiary device to escape before the explosion.

The plan was doomed from the start. On July 23, after a couple of minor operations, one of the bombs exploded in the pocket of Philip Natanson, a member of the Zionist network, at the entrance of cinema Rio in Alexandria. He was arrested by the police, and in the following days all the network members were caught.

Elie Cohen was arrested as well, but the search of his apartment failed to discover any incriminating evidence; he was released, but the Egyptian police opened a file on him. It included three photos and the record of Elie Shaul Jundi Cohen, born in 1924 in Alexandria, to Shaul and Sophie Cohen who had emigrated to an unknown destination in 1949 with Elie's two sisters and five brothers. The suspect was a graduate of the French college, and a student at the Cairo Farouk University.

The Egyptians didn't know that Elie's family had emigrated to Israel and settled in Bat Yam, a suburb of Tel Aviv.

In spite of the arrests, Elie decided to stay in Egypt and not run away. Fearing the worst for his friends, he collected every bit of information about their incarceration, beatings, and torture in Egypt's jail.

In October, the Egyptians publicly announced the arrest of "Israeli spies," and on December 7, their trial opened in Cairo. Max Bennet, an Israeli undercover agent who was arrested with the group, killed himself by cutting his wrists with a rusty nail he had pulled out of his cell door. At the trial, the prosecution asked for the death penalty for some of the detainees. Pleas for mercy streamed from the papal nuncio, the French foreign minister, the U.S. and Great Britain's ambassadors, members of the British House of Commons Richard Crossman and Maurice Auerbach, the chief rabbi of Egypt . . . All was in vain. On January 17, 1955, the Extraordinary Military Court announced the sentences: two of the accused were found not guilty; two were sentenced to seven years of prison with hard labor, two to fifteen years, and two to life. The two leaders of the network, Dr. Moshe Marzuk and the engineer Shmuel Azar, were sentenced to death and hanged, four days later, in the courtyard of Cairo prison. In Israel, a tremendous political scandal shook the government. Who had given the stupid, criminal order for that operation? Several boards of inquiry failed to reach a clear-cut answer. Lavon and Gibli pointed fingers at each other. Minister of Defense Lavon was forced to resign and was replaced by Ben-Gurion, who came back from retirement; Colonel Gibli was never promoted and after a short while had to leave the army.

In Egypt, Elie Cohen had lost some of his best friends. Although still a suspect in the eyes of the authorities, he stayed in Cairo and pursued his clandestine activities. Only in 1957, after the Suez War, did he immigrate to Israel.

The Cairo Martyrs is the name of a quiet, shady street in Bat Yam. Elie walked that street every day when coming to visit his family. His first steps in Israel were not easy. For a few weeks he was looking for a job. Thanks to his fluency in languages (Arabic, French, English, and even Hebrew) he found a position: translating weekly and monthly magazines for

Aman. His office on a Tel Aviv street was camouflaged as a commercial agency. Elie was paid a modest salary: 170 Israeli pounds ($95) a month. After a few months he was fired. One of his friends, also an Egyptian Jew, found him a new job: accountant at the department store chain Hamashbir. The job was boring, but the pay was higher. At that time his brother introduced him to a pretty, smart young nurse of Iraqi origin. A month after meeting her, Elie wed Nadia, the sister of a rising intellectual Sami Michael. One morning, a man walked into Elie's office. "My name is Zalman," he said. "I am an intelligence officer. I want to offer you a job."

"What kind of job?"

"Quite interesting, actually. You'll travel to Europe a lot. Perhaps you'll even have to go to Arab countries as our agent."

Elie refused. "I just got married," he said. "I don't want to travel to Europe or to any other place."

That was the end of the conversation but not the end of the affair. Nadia got pregnant and had to leave her job. Hamashbir had to restructure and fired a few employees, Elie among them. He couldn't find another job. And then, as if by chance, an unexpected visitor knocked on the door of his rented apartment.

It was Zalman again.

"Why do you refuse to work for us?" he asked Elie. "We shall pay you 350 pounds ($195) a month. You'll train for six months. Then, if you like it, you'll stay. If not—you'll be free to go."

This time, Elie didn't say no. And he became a secret agent.

Some of the Aman veterans tell a different version. They maintain that when he arrived in Israel, Elie didn't get a job at Aman, because the psychological tests he underwent showed him to be overconfident. He was gifted, courageous, and had an excellent memory, but had the tendency to overestimate himself and take unnecessary risks. These character traits, combined, made him unsuitable for Aman.

But in the early sixties, things changed. Aman's Unit 131, the special operations unit of the IDF intelligence branch, urgently started looking for a highly qualified agent in Damascus, the capital of Syria. In the last few years, Syria had become the most aggressive Arab country, and the sworn enemy of Israel. It never missed a chance to attack. Syria confronted Israel in bloody battles at the Golan Heights and on the shores of the Lake of Galilee; it dispatched squads of terrorists across the Israeli border. And now, it planned to carry out a grandiose engineering project, intended to divert the waters of the Jordan River tributaries and deprive Israel of water.

In the late fifties, Israel had launched a project of huge pipelines and canals that would carry a part of the Jordan water to the arid Negev region. The water was taken from the part of the river that passed through Israel's territory. The water project triggered a series of Arab summit conferences. The Arab nations solemnly decided to divert the Jordan tributaries and kill the Israeli project; the job itself fell to Syria.

Israel could not survive without Jordan's water. It could not let Syria succeed, and started planning a response. It needed an agent in Damascus, somebody trustworthy, confident, and daring. The same characteristics that had forced Aman to reject Elie before made him perfect now for Unit 131. (Fifty years later, it was revealed that Aman had tried to recruit somebody else for that job—Sami Michael, Nadia Cohen's brother! Michael refused, stayed in Israel, and became one of its great poets.)

Cohen's training was long and exhausting. Every morning, under some pretext, Elie would leave home and head for the Aman training center. For several weeks, he had only one instructor, a man named Yitzhak. First, he learned how to memorize things. Yitzhak would throw a dozen objects on the table—a pencil, a bunch of keys, a cigarette, an eraser, a few pins. Elie glanced at them for a second or two. Then he had to close his eyes and describe what they looked like. He also learned to identify the type and make of tanks, aircrafts, and cannons. "Let's go for a walk," Yitzhak would say. The two of them would stroll in the crowded Tel Aviv streets. "Do you see the newspaper stand over there?" Yitzhak would whisper. "Now, go there and pretend to be looking at the papers, but at the same time try to find out who is following you." When they returned to the center, Yitzhak would listen to Elie's report and then throw a batch of photos on the table. "You were right about this one; he followed you indeed, but what about that one, by the tree? He was also shadowing you."

One morning, Zalman introduced him to another instructor, Yehuda, who taught him how to use a small, sophisticated radio transmitter. He then sent Elie to undergo physical exams and psychological tests. After the tests were over, Zalman introduced Elie to a young woman, Marcelle Cousin.

"It's time for the decisive test, Elie," he said. "Marcelle will give you a French passport in the name of an Egyptian Jew who has immigrated to Africa and now has come to Israel as a tourist. With this passport you'll go to Jerusalem and stay there ten days. Marcelle will give you full details about your cover—your past in Egypt, your family, your work in Africa. In Jerusalem you'll only speak French and Arabic. You have to meet people, make friends, and establish new contacts without revealing your real identity. You must also make sure that you're not followed."

Elie spent ten days in Jerusalem. On his return he got a few days of leave. Nadia had just given birth to a daughter, Sophie. After Rosh Hashana—the Jewish New Year—Zalman introduced him to two other men, who didn't identify themselves. "You've passed your test in Jerusalem, Elie," one of them said with a smile. "It's time to get to more serious matters."

In a bare room at the Aman facility, Elie met a Muslim sheikh who patiently taught him the Koran and the Muslim prayers. Elie tried to concentrate, but kept making mistakes. "Don't worry," his instructors told him. "If somebody starts asking you questions, tell them that you're not a devout Muslim, and you only have vague religious memories from your days at school."

Now Elie was given a foretaste of his mission: he would soon be sent to a neutral country abroad, and after additional training he would proceed to an Arab capital.

"Which one?" he asked.

"You'll be told in due time."

Zalman went on. "You'll pose as an Arab, create local contacts, and establish an Israeli espionage network."

Elie agreed without hesitating. He felt confident that he could carry out the mission.

"You'll get papers of a Syrian or an Iraqi," his handlers told him.

"Why? I don't know anything about Iraq. Get me Egyptian papers."

"That's impossible," Zalman said. "The Egyptians have updated records of their population and of all the passports they have issued. That's too dangerous. Iraq and Syria don't have such records. They can't track you down."

Two days later, Zalman and his colleagues revealed to Elie his new identity. "Your name is Kamal. Your father's name is Amin Tabet, so your full name will be Kamal Amin Tabet."

Elie's case officers had prepared a detailed legend—a cover story—for their new agent. "You're the son of Syrian parents. Your mother's name is Saida Ibrahim. You had a sister. You were born in Beirut, in Lebanon. When you were three, your family left Lebanon and moved to Egypt, to Alexandria. Don't forget, your family is Syrian. A year later your sister died. Your father was a textile merchant. In 1946 your uncle emigrated to Argentina. Shortly after, he wrote to your father and invited your family to join him in Buenos Aires. In 1947 all of you arrived in Argentina. Your father and your uncle established a partnership with a third person, and opened a textile store, but it went bankrupt. Your father died in 1956 and six months later your mother died, too. You lived with your uncle and worked at a travel agency. You later went into business and were very successful."

Elie now needed a cover story for his family as well. "I got a job with a company that works with the Defense and Foreign Ministries," Elie told Nadia when he came back home. "They need somebody to travel in Europe, buy tools, equipment, and materials for Ta'as (Israel's military industry) and find markets for its products. I'll come home often, for long leaves. I know that the separation will be hard—for both of us—but you'll get my full salary here, and in a few years we'll buy furniture in Europe and set up the apartment."

In early February 1961 an unmarked car brought Elie to Lod Airport. A young man who identified himself as Gideon handed him an Israeli passport in his real name, $500, and a plane ticket to Zurich.

On his arrival in Zurich, Elie was met by a white-haired man, who took his passport and gave him a passport from a European country, in another name. That passport carried an entry visa to Chile and a transit visa to Argentina. "In Buenos Aires our people will extend your transit visa," the man said, slipping into Elie's hand a plane ticket to Santiago, with a stopover in Buenos Aires. "Tomorrow you'll arrive in Buenos Aires. The day after, at eleven A.M., you should come to Café Corrientes. Our people will meet you there."

Elie arrived in Argentina's capital and checked into a hotel. The following morning, at eleven o'clock on the dot, an elderly man came to his table at Café Corrientes, and introduced himself as Abraham. Cohen was instructed to settle in a furnished apartment, already rented for him. A local teacher would get in touch with him and teach him the Spanish language. "You'll have no other concerns," Abraham said. "I'll take care of your finances."

Three months later, Elie was ready for the next stage. He spoke passable Spanish, knew Buenos Aires well, dressed and behaved like thousands of Arab immigrants living in Argentina's capital. Another tutor trained him to speak Arabic with a Syrian accent.

Abraham met him again in a café, and handed him a Syrian passport in the name of Kamal Amin Tabet. "You must change your address by the end of the week," Abraham said. "Open a bank account in that name. Start visiting the Arab restaurants, the cinemas where Arab movies are shown, and the Arab cultural and political clubs. Try to make as many friends as possible, and establish contacts with the Arab community leaders. You are a man of means, a merchant and a brilliant businessman. You are in the import-export business, but you also are involved in transports and investments. Make generous contributions to the charity funds of the Arab community. Good luck!"

The Israeli spy, indeed, had plenty of good luck. In a few months, Elie Cohen successfully penetrated the core of the Arab-Syrian community in Buenos Aires. His personal charm, confidence, common sense, and fortune attracted quite a few Arabs, among the most important in

Argentina. He soon became a well-known figure in Arab circles. His breakthrough came in the Muslim club one evening when he met a dignified gentleman, well dressed, balding, his face adorned with a bushy mustache. He introduced himself as Abdel Latif Hassan, editor in chief of the *Arab World* magazine published in Argentina. Hassan was deeply impressed with the serious personality of "the Syrian immigrant," and the two of them became close friends.

The cultural events at the clubs were followed by more intimate gatherings in the company of the Arab community leaders. Elie made it to the Syrian embassy guest list, and was invited to posh parties and receptions. At an official reception at the embassy, Hassan steered his friend Tabet to an imposing-looking officer, dressed in the uniform of a Syrian general. "Allow me to introduce a real and devoted Syrian patriot," Hassan said to the general. And then, turning to Elie, he added: "Meet General Amin El-Hafez, the military attaché at the embassy."

Elie seemed to have completed the final stage in establishing his legend. Time had come for the real espionage mission. Elie was briefed in a short, surreptitious meeting with Abraham in July 1961. The next day he came to Hassan's office. "I am sick and tired of living in Argentina," he admitted. He loved Syria more than anything, and wanted to go back. Could Hassan help him with some letters of recommendation? The editor immediately wrote four letters: one to his brother-in-law in Alexandria, two to friends in Beirut (one of them a highly influential banker), and the fourth to his son in Damascus. Elie visited his other Arab friends, and his briefcase was soon full of enthusiastic letters of recommendation, written by the leaders of the Buenos Aires community.

At the end of July 1961, Kamal Amin Tabet flew to Zurich, changed planes, and proceeded to Munich. At the airport of the Bavarian capital, an Israeli agent approached him. His name was Zelinger. He handed Elie his Israeli passport and a plane ticket to Tel Aviv. In early August, Elie came home. "I'll spend some months at home," he said to Nadia.

The following months passed in intensive training. Elie's cover was perfect and he completely identified with his new character. His radio instructor, Yehuda, was back, and trained him in radio transmission in code. After a few weeks he was able to receive and transmit between twelve and sixteen words a minute. He compulsively read books and documents on Syria, its army, weapons, and strategy. After myriad briefings by specialists, he himself became an expert on Syrian internal politics.

In December 1961, Elie flew to Zurich again; but his final destination was Damascus, the lion's den.

The tension on the Syrian-Israeli border had grown as the Syrian regime had weakened. Since 1948, a long series of military coups had shaken the country. Very rarely did a Syrian dictator die a natural death anymore—they died on the gallows, in front of a firing squad, or by the good services of an assassin. The unstable country was in constant turmoil. Quite often, eager to distract the public's attention from inner problems, the Syrian leaders deliberately caused border incidents. Public executions were a common sight in Damascus's squares. One after the other, the hangmen put to death people labeled as conspirators, spies, enemies of the state, and supporters of the former regime. Not long before Elie arrived, there had been yet another coup, on September 28, 1961; it had put an end to the short-lived Syrian-Egyptian union, pompously named the United Arab Republic.

Before setting out on his mission, Elie met the ubiquitous Zalman, who gave him detailed instructions: "You'll get your radio transmitter from Zelinger, our man in Munich. After you arrive in Damascus, you'll be contacted by an employee of the Syrian broadcasting corporation. He, too, is an 'immigrant' like you, who has settled in Syria not long ago. He doesn't know your real identity. Don't try to find him! He'll find the right moment to establish contact with you."

In Munich, Zelinger had for him an impressive package of spying equipment: sheets of paper, on which the key to the transmission code was written with invisible ink; books serving as transmission codes; a special typewriter; a transistor radio, in which a transmitter had been inserted; an electric razor whose cord served as an antenna for the transmitter; dynamite sticks hidden in Yardley soap and cigars; and some cyanide pills for suicide, just in case . . .

Elie wondered how he would introduce all this equipment to Syria, where customs and immigration controls were thorough and severe.

Zelinger had the answer. "You'll buy a passage on the SS *Astoria* that sails from Genoa to Beirut in early January. Somebody will get in touch with you on the boat. He'll help you pass the border controls in Syria."

Elie set sail aboard the *Astoria*. One morning, when he was sitting close to a group of Egyptian passengers, a man approached him and whispered: "Follow me." Elie got up and strolled away from the group. The man told him: "My name is Majeed Sheikh El-Ard. I've got a car." That was a hint that he would drive Elie to Damascus.

El-Ard, a short, mousy man, was an international entrepreneur and a well-known—and shady—businessman in Damascus. He was married to an Egyptian Jewess, and yet he had chosen to pass the World War II years in Nazi Germany. His fickle and greedy character made him seem an un-savory partner, which attracted the Israeli services' attention; they soon made him their agent, even though he didn't realize it. He believed he was working for right-wing Syrian extremists who were acting undercover. He truly believed in Kamal Amin Tabet's legend, and in the coming years was to be of great help to the Israeli spy.

His first task was to make sure that Tabet's baggage would safely go through Syrian controls.

January 10, 1962. El-Ard's car, coming from Beirut, was stopped at the Syrian border. In the trunk were Elie Cohen's bags, full of transmission equipment and other incriminating items. Elie was sitting in the passenger seat, beside Sheikh El-Ard.

"We are going to meet my friend Abu Khaldun," El-Ard told Elie when they approached the border. "He happens to be in financial trouble. Five hundred dollars would certainly improve his situation."

And so, $500 quickly made their way from the Israeli agent's wallet to the pocket of Abu Khaldun, the Syrian customs inspector. The barrier was raised and the car sailed into the desert. Elie Cohen was in Syria.

In bustling Damascus, strewn with crowded mosques and colorful souks, it was not difficult to melt into the crowd. But Elie wanted the exact opposite. He wanted to be noticed, and fast. He rented a luxurious villa in the classy Abu Ramen neighborhood, close to Syrian Army Headquarters. From the villa's balcony, Elie could watch the entrance to the Syrian government's official guesthouse. His house stood among foreign embassies, rich businessmen's homes, and the official residences of the nation's leaders. Elie immediately concealed his secret equipment in various hiding places throughout the house. In order to avoid the risk of informers or traitors in his own household, he decided to refrain from hiring servants, and lived alone.

He was lucky again. He had arrived in Damascus at the right moment. The United Arab Republic collapse was regarded by President Nasser in Cairo as a personal affront and a humiliation to Egypt. The Syrian leaders, both politicians and military, were obsessed with the possibility of an Egyptian-inspired coup, and Israeli espionage was not on their agenda. On the other hand, they badly needed new allies, supporters, and sources of funding, both in Syria and among the Syrian émigrés overseas. Kamal Amin Tabet, the staunchly nationalist millionaire, armed with excellent letters of recommendation, was the right man at the right time.

Cohen established his contacts quickly and effectively. His letters of recommendation opened the gates to the high society, the banks, and the commercial circles that had inspired the coup of September 28. His new friends introduced Elie to top government officials, senior army officers, and leaders of the ruling party. Two rich businessmen courted the young and handsome millionaire, hoping he would marry one of their daughters. In a display of generosity, Tabet contributed a substantial sum of money to the building of a public kitchen for the poor of Damascus. His new popularity paved his way to the governing circles; yet he refrained from identifying with Syria's new rulers, because he intuitively felt that this was only temporary. Syria was still to go through major internal aftershocks following the separation from Egypt.

A month after his arrival in Damascus, Elie was visited by George

Salem Seif, a radio-show host in charge of Radio Damascus broadcasts for Syrians abroad. He was the man whom Zalman had mentioned at Elie's last briefing in Israel. Seif had "returned" to Syria a while before Tabet. Because of his position, he could supply Elie with inside information about the political and military situation. Seif also showed Elie the secret guidelines by the Ministry of Propaganda, outlining what he could broadcast and what he had to conceal from his audiences. At the parties held in Seif's house, Elie met several senior officials and well-known politicians.

Seif, like El-Ard, had no clue about Elie Cohen's real identity. He, too, believed Tabet was a fanatical nationalist who had his own political agenda.

Elie Cohen realized that he had become the loneliest spy in the world—with not even one friend and confidant; he didn't know if there was another Israeli network operating in Damascus. He needed nerves of steel to withstand the stress of his terrible solitude, and to play a dangerous role twenty-four hours a day. He knew that even during his rare visits home he couldn't share his secret with his wife, and had to mislead her, too.

He started transmitting his messages to Israel daily, at eight A.M.—and sometimes in the evening as well. His broadcasts were carried out under a foolproof cover. His transmitter was located in his villa, very close to the army headquarters, which was the source of endless transmissions. Nobody could discern the difference between Elie's broadcasts and the myriad messages emanating from the army communications center.

Six months after arriving in Syria, Kamal Amin Tabet had become a well-known figure in Damascus high society. He then decided to go abroad "for business." He first flew to Argentina, where he met several of his Arab friends, then traveled to Europe, changed planes and identities, and, on a hot summer night, landed in Lod Airport. Laden with presents, the "traveling salesman" arrived in his modest apartment in Bat Yam, where Nadia and Sophie were waiting for him.

At the end of fall, Elie Cohen flew to Europe. A few days later, Kamal Amin Tabet arrived in Damascus. During his stay in Israel, his superiors in Aman had equipped him with a miniature camera so he could photograph sites and documents. He had to conceal the microfilms in expensive boxes containing backgammon pieces. The boxes were made of polished wood embellished with a mosaic of nacre and ivory. The mosaic ornament could be dug out of the polished wood, and reinserted after the microfilm had been placed in the cavity. Tabet would send the backgammon sets to "friends in Argentina," who would dispatch them to Israel with the diplomatic pouch.

Some of the first documents sent by Elie were reports on the growing unrest in the army and the rising power of the Ba'ath (Resurrection) Socialist Party. Elie felt a profound change of mood in Syria, and let his intuition guide him. He established close contacts with the Ba'ath leaders and contributed large sums of money to the party.

He had done the right thing. On March 8, 1963, a new coup shook Damascus. The army deposed the government and the Ba'ath Party seized power in Syria. General Hafez, Elie's friend from Buenos Aires, was appointed minister of defense in Salah Al-Bitar's cabinet. In July a new coup took place, this time inside the regime. Hafez became president of the Revolutionary Council and head of state. Tabet's best friends were appointed to key positions in the cabinet and the military hierarchy. The Israeli spy was now a member of the inner circle of power.

A glamorous party in Damascus. One after the other, the luxury cars of ministers and generals arrive at the sprawling villa. A long line of guests in evening attire and resplendent uniforms proceeds into the house, where the host is warmly welcoming his guests. The guest list reads like a Who's Who in Damascus: several ministers, including the minister of defense and the minister for agrarian reform, a large number of generals and colonels, the top leaders of the Ba'ath Party, businessmen, and tycoons. Many of them are standing around Colonel Salim Hatum, the officer who led his tanks into Damascus on the night of the coup and actually handed General Hafez the presidency. President Hafez himself arrives later and warmly shakes the hand of the host, his friend Kamal Amin Tabet. He is accompanied by Mrs. Hafez, stunning in the mink coat presented to her by Tabet as a token of the Syrian emigrants' admiration for the president and his wife. She is not the only one to have received expensive gifts. Quite a few women wear the jewelry, and senior officials drive the cars, given them by Tabet. Important political dealers have deposited his money into their accounts.

In the living room, a group of officials and army officers, back from the Israel border, discuss the military situation; they are joined by entrepreneurs and engineers who work on the ambitious project of diverting the tributaries of the Jordan River. In the spacious hall, the directors of the government-sponsored Radio Damascus and the heads of the Ministry of Propaganda stand together. Tabet is one of them now—the government has asked him to run some radio broadcasts to emigrant communities overseas. Tabet has another radio show, where he analyzes political and economic issues.

That party, as many others, costs Tabet a fortune, but he doesn't even blink. He has reached the apex of success, and it seems that there is no door he can't open. He has good friends in the army headquarters, and he regularly participates in policy-making meetings of the Ba'ath Party.

Elie kept transmitting reports of military character, names and functions of senior officers, top-secret military orders, and other items to Israel. He photographed and dispatched military maps, mostly the detailed blueprints of the fortifications along the Israeli border, to Aman. He sent reports on new weapons introduced in the Syrian Army. He also described the Syrians' capacity to absorb new weapons. Months later, a Syrian general bitterly admitted: "There was no army secret that remained unknown to Elie Cohen . . ."

Elie transmitted every morning to Israel and didn't fear capture, thanks to the protective umbrella of the Syrian Army broadcasts from the nearby headquarters. But once, a friend, the army lieutenant Zaher Al-Din, paid him a surprise visit. Elie succeeded in hiding the transmitter, but a sheaf of papers with the secret code, in the form of grids filled with letters, remained on the table.

"What's this?" Zaher wanted to know.

"Oh, just crosswords," Elie said.

Besides the transmissions and the backgammon boxes for his "Argentinean friends," Elie developed a third way of communicating with Israel: Radio Damascus. He worked out with his superiors in Tel Aviv a code of words and phrases, which he inserted into his radio broadcasts and which were duly decoded by Aman.

He now took another step in his efforts to obtain top-secret information. A rumor started running in the governing circles in Damascus that Tabet held illicit sex parties in his villa. Only his close, intimate friends were invited to these parties, where the guests met a large number of pretty women. Some of them were street hookers; others, girls from good families. Tabet's guests enjoyed wild sex, but their host was the only one who did not lose his cool.

Tabet also supplied sexy—and generous—secretaries to his high-placed friends. One of these friends was Colonel Salim Hatum, whose mistress passed to Tabet every word she heard from her colonel.

Tabet showed extreme patriotic fervor when he spoke about Israel, which he defined as "the vilest enemy of Arab nationalism." He urged the leaders of Syria to increase their anti-Israeli propaganda and open a "second front" against Israel, besides Egypt. He even accused his friends of not doing enough against the Israeli aggressor. In doing so, he achieved his goal. His military friends were determined to prove him wrong, and to show him they were ready for battle with the enemy. On three occasions they took him to visit the Syrian positions along Israel's border. They let him see the fortifications and the bunkers, showed him the weapons concentrated in the area and described their defensive and offensive plans. Lieutenant Zaher Al-Din took him to the El-Hama military camp, where large quantities of new weapons had been stored. On his fourth visit to the Israeli border, Tabet was the only civilian in a group of Syrian and Egyptian high-ranking officers. The group was headed by the most respected Arab military leader, the Egyptian general Ali Amer, head of the United Arab Commandment, who commanded—at least on paper—the combined forces of Egypt, Syria, and Iraq.

Right after Amer's visit, the Ba'ath leaders charged Tabet with a vital assignment: he was sent on a mission of reconciliation to the elderly Ba'ath leader Salah Al-Bitar, who had been deposed by General Hafez, and was since "on a cure" in Jericho. Tabet traveled to Jordan and spent a few days with the former prime minister. Back in Damascus, Tabet accompanied to the airport the ailing President Hafez, who was on his way to get medical treatment in Paris. When Hafez returned a few weeks later, Tabet was once again in the welcoming line, waiting on the tarmac, his mission successfully completed.

In 1963, an important change took place in Israel. The new *ramsad* who replaced Little Isser, Meir Amit, had been for a few months in charge of both Aman and the Mossad. Amit decided to abolish Unit 131 and transfer all its men and operations to the Mossad. One morning, Elie Cohen learned that his employer had changed, and he was now a Mossad agent.

That same year, Nadia gave birth to a second daughter, Iris. But in November 1964, during his second visit to Israel that same year, Elie saw his secret dream come true: Nadia had a third child, a son! He was named Shaul.

"During that visit we noticed that Elie had changed," his family members said later. "He was withdrawn, nervous, and grim. He lost his temper several times. He didn't want to go out, didn't want to meet friends. 'Soon I'll quit my job,' he said to us. 'Next year I'll come back to Israel. I won't leave my family anymore.' "

At the end of November, Elie kissed his wife and three children goodbye and flew away again. Nadia didn't know that this was the last good-bye.

November 13, 1964, was a Wednesday. Syrian positions at the Israeli border, close to Tel-Dan, opened fire on Israeli tractors that were working in the demilitarized zone. The Israeli reaction was formidable. Tanks and cannon riposted with heavy fire, and minutes later Mirage and Vautour aircraft joined the battle. The aircraft pounded the Syrian positions, then dived toward the site of the deviation of the Jordan waters and blasted the canals dug by the Syrians. Heavy mechanical equipment, bulldozers, tractors, and shovels were systematically destroyed. The Syrian Air Force didn't interfere, as it had not yet mastered its newly acquired Soviet MiG fighters.

The world press almost unanimously validated the Israeli response to the Syrian aggression. Months later, Syrian officers would say that one of the Israeli attack's architects had been Elie Cohen, who was in Israel during the battle. Thanks to Cohen, the Israelis were fully aware of the poor state of the Syrian Air Force and its inability to go to battle at that stage. The Israelis also had detailed knowledge of the Syrian fortifications and the water deviation works. They knew exactly what kinds and quantities of weapons were positioned in each base and bunker.

But Elie Cohen knew much more than that. He had succeeded in befriending a Saudi entrepreneur who had been contracted to plan and dig the first canals of the Syrian project. Thanks to that friendship, the Israelis learned, months in advance, where the excavations would take place, how deep and wide the canals would be, what equipment would be used, and other technical details. The contractor also divulged to his friend Tabet the capacity of the canals to withstand bombing from the air and the full extent of the security measures. The name of Cohen's good friend was bin Laden, little Osama's father. Thanks to the detailed information he shared with the Israeli spy, Israel attacked the project several times, until the Arab countries decided to abandon it completely in 1965.

In mid-January 1965, a few weeks after Elie had left Israel, a beautiful postcard landed in Nadia Cohen's mailbox. "My dearest Nadia," Elie wrote in French. "Just a few lines to wish you a Happy New Year, which I hope will bring happiness to the whole family. Lots of kisses to my darlings—Fifi (Sophie), Iris, and Shaikeh' (Shaul), and to you, from the bottom of my heart—Elie."

When Nadia received that postcard, Elie was lying, beaten and tortured, on the rough stone floor of a Damascus prison.

For several months already, the Syrian Mukhabarat—the secret services—were on high alert. The alarm had been sounded by Chief Tayara, head of the Palestinian Department of the Mukhabarat. Tayara noticed that since the summer of 1964, almost every decision taken by the Syrian government in the evening—or even during the night—was broadcast the following day in the Arabic-language programs of Kol Israel—Israel's government-sponsored radio. Furthermore, Israel had made public some top-secret decisions that had been taken behind closed doors. Tayara was stunned by the precision of the Israeli bombings during the November 13 incident. His logical conclusion was that the Israelis had exact knowledge of the Syrian Army deployment at the front lines, and knew precisely where to hit and how. He became certain that Israel had a spy at the highest levels of the Syrian government. The spy's information was broadcasted by Kol Israel in a matter of hours. This meant he was transmitting his reports by wireless. But where was the transmitter?

In the fall of 1964, Tayara and his colleagues made great efforts to locate the secret transmitter with Soviet-made equipment, but failed.

And then, in January 1965, they got lucky.

A Soviet ship unloaded in Latakiyeh port several huge containers filled with new communications equipment. It was to replace the Syrian Army's obsolete instruments. The equipment upgrade took place on January 7, 1965. In order to put in place the new devices and check them out, all army communications were suspended for twenty-four hours.

When silence fell over all army communications throughout the country, an officer on duty by an army receiver discerned a single, faint transmission. The spy's broadcast. The officer reached for the telephone.

Mukhabarat's squads, equipped with Soviet locators, set out at once to find the transmission source. Unfortunately, the transmission stopped before they reached the place. But the technician's feverish calculations pointed in one direction: the home of Kamal Amin Tabet.

"That's a mistake," a senior Mukhabarat officer ruled. It was unthinkable that Tabet, whom the Ba'ath leaders wanted to appoint minister in the next cabinet, could be a spy. Tabet was above suspicion.

But in the evening, the transmission was there again. The Mukhabarat again sent its cars, and again got the same result.

At eight A.M. precisely, on a sunny January day, four Mukhabarat officers broke into the splendid house in the Abu Ramen neighborhood. They smashed the entrance door, tearing it from its hinges, and then darted toward the bedroom, guns in hands. The spy was there, but he was not sleeping. He was caught red-handed, in the middle of a transmission. He jumped on his feet and faced the officers; he didn't try to run away and didn't resist his captors. For once, the odds were against him. "Kamal Amin Tabet," thundered the commanding officer. "You are under arrest!"

The news spread through Damascus like wildfire. Fantastic, absurd, impossible, nonsense! There were no words to express the shock and the disbelief of Syria's leaders when they heard the news. Could one of the leaders of the ruling party, a personal friend of the president, a millionaire and a socialite, be a spy?!

But the evidence was irrefutable. The transmitter that Tabet would conceal behind the window shutters, the tiny reserve transmitter hidden in the large chandelier in the living room, the microfilms, the dynamite-stuffed cigars, the code pages . . . The man was a traitor indeed.

Panic-stricken, the heads of the regime ordered a thorough investigation. What exactly did Tabet know? Could he incriminate them? President Hafez himself came to interrogate him in his cell. "During the interrogation," Hafez later testified, "when I looked in Tabet's eyes, I was suddenly assailed by a terrible suspicion. I felt that the man before me wasn't an Arab at all. Very cautiously I asked him a few questions about the Muslim religion, about the Koran. I asked him to recite the Sura Al-Fatiha—the first chapter of the Koran. Tabet could barely quote a few verses. He tried to defend himself by saying that he had left Syria while still very young, and his memory was betraying him. But at this moment I knew: he was a Jew."

Damascus's torturers did the rest. While Tabet was still lying in his dark cell, unconscious, his face and body covered with ugly wounds, his nails pulled out, his confession was rushed to General Hafez. The man was not Tabet. He was Elie Cohen, an Israeli Jew.

On January 24, 1965, Damascus officially announced "the arrest of an important Israeli spy." A senior officer, livid with rage, roared at a press conference: "Israel is the devil, and Cohen is the devil's agent!"

Panic spread throughout Damascus. Was Cohen a lone wolf or the head of a spy ring? One after the other, sixty-nine people were arrested; twenty-seven of them women. Among the suspects were Majeed Sheikh El-Ard, George Salem Seif, Lieutenant Zaher Al-Din, senior officials of the Ministry of Propaganda, prostitutes, and other women whose identities were not revealed. Four hundred people who had been in contact with Tabet were questioned. The investigation exposed some serious problems. Many of Syria's political, military, and business leaders were among Cohen's closest friends. The investigators couldn't touch them. Their names couldn't be mentioned, as any public allusion to them could create the impression that they were complicit in Tabet's spying. The Syrians also found that Tabet had made every possible effort to prevent the publication of any contact between his various informants; therefore it was very difficult to establish the extent of the spy ring.

In Israel the military censorship imposed total blackout on any mention of Cohen's arrest. The Israelis still hoped to save him and were determined to prevent the news about him from reaching the local media. But there were some people who had the right to know. One evening a stranger visited Elie's brothers. "Your brother has been arrested in Damascus, and accused of spying for Israel," the man said. The brothers were stunned. One of them, Maurice, rushed to his mother's home in Bat Yam. "Mother, you should be strong," he said. "Elie was arrested in Syria."

The old woman was speechless. Finally, she managed, "In Syria? How? Did he cross the border by mistake?" When Maurice explained to her what Elie was doing in Damascus, the poor woman collapsed.

Nadia stood among her three children, astounded. Even though she had suspected all along that her husband didn't reveal everything to her, she never had guessed what his real line of work was. Elie's colleagues tried to calm her down. "You're flying to Paris right away," one of them told her. "We shall hire the best lawyers. We'll do everything possible to save him." Meir Amit personally took charge of the efforts to rescue Cohen.

On January 31, one of France's greatest lawyers, Jacques Mercier, came to Damascus. Officially, he had been hired by the Cohen family; actually, it was the State of Israel that covered his expenses and his fees. He came to Syria on a mission impossible. "From my first day in Damascus," he said later, "I realized that Elie Cohen's fate was sealed. He would hang. Now all I could do was try to gain time and work out a deal that could save his life."

At first Mercier tried to prevent a trial. He met with the regime's leaders and asked to be allowed to see Cohen in order to make him sign Mercier's appointment as his attorney.

His demand was flatly rejected.

Yet Mercier found out very soon that he had some allies in certain governing circles who treated the world public opinion with respect. They wanted a trial where the rights of the accused would be protected. They were supported—for a totally different reason—by the "hawks" in the military establishment, sworn enemies of Hafez, who wanted to expose the president's close ties with Tabet in open court. Such a trial, they thought, would make public the corruption of the regime and undermine its position.

But this approach was bitterly opposed by another group—all those who had maintained close ties with Tabet. They knew that a public trial could send them to the gallows as well. That faction had one single goal: to prevent a public trial at all costs and eliminate Cohen as soon as possible.

The trial finally took place before a special military court, behind closed doors, in front of an empty room; only some portions, duly selected, were broadcast on the state television. There were no prosecuting and no defending attorneys. When Elie Cohen asked the court for a defense attorney, the presiding judge exploded: "You don't need a defender. All the corrupt press is on your side, and all the enemies of the revolution are your defenders." The presiding judge assumed the functions of interrogator, prosecutor, and judge. But the worst of it was that the presiding judge was Brigadier General Salah Dali, formerly Tabet's good friend. Another close, even intimate, friend of Tabet, Colonel Salim Hatum, was among the judges. In order to disprove any rumors of his ties with Cohen, he asked him: "Do you know Salim Hatum?" And the accused, like an actor who follows a detailed script, turned to the empty courtroom, then looked Hatum in the eye, and answered: "No, I don't see him in this room."

That portion was shown on television. "All of Damascus was laughing at this episode," Mercier said. "That was not a trial. That was a tragicomedy, a circus."

The television cameras showed Elie Cohen's codefendants: El-Ard, Al-Din, Seif, a few prostitutes. But who were the other women? Senior officers' wives? "Secretaries"? Friends of Tabet and of the Ba'ath leaders? And what were the secrets that Cohen had communicated to his Israeli handlers? He was accused of espionage, but throughout the trial not one word was said about the things he did and the contents of his transmissions. The only thing the cameras couldn't hide was the nervous tremor of a muscle in Cohen's left cheek, and a repeated sharp tilting of his head. These were results of his torture by electrodes attached to his body and head.

Israel followed the trial in silence. Every evening, Elie's family met by the television set the Mossad had loaned them. The children, Nadia, the brothers, were softly crying at the sight of Elie's face on the screen. His mother, on an impulse, kissed the screen and pressed to Elie's face the small Star of David she was wearing on a chain. Sophie called: "This is my daddy! He is a hero!" Nadia wept in silence.

In Damascus, Mercier would wake up in the middle of the night, bathed in cold sweat and haunted by horrible nightmares. His inutility depressed him deeply. On March 31, the military court published its verdict: Elie Cohen, Majeed Sheikh El-Ard, and Lieutenant Zaher Al-Din were sentenced to death.

Mercier launched a new effort. In April and May of 1965, he visited Damascus three times. He brought substantial offers from Israel. The first one was a deal: Israel was ready to deliver to Syria medicines and heavy agricultural equipment, estimated worth millions of dollars, for the life of Cohen. The Syrians rejected the offer. Israel then made another offer: to send back to Syria the eleven Syrian spies that had been captured and jailed in Israel. The Syrians rejected that offer, too, but hinted that a presidential pardon wasn't out of the question.

On May 1, El-Ard's sentence was commuted to life in prison. On May 8, Elie Cohen's sentence was officially published. The Mossad braced for a last effort. In Paris, Nadia Cohen presented an appeal for clemency at the Syrian embassy. Other appeals came from all over the world. They were signed by world-famous figures like Pope Paul VI and British philosopher Bertrand Russell; statesmen like France's Edgar Faure and Antoine Pinay, Belgium's Queen Mother Elisabeth and politician Camille Huysmans, and Canadian John Diefenbaker; Italian cardinals and ministers; twenty-two members of British Parliament; the Human Rights League; the International Red Cross . . . If Elie had heard about them, he would have remembered the similar appeals that tried in vain to save his friends' lives in Cairo eleven years before.

On May 18, in the middle of the night, Elie Cohen was awakened by his jailers. They dressed him in a long white gown and took him to the Damascus marketplace. They let him write a letter to his family and exchange a few words with the Damascus rabbi, Nissim Andabo. Syrian soldiers then fastened to his chest a huge poster where his sentence was written in large Arabic letters, the television and newspaper cameras focused on the lone man who went up the stairs to the gallows between two rows of armed soldiers.

The hangman was waiting, and quickly fastened the noose around Elie's neck. He made the condemned man stand on a low stool.

Elie faced the crowd, silent, resigned, but not defeated. The crowd held its breath. They distinctly heard the thump when the stool was pulled out from under his feet; men and women yelled with delight watching the death throes of the Israeli spy.

Large crowds of Damascenes, mysteriously awakened in the wee hours, passed by the gallows, for the next six hours, to view the body. In Israel, the heavy veil of silence was removed in a single moment. In a few hours, Elie Cohen became a national hero. Hundreds of thousands participated in his family's grief. Schools, streets, and parks were named after him. Articles and books described his feats. Nadia did not marry again.

Even today, forty-six years after Elie Cohen's death, Syria refuses to return his body for burial in Israel. Elie Cohen is considered one of the Mossad heroes. But there are many who point an accusing finger at the Mossad. His family and various writers contend that the Mossad used Elie with extreme recklessness by having him transmit his reports daily, sometimes twice a day; the Mossad even ordered Elie to transmit regularly the debates of the Syrian parliament, even though their importance was almost nil. A pointless task that made Elie run unnecessary risks.

Elie Cohen was a great spy; and his end was the end of all great spies.

Their overconfidence, and the exaggerated demands of their handlers, led them to their deaths.

CHAPTER TEN

"I WANT A MIG-21!"

Meir Amit, Isser Harel's successor, was a special kind of man. He was firm, decisive, sometimes blunt and querulous, but he was also warm, charming, a soldiers' soldier and a man of many friends. Moshe Dayan told us once: "He was the only friend I ever had."

Meir Amit's life story symbolized the change in the Mossad's leadership. Isser Harel was born in Russia, and belonged to the pioneering generation, while Meir Amit, a Sabra (born in Israel), was the first of a long line of Israeli generals; he had fought in Israel's wars and joined the Mossad after many years in uniform. Isser's generation was unobtrusive, closemouthed, shrouded in a shadow of anonymity, conspiracy, and concealment. Meir Amit was an army man, with lots of friends and colleagues who knew what he was doing. Life in the shadows was not for him. And while Little Isser had charisma and mysteriousness on his side, Amit and his successors had the brutal directness and authority that rank and uniform gave them.

Born in Tiberias, raised in Jerusalem, and, finally, a member of kibbutz Alonim, Meir had spent most of his life in uniform. A member of the Haganah since the age of sixteen, a battalion commander when the IDF was created, he had been wounded in Israel's Independence War, and had later made a brilliant army career. Commander of the elite Golani Brigade, chief of operations during the Sinai campaign, chief of the Southern, then the Central Command, he was certainly on his way to becoming chief of staff, but an ill-fated parachute jump immobilized him for a year in a hospital bed. Partly recovered, after a long convalescence and studies at Columbia University, he was appointed chief of Aman. And there Ben-Gurion found him that dramatic afternoon in April 1963, when he needed a replacement for Little Isser.

Meir's first steps in the Mossad were not easy. Many of Isser Harel's colleagues, like Yaacov Caroz, couldn't stand his abrupt manners and his self-confidence. Some resigned right away, others took their time. Under Amit's leadership, a change of the guard began. But the internal turmoil against the new *ramsad* was nothing compared to what Little Isser did to him.

In the late spring of 1963, Ben-Gurion resigned from office and was replaced as prime minister and minister of defense by his close aide, Levi Eshkol. Eshkol launched several initiatives that infuriated his predecessor. One of them was appointing Little Isser as his adviser on matters of intelligence. Little Isser was bitter and disappointed after his departure from the Mossad. And when he heard that Meir Amit had done the Moroccans an unusual favor, he went straight for the jugular.

Meir Amit's Mossad had established very close relations with the Moroccan kingdom.

The Moroccan rapprochement had started during Isser's tenure. The first connections with the Moroccans had been made by Yaacov Caroz and Rafi Eitan. In the winter of 1963, Isser told Eitan, in the strictest confidence: "Hassan II, the king of Morocco, fears that Egypt's president Nasser plots to assassinate him because of his pro-Western policy. Hassan wants the Mossad to take care of his personal security."

The story seemed improbable. An Arab king turns to the Israeli secret service for help? The always practical Rafi Eitan and another agent, David

Shomron, flew right away to Rabat, the Moroccan capital, with false passports; they were whisked through a secret entrance into the king's palace. There they met the formidable General Oufkir, the king's minister of interior, whose name alone made people tremble. He was known for his cruelty, used torture against the king's enemies, and was responsible for the unexplained disappearances of many opponents of the regime. Nevertheless, he was the king's most valued adviser on intelligence matters, and any agreement between Israel and Morocco needed his approval. He came to Eitan with his deputy, Colonel Dlimi.

Right there, Eitan and Oufkir reached an agreement: the Mossad and the Moroccan secret service would establish close ties and permanent offices in both countries; the Mossad would train the Moroccan secret services and Morocco would give the Mossad agents a foolproof cover throughout the world; a special body would be created for the shared gathering of intelligence; the Mossad would also train the special unit in charge of the king's security. The agreement was sealed by a visit to the king; Eitan gauchely bowed and kissed his hand—and the Mossad got its first ally in the Arab world.

Two weeks later Oufkir was in Israel. The general, used to sumptuous palaces and posh hotels, spent his long visit in Eitan's tiny three-room apartment in a modest Tel Aviv neighborhood. Eitan did manage to get Philip, the legendary Mossad chef, to cook for his Moroccan guest. Oufkir left and came again; the relations of the two services kept improving. In 1965 Oufkir asked Meir Amit for a special favor.

The major opposition leader and the king's most dangerous enemy was a Moroccan called Mehdi Ben-Barka. After being accused of plotting against the king, he had been exiled, but kept directing subversive activities from his hideouts. Sentenced to death in absentia, he knew that his life was in danger; he operated with extreme caution and Oufkir's men had failed to find him. Could the Mossad help?

Amit's men helped indeed. Under a clever pretext, they established contact with Ben-Barka in Switzerland and convinced him to come to Paris for an important meeting. At the door of the famous Left Bank restaurant Brasserie Lipp, he was arrested by two French police officers, who—it turned out later—were on Oufkir's payroll. Ben-Barka was delivered to Oufkir and vanished, but a witness testified that he had seen Oufkir stab him to death. Meir Amit himself informed Prime Minister Eshkol: "The man is dead."

In France, Ben-Barka's disappearance caused an unprecedented political scandal. President de Gaulle was beside himself with rage, and when he heard of Israel's role in the abduction, he didn't spare it in his fury. Isser Harel was stunned. How could the Mossad participate in such an affair? How could Amit play a role in such a criminal, immoral operation—and jeopardize Israel's close alliance with France? He asked Eshkol to fire Amit immediately. Eshkol hesitated, but then appointed two boards of inquiry, which found no grounds for any measure against Amit. After all, Amit had lured Ben-Barka to Paris, but had not taken part in his abduction and assassination. Little Isser then resigned and demanded the immediate resignation of both Eshkol and Amit. He tried to launch a campaign in the press, but the military censorship strictly forbade any mention of the affair.

Isser kept doggedly fighting Amit, but the *ramsad* was already engaged in another operation that was utterly crucial to Israel's defense: a secret alliance with the Kurds in Iraq.

"At the end of 1965," Amit wrote in his memoirs, "our dream started to become a reality. The unbelievable happened. An official Israeli delegation settled in the camp of the Mullah Mustafa Barzani (the leader of the Kurdish rebels in Northern Iraq)."

The arrival of Mossad officers in Kurdistan was considered a tremendous victory for Israeli intelligence. For the first time a contact was established with one of the three components of the Iraqi nation—the Kurds, who were waging a stubborn, endless war against the Baghdad government. (The other two components were the Shiite and Sunni Muslims.) The rebels, led by Barzani, controlled a large area inside Iraq. If the Mossad succeeded in turning the Kurdish rebels into a strong military force, the Iraqi leaders would be compelled to focus their efforts on their internal problems and their capacity for fighting Israel would be diminished. The alliance with the Kurds could become a real boon for Israel.

The first two Mossad agents spent three months in Kurdistan. Barzani welcomed them in his inner circle, took them with him wherever he went, and revealed to them all his secrets. That first encounter laid the foundation for a close cooperation that was to last for many years. Barzani and the Kurdish military chiefs visited Israel; Meir Amit and his aides came to Kurdistan; Israel supplied the Kurds with weapons and defended their interests in international forums.

Beni Ze'evi, the senior Israeli agent who first visited Kurdistan, had left his wife, Galila, in London; she was expecting a child. Beni's son, Nadav, was born while his father followed Barzani in the jagged mountains of Kurdistan. A coded telegram reached Ze'evi. It was signed by "Rimon"— Meir Amit's code name—and read: "The mother and child are in excellent health. Mazal tov!"

When Barzani heard of the baby's birth, he took four stones and marked a lot with them. "This is my gift to your son," he said to Ze'evi. "When he grows up, he can come to our country and claim his piece of land."

And while his relations with the Kurds were developing, Meir Amit started planning another great Mossad operation, code-named "Yahalom" (Diamond), the operation he was perhaps most proud of.

During the year preceding Amit's death, we met him several times in his Ramat-Gan home. "The story started in one of my meetings with General Ezer Weizman, who was then chief of the air force," he began. "We used to have breakfast together every two or three weeks. In one of these meetings, I asked Ezer what I could do for him as *ramsad*. He said right away: 'Meir, I want a MiG-21.'"

"I told him: 'Have you gone mad? There is not even one such plane in the Western world.'" The MiG-21 was the most sophisticated Soviet fighter plane at that time; the Russians supplied many of those aircraft to the Arab states.

But Ezer stood his ground: "We need a MiG-21, and you should not spare any effort in getting us one."

Amit decided to entrust the operation to Rehavia Vardi, a veteran operations officer who had already tried in the past to get a MiG-21 in Egypt or Syria. "We spent many months working on this operation," Vardi said years later. "Our main problem was how to transform the idea into an operation."

Vardi sent out the feelers throughout the Arab world. After long weeks, he got a report from Yaacov Nimrodi, Israel's military attaché in Iran. Nimrodi wrote about an Iraqi Jew, Yossef Shemesh, who claimed he knew a pilot that could bring a MiG-21 to Israel. Shemesh, single, smart, a womanizer and a bon vivant, had an uncanny ability to befriend people and make them trust him. "He was a smooth operator and could be very persuasive," Nimrodi said. "He recruited the pilot in the most professional fashion. He worked on him for a year. Only he could do that, nobody else." Nimrodi decided to test Shemesh. He sent him to perform a few secondary espionage operations. Shemesh passed the test with flying colors, obtaining excellent intelligence. Then Nimrodi gave him the green light to launch his operation.

In Baghdad, Shemesh had a Christian mistress. Her sister, Camille, was married to the Iraqi Air Force pilot Munir Redfa, also a Christian. Shemesh knew that Redfa was frustrated and bitter; even though he was an excellent MiG-21 pilot, he was not promoted in rank. Moreover, he was ordered to fly an antiquated MiG-17 to fulfill a disgusting mission—to bomb the Kurd villages. He regarded this as a humiliation and a demotion. He complained to his superiors and was made to understand that as a Christian, he would never be promoted and never become a squadron leader. Redfa, a very ambitious man, concluded that there was no sense in living in Iraq anymore.

For almost a year, Shemesh held long conversations with the young pilot, and finally succeeded in convincing him to make a short trip to Athens. Using all his eloquence and powers of persuasion, Shemesh explained to the Iraqi authorities that Redfa's wife suffered from a serious illness, and the only way to save her was to have her examined by Western doctors. She must fly to Greece right away, he said, and asked on her behalf that her husband be allowed to join her, as he was the only one in the family who spoke English.

The authorities capitulated, and Munir Redfa was allowed to travel with his wife to Athens. There they met another pilot—Colonel Ze'ev Liron (Londner), an Israeli Air Force officer. Liron, born in Poland and a Holocaust survivor, was the chief of Air Force Intelligence. He had been asked by the Mossad to help in the Redfa case. Liron and Redfa had several tête-à-tête discussions. Liron pretended to be a Polish pilot working for an anti-Communist organization. Munir told him about his family, his life in Iraq, and his deep disappointment with his superiors who sent him to bomb Kurd villages. All the able Kurdish men had gone to fight, he said, and those who had stayed in the villages were women, children, and old people. These were the people he had to kill? For him it was the last straw that made his decision final: he would leave Iraq for good.

Following the Mossad's orders, Liron invited Munir to join him on a small Greek island. The Mossad gave Redfa a code name: "Yahalom" (Diamond). In the serene, tranquil atmosphere of the island, the two men continued their conversations and became good friends. Late one evening, Liron asked Redfa what would happen if he left Iraq with his plane.

"They would kill me," Redfa said. "Besides, there is no country that would agree to give me asylum."

"There is one country that will welcome you with open arms," Liron said, and revealed the truth to his astounded friend:

"I am an Israeli pilot, not a Pole."

There was a long silence.

"Let's talk about this tomorrow," Liron said and they parted for the night. The following morning, Redfa told Liron he had decided to accept his offer. The two of them started discussing the conditions for Redfa's defection and the sum of money he would get.

Redfa was very modest. "Meir Amit told me to offer Redfa a certain amount of money," Liron said later, "and to double it if needed. But Redfa immediately accepted my initial offer. We agreed that his family would join him in Israel."

From the Greek island they flew to Rome. Shemesh and his mistress arrived from Baghdad. A few days later, they were joined by Yehuda Porat, a research officer at Air Force Intelligence, who started debriefing Redfa.

"He was polite, very considerate, a man of honor," Porat recalled. "He was brave, not talkative; he had none of the inhibitions that you would expect of a man in his situation."

In Rome, Liron and Redfa discussed communication methods. It was agreed that when Redfa heard at Radio Kol Israel in Arabic the popular Arab song "Marhabtein Marhabtein," that would be the signal for him to be on his way. But he did not know that while he was meeting his handlers in various cafés in Rome, he was being watched by the heads of the Mossad.

"I decided," Meir Amit told us, "to have a personal look at the pilot before the operation got into its final stage. I flew to Rome and went to the café where the Iraqi pilot and my men were supposed to go. I sat at a neighboring table and waited. Then quite a few people walked into the café. The guy made a good impression; I signaled to our officer who was sitting with him that everything was all right; and I left."

During our meeting with Amit, he insisted on reading to us a passage from his book *Head On*, which described the group that had walked into the Rome café: "The Jewish lover (Shemesh), wearing slippers because of a wound in his foot; his mistress, a fat and almost ugly lady (I didn't understand what he saw in her); and Diamond (Munir's code name), a short, sturdy, and broad-shouldered man with a serious face. They didn't know they were being tested."

Only when he was convinced that he could trust Diamond did Amit give Rehavia Vardi the order to proceed with the next stage—briefing the Iraqi pilot in Israel. Liron and Redfa returned to Athens to catch a flight to Tel Aviv. But a snag at Athens Airport almost ruined the operation. By mistake, Redfa boarded a flight to Cairo instead of Tel Aviv. Only when he boarded the El Al flight, did Liron realize that Redfa had vanished.

"I was desperate," Liron reported later. "I was certain that everything was lost. But a few minutes later, Munir appeared beside me. It turned out that the flight attendants in the Cairo plane counted the passengers, found out that there was an extra passenger, checked the tickets, and sent Munir to the Tel Aviv flight."

Redfa spent only twenty-four hours in Israel. He was briefed, and even rehearsed the flight itinerary into Israel. In a Mossad compound, he was taught a secret code; his new friends then took him on a stroll down Allenby Street, one of Tel Aviv's main arteries, and in the evening hosted him in a fine restaurant in Jaffa, "to make him feel at home."

Redfa flew back to Athens, changed planes, and landed in Baghdad, in preparation for the last stage.

But . . . "at that moment, I almost got a heart attack," Amit recalled. "A few days before his desertion, the Iraqi pilot decided to sell his home furniture. Now try to imagine the implications of a sudden garage sale by a fighter pilot. I was scared to death that the Iraqi Mukhabarat (security service) would find out about the sale, would interrogate Redfa, arrest him, and the entire operation would collapse. Thank God, the Mukhabarat didn't hear about that, and the stupid sale of this miser's belongings didn't lead to his arrest . . ."

Then, another problem: how to get the pilot's family out of Iraq, first to England and later to the United States? He had quite a few sisters and brothers-in-law that had to be taken out of Iraq before he flew. His immediate family, it had been agreed, would be flown to Israel. Redfa's wife didn't know a thing about this, and he was afraid to tell her the truth. He had only told her that they were going to Europe, for a long stay. She flew with her two children to Amsterdam. Mossad people waiting there took them on to Paris, where Liron met them. She still had no idea who these people were.

"They were settled in a small apartment with one double bed," Liron recalled. "We sat on this bed, and there, on the night before the flight to Israel, I revealed to her that I was an Israeli officer, that her husband would land in Israel the next day, and that we are going there as well."

Her reaction was dramatic. "She wept and yelled all night," Liron reported to his superiors. "She said that her husband was a traitor; that this was treason against Iraq; and her brothers would kill Munir when they found out what he had done.

"She wanted to go right away to the Iraqi embassy and tell them what her husband intended to do. She didn't stop screaming and crying all night long. I tried to calm her down; I told her that if she wanted to see him, she had to come to Israel with me. She realized she had no other choice. With swollen eyes and a sick child, she got on the plane and we flew to Israel."

On July 17, 1966, one of the Mossad stations in Europe got a coded letter from Munir, informing them that his flight was approaching. On August 14, he took off, but a malfunction in the aircraft's electric system made him turn back and land at Rashid Air Base. "Later," Amit said, "he found out that it was not a serious hitch. The cockpit suddenly filled with smoke because of a burned fuse; if he stayed the course, he would have arrived without any problem. But he didn't want to take risks and returned to base, and I got some more white hairs . . ."

Two days later, Munir Redfa took off again. He stuck to the planned route, and on the Israeli radar screens a dot appeared, indicating the approach of a foreign aircraft to Israel's airspace. The new air force commander, General Mordechai (Motti) Hod, had let only a couple of pilots in on the mission. They would escort the Iraqi plane to their base. All the other units, pilots, squadrons, and bases of the air force were given an order by Hod: "Today you don't do anything, but absolutely anything, without a verbal order from me. And you know my voice." Hod didn't want some overzealous pilot to shoot down "the enemy aircraft" breaching Israel's perimeter.

The MiG-21 penetrated into Israel's air space. Ran Pecker, one of the aces of the air force, had been chosen to escort Redfa. "Our guest is slowing down," Ran reported to air force control, "and signals me with his thumb that he wants to land; he also tilts his wings, which is the international code indicating that he comes in peace." At eight A.M., sixty-five minutes after taking off from Baghdad, Redfa landed in the Hatzor Air Base in Israel.

A year after the operation started, and ten months before the 1967 Six-Day War, the air force got its MiG-21. The two Mirage fighters that had escorted it from the border landed with it. Meir Amit and his men had accomplished the impossible. The MiG-21, which at that time was considered the crown jewel of the Soviet arsenal and was regarded as the main threat to Western air forces, was now in Israel's hands.

After he landed, still stunned and confused, Munir was taken to the home of the Hatzor base commander. Several senior officers threw him a party, with inexcusable disregard for the man's feelings.

"Munir was surprised by the party and at first felt as if he had strayed into another man's wedding," Meir Amit recalled. "He sat down in a corner and kept quiet."

After a short rest, when he was assured that his wife and children were already on an El Al plane on the way to Israel, Munir Redfa was taken to a press conference. In his statement, he spoke about the persecution of Christians in Iraq, the bombing of the Kurds, and his own reasons for defection.

After the press conference, Munir was driven to Herzliya, an oceanfront city north of Tel Aviv, to meet his family. "We did our best to calm him down, encourage him, and compliment him for the operation," Meir Amit wrote. "I promised him to do all in my power to help him and his family to recover, but I feared the next stage, as we had learned that Munir's family was very problematic."

A few days after Munir had landed his MiG in Hatzor, his wife's brother—an officer in the Iraqi Army—arrived in Israel. He was accompanied by Shemesh and his lover, Camille. The officer was mad with rage. He had been told that he had to urgently visit his sister, who was very sick, in Europe, and to his amazement, he was taken to Israel. When he met with Munir, he blew his top, called him a traitor, jumped him, and tried to beat him up. He also accused his sister, Munir's wife, of being aware of her husband's plans all along, which made her an accomplice to an unspeakable crime. She denied his accusations, but in vain. A few days later, the brother left Israel.

The first to fly the MiG was Danny Shapira, a famous air force pilot and the best test pilot in Israel. Motti Hod called him the day after the plane's landing and told him: "You're going to be the first Western pilot to fly a MiG-21. Start studying this aircraft, fly it as much as you can, and learn its strengths and its flaws."

Shapira met with Redfa. "We met in Herzliya a few days after his arrival," Danny Shapira said. "When they introduced us, he almost jumped to attention. Later we met in Hatzor, by the plane. He showed me the switches, we went over the labels that were in Russian and Arabic, and after an hour I told him that I was going to fly the plane. He was amazed. He said: 'But you haven't completed a course!' I explained that I was a test pilot. He seemed very worried and asked to be beside the plane when I took off. I promised."

All the senior officers of the air force came to Hatzor to watch the maiden flight. Ezer Weizman, until recently the air force commander, was also there. "Ezer came to me," Shapira remembered, "patted my shoulder, and said: 'Danny, no tricks, bring the aircraft back, okay?'

"Redfa was also there. I took off, did what I did, and after I landed, Redfa came to me and hugged me. He had tears in his eyes. 'With pilots like you,' he said, 'the Arabs will never beat you.'"

After a few test flights, the air force experts understood why the West held the MiG-21 in such esteem. It flew very high and very fast and weighed a ton less than the French and Israeli Mirage III.

The MiG-21 operation made the headlines of the world press. The Americans were amazed. Soon after, they sent a delegation of technicians and asked to study and fly the aircraft. Israel, however, refused to let them near the plane before the United States shared with it its files on the SAM-2, the new Soviet antiaircraft missile. The Americans finally agreed; American pilots came to Israel, examined the MiG-21, and flew it.

Learning the secrets of the MiG-21 was a tremendous help to the Israeli Air Force and was essential in preparing for the confrontations with the MiGs that finally occurred ten months later, in the Six-Day War of June 1967. "That MiG had an important part in the victory of the Israeli Air Force over the Arab air forces, and in particular in the destruction of the Egyptian Air Force in a few hours," Amit proudly said.

The Mossad and the Israeli Air Force had indeed achieved a tremendous victory, but Munir Redfa and his family paid dearly for it. "After his arrival, Munir had a very hard, miserable, and sad life," a senior Mossad officer said. "Building a new life for an agent [out of his country] is almost a mission impossible. Munir felt frustrated, but his family suffered, too. A whole family was broken."

For three years, Munir tried to make Israel his home, and even flew Dakota aircrafts for the Israeli oil companies to the Sinai and back. His family lived in Tel Aviv; they were given a cover, as Iranian refugees. But Munir's wife, a devout Catholic, was unable to make friends, felt isolated, and couldn't adapt to life in Israel. They finally left and moved to a Western country under false identities. Even there, far from home and relatives, surrounded by local security agents, they felt lonely and feared the long arm of the Iraqi Mukhabarat.

In August 1988, twenty-two years after his desertion, Munir Redfa died at his home of a sudden heart attack. His wife, in tears, called Meir Amit (who had long ago left the Mossad) and told him that earlier that morning, her husband had come down from the second floor of their house and, while standing next to their son, suddenly collapsed in the entrance hall and died instantly.

The Mossad held a memorial service for Munir Redfa. Veteran officers couldn't hold back their tears. "It was a surreal sight," Liron said. "The Israeli Mossad mourns an Iraqi pilot . . ."

Following the success of Operation Diamond and the subsequent astounding victory in the Six-Day War, Meir Amit saw an opportunity to launch a new operation. He requested that his superiors demand the release of the Lavon Affair prisoners as part of a POW exchange. The young captives had been rotting in prison for thirteen years, with no chance of pardon or early release. Israel, Amit felt, seemed to have forgotten them. Now that the Six-Day War was over, Israel was in negotiations with Egypt. Israel had captured 4,338 Egyptian soldiers and 830 civilians—while Egypt only captured 11 Israelis. Yet the Egyptians firmly refused to include the Lavon Affair prisoners in the deal.

Meir Amit wouldn't let go. "Forget about it, Meir," Minister of Defense Moshe Dayan told his friend. "The Egyptians will never release them." Prime Minister Eshkol agreed. But Amit refused to give up. He finally sent a personal note to President Nasser, "as a soldier to a soldier," and demanded the prisoners' release, as well as that of Wolfgang Lutz, the "Champagne Spy," who had been arrested during the German scientists affair.

Amit negotiated for a prisoner exchange with the Syrians as well. He had a personal stake in this negotiation. He asked the Syrians to help release Mrs. Shula Cohen from her Lebanese jail. Shula Cohen (code-named "the Pearl") was one of the legendary Mossad spies. A simple housewife, she had established relations with high-placed leaders in Lebanon and Syria, organized the clandestine emigration of thousands of Syrian and Lebanese Jews, and directed a highly successful spy ring.

To his amazement, his plea to Nasser worked, and the Syrians followed suit soon after. Meir Amit won. In a covert transaction, the Lavon Affair prisoners, Lutz, and Shula Cohen were returned to Israel.

Sometimes the missions to bring home a nation's own are the most meaningful.

CHAPTER ELEVEN

THOSE WHO'LL NEVER FORGET

In early September 1964, a bald, sturdy man in his mid-forties, wearing sunglasses, arrived in the Rotterdam railway station in Holland on the express train from Paris. He checked into the luxurious Rheinhotel in the city center under the name "Anton Kunzle," an Austrian business-man. He then went to the nearby post office and rented a P.O. box under the same name. From the post office, he went to Amro Bank, opened an account, and deposited $3,000. At a printer's shop, he ordered business cards and stationery in the name of Anton Kunzle, manager of an invest-ment company in Rotterdam. From there, he hurried to the Brazilian consulate and filled out forms for a tourist visa to Brazil. At a doctor's clinic, he underwent a perfunctory checkup and got a medical certificate about his health, then visited an optometrist, cheated during the test, and ordered thick magnifying glasses, even though he didn't need them at all.

The following morning, he made a short trip to Zurich and opened an account in the Credit Suisse bank, in which he deposited $6,000. Then he returned to Paris, where a makeup artist attached a bushy mustache to his face; a photographer took his pictures with his new glasses and handed him a set of passport photos. Back in Rotterdam, he brought the photos to the visa clerk at the Brazilian consulate, and the tourist visa to Brazil was stamped in his Austrian passport. Now he could buy his plane tickets to Rio de Janeiro and, from there, to São Paulo and Montevideo, in Uruguay. Wherever he went, the loquacious Kunzle spoke of his flourishing business in Austria. The generous tips that he spread on his way, his choice of the best hotels and the most exclusive restaurants spoke for themselves—Kunzle, indeed, was a rich and successful businessman.

By these seemingly simple actions, Mossad agent Yitzhak Sarid (not his real name) built a foolproof cover for himself. Somewhere between Paris, Rotterdam, and Zurich, Yitzhak Sarid evaporated into thin air and a new man emerged in his stead: Anton Kunzle, an Austrian businessman, with an address in Rotterdam, bank accounts, business cards, a visa, and a plane ticket to Brazil.

Only a few days earlier, on September 1, Yitzhak Sarid had been summoned to a meeting in Paris. Sarid was a member of the Mossad operational team code-named "Caesarea." In a safe house on Avenue de Versailles, he met with Caesarea's commander, Yoske Yariv, a sturdy, muscular man admired by his subordinates. Yariv, a former army officer, had replaced Rafi Eitan as the head of the operational team; Eitan had been appointed head of Europe station, based in Paris.

Yariv started by saying that in a few months, the West German parliament would adopt a statute of limitations regarding war crimes, which meant that Nazi criminals—living now undercover—would be able to re-emerge from hiding and resume normal lives, as if they had never committed their atrocious acts. Yariv said that many Germans wanted to turn the page and leave Germany's horrid past behind them. Even other nations that had suffered under the Germans were not eager to keep searching for Nazi criminals. Since Eichmann's capture four years before, awareness about Nazi crimes had diminished, as if Eichmann's trial and execution had closed a chapter in the world's history. It was imperative, Yariv said, to make sure that the statute of limitations on Nazi crimes did not become law. The world needed to be reminded that monsters were still at large.

"We should kill one of the greatest Nazi criminals," Yariv said to Sarid. And a Mossad agent on a mission in South America had found the one. "The Butcher of Riga," a Latvian Nazi, guilty of massacring thirty thousand Jews, had been positively identified. He was living in Brazil under his real name, Herberts Cukurs. The *ramsad*, Meir Amit, had given the green light for the operation.

Yariv now turned to Sarid. And not only because of Sarid's record as a smart and resourceful agent, who had participated in the Eichmann operation. He also knew Sarid was born in Germany, and both his parents had died in the Holocaust. Sarid had escaped to Palestine, but had sworn to fight Hitler and had been one of the first Palestinian volunteers in the British Army during the war. Yariv did not have to worry about Sarid's motivation.

"I want you to build yourself a cover as an Austrian businessman," the Caesarea commander said to Sarid. "Your job will be to fly to Brazil, find Cukurs, and win his confidence. That is the first step toward his execution." In the detailed briefing that followed, Yariv gave Sarid his new name: "Anton Kunzle."

Ten days after the meeting in Paris, Anton Kunzle boarded a Varig plane to Rio de Janeiro. He was excited and yet troubled by his mission. He had never been in such a situation before. He had to operate, completely alone, in a foreign country, and try making friends with a monster with sharp senses who certainly expected that one day somebody would try to kill him. Kunzle knew well that a single mistake could cause the failure of the entire operation; just one misstep could cost him his life.

During the flight, Kunzle perused a voluminous file of documents, testimonies, and press cuttings about Herberts Cukurs. He had become famous in the thirties as a gifted and bold pilot, who had flown from Latvia to Gambia, in Africa, in a small plane he had built with his own hands. Overnight, the young, handsome pilot had become a national hero in Latvia. He was awarded the international Santos Dumont medal in honor of the Brazilian aviation pioneer; the press called him "the Eagle of Latvia" and "the Latvian Lindbergh." The War Museum in Riga was assailed by multitudes eager to see Cukurs's plane, on display there.

Cukurs was a right-wing Latvian nationalist, yet he had many Jewish friends. He even traveled to Palestine and came back deeply impressed by the Zionists' achievements. His enthusiastic speeches about the pioneers in Palestine made him seem an ally to Latvian Jews.

Yet when World War II erupted, things suddenly changed. Latvia was first occupied by the Soviets, who quickly won the people's hatred and who persecuted those like Cukurs. But the Red Army retreated after Hitler's invasion of Russia—and Latvia was conquered by the German Army. Cukurs now transformed completely. As staunch nationalist and a leader of the fanatic Fascist organization Thunder Cross that volunteered to serve the Nazis, Cukurs became the most cruel and sadistic murderer of the Riga Jews. Early on, he and his soldiers herded three hundred Jews into a local synagogue and set it on fire, murdering everyone inside. He arrested Jews, beat them to death with his revolver, shot hundreds of others, humiliated and killed Orthodox Jews, smashed babies' heads on the city walls. One night, he made a Jewish girl undress in front of a group of Jewish prisoners, then forced an old rabbi to stroke and lick her, to the drunken laughter of the Latvian guards. In the summer, he ordered the drowning of twelve hundred Jews in the Kuldiga Lake, and in November 1941, he led thirty thousand Riga Jews to the killing field in the Rumbula forests, where they were undressed by German soldiers and shot in cold blood.

Reading the depositions of some Jews who miraculously survived, Kunzle was deeply shocked. The documents in the file described Cukurs's flight to France with forged papers at the end of the war. Posing as a "farmer," he managed to get on a boat bound for Rio de Janeiro. He took with him a strange "insurance policy"—a young Jewish girl, Miriam Keitzner, whom he had protected during the war. Miriam, who served as his champion now, was speaking throughout Brazil about her noble "savior from Riga."

In Rio, Cukurs quickly established warm relations with many Brazilian Jews. He loved describing to his audiences Miriam's fascinating story. "The Nazis caught her in Latvia," he used to say. "She was to die a horrible death, but I saved her, risking my life." Such a valiant hero and a savior of Jews didn't come to Rio every day, and the city Jews did their best to show the brave Latvian how much they valued his noble deeds.

Cukurs became very popular in the Jewish community—till the night when the brave Latvian had too much to drink. The alcohol loosened his tongue, and the inebriated Cukurs told now a very different story to his audience. He spoke of Jews indeed, but now he called them pigs and scum. He spoke with enthusiasm of the means he and his Nazi friends had used to slaughter the Jews of Europe, of Jews who were burned, drowned, shot, and beaten to death . . . The Latvian's Jewish friends were stupefied; they started investigating—and the results of their research were horrifying.

When his real identity was exposed, Cukurs vanished. He didn't leave Rio, only moved to a distant neighborhood of the sprawling city. He abandoned Miriam Keitzner, whom he didn't need anymore. Miriam would later marry a local Jew and assimilate in the Brazilian society. As for Cukurs, he brought over his wife and three sons.

Ten years went by. Cukurs had become the respected owner of the Air Taxi company. But then, by chance, he was discovered again by the Rio Jewish community. They marched to raise public awareness. Students broke into the Air Taxi offices, smashed windows, destroyed equipment, and emptied files . . . Cukurs left Rio with his family right away and settled in São Paulo.

Even though nobody bothered him there, Cukurs felt he was still in danger. He was haunted by fears and suspected every approaching stranger. In June 1960, a few days after Eichmann's capture, Cukurs came to police headquarters in São Paulo and asked for police protection. His request was granted—but it was also publicized in the media, and relatives of Cukurs's victims all over the world now knew where he lived.

As years passed, Cukurs's fears only grew. He told his wife and sons that Jewish avengers could discover his whereabouts and come to murder him at any time. He even prepared a list of his most dangerous enemies, most of them important Brazilian Jews from Rio. At the top of the list were Dr. Aharon Steinbruck, a senator; Dr. Alfredo Gartenberg; Dr. Marcus Constantino; Dr. Israel Skolnikov; Mr. Klinger; Mr. Pairitzki.

Cukurs kept his real name, but built his houses like fortresses and apparently paid substantial bribes for protection by the police and the security services.

He launched several business ventures, but they all failed. According to Kunzle's file, his last address was a marina on an artificial lake outside São Paulo. Cukurs used to rent a few boats, and take tourists on aerial promenades over the city in his seaplane.

Kunzle knew well that if he tried to approach Cukurs directly, he would certainly arouse his suspicions, so, first, he spent a few days in Rio. His stay in the stunning Brazilian city stood in sheer contrast to the dark mission he had undertaken. He walked on the Copacabana and Ipanema beaches, staring at mulatto beauties in minimal bikinis, gazed at the breathtaking Sugarloaf and the huge statue of Christ on top of the Corcovado, watched a Macumba (the Brazilian voodoo) ceremony, absorbed the warm sunshine and the rhythms of samba. He was a typical tourist, but he got acquainted with several senior officials and private investors in the tourism business, met with the local minister of tourism, and introduced himself as an investor interested in tourist enterprises in Brazil. He got a few letters of recommendation to major figures in the tourism business in São Paulo.

Kunzle arrived in São Paulo and immediately found Cukurs's marina. By the pier, a little apart from the pleasure boats, he saw an old seaplane and, beside it, a tall, lean man wearing a pilot's overalls. Herberts Cukurs.

Kunzle approached the pretty German girl who sold tickets for Cukurs's boat excursions, and asked her for information about tourism in that area. He didn't know then that the young woman was the wife of Cukurs's oldest son. She admitted she didn't know very much about tourism, but pointed at the man in the overalls. "Ask him, he will help you."

Kunzle walked to the pilot and introduced himself as an Austrian investor. He asked a few professional questions and Cukurs reluctantly answered; but his attitude changed when Kunzle asked to hire him and his plane for a tour over the city. A few minutes later, they were high in the air. The two men had a long, friendly chat; Kunzle knew how to make friends. On their return, Cukurs invited him to his boat, for a shot of brandy.

While they were drinking, Cukurs suddenly erupted in a furious diatribe against his accusers. "I was a war criminal?" he shouted. "I saved a Jewish girl during the war." Kunzle suspected that Cukurs's indignation was fake and the Latvian only wanted to provoke his reaction.

"Did you serve in the war?" Cukurs asked.

"Yes," Kunzle said, "on the Russian Front." But the tone of his answer seemed to indicate the opposite, to imply that Kunzle had served in the army but certainly not on the Russian Front. He also unbuttoned his shirt and showed Cukurs a chest scar. "From the war," he said, without elaborating.

Kunzle made a quick assessment of his host. Cukurs was in a bad economic situation; the frayed overalls, the ramshackle plane, the sorry state of the boats—all of which indicated a low standard of living. Kunzle realized that he had to make Cukurs believe that he, Kunzle, was his chance to overcome his troubles; he was the man who could bring him large profits. He therefore kept talking about his company and his partners, and their grandiose projects to invest a lot of money in tourism in Latin America. He hinted that Cukurs could perhaps join their group, as he knew the Brazilian tourist scene well.

Cukurs seemed interested in his guest's words, but Kunzle suddenly got on his feet. "Well," he said, "I shouldn't be bothering you anymore. You must be very busy."

"No, not at all," Cukurs said, and suggested that Kunzle come to his home one of these days, after work, "so that we could discuss our common interests."

The contact was established. The bait was cast. Now Cukurs should be persuaded to swallow it.

That evening, Kunzle dispatched a coded telegram to Yoske Yariv. For the first time, he used the code name that Yariv had chosen for Cukurs: "the Deceased."

Cukurs, too, did some writing that night. He took the list of his most dangerous enemies and added another name to it.

Anton Kunzle.

A week later, a taxi stopped by a house in the Riviera neighborhood in São Paulo. The house was modest but protected like a fortress: it was surrounded by a wall and barbed wire, the entrance was barred by an iron gate, and beside it stood a young man and a fierce-looking dog.

Kunzle asked the youngster—who turned out to be one of Cukurs's sons—to inform the pilot of his arrival. Cukurs welcomed him warmly, walked him through the house, introduced him to his wife, Milda, then pulled out a drawer and showed Kunzle about fifteen medals from the war days; many of them were adorned by a swastika.

Cukurs opened another drawer and showed the amazed Kunzle his private armory: three heavy revolvers and a semiautomatic rifle. Cukurs proudly revealed that the Brazilian secret service had given him permits for all these weapons. "I know how to defend myself," he added.

Kunzle took Cukurs's words as a veiled threat. If you try to hurt me, his host seemed to say, you should know that I am armed and dangerous.

Cukurs suddenly had an idea. "Why don't you come with me on a trip to my farms? They are in the country; we can spend a night there."

Kunzle readily agreed. But on his way to his hotel, he stopped at a hardware store and bought a switchblade. Just in case.

A few days later, the two of them got into Kunzle's rented car and headed for the mountains.

It was an eerie, tense trip. Here was Anton Kunzle, armed only with a knife, fearing Cukurs and yet determined to tempt him with the prospects of easy money, and lead him to his death.

And sitting in the car beside him was Herberts Cukurs, strong, sober, but poor, suspicious of his new friend, armed with a heavy handgun but unable to resist the bait Kunzle was dangling before him.

Kunzle thought that perhaps he was the victim in this cat-and-mouse game; perhaps Cukurs did not believe his cover story, perhaps he was taking him to the mountains to murder him there?

Along the way, they visited a neglected farm. All of a sudden, Cukurs drew his semiautomatic rifle out of his bag. Kunzle started. Why did Cukurs bring over both a handgun and a rifle?

"What about a shooting contest?" Cukurs asked him. Kunzle understood right away: Cukurs wanted to test his abilities as a former fighter on the Russian Front and see if he knew how to shoot. The Latvian fixed a paper target to a tree, loaded his rifle, and fired ten bullets in rapid succession. The hits formed a cluster ten centimeters in diameter. Cukurs took from his bag a second paper target, loaded the rifle again, and handed it to Kunzle. A veteran of the British Army and the IDF, Kunzle was an excellent marksman. He picked up the weapon and without any delay fired ten bullets, making a cluster of three centimeters. Cukurs nodded with approval. "Excellent, Herr Anton," he said.

The two of them got back in the car and traveled to a second farm. It was much larger, and included a dense forest and a river, where alligators lazily lingered. Cukurs led the way into the forest, and Kunzle again was assailed by fears. Was this a trap? Did Cukurs bring him here so he could murder him without leaving evidence?

He kept walking at Cukurs's side. All of a sudden, he stepped on a rock; a nail got loose in his shoe and deeply punctured his heel. Doubling over in pain, Kunzle kneeled and removed his shoe. Blood was dripping from a wound in his heel.

Cukurs bent over him and drew his gun. Kunzle was exposed, completely defenseless. That's it, he thought, his last moment had arrived. The Latvian would shoot him as a dog. But Cukurs handed him the gun. "Use the butt," he said, "hammer it down."

Kunzle took the gun. All of a sudden, the roles were reversed. They were all alone in a mountain farm. There was not a living soul for miles around. The gun was loaded. He could terminate Cukurs that very moment. Just point the gun and press the trigger.

Instead, he bent down and forcefully pounded the nail's sharp end, then returned the gun to its owner.

At nightfall the two of them reached a ramshackle hut and improvised dinner with some food they had brought with them. They spread their sleeping bags on two old iron beds. Kunzle saw Cukurs slipping his gun under his pillow. Troubled by ominous thoughts, he pulled his knife out of his pocket and held it ready, but he couldn't sleep.

In the middle of the night, he heard a noise coming from Cukurs's bed. The Nazi got up, took his gun, and quietly stepped out. Why? Kunzle thought. He tried to listen to the sounds outside, and suddenly he heard an easily recognizable noise. Cukurs was standing outside and urinating. There were probably wild animals prowling around.

The following day, they returned, safe and sound, to São Paulo. Kunzle let out a sigh of relief when he walked into his hotel.

During the following week, Kunzle invited Cukurs to gourmet restaurants, expensive nightclubs, and bars. He noticed Cukurs's hungry stare and realized that it had been years since the man last tasted all those pleasures that money could buy. His next move was to ask Cukurs to join him in several domestic flights—on Kunzle's expense account, of course. They visited some major tourist locations, and Cukurs enjoyed the best food and lodging.

Now Kunzle suggested that they flew to Montevideo, the capital of Uruguay. His partners, he said, wanted to establish their South American business center there and he wanted to check the availability of office buildings and other facilities. He even paid for Cukurs's new passport.

Kunzle flew to Montevideo, and a few days later, Cukurs joined him. But the Latvian's suspicions had not faded away; he had brought his camera. As he came out of the plane in Montevideo airport, he saw Kunzle, who was waiting for him. Cukurs took out his camera and snapped several photos of Kunzle, catching him by surprise. His friend, his partner, and his funder had become in Cukurs's eyes the major suspect in a plot to assassinate him.

In the meantime, Kunzle had rented a big American car. He was quite embarrassed by its color—shocking pink—but that was the only car available at the rental agency. He also had reserved rooms for both of them in the best hotel in town, the Victoria Plaza. They spent a few days in Montevideo, looking for a building that could serve as headquarters for Kunzle's company. They didn't find a place, but enjoyed a dreamlike vacation. Again, Kunzle invited Cukurs to the best restaurants, took him to nightclubs, on sightseeing tours, to the casino, where he shared his winnings with his guest. Cukurs was delighted. Finally they parted, and Kunzle left for Europe, after promising Cukurs he would be back in a few months to continue developing their project. Cukurs went back to São Paulo, but told his wife that in Montevideo somebody had been following him, so now he had to stay alert and be ready to defend himself.

In Paris, Kunzle again met Yariv and his friends, and they immediately started to prepare the operation. It was decided that Cukurs would be executed in Montevideo, for a few reasons: in Brazil, Cukurs was protected by the local police, and that could create some problems; in Brazil, the large Jewish community was vulnerable to attacks by neo-Nazis or Germans seeking revenge; and finally, Brazil still had the death penalty, and if a hit team was caught and tried, they could be killed.

The hit team consisted of five agents and was headed by Yoske Yariv himself. One of the agents was Ze'ev Amit (Slutzky), a cousin of the *ramsad*, Meir Amit; the other members were Kunzle, Arye Cohen (not his real name), and Eliezer Sudit (Sharon), who also got an Austrian passport in the name of Oswald Taussig.

The team members arrived in Montevideo in February 1965. Oswald Taussig rented a green Volkswagen; he also rented a small house, the Casa Cubertini, on Cartagena Street, in the Carrasco neighborhood. At the last moment, Yariv charged him with a chilling task: to buy a large trunk, like the travel trunks that were used in the nineteenth century. The trunk would be used as a makeshift coffin for the Nazi's body when the operation was over.

Kunzle invited Cukurs to Montevideo again.

On February 15, 1965, Cukurs went to police headquarters and was received by an officer, Alcido Cintra Bueno Filho. "I am a businessman," the Latvian said. "For several years I've been under the protection of the Brazilian police, because I have good reason to fear for my life. Now a European business partner is asking me to travel to Montevideo to meet him. What do you think, can I travel to Uruguay? Isn't it risky?"

"Don't go!" the officer firmly said. "Here you live in peace because we protect you. But don't forget—the moment you leave Brazil, you aren't protected anymore. You expose yourself to your enemies. And if you've got enemies, I assume that they haven't forgotten you."

Cukurs thought awhile, seemed to hesitate, but finally got up and said: "I was always a brave man. I am not afraid. I know how to defend my life. I always carry a gun. And believe me—in spite of all the years that have passed, I am still a fine shot."

Kunzle met Cukurs in Montevideo on February 23. The trap was set. Kunzle drove Cukurs in a rented black Volkswagen toward the Casa Cubertini, where the hit team was waiting. On the way, they stopped several times "to check" some other houses that could serve as an office for the company. Finally, they reached the Casa Cubertini. They saw some men at work, repairing the neighboring house. Taussig's green car, also a Volkswagen, was parked by the house. Kunzle turned off the engine, got out of the car, and walked purposefully toward the door. Cukurs followed him. Kunzle opened the door and saw a terrifying sight: in the dark house, the members of the hit team stood by the walls, wearing only their drawers. They knew they couldn't overcome Cukurs without a bloody fight, and had undressed so their clothes wouldn't be soiled by his blood. There was something appalling in that sight of a group of people in drawers, waiting in the dark for their victim.

Kunzle moved aside and Cukurs entered the house. As soon as he stepped in, Kunzle slammed the door behind him. Three men leaped on Cukurs. Ze'ev Amit tried to grab him by the throat, as he had been trained in Paris. The others jumped him from both sides.

The Latvian fought back. He succeeded in shaking off his attackers and made for the door. He yanked the door handle, then tried to draw the gun he was carrying in his pocket, while shouting in German: *"Lassen Sie Mich sprechen!"* ("Let me speak!")

During the fight, Yariv tried to cover Cukurs's mouth with his hand, to prevent him from shouting. Cukurs fiercely bit his hand and almost tore off one of Yariv's fingers. Yariv cried in pain. At that moment, Amit grabbed a heavy construction hammer and landed a blow on Cukurs's head. Blood spurted from the wound. The bodies of the attackers and their victim turned into a convulsing heap on the floor, while Cukurs desperately tried to draw his gun. It was a matter of seconds. Arye pressed his gun to Cukurs's head and fired twice. The silencer muffled the sound of the shots.

Cukurs's body collapsed. His blood flowed on his clothes and the floor tiles. The hit team members were covered with blood.

Oswald Taussig hurried to the yard and turned on the main water pipe. His friends washed the blood off their bodies, then cleaned the floor and the walls; yet some large bloodstains remained on the house tiles.

One of the members of the hit team claimed afterward that their intention had been to capture Cukurs alive and make him stand for an improvised court-martial before executing him. But flawed planning or a gross underestimation of the Latvian's physical strength turned the mission into a repulsive bloodbath that was unplanned and unnecessary. The Mossad agent had rented the house on Cartagena Street at the very last moment; the travel trunk was bought at the last moment as well. Instead of jumping their victim in their drawers, the Mossad agents could have shot him right away. But, as some of the hit team members told us, the mission was accomplished.

The agents placed Cukurs's body in the trunk, to make the police believe that they intended to abduct him and smuggle him out of Uruguay. Then they left a typewritten letter in English on the body, which had been prepared beforehand: "Considering the gravity of the crimes of which Herberts Cukurs was accused, notably his personal responsibility in the murder of thirty thousand men, women, and children, and considering the terrible cruelty shown by Herberts Cukurs in carrying out his crimes, we condemned the said Cukurs to death. The accused was executed on February 23, 1965, by 'those who will never forget.' "

The team left the building and departed in the two rented Volkswagens. In the neighboring house, the workmen kept pounding and hammering; they had not heard a thing. Yariv suffered terrible pain in his hand; till his death, he wouldn't be able to properly use one of his fingers. Taussig and Kunzle returned the cars and left their hotels; the entire team left Montevideo and went back by complex routes to Europe and to Israel. Ze'ev Amit returned to Paris "wounded in his body and hurt in his soul." Terrible nightmares haunted him for many months and he couldn't overcome his shock and pain.

When all the hit team members had left Latin America, a Mossad agent called the news agencies in Germany and reported the execution of a Nazi criminal in Montevideo by "those who will never forget."

The reporters who got the message discarded it right away, believing it was a prank. Seeing that nothing happened, the Mossad agents prepared a much more detailed and credible message and dispatched it to the news agencies and to a reporter in a Montevideo newspaper, who alerted the police. On March 8, more than ten days after Cukurs was killed, the police finally arrived at Casa Cubertini.

The next day, the world press announced, in banner headlines, the discovery of Cukurs's body in an empty house in Montevideo. In the media reports, two names were singled out as suspects in the killing: Anton Kunzle and Oswald Taussig. A few days later, a Rio de Janeiro weekly published a huge photo of Anton Kunzle that had been taken by Cukurs. The magazine called Kunzle "the smiling Austrian." The photo was reproduced on the front page of the Israel newspaper *Maariv*. Some friends of the Mossad agent immediately identified Anton Kunzle.

After a few more days, a letter arrived to Cukurs's house. It was a rather poor effort by Anton Kunzle to cover his tracks.

My dear Herberts,

With God's help and that of some of our compatriots, I have safely reached Chile. I am now resting after a tiring journey, and I am sure that you, too, will very soon be back home. Meanwhile, I've discovered that we were followed by two people, a man and a woman. We must be very careful and take every precaution. As I've always said, you are running a great risk in working and traveling under your own name. It could be disastrous for us, and also lead to my real identity being discovered.

So I hope that the complications in Uruguay have taught you a lesson for the future, and that you'll be more prudent now. If you notice anything suspicious in or around your house, remember the advice I gave you: go and hide among Von Leeds's men (a Nazi leader who had escaped to Cairo with a group of German exiles) for a year or two, until the question of an amnesty is settled.

When you get this letter, reply to the address you know of, in Santiago, Chile.

Yours, Anton K.

The letter, of course, did not fool anybody. Cukurs's wife, Milda, was adamant: Kunzle was the murderer.

Most of the participants in the Cukurs killing are dead. Ze'ev Amit, whom the authors of this book knew well, was killed in the Yom Kippur War in 1973.

Their mission paid off. The parliaments of Germany and Austria rejected the statute of limitation on the Nazi crimes.

Years later, former *ramsad* Isser Harel called one of the authors of this book and told him that a good friend of his wanted to meet. He didn't give any details, just an address in North Tel Aviv. The author found there a neat little house. A sturdy, bald man wearing glasses opened the door. The author recognized him right away.

He said to the man: *"Guten Abend, Herr Kunzle."*

CHAPTER TWELVE

THE QUEST FOR THE RED PRINCE

On September 5, 1972, at four thirty A.M., eight armed terrorists wearing ski masks broke into the apartment of the Israeli team at the Munich Olympics. They killed Moshe Weinberg, the coach of the wrestling team, who tried to bar their way, and Joe Romano, a weight-lifting champion. A few athletes, awakened by the shouts and the gunfire, escaped by jumping out the windows; nine were taken hostage by the terrorists.

The German police arrived, followed by reporters, photographers, and television crews that covered the drama unfolding in the Olympic Village. For the first time in history, the whole world watched a murderous terrorist attack in live broadcast on its television screens. So, too, did Golda Meir, Israel's prime minister, who was awakened by her military adjutant. Golda felt trapped: the attack happened in a friendly country and the responsibility for rescuing the hostages fell on Germany's shoulders. The authorities of the State of Bavaria, where the attack had occurred, politely rejected Israel's suggestion to send over Sayeret Matkal, the best Israeli commando unit. You have nothing to worry about, the Germans said to the Israeli representatives, we shall free all the hostages. But Germany lacked the experience, the creativity, and the courage to face a deadly, cunning terrorist organization. After an exhausting negotiation between the terrorists and the German authorities, which lasted a whole day, the terrorists and the hostages were driven to Fürstenfeldbruck Airport, outside Munich. There, the Germans had promised the terrorists, they would board a plane that would take them to the destination of their choice. But the police actually had laid a childish and amateurish trap at the airport. They had hauled an empty and unmanned Lufthansa aircraft to the center of the airport. Incompetent sharpshooters had been placed on the roofs. The terrorists' leader came to inspect the plane. That plane, with no air crew, its engines cold, was going to take off in a few minutes? The terrorists right away realized they were being deceived; they opened fire and threw hand grenades. During the ensuing shoot-out with the police, they murdered all the hostages. A German police officer was also killed, as well as five of the eight terrorists (the other three would be captured, but released shortly afterward, following the hijacking of a Lufthansa aircraft by the terrorist organization). Israeli general Zvi Zamir, who had recently replaced Meir Amit as *ramsad*, helplessly watched the bloody drama from the control tower. He had been sent to Munich by Prime Minister Golda Meir, but had no right to interfere with the German operation. His hosts kept assuring him that their plan was excellent, and he just had to watch and see. What the *ramsad* saw was the massacre of the Israeli athletes. He now realized that Israel had a new enemy: a terrorist organization that called itself "Black September."

Black September. That was how the Palestinian terrorists had renamed September 1970, the month when King Hussein of Jordan had massacred thousands of them in his kingdom. In the years that had passed since the 1967 Six-Day War, the terrorists gradually had gained control over large chunks of Jordanian territory and many neighborhoods in the capital, Amman; towns and villages along the Israeli border became their exclusive bases and they would wander in their streets with their weapons. They rejected King Hussein's authority and step by step had become the real masters of Jordan. The king knew this—but didn't do anything. In one of his visits to an army camp, he saw a brassiere flying like a flag from a tank antenna. "What's this?" he angrily inquired.

"This means that we are women," the male tank commander replied. "You don't let us fight."

Finally, Hussein could take that no more. He could not continue burying his head in the sand like an ostrich while his kingdom was slipping through his fingers. On September 17, 1970, the king unleashed his army against the terrorist bases and camps. It was a terrible massacre. Terrorists were shot in the streets, hunted, captured, and executed without trial. Some of them found shelter in the Palestinian refugee camps, but the Jordanian artillery shelled the camps without a shadow of remorse, killing thousands. Scores of panicked terrorists crossed the Jordan River and surrendered to the Israeli Army. They preferred to rot in Israeli prisons than die by Jordanian guns. During the massacre, most of the surviving terrorists escaped to Syria and Lebanon. Until this very day, the number of dead terrorists in Black September remains unknown; the figures are between two thousand and seven thousand people.

Yasser Arafat, chief of Fatah, the major Palestinian terrorist organization, became obsessed with revenge. He created, inside the Fatah, a secret inner organization, an underground within an underground. The regular Fatah members and commanders didn't even know of its existence. He called it "Black September." This organization did not comply with the "respectable" lines of conduct that Arafat now tried to impose on his group in order to achieve international recognition and sympathy. It was to be a cruel, unrestrained group that would attack the "enemies of the Palestinian people" in every possible way, without mercy. Formally, Black September did not exist, and Arafat would deny any connection to it, but secretly he was its creator and leader. He appointed Abu Yussef, one of the senior Fatah commanders, as the head of Black September; as chief of operations, he selected Ali Hassan Salameh, a young man with fanatic views but no less brave or smart. Ali was the son of Hassan Salameh, who had been the last supreme commander of the Palestinian forces during the 1948 Arab-Israeli

War. Hassan Salameh had been killed in battle, and his son Ali had vowed to continue his father's struggle.

Black September's first operations didn't worry Israel too much, as they were mostly directed against Jordan. The terrorists bombed the Rome offices of the Jordanian national airline; attacked the Jordanian embassy in Paris with Molotov cocktails; hijacked a Jordanian airliner to Libya; sabotaged the Jordanian embassy in Berne, an electronics plant in Germany, and oil reservoirs in Hamburg and Rotterdam; in the cellar of a house in Bonn, they murdered five Jordanian secret agents. In their most appalling operation, they murdered former Jordanian prime minister Wasfi Al-Tal in the lobby of the Cairo Sheraton. One of the assassins crouched over the body and lapped his victim's blood.

With Israel's victory in the 1967 Six-Day War, the terrorists now took upon themselves to continue the war against the Jewish state. They hijacked aircraft, crossed Israel's borders, and assassinated civilians, planted bombs and explosive charges in the big cities. The Shabak and the Mossad had to fight a new enemy now, penetrate the terrorist organizations, foil their plans, and arrest their activists. Fatah was the major organization Israel had to confront now; Black September was not.

But Black September soon crossed the limits it had originally set to its activities and started acting against Western nations—first and foremost, against Israel.

The Munich massacre was their first, bloody assault.

And that was how Ali Hassan Salameh earned his nickname. He was the brains behind the Munich operation. The rumors about his obsession with killing and blood spread among the terrorists, and they started calling Hassan Salameh's son the "Red Prince."

In early October 1972, two retired generals asked to meet with Prime Minister Golda Meir, who had replaced Levi Eshkol after his sudden death in 1969. They were the new *ramsad*, Zvi Zamir, and the prime minister's adviser on counterterrorism, former Aman chief Aharon Yariv.

Golda Meir had been utterly traumatized by "Munich night," when the

Israeli athletes had been murdered. "Once again, bound and tied Jews are being murdered on German soil," she had said. Golda was a strong, tough woman; it was clear that she wouldn't let the Munich massacre go without punishment.

That was exactly what Zamir and Yariv came to propose.

Zvi Zamir, skinny, balding, and freckled, with sharp features jotting out of a triangular face, was a former Palmach fighter but was not regarded as an outstanding general. The highest position he had reached during his military service was commander of the Southern Front. He later served as military attaché and representative of the Israeli Ministry of Defense in Great Britain. In 1968, he was appointed *ramsad* to replace Meir Amit, who had completed his term. Many criticized Zamir's appointment; he was a bland and shy man with no experience in secret operations; lacking charisma, he didn't consider himself the Mossad chief like Harel and Amit before him. He preferred to act as a sort of chairman of the board, and delegated authority to many of his senior aides. He would achieve his fame only in the Yom Kippur War (see chapter 14), but in 1972 he couldn't claim any substantial success. And some of the veteran agents of the Mossad, like Rafi Eitan, disliked him and left the service in protest.

Yariv, like Zamir, was more a man in the background than a man of limelight. He had been an outstanding Aman chief during the Six-Day War, but he was admired mostly because of his learned, analytical mind. Slim, soft-spoken, bespectacled, with a clear forehead, the well-mannered Yariv looked more like an erudite professor than a master spy.

Yariv and Zamir had a lot in common. They were supposed to be rivals, because of their overlapping functions; yet they worked in harmony and mutual trust. They both were quiet, low-key, reserved, and rather shy. They hated to take center stage and were very cautious in their analyses and planning. But the idea they presented to Golda that October afternoon was surprisingly brutal: the secret services would identify and locate the Black September leaders, and kill them. All of them.

Since Munich, Yaniv and Zamir had engaged in feverish activity and had gathered top-notch intelligence about Black September. They came to Golda prepared. Black September, they said, intended to launch an all-out war against Israel. This was a group that had sworn to kill as many Jews as possible—military, civilians, women and children. The only way to stop it was to kill all its leaders, one after the other. Crush the snake's head.

Golda hesitated. It was not easy for her to make a decision that would mean sending young people to a risky assassination campaign. Israel had never done that before. She sat quiet for a long time. Then she started speaking, in a barely audible voice, as if she were talking to herself; she mentioned the horrid memory of the Holocaust and the tragic march of the Jewish people through the ages, always persecuted, hunted, and massacred.

Finally, she raised her head and looked at Yariv and Zamir. "Send the boys," she said.

Zamir immediately started preparing the operation. He called it Wrath of God.

But Golda, too, had her say. As a prime minister of a democratic Jewish state, Golda could not rely only on the promise of Yariv and Zamir that "the boys" would hurt no one but the leaders and the major militants of Black September. Promises were not enough. She knew well that such an operation would be outside the law, and that if the civilian supervision of Mossad's actions was loosened, there was a real danger that innocent people might also be killed. Therefore she decided to establish a tight control over Wrath of God. She created a secret committee that included, besides her, Minister of Defense Moshe Dayan and Deputy Prime Minister Yigal Allon, a brilliant former general. The three of them became a secret tribunal that had to review and approve every individual case in the operation. They were called the X Committee. Yariv and Zamir had to submit every file and name to the trio, and only after getting their approval could the Mossad hit team enter the scene.

Massada (Caesarea), the operational department of the Mossad, was assigned to carry out Wrath of God. It was headed by Mike Harari, a black-haired, rugged, and secretive agent. Almost all the hits were to be carried out in Europe, where Black September had deployed its men and where they were protected by sophisticated covers.

Harari picked his men from Kidon, the Massada operational team. Each unit sent against a Black September operative was composed of several secondary crews. A crew of six men and women would be charged with identifying and following the suspects. They had to make sure that the man they targeted was indeed the right one, the wolf in sheep's clothing. They would arrive in the city where the suspect terrorist operated, follow him, secretly photograph him, learn his habits, locate his friends, find his exact address, the bars and restaurants he visited, his routine, hour by hour. A smaller unit, in most cases just a man and a woman, was in charge of the logistics—renting apartments, hotel rooms, and cars. Another small crew was in charge of communications with the advanced operational headquarters established in the respective European cities and with the Mossad headquarters in Israel.

The hit team itself consisted of several Mossad agents, who were the last to arrive on the ground. Their task was to get to a certain address, at a certain time, and kill the man whose photograph and other identifying details had been given to them. While they operated in the targeted city, they were protected by another team—a crew of armed agents and drivers, who were positioned nearby, with vehicles ready to move and escape routes designed and rehearsed. Their task was to protect—with weapons, if necessary—the members of the hit team. Immediately after the operation was over, all hit team members and their security details would leave the country.

The crew that identified and followed the suspect would have left the country before the operation. The others would stay a few more days to cover up the traces, pack equipment, and return rental cars used for the operation.

The first city chosen for a Wrath of God operation was Rome.

In the Eternal City, the advance team identified and followed a man who could never be suspected of terrorism: a low-level clerk in the Libyan embassy, a Nablus-born, thirty-eight-year-old Palestinian, Wael Zwaiter. He was slim, gentle, and soft-spoken, the son of a well-known man of letters and translator into Arabic. Wael himself was known for his excellent translation of fiction and poetry into and from Arabic. He also was a devoted art lover. He worked as an interpreter at the Libyan embassy for the meager salary of 100 Libyan dinars a month, led a very modest life, and lived in a tiny apartment on Piazza Annibaliano. His friends knew him as a moderate man who rejected any form of violence and often expressed his disgust toward terrorism and killing.

But even Zwaiter's closest friends were not aware of his secret: their good friend was a cruel fanatic, who commanded the Black September operations in Rome with ruthless determination. Recently, he had devised and carried out a lethal operation: he identified two young Englishwomen who spent the first days of their vacation in Rome before continuing to Israel. Zwaiter instructed two young, handsome, and charming Palestinians to establish contact with the girls and try to seduce them. And indeed, soon the young Casanovas landed in the Englishwomen's beds. When parting from their lovers, one of the Palestinians asked his girl to take a small record player with her, a gift for his family on the West Bank. The silly girl readily agreed, and the record player was duly checked with the ladies' other luggage at the El Al counter in Rome's airport. They did not know that Zwaiter and their charming lovers were sending them to their death. Under Zwaiter's supervision, the Black September agents had taken the record player apart, stuffed it with explosives, then repacked it in a brand-new box. The booby-trapped device was programmed to explode as soon as the aircraft reached its cruising altitude. The plane and all its passengers were doomed.

Fortunately, the terrorists did not know that after a Swissair liner headed for Israel had been blown up by a similar device, the storage compartments of El Al's planes had been covered with thick armor plate, so that no explosion could wreck the aircraft. The record player did explode, but the blast was contained by the armor. The El Al pilot, alerted by a flashing red light, immediately returned to the airport. The stunned English girls were interrogated and revealed their involvement with their Palestinian lovers; but those two had left Italy right after they bid a heartbreaking farewell to the girls they were sending to their deaths.

The first crews of the hit team arrived in Rome and followed Zwaiter for several days. A young couple strolled in front of the Libyan embassy and the woman clicked a camera concealed in her handbag every time Zwaiter went in or out of the embassy. Some "tourists" arrived in Rome by various flights. One of them, a forty-seven-year-old Canadian by the name of Anthony Hutton, rented an Avis car and told the clerk he was staying at the Excelsior Hotel on Via Veneto. If the clerk had checked the information, he would have found that no such person was staying at the Excelsior, exactly like some other "tourists" who had rented cars that same week and given false addresses to the car rental agencies.

On the night of October 16, Zwaiter returned home and was about to put a ten-lira coin in the elevator slot. The house entrance was dark and somebody on the third floor was playing a melancholy tune on the piano. Suddenly two men emerged from the shadows and pumped twelve 0.22 Beretta bullets in Zwaiter's body. Nobody heard the shots; the two agents jumped into a Fiat 125 parked on the Plaza Annibaliano. A few hours later, they were out of the country.

Now that Zwaiter had been killed, his deep cover was no longer necessary. A Beirut paper published his obituary, signed by several terrorist organizations that mourned Zwaiter as "one of our best combatants."

The leader of the small team that killed Zwaiter was an Israeli in his mid-twenties, David Molad (not his real name). He was born in Tunisia and emigrated to Israel as a child. From his parents, both teachers and Zionists, he had inherited a perfect mastery of the French language, a profound, deeply emotional love for the State of Israel, and a burning patriotism. Since a young age, he had dreamed of serving Israel, even at the risk of his life. In the army, he had volunteered for an elite commando unit in the IDF and amazed his commanders with his daring and creativity. After his discharge, he had joined the Mossad and had quickly become one of its best agents, participating in the most hazardous operations. Because of his fluent French, he could easily assume the identity of a Frenchman, Belgian, Canadian, or Swiss. He married young, and soon became the father of a little boy; but this did not cool his urge to serve on the front lines of the Mossad fighters.

After Zwaiter's death, Molad spent a few days in Israel, then flew to Paris.

A few days later, the phone rang in an apartment on 175 Rue Alesia, in Paris. Dr. Mahmoud Hamshari answered the call. "Is this Dr. Hamshari? The PLO (Palestine Liberation Organization) representative in France?" The caller had a strong Italian accent. He introduced himself as an Italian journalist who sympathized with the Palestinian cause, and asked to interview Hamshari. They agreed to meet in a café, far from Hamshari's home. Hamshari, a respected historian who lived in Paris with his French wife, Marie-Claude, and their little daughter, had been taking very strict precautions lately. When walking the streets, he kept watching for people who might be shadowing him; he left cafés and restaurants before his order was filled; he often checked with his neighbors if any strangers had asked about him.

On the face of it, he had nothing to worry about. He was an academic, a moderate man, well integrated in the Parisian intellectual circles. "He does not need any precautions," wrote Annie Francos in the *Jeune Afrique* weekly, "because he is not dangerous. The Israeli secret services know that well."

But the Israeli secret services knew a few more things: Hamshari's participation in the foiled attempt to assassinate Ben-Gurion in Denmark in 1969; his involvement in the midair explosion of a Swissair liner in 1970 that took the lives of forty-seven people; his connections with mysterious young Arabs, who would sneak into his apartment at night, carrying heavy suitcases.

The Israeli secret services also knew that Hamshari was now the second in command of Black September in Europe.

So, on the day Hamshari left for his interview with the Italian reporter, a couple of men broke into his apartment and left fifteen minutes later.

The following day, the strangers waited until Hamshari's wife and daughter left the apartment and he remained there by himself. The telephone rang and he picked up the receiver.

"Dr. Hamshari?" The Italian journalist again.

"Yes, speaking."

At that moment, Hamshari heard a shrill whistle—and, after it, a thunderous explosion. An explosive charge that had been concealed under his desk blew up and Hamshari collapsed, gravely wounded. A few days later he died in the hospital, not before blaming the Mossad for his death.

A few weeks after Hamshari's death, Mike Harari and a man named Jonathan Ingleby arrived on the island of Cyprus. They checked into the Olympia Hotel in Nicosia. Lately, because of its location, close to Israel, Syria, Lebanon, and Egypt, Cyprus had become a battlefield between Israeli and Arab agents. This time, the two Israeli agents shadowed a Palestinian by the name of Hussein Abd el Hir. A few months before, Abd el Hir had been appointed the Black September resident in Cyprus; he was also in charge of relations with the Soviet Union and the Eastern bloc nations that had become a paradise and a safe haven for the terrorists. In Russia, Czechoslovakia, Hungary, Bulgaria, Palestinian terrorists trained in army installations and special forces' units. Those countries sent shipments of weapons and equipment for the terrorist organizations; quite a few Palestinian leaders, enthusiastic believers in the Soviet ideology, studied at the Patrice Lumumba University in Moscow.

Abd el Hir also was in charge of infiltrating terrorists into Israel, and eliminating Arab spies who came to Cyprus to meet their Israeli handlers. The X Committee sentenced him to death.

That night, Abd el Hir returned to his hotel room, turned off the lights, and went to bed. Jonathan Ingleby made sure that the man was asleep, then pressed a button on a remote-control monitor. A shattering explosion shook the hotel. In a third-floor hotel room, a couple of Israeli honeymooners dived under their bed for protection. The reception clerk rushed to Abd el Hir's room. When the smoke cleared, he saw a terrifying scene that made him faint: Abd el Hir's bloodied head was facing him, stuck in the lavatory pan.

* * *

lack September's revenge was instantaneous.

On January 26, 1973, an Israeli by the name of Moshe Hanan Ishai met with a Palestinian friend at the Morrison Pub on Jose Antonio Street in Madrid. After they left the pub, two men appeared in front of them and blocked their way. The Palestinian escaped, while the two men drew their weapons, sprayed Ishai with bullets, and vanished.

Only a few days later, it was established that Ishai's real name was Baruch Cohen, a veteran Mossad agent who had established a network of Palestinian students in Madrid. The young man he had met at the pub was one of his informants, who actually had been planted in the network by Black September. His comrades avenged Abd el Hir's death by taking out Baruch Cohen.

Black September was also suspected of shooting and wounding another Israeli agent, Zadok Ophir, in a Brussels café, and of assassinating Dr. Ami Shechori, an attaché at the Israeli embassy in London, by a letter bomb.

Two weeks after Abd el Hir's death, Black September appointed a new agent in Cyprus. Barely twenty-four hours after arriving in Nicosia, the Palestinian met with his KGB contact, returned to his hotel, turned off the light—and died in the same way as his predecessor.

Arafat and Ali Hassan Salameh decided, therefore, to carry out a massive act of revenge. They planned to hijack a plane, load it with explosives, and have it flown to Israel by a suicide commando. The aircraft would then be crashed in the midst of Tel Aviv, killing hundreds. It was an early version of the 9/11 attack on the Twin Towers in New York.

The Mossad informants got wind of the preparations, and several agents started following a group of Palestinians in Paris, who were apparently in charge of the project. One night, the agents noticed an older man who had joined the group. They dispatched the man's photos to Mossad headquarters and the stranger was identified as Basil Al-Kubaissi, a senior leader of Black September. Kubaissi was a well-known jurist, a law professor at the American University in Beirut, and a respected scholar. But he, too—like Zwaiter and Hamshari and quite a few others—secretly was a dangerous man. In 1956, he had tried to assassinate Iraq's king Faisal by placing a car bomb on the path of the royal convoy; the bomb exploded prematurely, and Al-Kubaissi escaped to Lebanon, and then to the United States. A few years later, he tried to assassinate Golda Meir, who was visiting the United States. When this attempt failed, he tried to murder Meir at the Socialist International summit in Paris. It was another failure. Al-Kubaissi didn't give up; he joined the Popular Front for the Liberation of Palestine and became the deputy of George Habash, the group's leader. He participated in the planning of the May 30, 1972, massacre, in which innocent passengers in the Lod Airport were attacked by Arab and Japanese terrorists. Twenty-six people died in the attack, most of them Puerto Rican pilgrims to the Holy Land. Later, Al-Kubaissi joined Black September, and now he was in Paris, probably to direct the suicide-plane operation. He checked into a small hotel on Rue des Arcades, off the Place de la Madeleine.

On April 6, after having dinner at Café de la Paix, Al-Kubaissi was on his way back to his hotel. At the Place de la Madeleine, the Mossad's hit team was waiting. Two people had been placed on the street, two more in a car. One of them was wearing a blond wig. As Al-Kubaissi came closer, the two agents approached him, cocking their guns. But something unexpected happened. A flashy car stopped next to Al-Kubaissi, and a pretty young woman leaned out of the window. They exchanged a few phrases, and Al-Kubaissi got into the car, which left immediately. The frustrated agents realized that the woman was a prostitute, and had just propositioned Al-Kubaissi.

The entire operation was going to fail because of a hooker!

But the team commander, who was present, calmed his disappointed warriors. Wait and see, he said knowingly, she'll bring him back here shortly. They didn't ask how he knew, but the man was right. Barely twenty minutes later, the car was back. Al-Kubaissi parted from the prostitute and started walking toward his hotel. He had only taken a few steps when two men emerged from the shadows, blocking his way. One of them was David Molad.

Al-Kubaissi immediately understood. "No!" he shouted in French. "No! Don't do that!"

Nine bullets pierced his body and he collapsed by the Madeleine church. The Mossad agents jumped in the getaway car and left the square.

The following day, as in the Zwaiter case, the spokesmen of the Popular Front for the Liberation of Palestine revealed the real role of the law professor.

In the following months, Molad and the members of Kidon killed several Black September envoys who had come to Greece to buy ships, load them with explosives, and sail them to Israel's ports.

But one question remained unanswered: Where was the mastermind behind Munich? Where was Salameh?

Salameh was in his Beirut headquarters, planning his next moves. The first was the takeover of the Israeli embassy in Thailand by a Black September team. But the operation had failed. Threatened by the tough Thai generals and pressured by the Egyptian ambassador in Bangkok, the terrorists released their hostages and left Thailand utterly humiliated.

Salameh's next operation was more reckless: his men, armed to the teeth, broke into the Saudi embassy in Khartoum during a farewell party for a European envoy, and captured almost the entire diplomatic corps in the Sudanese capital. By Arafat's order, they released most of the hostages, and kept only the U.S. ambassador, Cleo A. Noel; the deputy chief of the U.S. mission, George C. Moore; and the Belgian acting ambassador, Guy Eid. Following Salameh's instructions, they murdered them with horrific cruelty, firing first at the feet and legs of their victims, then slowly raising the barrels of their Kalashnikov assault rifles till they ripped open their chests.

The terrorists were arrested after the massacre but released a few weeks later by the Sudanese government.

The world reacted with fury and disgust to the appalling assassination of the diplomats. Israel felt that it was time to deal Black September a mortal blow.

In Jerusalem, Golda Meir gave the go-ahead to Operation Spring of Youth—a new phase in the ongoing Operation Wrath of God.

* * *

On April 1, 1973, a thirty-five-year-old Belgian tourist named Gilbert Rimbaud checked into the Sands Hotel in Beirut. The same day another tourist, Dieter Altnuder, also checked into the hotel. The two men apparently didn't know each other; both were given rooms with ocean view.

On April 6, three more tourists arrived in the hotel. The dapper, impeccably dressed Andrew Whichelaw was British; David Molad, who arrived two hours later on the Rome flight, produced a Belgian passport in the name of Charles Boussard; George Elder, who arrived in the evening was British, too, but quite the opposite of his fellow countryman. Another British tourist, Charles Macy, checked into the Atlantic Hotel on El-Baida beach. And, like a real Englishman, he inquired twice a day about the weather forecast.

Each on his own, the six men toured Beirut, walked the streets, and got familiar with the main traffic arteries. At the Avis and Lenacar agencies, they rented three Buick Skylarks, a Plymouth station wagon, a Valiant, and a Renault-16.

On April 9, a flotilla of nine missile boats and patrol vessels of the Israeli Navy took to the high seas and blended into the international traffic lanes. The MB *Mivtah* carried a paratrooper unit under the command of Colonel Amnon Lipkin, which was to attack the headquarters of the Popular Front for the Liberation of Palestine. Two other units had embarked on the MB *Gaash*: another paratrooper platoon and the Sayeret Matkal unit, under Colonel Ehud Barak. They had a different mission. Before embarking, each of them had received the photos of four people. Three of them were Abu Yussef, the supreme commander of Black September; Kamal Adwan, the Fatah top operations commander, who was also in charge of Black September's operations in the Israeli occupied territories; and Kamal Nasser, Fatah's main spokesman. All three, the soldiers were told, lived in the same apartment building on Rue Verdun.

The fourth photo was of Ali Hassan Salameh. Nobody knew where he was.

The commandos were wearing civilian clothes. At nine thirty P.M., as the boats approached Beirut, they donned wigs and hippie clothes. Ehud Barak put on women's clothes, assuming the appearance of a voluptuous brunette; in his brassiere, he concealed several explosive charges.

Out of the dark, several rubber dinghies emerged on the deserted Beirut beach, bringing over the paratroopers from the mother ships. In front of them, they saw the six cars, with one of the "tourists" behind each wheel. Each soldier knew to which car he was assigned. In a matter of minutes, the cars darted in different directions. A few of them turned to the headquarters of the Popular Front. Other vehicles, one of them driven by Molad, headed for the apartment building where the leaders of Black September lived.

The military commando unit that headed for the Popular Front headquarters had rehearsed the attack before, using an unfinished building in a Tel Aviv suburb. One night, when Chief of Staff David (Dado) El'azar had come to watch the training, he had been approached by a young, handsome lieutenant, Avida Shor. "We are going to use a hundred twenty kilograms of explosives to bring down the building in Beirut," Avida said. "But this is unnecessary and dangerous. The explosion would affect the neighboring buildings, and there are lots of civilians there." He took a notebook from his pocket. "I made some calculations. We should use only eighty kilograms of explosives. That will bring the building down without harming innocent people in other houses." El'azar had the figures checked, and agreed to Shor's suggestion. He instructed the operation commander to use a charge of no more than eighty kilograms.

Now, the paratroopers reached the Popular Front headquarters. After a short shoot-out, in which two Israeli commandos lost their lives, the paratroopers took over the entrance lobby of the building and planted the eighty kilograms of explosives. The explosion turned the building into a heap of ruins, killing scores of terrorists; but not one of the neighboring houses was damaged.

One of the commandos killed was Lieutenant Avida Shor.

* * *

At the same time, other units of paratroopers and naval commandos attacked several terrorist camps south of Beirut, in a diversionary move intended to draw the response of the terrorists and the Lebanese Army. But there was no such response.

At that very moment, the Sayeret Matkal commandos reached the building on Rue Verdun. They were about to enter, when two Lebanese police officers passed by. But all they saw was a pair of lovers tenderly embracing on the sidewalk. The Romeo was none other than Muki Betzer, one of the best Sayeret fighters, and his curvaceous Juliet was Ehud Barak. As soon as the policemen had turned the corner, the Israelis stormed the building. They simultaneously broke into the apartments of Kamal Adwan, on the second floor; Kamal Nasser, on the third floor; and Abu Yussef, on the sixth.

The terrorist leaders had no chance whatsoever. When the paratroopers broke into their flats, they reached for their weapons, but the soldiers were faster. In minutes, the three terrorists were killed. Abu Yussef's wife tried to shield him with her body and was hit as well. Another casualty was an old Italian woman who lived across the landing from Adwan's apartment. She heard the shots, opened the door—and was slain with a burst of gunfire.

During the operation, the commandos collected documents that they found in the cupboards and drawers of the Black September leaders. Then they collected their wounded and dead and rushed to the cars headed for the beach, where the rubber dinghies were waiting.

On the beach, the six Mossad "tourists" parked their rented cars in a neat row, leaving the keys in the ignitions. A few days later, the rental companies received the payment via American Express.

The task force was reunited on the mother ship and sailed to Israel. The operation was a total success. The PFLP headquarters was no more, the Black September leaders had been killed; among them, Abu Yussef, the organization commander.

But the commandos didn't know that barely fifty yards away from the house on Rue Verdun, Ali Hassan Salameh was sleeping peacefully in an inconspicuous apartment. He had not been disturbed. The next day, when

Abu Yussef's death was announced, he became Black September's leader.

Spring of Youth heralded the end of Black September. The organization would never recover, after all its leaders had been killed.

All but one.

In Tel Aviv, the documents seized during Spring of Youth helped solve a mystery that had preoccupied the Mossad for the previous two years. That was the Passover Affair.

In April 1971, two young, pretty Frenchwomen landed at Lod Airport and tried to go through immigration with fake French passports. The airport security had received an early warning about their arrival. The girls were taken to a side room where they were searched by policewomen and Shabak female officers. The search revealed something strange: the women's clothing, including their underwear, weighed twice what would feel like its normal weight. The policewomen found that the Frenchwomen's clothes were saturated by some white powder. Apparently, the clothes had been immersed in a thick solution that contained the white powder. When the garments were shaken and rubbed, large quantities of the powder dropped off. More white powder was found in the heels of the ladies' exquisite sandals. The two girls were carrying about twelve pounds of white powder that turned out to be a powerful plastic explosive. In a box of tampons, in one of the girls' suitcase, the police found scores of detonators.

The girls broke down under interrogation and admitted that they were sisters, daughters of a rich Moroccan businessman; their names were Nadia and Madeleine Bardeli. They had been contacted by a man in Paris, and being adventurous by nature, had agreed to smuggle the powder.

"And who else is in this with you?" the police detectives asked.

That afternoon, several police officers raided the small hotel Commodore in Tel Aviv and arrested an old French couple, Pierre and Edith Bourghalter. When they disassembled the transistor radio of the couple, they found it had been stuffed with delayed action fuses for the manufacture of explosive charges. Pierre Bourghalter burst into tears.

The next day, the unsuspecting commander of the operation landed in Israel as well: an attractive twenty-six-year-old Frenchwoman, carrying a passport in the name of Francine Adeleine Maria. Her true name was Evelyne Barges and she was well known to the Mossad as a professional terrorist, a fanatic Marxist who already had participated in several terrorist attacks in Europe.

When interrogated by police, the members of the so-called Passover Team confessed that they had intended to blow up their plastic charges in nine major Tel Aviv hotels, at the peak of the tourist season, and kill as many tourists and Israelis as possible, dealing Israel a heavy blow.

This nice bunch went to jail, but the man who pulled the strings behind the scenes had not been caught. He was Mohammad Boudia, a charming Algerian, a director of a Paris theater and an actor himself. Again, a Dr. Jekyll and Mr. Hyde: a man of culture, an intellectual and an artist, whose life on stage was but a cover for his criminal activities. He was Evelyne Barges's lover, and involved in so many love affairs that the Mossad agents called him Bluebeard.

Boudia was originally under the orders of George Habash and the PFLP. A year after the Passover Team had been captured, he had joined Black September and was appointed head of the organization in France. He was involved in the murder of Khader Kanou, a Syrian reporter in Paris who was suspected of being a Mossad informant. Boudia was also in charge of Black September's operations in Europe, and planned an attack on a transit camp for Jewish immigrants from Russia. After Hamshari's assassination, Boudia became extremely cautious and following him became incredibly difficult.

In May 1973, a hit team of the Massada group arrived in Paris and tried to find Boudia. They had the name and address of Boudia's new lover. The agents waited patiently around the corner of the building where she lived. Finally, Boudia emerged out of nowhere and snuck inside. But the next day, when most of the residents left the building for work—he was not among them! Only after a frustrating month, when the agents had compared notes, did they notice something strange: every morning, after the torrid nights Boudia spent with his lover, a tall, big woman would be among the people coming out of the house. At times, she would be a blond, at other times, brunette . . . At last the agents solved the riddle: using his actor's talents, Boudia disguised himself as a woman before leaving the building.

But now, for some reason, he stopped visiting his mistress, and the Mossad lost track of him. The only lead they still had was that every morning he traveled by subway to his meetings, and took a connecting train at the Étoile station, under the Arc de Triomphe. That metro station was a major hub—scores of trains passed through it, millions of people ran through the underground passages, switching lines. How could they find Boudia, "the man with a thousand faces"?

But there was no other choice. Mossad agents were alerted from all over Europe. Scores of Israelis received Boudia's photos and were positioned in the corridors, passages, hallways, and platforms of the giant Étoile station. One day passed, then two and three, and nothing happened. But on the fourth day, one of the agents spotted Boudia—disguised, made-up, but still the man they were looking for. This time they stuck to him like shadows till he got into his car that was parked near the metro exit. They followed the car and watched it through the night, while Boudia stayed in a house on the Rue des Fossés-Saint-Bernard, probably his new lover's abode. The next morning, June 29, 1973, Boudia approached his car, inspected it thoroughly from the outside, peeked under the chassis, and, apparently satisfied, unlocked it and took the driver's seat. A deafening explosion turned the car into a heap of twisted, blackened metal and killed Boudia. According to European reporters, the *ramsad*, Zvi Zamir, watched the explosion from a street corner.

But the heads of Mossad had no time to celebrate their success. An urgent message reached headquarters: a special Black September messenger, the Algerian Ben Amana, had been sent to meet with Ali Hassan Salameh; Ben Amana had crossed Europe in an odd, tortuous route, and had reached Lillehammer, a resort town in Norway.

A few days later, the Kidon hit team, under Mike Harari's command, was positioned in Lillehammer. Nobody had any idea what Salameh was doing in the quiet mountain town. The first crew followed Ben Amana to the town's swimming pool and saw him establishing contact with a Middle Eastern–looking man. Three members of the crew looked at the photographs they carried and concluded that the man undoubtedly was Salameh. They overruled their fourth colleague, who had overheard the man speaking with other people and pointed out that it was impossible that Salameh could speak Norwegian.

The agents were cocksure in the identification; they followed Salameh in Lillehammer's streets and saw him in the company of a young, pregnant Norwegian woman.

The operation entered its final stage. More agents arrived from Israel; Zvi Zamir was among them. Salameh's elimination was to be the last step in the total destruction of Black September, and Zvi Zamir wanted to be there for the finale. The killers were to be the ubiquitous Jonathan Ingleby, along with Rolf Baehr and Gerard Emile Lafond. David Molad did not participate in that operation. The support crew rented cars and hotel rooms. Some maintain that the town residents immediately noticed the unusual activity; the presence in Lillehammer of many "tourists," whose cars whooshed in all directions, was not a common sight in Lillehammer during the summer.

On July 21, 1973, Salameh and his pregnant friend came out of a cinema where they had seen Clint Eastwood in *Where Eagles Dare*. The couple took the bus and got off on a quiet, deserted street. Suddenly a white car braked beside them; a couple of men jumped out on the sidewalk, Beretta guns in their hands, and sprayed Salameh's body with fourteen bullets.

The Red Prince was dead.

The operation over, Mike Harari ordered his men to leave Norway right away. The pullout was done according to the rules: the killers left first, abandoning their white car in Lillehammer's center, and took the first flights out of Oslo, the capital. Most of the agents and Mike Harari were the next to depart, leaving behind the crew that was to evacuate the safe houses and return the rental cars. But an unexpected coincidence turned everything upside down. A woman who lived near where the shooting took place noticed the color—white—and the make—Peugeot—of the killers' car; a police officer, manning a roadblock between Lillehammer and Oslo, saw a white Peugeot driven by a striking-looking woman and noted the car's license plate. The following day, when the car was returned at the airport car-rental desk, the police arrested its occupants, Dan Aerbel and Marianne Gladnikoff. Their interrogation brought about the arrest of two more agents, Sylvia Raphael and Avraham Gemer. Another two agents were arrested the same day. Aerbel and Gladnikoff broke down under the intensive interrogation. They revealed top-secret information about the operation, addresses of safe houses in Norway and throughout Europe, conspiracy rules, phone numbers, and modus operandi of the Mossad. The police raided an apartment in Oslo and found a trove of documents there; they also discovered that Ig'al Eyal, the Israeli embassy security officer, had a connection with the Mossad. It was a disaster.

The next day, Norway's media published the news about the Israeli agents' arrests. It was a terrible blow to the Mossad's prestige and credibility. But the media published another piece of news, even more devastating: the Mossad had killed the wrong man.

The man killed in Lillehammer was not Ali Hassan Salameh. He was Ahmed Bushiki, a Moroccan waiter who had come to Norway looking for a job. He had also married a Norwegian woman, the blond Torril, who was seven months pregnant.

Sensational headlines sprouted all over the world's newspapers. The captured agents stood trial and some of them were sentenced to long prison terms. One of them, Sylvia Raphael, made a strong impression on the Norwegians by her proud and noble appearance. Her trial brought her an unexpected prize: she fell in love with her Norwegian attorney, and after her release from jail she married him and lived happily with him till she died of cancer in 2005.

After the Lillehammer fiasco, the heads of the Mossad had to clean house—change conspiracy rules, abandon safe houses, establish new contacts . . . They had to admit their responsibility for Ahmed Bushiki's death and pay $400,000 to his family. But the worst was that the legend of the glorious, invincible Mossad had been shattered.

Golda Meir ordered Zvi Zamir to end Wrath of God immediately. But soon the failure was obscured by more dramatic events. On October 6, the armies of Egypt and Syria launched a surprise attack on Israel. The Yom Kippur War had begun. (See chapter 14.)

Two years passed.

On a balmy spring evening in 1975, a Beirut family hosted the most beautiful woman in the world. Georgina Rizk certainly deserved that title, as four years before she had been elected Miss Universe in the flashy beauty contest at Miami Beach, Florida. The gorgeous Lebanese beauty had won fame, awards, trips, meetings with world leaders. Back in Lebanon, she had developed a brilliant career as a supermodel and owner of fashion boutiques.

That evening, in her friends' home, she met a handsome, charismatic young man. They fell in love. Two years later, on June 8, 1977, they got married. The happy groom was Ali Hassan Salameh.

His career, too, had soared in the previous few years. At the end of 1973, Black September ceased to exist. Despite the collapse of his organization, Salameh had become Arafat's right hand and his "adopted son"; rumor had it that he would be appointed Arafat's successor at the helm of the PLO.

After the fall of Black September, Salameh was made head of Force Seventeen, which was in charge of personal security of the Fatah leaders and of all unorthodox coups de main. Salameh accompanied Arafat on a trip to New York. Arafat entered the United Nations General Assembly holding an olive branch in his hand but carrying his gun on his belt. Salameh was at Arafat's side when the latter traveled to Moscow and met with powerful world leaders. To Israel's amazement, he was also courted by the CIA.

In another of its great oversights, the Central Intelligence Agency decided to ignore the bloody past of the "Red Prince," his role in the Munich Massacre, the savage assassination of American diplomats in Khartum that he masterminded, the simple fact that Salameh was one of the most dangerous terrorists in the world, and recruited Salameh as its informant. The CIA hoped that Salameh would become a loyal servant of American interests. The CIA offered Salameh hundreds of thousands of dollars, but he refused. On the other hand, he agreed to spend a long vacation with Georgina in Hawaii, all expenses covered by the agency.

Salameh's lifestyle had changed, and his friends had started to believe that his life was no longer in danger. But he felt that his days were numbered. He did not stop speaking about his death. "I know," he said to a reporter, "that when my fate is sealed the end will come. Nobody will be able to save me."

Israel decided to seal his fate.

Many changes had taken place in Israel since the downfall of Black September. Golda Meir had gone; her successor, Yitzhak Rabin, had resigned; and a new prime minister, Menachem Begin, was now in power. Zvi Zamir had been replaced as *ramsad* by General Yitzhak (Haka) Hofi, a former commander of the Northern region. The Palestinian terror against Israel continued, in sporadic outbursts. In 1976, the hijacking of an Air France plane to Entebbe, in Uganda, had resulted in a daring rescue raid by Israeli paratroopers and Sayeret Matkal. In 1978, Fatah terrorists landed in Israel, hijacked a civilian bus, and proceeded to Tel Aviv. They were stopped by a roadblock in the city outskirts, and were finally overpowered, but not before murdering thirty-five civilian passengers. Civilian men, women, and children were regularly brutally murdered in terrorist incursions into Israeli territory.

Menachem Begin felt that no terrorist with blood on his hands could be left in peace. In the late seventies, Salameh's name was on the avengers' list once again.

An undercover Mossad agent was sent to Beirut, and managed to join the health club where Salameh exercised. One day, as he walked into the sauna, he found himself face-to-face with the naked Salameh.

This stunning discovery triggered a fiery debate at Mossad headquarters. A naked Salameh in his health club was an easy prey. On the other hand, any attempt to kill him there could result in the death of civilians; therefore, the plan was abandoned.

Enter Erika Mary Chambers.

She was a single Englishwoman, eccentric and strange, who had lived in Germany for the last four years. She arrived in Beirut and rented an apartment on the eighth floor of a building at the corner of Rue Verdun and Rue Madame Curie. Her neighbors nicknamed her Penelope. She told them she did volunteer work for an international organization taking care of poor children. She was seen, indeed, in hospitals and relief agencies; some even said she had met with Ali Hassan Salameh. She seemed to be a very lonely woman. Always disheveled, shabbily dressed, Penelope would emerge on the street with plates full of food for stray cats; her apartment was also said to be full of her beloved felines. She was also a passionate painter, but those who saw her canvases quickly realized that her talents were rather limited.

But besides painting Lebanon's landscapes, what really interested Miss Chambers was the busy traffic in the street below and, more specifically, the daily passage of two cars under her windows: a tan Chevrolet station wagon, always followed by a Land Rover jeep. Using a code, Erika scrupulously noted the times and directions of the vehicles' movements. Every morning they came from the Snoubra neighborhood, down Verdun and Curie streets, heading south toward the Fatah headquarters; they came back at lunch time, and reappeared in the early afternoon, heading to headquarters again.

Watching the cars with a pair of binoculars, Erika identified Salameh sitting in the backseat of the Chevrolet between two armed bodyguards; several other armed terrorists rode in the Land Rover that followed.

Salameh's guards perhaps could protect him, but they could not save him from the worst enemy of a secret agent: routine. Since his marriage to beautiful Georgina, Salameh's life had fallen into a steady pattern: he had settled with his wife in the Snoubra neighborhood, and would go to work, like a clerk, every morning at the same time, come home for lunch and rest, return to work after the siesta. He was ignoring the basic rules of secret activity: never develop regular habits, never stay at the same address for too long, never use the same itinerary twice, never travel at the same time of day.

On January 18, 1979, a British tourist, Peter Scriver, arrived in Beirut, checked into the Mediterranee Hotel, and rented a blue Volkswagen Golf at the Lenacar agency. The same day he met with a Canadian tourist, Ronald Kolberg, who stayed at the Royal Garden Hotel and rented a Simca Chrysler, also at Lenacar. Kolberg was none other than David Molad. The third client of the popular rental agency walked into its office the following day. That was Erika Chambers, who asked to rent a car "for a trip in the mountains." She signed out a Datsun, which she parked close to her home.

That night, three Israeli missile boats approached a deserted beach between Beirut and the port of Jounieh, and left a large load of explosives on the wet sand. Kolberg and Scriver were there; they loaded the explosives in the Volkswagen.

On January 21, Peter Scriver checked out of his hotel, drove the blue Volkswagen to Rue Verdun, and parked it in full view of Erika Chambers's windows. He then took a cab to the airport and boarded a flight to Cyprus. Ronald Kolberg checked out of his hotel, too, and moved to the Montmartre Hotel, in Jounieh.

At three forty-five P.M., as usual, Ali Hassan Salameh entered his Chevrolet. His bodyguards took the Land Rover, and the small motorcade headed for the Fatah headquarters. The cars moved down Rue Madame Curie and turned into Rue Verdun.

From the eighth floor of the corner building, Erika Chambers watched them approach. Molad stood beside her, holding a remote control device.

The Chevrolet sailed smoothly past the blue Volkswagen. At that moment, Molad pressed the switch on the remote control.

The Volkswagen exploded, turning into a huge ball of fire. The Chevrolet, engulfed by the flames, blew up in turn. Chunks of metal and splinters of glass were projected violently upward. Windows in the neighboring houses were shattered and pieces of glass rained down on the sidewalk. Horrified passersby stared at the bodies of the Chevrolet's passengers, strewn about the smoldering debris.

Police cars and ambulances rushed toward the scene and the medics pulled out of the Chevrolet's twisted chassis the bodies of the driver, the two bodyguards, and Ali Hassan Salameh.

In Damascus, a harried messenger brought an urgent telegram to Yasser Arafat, who was presiding over a meeting at the Meridien Hotel. Stunned, Arafat perused the telegram and burst into tears.

That same night, a rubber dinghy, launched from an Israeli missile boat, landed at Jounieh beach. Ronald Kolberg and Erika Chambers jumped onto the dinghy that took them to its mother ship. A few hours later, they were in Israel. The Lebanese police found their rented cars parked on the beach, keys in the ignition.

Erika Mary Chambers was the real name of a Mossad agent, a British Jewess, who had lived in England and Australia before immigrating to Israel, and was recruited by the Mossad during her studies at Hebrew University. She returned to Israel and was never heard of again.

That was the end of the Quest and the end of Operation Wrath of God. Black September was eliminated.

Many years later, some of the operation's details came to light. General Aharon Yariv admitted in a television interview that he had advised Prime Minister Golda Meir "to kill as many of the Black September leaders as possible." He admitted that he was surprised by the fact that "a military operation by our forces in Beirut and a few killings in Europe were enough to make the Fatah leaders stop the terrorism abroad. That proves that we were right by using this method for a certain time."

But that dark affair had a surprising and promising epilogue. In 1996, the Israeli journalist Daniel Ben-Simon was invited by friends to a merry party in Jerusalem. He met a young, pleasant Palestinian there, impeccably dressed and speaking fluent English. He introduced himself as Ali Hassan Salameh.

"That's the name of the man who masterminded the massacre of the Israeli athletes in Munich," Ben-Simon said.

"He was my father," the young man said. "He was murdered by the Mossad." He told the amazed Ben-Simon that he had lived for years with his mother in Europe, and finally had come to Jerusalem as Yasser Arafat's guest. "I would never have believed," he added, "that the day would come when I'd be dancing together with young Israelis at a party in Jerusalem." He described his voyage throughout Israel, the warm hospitality of the Israelis he had met, and expressed his desire to help conciliate Israelis and Palestinians.

"I am a man of peace, a hundred percent," young Salameh said. "My father lived in times of war and paid for that with his life. Now a new era has begun. I hope that peace between Israelis and Palestinians will be the most important event in the life of those two peoples."

CHAPTER THIRTEEN

THE SYRIAN VIRGINS

On a stormy night in November 1971, an Israeli Navy missile boat was struggling against the raging Mediterranean waves as it plowed its way toward the Syrian coast. It had left the big naval base in Haifa in the early evening, sailed along the Lebanese coast, and entered the Syrian territorial waters. The darkened boat passed by the illuminated Latakiyeh port, and kept its northbound course. It finally moored at a safe distance from a deserted beach, close to the Turkish border. Naval commandos of Flotilla 13 emerged on board of the wildly swaying boat and launched a few rubber dinghies into the water.

When they were ready to depart, the door of a locked side cabin opened, and three men in civilian clothes came out. Their faces were concealed by checkered *keffiyeh*s and in their watertight bags they carried small transceivers, forged passports, personal belongings, and loaded revolvers. Without uttering a word, they jumped into the dinghies and headed toward the beach. The commandos were not told their identities or the reason they were bringing these men to Syria. As they approached the coast, shortly before daybreak, the three civilians dove into the icy waters and swam toward the beach. They crouched in the surf till they saw the silhouette of a man waiting in the sand. They swam the last few yards and joined him. This was Yonatan, code-named "Prosper," their leader. He had brought dry clothes for his shivering friends and they changed right away. He took them to his concealed car close by. A stranger, apparently Mossad's local auxiliary, was waiting at the wheel; he started the car and deftly merged into the traffic on one of Syria's main highways. A few hours later, they entered Damascus.

They checked into two hotels. After a long sleep, they got together and set out to reconnoiter the Syrian capital. They all were former Flotilla 13 commandos, now Mossad agents, and were on the most unusual mission of their lives. Among them was David Molad.

The operation had been planned a few weeks earlier, at Mossad headquarters in Tel Aviv. The *ramsad*, Zvi Zamir; the head of Caesarea, Mike Harari; and a few other department heads met with the four young men, who were between twenty-three and twenty-seven years old. The four of them were close friends, had participated in several operations together, mixing their naval commando skills with their Mossad training. All of them were born in North Africa and spoke excellent French and Arabic. They called themselves the "Cosa Nostra," like the Sicilian Mafia. Zamir began to brief them.

Two years ago, a message had come from Syria. It had been sent by the leaders of the dwindling Jewish community. The autocratic regime of President Hafez Al-Assad, who had seized power in 1970, oppressed and persecuted the local Jews. Many of them had trickled out of the country, leaving behind a tiny, aging community. The young and able men had escaped from Syria, leaving behind Jewish girls who had no hope of finding husbands. Their best option was to escape to Israel.

Some of the girls, Zamir told the Cosa Nostra, had tried to escape via Lebanon, with the help of smugglers they had bribed. Some of them had been captured, beaten, tortured, even shot. A few had still managed to get to Beirut. All of them had the address of a safe house in the Lebanese capital. Local Mossad helpers had taken care of them until they could be brought to Israel.

One night, in the winter of 1970, an Israeli missile boat approached the port of Jounieh, north of Beirut, and local fishermen brought over the twelve Jewish girls who had fled Syria.

The captain of the Israeli boat was a veteran sea wolf and a submariner, Colonel Avraham (Zabu) Ben-Ze'ev. Before the operation, he and his men had undergone very rigorous training on a model they had built at a navy base. The training had been excellent, and the transfer of the girls on board had been smooth and efficient. Zabu had his men throw blankets on the badly frightened, shivering girls, served them sandwiches and coffee, and then sailed full-throttle to Haifa. He docked at four A.M. and, to his great surprise, saw the unmistakable figure of Prime Minister Golda Meir waiting on the wharf, along with the chief of the IDF staff, General Haim Bar-Lev, and his deputy, General David (Dado) El'azar. Golda threw a modest party for the Syrian girls and was deeply shaken by their stories. During the following year, Ben-Ze'ev and his successor on the job, Amnon Gonen, carried out a few more operations, bringing a few more young Syrian girls from the Lebanese coast to Israel. But crossing the Syrian-Lebanese border had become a very risky business, and the Arab smugglers and fishermen could not be trusted. Golda decided then that she must bring the remaining girls directly from Syria to Israel.

She called Zamir and instructed him to rescue the Syrian girls.

At the meeting with the Cosa Nostra, Zamir addressed the four young men. "You have to rescue those girls. That's your assignment."

A heated debate broke out in the conference room. Is this a job for Mossad agents? one of the men asked. This task should be given to the Jewish Agency. Another angrily added that the Mossad was not a matchmaking agency, and its officers should not have to risk their lives in one of the most dangerous and cruel Arab countries just to ensure that a few Jewish virgins would find grooms.

The *ramsad* did not budge. He reminded his men that rescuing the Jewish communities in enemy countries was one of the Mossad's missions from its very inception.

The operation was code-named "Smicha"—Hebrew for "blanket."

The day after the Cosa Nostra landed on Syrian territory, their self-confidence improved. They walked the streets of Damascus, chatting in French. They checked their surroundings and made sure they were not followed by the Mukhabarat, the dreaded Syrian Intelligence service. Later that day, they strolled in the illuminated markets of the city, and entered a jewelry store. "Prosper" and "Claudie" (Emanuel Allon) were examining the jewelry, conversing in French, when the merchant bent toward them and whispered: "You are from Bnai Amenu (Hebrew for 'our people'), aren't you?"

The agents were stunned. If they were so easy to identify, they were in mortal danger. They ignored the merchant's remark and quickly slipped out of the store and disappeared in the crowd.

The news about the chance to escape Syria and reach Israel had spread among the young girls of the Jewish community. "Our situation in Syria was very bad," Sara Gafni, one of the young women, said later. "We were under pressure to marry—but whom? There was nobody. We heard a lot of stories and rumors, and we became obsessed with the idea: to get to Israel, to the land of the Jews."

A message was secretly delivered to Prosper: tomorrow evening, the girls will be waiting in a small truck not far from your hotels.

The following evening, indeed, the Cosa Nostra found the small truck, its back covered with a canvas roof, parked in a dark street. The agents had previously checked out of their hotels and carried their bags with them. Two of the Cosa Nostra sat in the front of the car, and two others got in the back; under the canvas roof were several girls, between the ages of fifteen and twenty, and a teenage boy. The Cosa Nostra were wearing *keffiyeh*s again, covering their heads and leaving just a narrow slit for their eyes. They knew that on the Syrian highways, the army and police often established barriers and checkpoints. They decided that if they were stopped by the police, they would say that the truck was taking the girls to a high school field trip.

The local auxiliary, who had brought over the truck, was driving. He picked up a couple of girls in prearranged locations and then headed north, toward Tartus. They reached a deserted beach; the young Syrian Jews and the agents hid in an abandoned hut. Far from the beach, an IDF missile boat was waiting. Prosper signaled the boat with his flashlight and called them on his radio. The rubber dinghies, manned with Flotilla 13 commandos, started making their way toward the beach.

All of a sudden, bursts of gunfire echoed very close to Prosper and his friends. They scrambled for cover, but soon found out that the shots were not aimed at them. Who was firing? Had the Syrians detected the flotilla dinghies? "Mess on the beach," the naval commandos' chief, Gadi Kroll, radioed to Israel. But he did not give up. He called back the flotilla dinghies and sailed north, to an alternative beach that had been selected beforehand. Simultaneously, Prosper and his men rushed the girls back to the truck, drove north, and again made contact with the navy boat. This time, the beach was quiet. The girls and the Cosa Nostra men, their *keffiyeh*s again masking their faces, waded in the water up to their waists, and jumped into the dinghies that took them to the open sea; after a long and bumpy sail in the stormy waters, they finally boarded the navy boat that turned back to Israel. The agents disappeared in a cabin; the girls were taken to another, and ordered never to say a word to anybody about their escape from Syria. They had left their families in Damascus, and if their flight to Israel became known, their parents could pay for it with their lives.

The local auxiliary drove the truck back to Damascus, to prepare for the next operation.

The missile boat arrived to Haifa without any further incident. But before sending out the boys on their next mission, the Mossad tried to find out who had fired that night on the beach. The intelligence department checked spies' reports, activated its sleepers in Syria, contacted its sources in the army—but to no avail. They concluded that the incident might have been a badly planned ambush or a nervous response by Syrian soldiers to suspicious movements in the water.

The next time, the Cosa Nostra arrived in Damascus by air. They came from Paris, using the cover of archaeology students, coming to visit Syria's antiquities. They carried false papers, and their pockets were full of metro (the Parisian subway) tickets, coins, receipts from cafés and restaurants, and other tangible proof of their assumed identities. Their documents were in order, yet they were nervous and edgy; perhaps the Mukhabarat had blown their cover? They went through immigration without any problems, and yet they could not calm down. They crossed the crowded arrival hall of the airport and left for the city in several taxis. The Cosa Nostra settled in different hotels. Claudie checked into the Damascus Hilton.

This time, the first night they spent in Damascus was tense. The four young men knew well that if they were caught, their fate was sealed: torture and horrible death. They asked the auxiliary to take them to the square where a few years ago the Syrians had hanged Israel's greatest spy, Elie Cohen. Standing at the very place where the body of Cohen had hung from the gallows, while a fanatic crowd cheered and waved its fists, was too much for them. Claudie left his friends and ran back to his hotel; he was deeply shaken by the experience.

Haunted by the sinister image of the square, he tossed and turned on his bed, but could not sleep. Suddenly, at midnight, he heard a noise coming from the door, and immediately knew what it was: a key being inserted in the keyhole. That's it, he thought. They've got me. I'll be the next to hang in the city square. He rushed to the door and looked through the peephole. What he saw was an elderly American tourist trying in vain to open the door. After several failed attempts, she walked away. It turned out that the lady had got off the elevator on the wrong floor. Claudie felt reborn.

While they waited for the next group of girls to be prepared, they walked Damascus's streets and visited cafés and restaurants. The waiters gaped in amazement at the quartet of *Fransaouees* (Frenchmen) who split their sides laughing during the meals. It was all Claudie's fault: he repeatedly succeeded in dispelling his buddies' tremendous tension—and his own—by improvising bombastic speeches in French, inserting words and jokes in Hebrew slang.

This and future operations were flawlessly executed, until the day when Prosper and his friends noticed unusual traffic and large concentrations of troops along the beach. They could not risk an operation on the heavily patrolled coast. Prosper decided to change the itinerary.

"Go to Beirut!" he told his helper and they raced to Lebanon's capital, a hundred kilometers away. After crossing the border into Lebanon, Prosper headed for Jounieh, a port north of Beirut, inhabited mainly by Christians. In no time he rented a boat, a midsize yacht, after explaining to its owner that he wanted to take about fifteen guests on a pleasure cruise, a "surprise party" for one of his friends' birthday. Once the boat was secured and ready for departure, he cabled in code his superiors in Paris and informed them of the change in plans. Shortly after, he received confirmation by the same channel.

That night, the truck came from Damascus, carrying its usual load of young Jewish women. Claudie was at the wheel. The truck stopped a few kilometers from the Lebanese border and unloaded its human cargo. Claudie continued, alone in the truck, presented his papers at the border checkpoint, and crossed into Lebanon. There he stopped the truck on the roadside and waited. The young women, carrying their heavy suitcases, escorted by the Mossad agents, walked in the darkness for hours, stumbling on the rock-strewn ground and bypassing the border control barrier. After an exhausting march, they reached the road on the other side of the border, and met with Claudie, who drove them to Jounieh. They boarded the yacht, one by one, and finally the yacht sailed on its "birthday voyage." In the open sea, the girls were transferred to a navy boat.

The Cosa Nostra spent the following day in Beirut, strolling and shopping. At night, they headed back to Damascus by the same way they had come; a few kilometers before the border, three of the agents got off and made their way in the dark fields around the checkpoint. Claudie crossed legally with his vehicle, met his friends down the road, and took them back to Damascus.

The day after, they were on their way back to Paris, and to Tel Aviv.

The operation ended in April 1973, when Golda Meir came to Haifa naval base to personally thank Prosper, Claudie, and their friends for what they had done. Between September 1970 and April 1973, the Mossad and the navy had carried out about twenty operations for bringing young Jews and Jewesses from Syria via the Tartus beaches and the Lebanese coast. All the operations were successful, and about 120 young people were brought to Israel. The operation was kept secret for more than thirty years.

That was the end of the Cosa Nostra. Its members turned to more peaceful activities, like business, tourism, and civil service, even though they were still called back for special Mossad operations once in a while.

Time passed, and Emanuel Allon (Claudie) was invited to the wedding of a relative. He was introduced to the bride and recognized her immediately: she was one of the virgins he had helped bring over from Syria. He asked her: "Where do you come from?"

The girl paled. She felt she was still bound by the secret of her past. Allon smiled at her: "Didn't you come from Syria? By sea?"

The stunned woman almost fainted, and then all of a sudden grabbed his arms, hugged and kissed him warmly. "It was you," she mumbled. "You took me out of there!"

"This moment," Allon said later, "was worth all the risks we took."

CHAPTER FOURTEEN

"TODAY WE'LL BE AT WAR!"

O n October 5, 1973, at one A.M., Mossad agent code-named "Dubi" got a phone call from Cairo. Dubi, a senior case officer, operated from a safe house in London. The phone call was a tremendous shock. On the line was the most important and most secret agent of the Mossad, whose very existence was known only to a select few. He was known as the Angel (in some reports, he was code-named "Rashash" or "Hot'el"). The Angel uttered a few words, but one of them made Dubi shudder. It was "chemicals." Dubi immediately called the Mossad headquarters in Israel and conveyed the code word. As soon as it reached the *ramsad*, Zvi Zamir, he told his chief of staff, Freddie Eini: "I am going to London."

He knew he had no time to lose. The code word "chemicals" carried an ominous message: "Expect an immediate attack on Israel."

Israel was expecting an attack by its Arab neighbors since the 1967 Six-Day War, in which it gained large chunks of territory: the Sinai Peninsula and the Gaza strip from Egypt, the Golan Heights from Syria, the West Bank and Jerusalem from Jordan. The IDF was now deployed on the Golan Heights, on the eastern shore of the Suez Canal, and along the Jordan River. The Arab countries were rattling their sabers, promising revenge, but in the war of attrition that had followed the Six-Day battles, Israel had the upper hand. All its efforts to trade the newly conquered territories for peace had been angrily rejected by the Arab states. In the meantime, Egypt's fiery President Nasser had died and been replaced by Anwar Sadat, a man lacking charisma, regarded by the Israeli experts as weak, irresolute, and unable to lead his people to a new war. After the death of Prime Minister Eshkol, Israel's leadership had been entrusted to the strong hands of charismatic Golda Meir, a tough and powerful stateswoman, assisted by the world-famous minister of defense Moshe Dayan. Israel's security, it seemed, couldn't be in better hands.

A few weeks before the phone call, in utmost secrecy, King Hussein of Jordan had flown to Israel and warned Golda that the Egyptians and Syrians were planning an attack on Israel. Hussein had become Israel's secret ally and was engaged in intensive negotiations with Golda's envoys. But, at the time, Golda was not focused on Hussein's warnings. She was much more interested in the forthcoming elections, and Golda's Labor Party campaigned under the slogan "All Is Quiet on the Suez Canal."

Barely eighteen hours before Yom Kippur, it appeared that nothing was quiet on the Suez Canal. Zvi Zamir took the Angel's warning very seriously. According to the prearranged procedures, triggered by the code word, the *ramsad* was to meet his agent in London, as soon as he got the signal.

Zamir boarded the first flight to London. On the sixth floor of an apartment building in the British capital, not far from the Dorchester Hotel, the Mossad kept a discreet safe house. The apartment was bugged, serviced, and secured by Mossad agents. It had been acquired and equipped for only one purpose: meetings with the Angel. As soon as Zvi Zamir arrived, a detachment of ten Mossad agents took positions around the building, to protect their chief in case the signal from Cairo was part of a plot to capture or injure him. The head of the unit was veteran Zvi Malkin, the legendary agent that had helped catch Eichmann in Argentina.

Zamir, tense and agitated, waited for the Angel all day long. His agent apparently had made a stopover in Rome, on its way from Cairo, and reached London only in the late evening. The two men met at the safe house at eleven P.M.

In the meantime, Yom Kippur—the holiday of prayer, fasting, and atonement—had settled upon Israel. All work had ceased, the television and radio had stopped their broadcasts, no cars moved on the roads. Skeleton army units manned the borders of the Jewish state.

The meeting between Zamir and the Angel lasted two hours. Dubi noted every word.

It was close to one A.M., when the meeting ended. Dubi invited the Angel into another room, where he paid him his customary fee of $100,000. Zamir, frantic, hurriedly composed an urgent telegram to Israel. But the Mossad agents couldn't find the embassy encoder to transmit the vital message. Finally, Zamir lost his cool and placed a call to Freddie Eini's home. The calls were not answered and the harried operator told him: "There is no answer, sir. I think today is an important holiday in Israel."

"Try again!" Zamir growled. Finally, the ringing woke up his chief of staff and he picked up the phone. He sounded half-asleep. "Take a basin of cold water," Zamir said to him. "Put your feet in it and pick up pen and paper." When Freddie did as he was told, Zamir dictated the code phrase: "The company will sign the contract by the end of the day."

Then Zamir added: "Now get dressed, go to headquarters, and wake everybody up."

Freddie followed Zamir's orders to the letter. He started calling the political and military leaders of Israel. His message to them could be summed up in one sentence: "War will break out today."

Shortly afterward, the telegram that Zamir had written finally arrived in Tel Aviv: "According to the plan, the Egyptians and the Syrians are going to attack in the early evening. They know that today is a holiday and they believe that they can land [on our side of the Suez Canal] before dark. The attack would be carried out according to the plan which is known to us. He (the Angel) believes that Sadat cannot delay the attack because of his promise to other Arab heads of state, and he wants to keep his commitment to the last detail. The source estimates that in spite of Sadat's hesitation, the chances that the attack will be carried out are 99.9 percent. They believe they'll win, that's why they fear an early disclosure that may cause an outside intervention; this may deter some of the partners who then will reconsider. The Russians will not take part in the operation."

The *ramsad*'s dramatic report was not accepted by everybody at face value. General Eli Zeira, the handsome, confident chief of Aman, was convinced that there was no danger of war, in spite of the worrying reports by intelligence sources. He believed that the huge concentrations of Egyptian soldiers and armor on the African shore of the Suez Canal were nothing but a part of a large army maneuver. Zeira also admitted, in a conversation with Zamir, that he had "no explanation" as to why a report by Unit 848 (later renamed Unit 8200, 848 was the listening and monitoring installation of the IDF) stated that the families of the Russian military advisers in Syria and Egypt were urgently leaving those countries—a surefire indication of imminent war.

The chief of Aman and most of the defense community leaders were firm believers in "conception"—a theory that Egypt would attack Israel only under two conditions: first, that it would receive from the Soviet Union fighter jets able to face the Israeli fighter aircraft, as well as bombers and missiles that would reach Israel's population centers; and second, that it would assure the participation of the other Arab countries in the onslaught. As long as these two conditions had not been met, the conception said, there was no chance that Egypt would attack. Egypt would make threats, would tease and provoke, would carry out mammoth maneuvers— but wouldn't go to war.

But the theory had already failed before, in 1967. That year, a large part of the Egyptian Army was in Yemen, where it waged a prolonged war against the royal army. Israel was convinced that Egypt wouldn't initiate any provocative or aggressive action as long as part of its army was tied up in the Yemenite quagmire. But on May 15, 1967, the elite units of the Egyptian Army suddenly crossed the Sinai and reached the Israeli border while President Nasser expelled the United Nations' observers and closed the Straits of the Red Sea to Israeli shipping. Israeli experts should have realized the failure of their logic, but in the afterglow of the astonishing victory of the Six-Day War, it was forgotten.

The "conception" theory hovered over the extraordinary cabinet meeting called in the early hours of October 6, 1973. Not only Zeira, but several cabinet ministers as well doubted the report about an imminent Egyptian-Syrian surprise attack. Twice in the past, in November 1972 and May 1973, the Angel had flashed Israel a warning about a forthcoming attack. True, he had retracted at the last moment, but in May 1973, huge numbers of reserve soldiers had been urgently mobilized, and the operation had cost Israel the staggering sum of $34.5 million.

At this morning's cabinet meeting, everybody was conscious of the gravity of the situation. Nevertheless, they only decided on a partial mobilization of reservists. The ministers also decided not to launch a preventive strike on the huge Egyptian concentrations of troops along the canal.

Zamir returned to Israel and stuck to his guns: war is imminent! He quoted the Angel's warning of a joint offensive by the Egyptian and Syrian armies, shortly before sunset.

At two P.M., Zeira summoned the military correspondents to his office and stated that there was only a low probability of war breaking out. He was still speaking, when an aide walked into his office and handed him a short note. Zeira read it, and without another word grabbed his beret and hurried out of the room.

A few moments later, the wail of the air-raid sirens shattered the silence of Yom Kippur. The war had begun.

After the war, senior Aman officers angrily accused the Angel of having misled Zamir by mentioning the end of the day as the H-hour for the attack, while the real offensive had started at midday. Only later it was established that the H-hour had been modified at the last moment, in a phone conversation between the presidents of Syria and Egypt. The Angel was already in the air, on his way to London.

It seems strange that the Aman chiefs were disturbed by the Angel's mistake, or by his former mistaken warnings. Apparently, Aman's chiefs regarded the Angel not as an intelligence source but as the Mossad's representative in the office of Egypt's president, who was supposed to report, in full detail, everything that happened there. They ignored the fact that, in spite of his senior position, the Angel was only a spy; he produced excellent reports, but did not always know everything, as is the case with any other spy.

During the Yom Kippur War that broke out that day, the Angel kept supplying Israel with first-rate intelligence. When the Egyptians fired two Scud missiles at IDF troop concentrations, a reassuring report by the Angel calmed the Israelis. The Egyptian Army had no intention of using more missiles during the fighting, he said, and Egypt wouldn't escalate the war against Israel.

The Yom Kippur War ended on October 23. In the Golan Heights, the Syrian Army had been routed, and the Israeli cannons were positioned twenty miles from Damascus. In the south, the Egyptians had occupied a strip five miles wide on the Israeli shore of the Suez Canal, but their Third Army was completely surrounded by the Israelis, who had established a bridgehead in Egyptian territory, broken the Egyptian lines, and attained new positions barely sixty-three miles from Cairo.

Still, Israel could not rejoice with this victory. The war had cost them 2,656 lives, wounded 7,251, and the myth of its superior power had been destroyed.

Yet negotiations had started between Israelis and Egyptians and accords were signed, first for the ending of hostilities, then for establishing durable peace between the two nations. Syria refused to join the peace process.

Zvi Zamir completed his tour of duty and was replaced by general Yitzhak (Haka) Hofi.

Zamir retired amid general praise for his achievements. He was acclaimed for being the only one in the intelligence community to have warned about the military preparations of the Syrians and the Egyptians, and for bringing the crucial report about the imminent attack on Israel. If

Israel's leaders had been more attentive to his warnings, and ordered an immediate preventive strike, it is highly probable that the results would have been far better for Israel. Certain cabinet ministers maintained that Israel refrained from preventive action so that it could not be accused of starting the war. Not only does this seem contrived, it seems a nearsighted decision. For what was more important—that Israel not be "accused" of triggering the war or that it protect itself with all the means at its disposal?

And yet, the Israeli historian Dr. Uri Bar-Yossef maintains that the Angel's warning saved the Golan Heights. On the morning of October 6, he wrote, tank crews had been urgently mobilized following the Angel's report; these crews reached the Golan in the afternoon and stopped the Syrian advance in the Nafah sector.

At the war's end, under unprecedented public pressure, Israel's government appointed a board of inquiry, headed by Supreme Court Judge Shimon Agranat, to investigate the decision-making process during the Yom Kippur War. The board ordered the immediate discharge of General Eli Zeira (and several other officers, including Chief of Staff David El'azar).

But who was the Angel? An unending flow of stories, reports, and books— all of them erroneous—about his identity have been published throughout the years. It was obvious that the Angel was somebody very close to Egypt's governing circles and Egyptian Army's supreme command; but no one ever pierced the armor of secrecy that protected his real identity. Journalists and analysts called him by several code names and painted a figure blessed with legendary talents. He became the hero of many spy stories and even some bestselling novels.

After his discharge, General Zeira carried his frustration deep in his heart. He was determined to prove his innocence and reveal his version of the 1973 events to the world.

He finally decided to write a book, and give his own answer to the question: Why did he reject the Angel's report?

The general wrote that the Angel was nothing less than a double agent who had been planted in the Mossad by the wily Egyptians in order to mislead the Israelis.

Some reporters bought Zeira's story, and wrote that the Angel was indeed a double agent par excellence. The Angel's role, they explained, was, over a length of time, to deliver to Israel truthful and accurate intelligence, in order to win its trust—and then, when the Mossad was practically eating out of his hand, feed it a monstrous lie that would destroy it.

It was a great story. It explained everything, almost . . . Because both Zeira and his followers chose to disregard one single fact: all the Angel's reports, from the very beginning and till the very end, had been absolutely accurate. So where was the lie?

And when the Angel could mislead Israel and inform it that the massing of troops on the Suez Canal's shore was just a maneuver, and there was no danger of war—the "double agent" chose the opposite solution: he called Zamir's aide in England and sent him the warning—"chemicals"—then flew to London and warned Zamir that the surprise attack was imminent.

But Zeira could not be stopped. In 2004, when a new edition of his book was published, he went a step further and revealed the Angel's identity to the public. In a series of interviews, culminating with a television news show hosted by veteran journalist Dan Margalit, Zeira used the Angel's real name.

Ashraf Marwan.

The name stunned all those familiar with the Egyptian political circles. They could not believe that Marwan might be an Israeli spy.

But who was this master spy? Who was Ashraf Marwan?

In 1965, a sweet, shy Egyptian girl met a charming and handsome young man at the Heliopolis tennis court. The girl, Moona, was the third daughter in her family and not exactly the smartest. Her sister Huda was more gifted and an A-student at the Giza high school. But Moona was cute, charming, and her father's favorite child. The young man she had met came from a respectable and well-off family; he had just graduated with a B.S. in chemistry and had joined the army. And Moona fell for him, head over heels.

Shortly afterward, she introduced her boyfriend to her family. That's how the young man met Moona's father, Egypt's president Gamal Abdel Nasser.

Nasser was not sure that his daughter had met the ideal match, but she did not leave him any choice. Finally, Nasser invited the young man's father, a senior officer in the President's Guard, to his office, and the two men agreed that their children should get married. A year later, in July 1966, the young people were wed. Soon after, Moona's young husband was posted at the chemical department of the Republic Guards, and at the end of 1968 was transferred to the presidential department of science.

The name of the president's son-in-law was Ashraf Marwan.

The young man apparently was not satisfied with his new job. He asked Nasser for permission to pursue his studies in London. Nasser agreed, and Ashraf Marwan, alone, settled in England's capital, under the close supervision of the Egyptian embassy.

But the supervision, apparently, was not close enough. Ashraf Marwan loved the good life, the parties, the adventures—and London of the sixties generously supplied all of that. It didn't take long for the young Egyptian to spend all his allowance. He needed another source of financing for his nightly pleasures—and soon he found it.

Her name was Suad, and she was married to the Kuwaiti sheik Abdallah Mubarak Al-Sabah. Ashraf charmed the romantic lady and she opened her purse in return. But the arrangement did not last long. The affair was exposed and an angry Nasser had the bad boy sent home in disgrace. Nasser demanded that Moona divorce the adulterer, but she flatly refused. Nasser finally decided that Marwan would remain in Egypt and be allowed to go to London only to deliver his papers to his professors; Marwan also had to pay back all the money he had received from Suad Al-Sabah. He got a job in Nasser's office, and once in a while he would be charged with petty tasks or missions.

In 1969, Ashraf Marwan came to London again, to submit an essay to the university. But on that occasion, he also took the first step to betraying his father-in-law. His humiliation by Egypt's president had left him bitter and frustrated. He did not hesitate: he phoned the Israeli embassy and asked to speak to the military attaché. When an officer answered, Marwan identified himself by his real name, and bluntly said that he wanted to work for Israel. He asked that his offer be forwarded to the people dealing with this kind of activity. The officer who received his call did not take him seriously and did not report the call; Marwan's second call also remained unanswered. But the story reached some Mossad officials. The chief of the Mossad European section, Shmuel Goren, received a phone call from Marwan. Goren knew who Marwan was, was aware of the man's important position, and asked Marwan not to call the embassy anymore; he gave him an unlisted number and immediately alerted some of his colleagues.

Goren's top-secret report was handed to Zvi Zamir and to Rehavia Vardi, the head of Tzomet, the Mossad department for agent recruitment. The two of them appointed a special team to check Marwan's offer in-depth. On the one hand, Marwan's move had all the characteristics of a classic sting operation: somebody high up in an enemy organization volunteers as an agent, and no effort is needed to recruit him. That seems very suspicious. The man can be a double agent, sent over as bait by the Egyptian services.

But on the other hand—the same equation might have the opposite meaning. Somebody high up in the enemy organization volunteers as an agent. He certainly must have access to ultrasecret material that nobody else can provide. Perhaps, after all, he was the ideal agent, the one every secret service in the world dreamed about? Besides, Vardi's men knew who Marwan was—an ambitious young man, a hedonist, therefore somebody who loved money. The temptation for Mossad recruiters was great.

Goren returned to London and asked to meet Marwan. Marwan agreed and arrived elegantly dressed, ever the handsome young man. He openly told Goren that he had been deeply disappointed by Egypt's defeat in the 1967 Six-Day War, and had decided to join the winner. But beside that "ideological" motive, Marwan asked for lots of money: $100,000 for every meeting in which he would deliver a report to his handlers.

Goren was inclined to accept the offer, in spite of the huge cost. Such sums had never before been paid to a Mossad agent. But first, Goren needed tangible proof that Marwan was as good as his word. He asked him for a sample of the secret documents he could deliver. The delivery of the documents would also tie Marwan to the Mossad. It was self-incriminating, solid proof that Marwan had become an Israeli agent. From the Egyptian point of view, that would make him a traitor and an enemy agent.

Marwan did not let Goren wait long, and brought the full minutes of the talks held by President Nasser with the leaders of the Soviet Union in Moscow, on January 22, 1970. In that visit, Nasser demanded that the Soviets supply him with modern, long-range jet bombers that could carry out bombings deep inside Israel.

The document astonished all those who read it. They had never seen such a paper; its authenticity was beyond doubt. Now the Mossad chiefs realized that they had a fabulous treasure in their hands. They appointed Dubi as Marwan's handler and sent him to London. They also took immediate care of all the arrangements: renting an apartment in London for the meetings with the Angel, equipping it with hidden listening and recording devices, securing it, establishing a special fund for the financing of their star agent. The games could start.

The meetings were initiated by Marwan himself, whenever he had something to report. According to the rules established with Dubi, Marwan would make a phone call to a middleman (some sources claim that he used to call Jewish women in London), and the Mossad would be alerted. Marwan provided his handlers with lots of intelligence and top-secret political and military documents. Colonel Meir Meir, the head of Branch 6 (Egyptian Army) in Aman, participated in several of those meetings. Meir used to fly to London under an assumed identity; all identifying labels would have been removed from his clothes. He used to move around London for hours, by foot, in cabs and buses, to make absolutely sure he was not followed, then, finally, reach the apartment building and go up to the sixth floor. When he came to the apartment the first time, he met there a handsome but unpleasant man, who openly disdained him and condescendingly glowered at him. Marwan softened up only when he realized that Meir was a man of vast knowledge and experience. Once, Meir was asked by his Mossad friend to bring a briefcase to Marwan. When he asked what was in the case, his friend winked at him and said "a penthouse in Hamedina Square" (the most exclusive neighborhood in Tel Aviv), hinting that it carried a fabulous sum of money. According to Mossad estimates, Marwan's reports during his secret service for Israel cost the Jewish state more than $3 million.

Nasser died on September 28, 1970, and was replaced by Anwar Sadat. Professor Shimon Shamir, one of the foremost Egypt scholars in Israel, analyzed Sadat's character for the Mossad. A feeble, dull man, Shamir said; he stressed that Sadat would not stay long in power or go to war. Many of Egypt's leaders thought the same, but Marwan decided to back Sadat unconditionally. He took the keys to Nasser's personal safe from his wife, collected the most important files and documents, and brought them to the new president.

He stood by him again in May 1971, when some of Egypt's leaders conspired to carry out a pro-Soviet coup. Some of the most famous names in Egypt were among the conspirers: Ali Sabri, a former vice president; Mahmoud Fawzi, a former minister of war; Sharawi Guma, minister of the interior, and other ministers and members of parliament. The plan was to assassinate Sadat during his visit to Alexandria University. But Sadat moved first, and arrested all the conspirators. Marwan stood by him, and assisted Sadat when he smashed the conspiracy.

The results were not long coming. Marwan's position in the Egyptian hierarchy vastly improved. He was appointed presidential secretary for information and special adviser to the president. He accompanied Sadat on his trips throughout the Arab world and took part in top-level political talks.

As Marwan's status improved, so did his reports. In 1971, Sadat traveled to Moscow several times, and presented Leonid Brezhnev with a shopping list of the weapons he needed to attack Israel. The list included, among other things, MiG-25 aircraft. Marwan delivered the list to his Mossad handlers; when they asked for the minutes of the Sadat-Brezhnev talks, Marwan brought that, too. Zvi Zamir was profoundly impressed by Marwan's reports, and met him in person. The material provided by Marwan was distributed to a few senior Mossad and Aman officers, the IDF chief of staff and his deputy, Prime Minister Golda Meir, Minister of Defense Moshe Dayan, and Golda's confidant, minister without portfolio Israel Galili.

Some of Marwan's material apparently landed on the desks of other secret services. He approached the Italian secret service and offered to work for it as well; according to one source, he also established contact with the British MI6. That explains why, on that fateful October 5, when he was on his way to meet with Zvi Zamir in London, he made a stopover in Rome: he informed the Italians, too, about the forthcoming war.

Another one of his reports had reached the Italians before, but this was by means of the Mossad. A month before the Yom Kippur War, Libya had asked for Egypt's help. Palestinian terrorists, in the service of Libya's leader, Muammar Khaddafi, intended to shoot down an El Al plane during its takeoff from Rome's airport.

This was meant to be an act of vengeance against Israel for mistakenly shooting down a civilian Libyan aircraft over Sinai in February 1973. The Mossad had obtained evidence that Palestinian terrorists were planning to hijack a plane, load it with explosives, and crash the plane in one of Israel's big cities (see chapter 12). When a plane flying the Libyan colors emerged over Sinai, refusing to identify itself and to leave the Israeli-controlled space, the Israeli Air Force controllers concluded that this was the suicide bombers' aircraft. They launched a couple of fighter jets that shot the plane down. It was later established that the airliner had strayed from its course because of a sand storm that raged over Sinai. The Israeli medics found 108 bodies among the aircraft's smoldering debris.

Khaddafi swore to avenge the victims. The team to carry out the operation numbered five Fatah terrorists, led by Amin Al-Hindi. President Sadat decided to help the Libyans and ordered Marwan to deliver two Russian-made Strela missiles to the terrorists. Marwan sent the surface-to-air missiles to Rome via the diplomatic pouch. In Rome, Marwan loaded the missiles into his car; met with Al-Hindi in a shoe store on the world-famous Via Veneto; entered a carpet store with him, and bought two large carpets. Together they wrapped the missiles in the carpets and transported them, by subway, to the Palestinians' safe house . . . The terrorists prepared to launch the missiles, unaware that Marwan had already alerted the Mossad, and the Mossad warned the Italians. On September 6, the anti-terror squad of the Italian police broke into an apartment in Ostia, close to the Rome airport. The Italians arrested some of the terrorist team members and seized the missiles. The other members of the team were apprehended in a Rome hotel. The Italian press named the Mossad as the source that had alerted the Italian services; some maintained that during the operation, Zvi Zamir himself was present in Rome.

A month later, the Yom Kippur War broke out.

After the war, Marwan kept fulfilling major secret tasks for Sadat. He was sent as Sadat's envoy to Arab capitals, and was active in the separation of forces between Syria and Egypt—and Israel. He was also present at the talks between U.S. secretary of state Henry Kissinger and King Hussein of Jordan in Amman. The separation of forces gave Marwan the opportunity to connect with another secret service—the American CIA, which was looking for credible intelligence about Egypt's policy after the interim agreements with Israel. According to American sources, the secret relations between Marwan and the CIA lasted almost twenty-five years. He visited the United States several times for medical treatment and enjoyed a warm welcome and generous hospitality, courtesy of the CIA.

But even his senior position and secret activities lost their appeal, and Marwan started a second career, in business. He bought a luxurious apartment in London, at 24 Carlton House Terrace, and started investing his money in various projects. In 1975, Ashraf Marwan was appointed chairman of the Arab Industrial Union—an organization founded by Egypt, Saudi Arabia, and the Gulf Emirates in order to produce conventional weapons by Western methods. The project failed, but it helped Marwan to establish valuable contacts in the business world. After a short term, he was removed from his position, and in 1979 he moved to Paris. Two years later, after the assassination of President Sadat by fanatic terrorists, he moved to London and started a brilliant business career, which made him a very rich man. He hosted his Mossad handler Dubi in a hotel he owned in Majorca, in the Balearic Islands, and let him know that he was retiring from the world of espionage. Some claim that by the end of the seventies Marwan felt the Egyptian soil burning under his feet, and that he was suspected of maintaining secret ties with Israel, so he decided to leave both Egypt and the Mossad for good.

In the following years, Marwan made a series of fabulous business deals. He invested his money well, and soon bought a part of the Chelsea Football Club, while competing with Mohamed Al-Fayed, the father of Princess Diana's boyfriend Dodi, for the purchase of the upscale Harrods department store in London. He stuck to his hedonistic lifestyle, was always well dressed, and a string of love affairs trailed in his wake. Some CIA agents, who came to see him once in his New York hotel, had to wait outside until his current paramour dressed and cleared out of his suite.

In the eighties, Marwan's name was linked to several arms-running deals for Khaddafi's regime in Libya and the terrorists in Lebanon. An American journalist reported that he invited a CIA agent to his home, led him to the terrace, and pointed to a shiny Rolls-Royce parked outside. "This is a present from Khaddafi," he said.

The story about Marwan's terrorist connection seems to be pure fabrication. Marwan wouldn't have dealt with terrorists and risked a confrontation with the Mossad that could expose his past as an Israeli agent, sentencing him to certain death. If Marwan had delved into shady deals with Libya or the terrorists, it could have been only in full cooperation with the Mossad.

But years passed by, and in 2002, a book titled *A History of Israel* came out in London. The book was written by the Israeli scholar Ahron Bregman, and mentioned the spy who had warned Israel of the forthcoming Yom Kippur War. Bregman called the spy "the son-in-law." This was a hint that the spy was close to an important personality; and the Angel was Nasser's son-in-law. Bregman wrote that the man had been a double agent, who provided Israel with false information.

The book did not reveal Marwan's name, but it did rouse his anger. He reacted in an interview in the Egyptian *Al-Ahram* newspaper, in which he mocked Bregman's research and called it "a stupid detective story."

Bregman, offended, decided to defend his honor, and in an interview with *Al-Ahram* openly stated that "the son-in-law" was indeed Ashraf Marwan. This was a grave accusation, but it lacked any proof. It did not have any impact—till the day when Eli Zeira declared that the double agent who "fooled" Israel was, indeed, Ashraf Marwan.

Such a thing had never happened in Israel before. The identity of former spies was not revealed, in many cases, even after their death. And Ashraf Marwan was alive, vulnerable, an easy prey for the killers of the Egyptian Mukhabarat. Zvi Zamir came back from thirty years of retirement and tried to establish contact with Marwan, but the Angel refused to speak with him. "He didn't want to," Zamir dolefully said, "because he felt I didn't protect him. I did all I could to protect him, but I did not succeed."

Following Zeira's revelations, Zamir broke his self-imposed silence and harshly attacked the former Aman chief. He accused him of revealing state secrets. Zeira hit back, claiming that the former *ramsad* was protecting a man who was nothing but a double agent.

Israeli journalist Ronen Bergman, who watched a live television broadcast of an official ceremony in Egypt, saw President Hosni Mubarak warmly shaking the hand of Marwan, who accompanied him in laying a wreath on Nasser's tomb. After the broadcast, Bergman wrote that Marwan had been a double agent. As for President Mubarak, he flew to the succor of Marwan and firmly rejected the rumors of his being an Israeli spy.

Israel was engulfed in a flood of accusations and counteraccusations. The Mossad and Aman established two boards of inquiry that reached the same conclusion: Marwan was not a double agent and did not cause any harm to Israel. Zeira did not give up and sued Zamir in a court of law. The former justice Theodore Or, who had been appointed arbitrator by the court, firmly ruled that Zamir's version was the true one.

Zeira and his supporters apparently chose to ignore the fact that Marwan had been one of the leading figures of the Egyptian government, the son-in-law of Nasser and close adviser of Sadat. The leaders of Egypt did not want to admit that one of their own had been a traitor and a Zionist spy. Such an admission would have shocked the Egyptian public opinion and shaken the Egyptians' trust in their leaders. So they chose a different approach: to laud and praise Marwan in public, but seal his fate in secret.

In early June 2007, Justice Or published his findings. On June 12, an Israeli court officially confirmed Zamir's account on Marwan's role in the service of the Mossad. Two weeks later, on June 27, Marwan's body was found on a sidewalk, under his terrace.

Israeli observers accused the Egyptian secret service of the murder. Many accused Zeira, claiming that by his reckless behavior he had caused Marwan's death. On the other hand, in a hardly surprising statement, Marwan's widow accused the Mossad of murdering her husband. Eyewitnesses said that they had seen men with Middle Eastern features standing with Marwan on his terrace, minutes before his death.

The Scotland Yard closed and reopened the case, and finally stated that it was unable to find the perpetrators. The Angel's murderers still remain free.

CHAPTER FIFTEEN

A HONEY TRAP FOR THE ATOM SPY

Except for carrying a sign that read I AM A SPY, Mordechai Vanunu seemed to have done all he could to expose his secret life.

He was a technician at the Dimona atomic reactor, the most secret and secure installation in Israel. The foreign press, as well as many governments, was convinced that Israel was building nuclear weapons in that top-secret facility. Anybody who applied for a job at Dimona had to go through a long, rigorous process of filling out forms, submitting to interrogations, undergoing background checks by the Shabak and other security specialists, until—at the end of the exhausting procedure—they were cleared to enter the secret compound. The intensive surveillance and close scrutiny continued throughout one's employment at Dimona.

Vanunu applied for a job at Dimona after he saw an ad in a daily newspaper. He filled out a form at the "nuclear research facility" office in nearby Beersheba, was subjected to a routine security investigation, and got the job without any problems.

How was this possible? He was a left-wing radical, his friends were Arab members of the Communist, anti-Zionist Rakah Party; he participated in protests at their side, was photographed in extreme pro-Palestinian rallies, carried signs, made speeches, and gave interviews to the media.

He also hosted Rakah militants in his small Beersheba apartment, and asked to join their university cell, exclusively composed of young Arab radicals, openly hostile to the State of Israel. In Ben-Gurion University, where he was registered as a student, he was known for his extreme views.

He was a gifted but unstable young man. Before he became a Rakah supporter, he had been a right-wing extremist and an admirer of the racist Rabbi Kahane. He later supported the extreme right-wing party Hatechiya (Revival), voted for the Likud, and finally landed in the extreme left. He claimed that the controversial 1982 Lebanon War had made him change his political opinions. A loner, with almost no friends, he firmly believed that he was discriminated against because of his Moroccan origins. That conviction grew when he failed the admission tests for the Air Force Academy, and was posted to the Engineer Corps. After his discharge from the IDF, he started engineering studies in Tel Aviv, changed his mind and moved to Beersheba, where he started studying economics, changed his mind again and switched to philosophy. He became a vegetarian, then a vegan.

His classmates were impressed by his lust for money. He boasted that he did not have to work, just to invest smartly in the stock market. In his diary, he gave the stock market "top priority," before philosophy and English. He drove a red Audi, made some money as a nude model, and, at a student party, pulled down his drawers to win a prize.

His way of life was his own business, of course, but his political activity as a Rakah sympathizer and a Palestinian supporter should have sounded a thousand alarms. Instead, he was called to a meeting with Shabak officials, who told him to stop these activities and asked him to sign a document stating that he had been warned. He did not sign and did not stop.

The Shabak described Vanunu's activities in a routine report to the director of security in the Ministry of Defense. The director conveyed the report to the director of security at the Dimona reactor, who filed it in one of his folders, and that was it. No action was taken, and no surveillance of Vanunu was initiated. A remarkable oversight. A whole chain of people—Shabak officials at local and national levels and the directors of security at the ministry and Dimona—had failed to do their duty.

Vanunu continued his political activities and was not bothered anymore.

He was an "operator" at Institute 2, the most secret department in the Dimona compound. Out of the 2,700 employees at Dimona, only 150 were allowed entrance into Institute 2. Vanunu had two badges: 9567-8 for entering the Dimona facility, and 320 for entering Institute 2.

From the outside, the institute looked like a modest two-story building that could be a storage facility or a marginal utility unit. But people with inquisitive minds would notice an elevator cabin on the flat roof, and wonder why a two-story house needed an elevator. The key to this mystery was the real secret of Institute 2: the elevator was needed to go not up but down, to the six underground floors that were artfully concealed. Vanunu was in charge of the night shift and knew the building well. The first floor was divided between several offices and a cafeteria. A few gates on the ground floor were used for the transfer of uranium rods used in the reactor; on the same floor were some more offices and some assembly labs. On the first underground floor were pipes and valves. On the second, the central control room and a sort of terrace, called "Golda's balcony." Important visitors with maximum clearance could watch the production hall beneath from that balcony. On underground floor three, technicians worked on the uranium rods that were lowered from above. On level four was a large underground space, rising to the height of three floors for the production plant and the separation facility, where the plutonium produced in the reactor was removed from the uranium rods. The fifth floor housed the metallurgic department and the lab where the components of the bombs were produced; and on the sixth underground floor, chemical waste was loaded into special containers.

Vanunu knew that during the normal operation of the nuclear reactor, the chain reaction produced plutonium that accumulated on the uranium rods. After being "shaved" from the rods, it was used on levels four and five, and in the assembly of Israel's atomic weapons.

One day, for no particular reason, Vanunu took a camera to Institute 2. He brought it in his bag, stuck among the books that he would take later to class at Ben-Gurion University. If he was asked by the security screeners why he had brought a camera to Dimona, he intended to say that he had taken it to the beach and forgotten it in his bag. But nobody checked his bag, nobody asked questions, and he stored the camera in his personal locker. During the lunch and evening breaks, when nobody was in the building, Vanunu would wander in the underground floors; photograph the labs, the equipment, and the halls; draw detailed sketches; enter the empty offices; and peruse documents in open safes. Nobody saw him and nobody suspected him. The security guards seemed to have evaporated into thin air. Vanunu's superiors had no idea about his dangerous hobby, and evaluated him as a quiet, serious, and diligent technician.

At the end of 1985, Vanunu was fired after nine years in Dimona. His dismissal was not connected to his political activities but was part of budgetary cuts at Dimona. He was let go like many others. He received a 150 percent severance package and eight months' wages as an "adaptation grant." Yet, again, he was angry and frustrated. He decided to go abroad for a long trip—and perhaps never return, if he could find a new home, like 12 million Jews who lived outside Israel. He sold his apartment and his car and liquidated his bank accounts.

The thirty-one-year-old Vanunu shouldered his backpack and set off on his trip. He had gone on long trips before—once to Europe and once to the United States. Now he headed for the Far East. In his bag he carried the two films he had shot at Dimona.

His first stop was Greece, then Russia, Thailand, and Nepal. In Kathmandu, he met an Israeli girl and courted her bashfully. He introduced himself as "Mordy" and openly admitted that he was a left-wing pacifist, and perhaps he would not return to Israel. He visited a Buddhist temple and toyed with the idea of becoming a Buddhist himself.

After Kathmandu, Vanunu traveled the Far East and finally landed in Australia. For a few months, he worked at odd jobs in Sydney, but most of the time he was lonely and miserable. One evening, he strolled through one of the most disreputable neighborhoods of the city, a haven for prostitutes, petty thieves, and drug dealers. From the darkness, in front of him, emerged the spire of the St. George church, a known refuge of tormented souls—desperate people, criminals, homeless wanderers, poor and oppressed men and women. He walked in and met the Anglican priest John McKnight. The good priest immediately realized that Vanunu was looking for a home and a family. He established a close and warm contact with his shy, insecure guest. In the next weeks, the two of them had long and sincere conversations, and finally—on August 17, 1986—Vanunu was baptized Christian, and chose a new name: John Crossman.

It was a huge transition for an observant Jew, born in Marrakesh, who had spent his youth in the Talmudic schools and yeshivas of Beersheba. True, his religious zeal had waned years ago, but his conversion was more a product of his instability and confusion than of his disappointment with Judaism. If he had not walked into St. George church and met Father John, he might have converted to Buddhism or some other religion. But by turning his back on Judaism, he also turned his back on Israel. His aversion to his country gradually became one of the major motives for his future actions.

During a social meeting at the church, Vanunu told his new friends about his work in Israel, described the Dimona reactor, and offered to make a slide show with the photographs he had taken. They gazed at him vacantly; they had no idea what he was talking about. But there was one man in his audience who became intrigued by his words: Oscar Guerrero, a Colombian wanderer and an occasional journalist. The two of them had painted the church fence, and had lived in the same apartment for a while. Guerrero realized the importance of the photos and fired up Vanunu's imagination with promises of fortune and glory.

Vanunu badly wanted money, but he also thought he could use the promised glory to promote peace between Jews and Arabs. This was not his original plan: peacemaking had not been the reason why he left Israel and carried the two rolls of film around the world for many months. But making peace and saving the world from Israel's atomic bomb became an allegedly noble motive for his actions. His private war against the Israeli nuclear project gained steam as the days went by, and turned into a major reason for publishing the Dimona photographs. But Vanunu also understood that if he did so, it would be his end as an Israeli. He would never be able to return to Israel, where he would be branded as a traitor and enemy of the state.

Still, the temptation was great. Vanunu and Guerrero went together to a photo lab in Sydney. They developed the pictures he took of Institute 2, and tried to peddle them to the local offices of American magazines and Australian television stations, but in vain. They were regarded as either oddballs or swindlers trying to make an easy dollar. Nobody believed that the shy, ascetic young man held Israel's most guarded secret in his hands.

Finally Guerrero flew to Spain and England, and this time he struck gold. The editors of the London *Sunday Times*, who heard his story, realized the dramatic potential of an article on Israel's nuclear reactor, based on exclusive photographs and drawings. Yet they had to be extremely cautious. Not long ago they had been badly hurt by buying "Hitler's diaries," which turned out to be a second-rate hoax. Therefore, they asked to thoroughly examine the material that Guerrero had brought over.

In the meantime, an official of Australian television got in touch with the Israeli embassy in Canberra and inquired if the strange man who had offered them the photos of the Dimona reactor was indeed an Israeli citizen. The story came to the attention of an Israeli journalist, who reported it to his newspaper in Tel Aviv.

Like a thunderbolt, a stunning blow shook Israel's secret services: a former operator at Institute 2 in Dimona was trying to sell Israel's most vital secret. "The system failed, we did not get to him in time," helplessly admitted Haim Carmon, then director of security at the Ministry of Defense.

The news was rushed to "The Prime Ministers' Club"—Prime Minister Peres and former prime ministers Rabin and Shamir—who were members of the National Unity government. They decided to find Vanunu at once and bring him to Israel. Some of their aides suggested killing Vanunu instead of bringing him back, but that idea was dismissed. The prime minister picked up the phone and called the *ramsad*.

The Natanz nuclear site—thanks to the watchfulness of a Mossad intelligence officer. *(Google Earth)*

Ali Mohammadi. Explosives in a motorcycle. *(Wikipedia)*

Meir Dagan. His soldiers called him "King of Shadows." *(Dan Balilti)*

Dagan: "This old man is my grandfather." *(Courtesy of Yad Vashem)*

Isser Harel. Ben-Gurion told him, "Bring Eichmann dead or alive." *(Amit Shabi)*

Adolf Eichmann on trial in Jerusalem. *(Israel Government Press Office)*

Madeleine Ferraille, also known as Ruth Ben-David—Mata Hari of the ultra-orthodox Jewish world. *(Yedioth Ahronoth archives)*

Yossele Schuchmacher with his parents, after he was found and returned to Israel. On the right is Yechezkel Adiram, the *Yedioth Ahronoth* reporter. *(David Rubinger)*

Al-Qahir, "The Conqueror"—the missile the German scientists built in Egypt. (*Yedioth Ahronoth archives*)

Professor Eugen Sänger with Otto Joklik.

The Italian dictator Benito Mussolini and his rescuer Otto Skorzeny.

Elie Cohen and his family in a rare moment of happiness.

Elie Cohen on trial in Damascus.

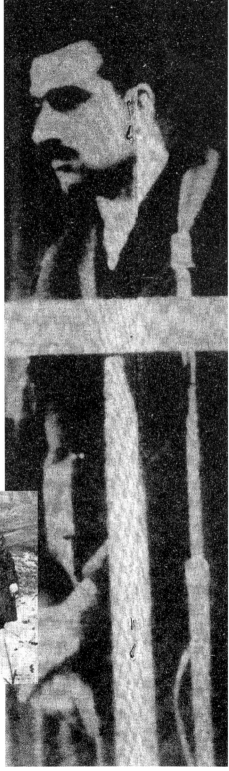

"Kamal Amin Tabet" in the company of Syrian officers on the Golan Heights.
(*Yedioth Ahronoth archives*)

ידיעות אחרונות

בוקורס, רוצח יהודי ריגה, נחטף
נמצא הרוג בארגז באורוגוואי

Front page of *Yedioth Ahronoth* on March 7, 1965, announcing the killing of Cukurs.

The crate where Cukurs's body was found in Montevideo.

Anton Kunzle as he was photographed by Herbert Cukurs. "If I'll be murdered, my murderer is in these pictures."

MiG-21. Ezer Weizman wanted one. *(Zvika Tishler)*

Heads of the Mossad (*ramsads*) Meir Amit and
Efraim Halevi. *(Michael Kremer)*

Golda Meir: "Send the boys." *(David Rubinger)*

The "Red Prince" and the most beautiful woman in the world.

The funeral of the Red Prince—Yasser Arafat and Ali Hassan Salameh's son.

Zvi Zamir: "Today we'll be at war!"
(Israel Government Press Office)

Ashraf Marwan, our man in the
Egyptian president's office. (Wikipedia)

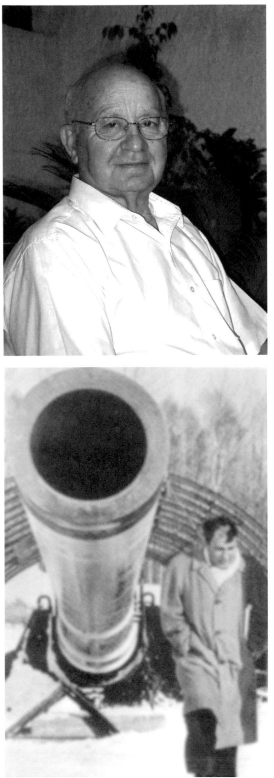

Yitzhak (Haka) Hofi.
Haka's forces in Sudan.
(David Rubinger)

Gerald Bull, the man
who sold his soul to
the devil. *(Wikipedia)*

Nahum Admoni, in the footsteps of Vanunu. (*Yedioth Ahronoth archives*)

The eternal Rafi Eitan, receiving a certificate of merit for the capture of Eichmann. *(Israel Government Press Office)*

"John Crossman" (Mordechai Vanunu) leaving jail. *(Israel Government Press Office)*

Heads of the Mossad: Danny Yatom and Shabtai Shavit. *(Meir Partush)*

A honey trap named "Cindy." *(Yedioth Ahronoth archives)*

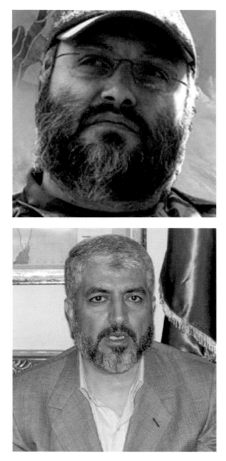

Imad Mughniyeh, Number 1 on the FBI's Most Wanted List. *(Hezbollah)*

Khaled Mash'al. The foul-up that saved his life. *(Israel Government Press Office)*

The Syrian nuclear reactor, before and after the visit of the Israeli Air Force. *(U.S. government)*

Mahmoud Al-Mabhouh. The cameras were rolling. *(Wikipedia)*

The Mossad agents in action. *(Courtesy of the Dubai police)*

"The dream will be fulfilled; soon we will arrive in the Land of Israel." *(Elad Gershgoren)*

Tamir Pardo, *ramsad. (Tomeriko)*

* * *

Since 1982, the Mossad had a new director: Nahum Admoni. After almost twenty years of generals parachuted from the IDF to the helm of the Mossad, the organization finally had a new chief, one who had worked his way up from the inside. Nahum Admoni, born in Jerusalem, was a veteran of the Shai and of Aman. He had been Yitzhak Hofi's deputy, and reached the coveted post of *ramsad* after Hofi retired in 1982. He was to spend seven years as *ramsad*, but these were not to be the best years of the intelligence community. Between 1982 and 1989, several incidents embarrassed the Mossad: the Pollard Affair, which erupted when a Jewish civilian intelligence analyst was arrested in Washington for spying for a secret Israeli intelligence unit; the Iran-Contra affair, in which Israel was involved; arrests of several Mossad agents in foreign countries because of careless blunders; but the worst damage to Israel was certainly caused by Mordechai Vanunu. As soon as Peres called him, Admoni launched an operation for capturing Vanunu. The Mossad computer spewed out the operation's code name: "Kaniuk."

Nahum Admoni urgently sent a Caesarea unit to Australia to find Vanunu. But on their arrival, the agents found out that they had come too late. The bird had flown the coop—to England.

Shortly after interviewing Guerrero, the *Sunday Times* editor sent Peter Hounam, a star of the Insight section of the weekly, to Australia, to meet Vanunu. When he boarded his flight, Hounam already knew that British scientists had examined some of the photos brought by Guerrero and confirmed their authenticity. The meeting with Vanunu in Sydney convinced Hounam, as well, that his story was true. He was particularly impressed by Vanunu's denial of Guerrero's exaggerated claims that he was "an Israeli scientist." Vanunu told him the truth: he had been only a technician at Dimona.

Vanunu and Hounam flew to London, leaving Guerrero behind. In London, Vanunu was subjected to several intensive interrogations by the *Sunday Times* people. He told them everything he knew, and revealed to the British that Israel was also developing a neutron bomb, capable of destroying living things but leaving buildings and structures intact. He also described the process of assembling the bombs at Institute 2. Yet, all along, he seemed scared and nervous. He feared being killed or kidnapped by the Israeli services. The *Sunday Times* people tried to calm him down; they moved him to another hotel, and recruited all their staff to serve, in turns, as "babysitters" for their precious guest. They insisted—in vain—that he not walk the streets alone.

When the interrogations were over, they offered him a fantastic deal: $100,000 for his story and photos, 40 percent of the distribution rights of the newspaper articles, and 25 percent of the book rights—if there were to be a book. They told him that the *Sunday Times* owner, Rupert Murdoch, also owned the film company Twentieth Century Fox, and he was thinking of making a movie about his life and times. The role of Vanunu would be played by Robert de Niro.

Vanunu's hosts in London offered him all the possible temptations except one: a woman. Vanunu hungered for sex and for a woman's warmth, and could not get them. When Insight staff member Rowena Webster kept him company, he desperately tried to convince her to have sex with him, but she refused. Sex was Vanunu's Achilles' heel, but the smart editors of the *Sunday Times* failed to realize this.

They also failed to realize that Vanunu's fears of the Israeli services were justified. One of the Insight reporters was sent to Israel to find out if Vanunu indeed was who he claimed to be. He spoke about him with an Israeli journalist, who immediately alerted the Shabak. A few hours later, several members of the Mossad operational team landed in London. The team was headed by the *ramsad*'s deputy, Shabtai Shavit. The operation was commanded by the *ramsad*'s second deputy and Caesarea's head, Beni Ze'evi.

Two Mossad agents, posing as press photographers, lingered by the *Sunday Times* building and took pictures of protesting workers, who happened to be on strike. After a few days, they saw and photographed Vanunu and followed him on London's streets, using the "comb" method developed by veteran Mossad agent Zvi Malkin. Besides following their "mark," the agents combed the areas that he might visit, and were in place even before he arrived. And so, on September 24, Vanunu arrived at Leicester Square, a favorite site for tourists and visitors. By a newspaper stand, he saw a girl "that looked very much like Farrah Fawcett, the star of the TV show *Charlie's Angels*."

She was a pretty blonde and to him she looked "beautiful and angelic." He stared at her longingly while she stood in line in front of the newsstand. She turned her head and looked back at him, a long and meaningful look. Their eyes locked for a moment, but her turn came, she bought her paper, and went her way. He turned to go in another direction, but gathered all his courage, came back, and asked her if he could talk to her. She agreed with a smile. A casual conversation followed between the two of them. She introduced herself as Cindy, a Jewish beautician from Philadelphia, on a vacation to Europe.

Vanunu was suspicious. The last few days had been nerve-racking for him. The *Sunday Times* people kept interrogating him endlessly, and postponed the publication of his story. His fears of the Israeli services increased after he learned that the *Sunday Times* was going to ask the Israeli embassy in London for their comment on the story. They explained to him that a respectable paper like the *Sunday Times* always had to ask for the other side's comments. He was not convinced. He felt lonely, angry, and impatient.

And all of a sudden—Cindy.

"Are you from the Mossad?" he asked, half-jokingly.

"No, no," she said. "No. What is Mossad?"

She asked him for his name.

"George," he said. That was the name he had used when he checked into the hotel.

She smiled. "Come on," she said. "You're not George."

When they settled in a café, he revealed his real name to her, and told her about the *Sunday Times* and his problems. She immediately suggested that he come to New York, where she could find good newspapers and good lawyers for him.

But he did not listen, not really. Mordechai Vanunu fell in love at first sight. He met with Cindy several times in the next few days, and, according to him, these were the best days of his life. They walked in the parks, holding hands, went to the movies and watched *Witness* with Harrison Ford and Woody Allen's *Hannah and Her Sisters*. They also saw a musical, *42nd Street,* and kissed a lot. The warm hugs and the sweet kisses he would never forget.

Cindy gave him her sweet kisses—but firmly refused to sleep with him. She told him she could not invite him to her hotel, because she shared a room with another girl; she also refused to come to his hotel room. You are tense and edgy, she kept saying, it won't work. Not in London.

Then she had an idea. "Why don't you come with me to Rome? My sister lives there, she's got an apartment, we can have a real good time, and you'll forget all your troubles."

At first, he refused. But she was determined to go to Rome, and bought a business-class ticket, and when she finally convinced him, she bought him a ticket, too. "You'll pay me back later," she said.

And he succumbed to temptation.

If he were a more serious and reasonable man, he would have realized right away that he had fallen into a "honey trap"—the secret services' term for a seduction by a woman. Just like that, he meets a girl in the street, and she falls for him head over heels, and is ready to do anything for him—take him to her sister's home in Rome, buy him a plane ticket even though she barely knows him. She cannot sleep with him in London, but she can sleep with him in Rome. A sensible man would have concluded that Cindy's story was suspicious, even ridiculous. But the Mossad psychologists had done an excellent job this time: they knew exactly what Vanunu wanted, and predicted that he would be driven blind by the sweet kisses and the even sweeter promises of a gorgeous, sexy woman.

Peter Hounam of the *Sunday Times* was a sensible man. As soon as he heard about Cindy, he felt something was very wrong. He tried his best to persuade Vanunu not to see her, but in vain. Vanunu had swallowed the bait already and nothing in the world could make him change his mind.

Once, he asked Peter to drive him to the café where Cindy was waiting for him, and Peter caught a glimpse of the young woman (later he would be able to sketch her face, based on their brief encounter). When Peter learned of Vanunu's intention to leave town "for a couple of days," he again tried to talk him out of it, but to no avail. Still, he warned Vanunu not to leave England and not to leave his passport with the reception clerks at the hotel. But even Peter Hounam could not imagine that Vanunu would fly to Rome so he could, at last, sleep with his Cindy.

Cindy had agreed to sleep with Vanunu in Rome for a totally different reason. Israel did not want to abduct Vanunu on British soil. Prime Minister Peres did not want to confront the formidable "Iron Lady," Margaret Thatcher. The Mossad did not feel comfortable in Great Britain, either. Only a few months before, the German authorities had found in a telephone booth a case containing eight false British passports. Unfortunately, the case also carried a tag announcing the identity of its owner and his connection to the Israeli embassy. The British government was furious; the Mossad had to promise not to infringe on British sovereignty again. Therefore, neither Peres nor the Mossad could even think of launching a covert operation in Great Britain.

Rome became the best possible choice. The relations between the Mossad and the Italian secret service were close and solid. The *ramsad* Nahum Admoni and Admiral Fulvio Martini, the head of the Italian secret service, were good friends. And with chronic chaos reigning in Italy, it was almost certain that the Italians could never prove that Vanunu was abducted on their soil.

Cindy and Mordy, hand in hand, boarded British Airways flight 504 to Rome on September 30, 1986. When they landed at nine P.M., the two lovers were met by a jolly Italian holding a huge bunch of flowers. He took them in his car to Cindy's sister's place. During the trip, Cindy kept hugging and kissing her blissful Mordy.

The car stopped by a small house, and a girl opened the door. Vanunu was the first to enter. Suddenly the door was slammed shut behind him, and two men jumped him, hit him hard, and threw him to the floor. He noticed that one of them was blond. While they tied his hands and feet, the girl bent over him and plunged a needle in his arm. Everything became a blur, and he sank into a deep sleep.

A commercial van carrying the unconscious Vanunu headed to the north of the country. The vehicle traveled for several hours; on Vanunu's side sat two men and one woman. After a few hours, Vanunu got another injection. Cindy had vanished. The car reached the port of La Spezia; Vanunu, strapped to a stretcher, was put aboard a fast speedboat that sailed to the open sea, where an Israeli freighter, *Tapuz*, was waiting (according to another source, it was SS *Noga*). The ship's crew members were ordered to enter the crew lounge and stay inside. But those on duty saw the speedboat arrive. A rope ladder was thrown overboard and two men and one woman cautiously climbed aboard. They were carrying an unconscious man and brought him to the first mate's cabin, locking the door behind them. The ship immediately sailed toward Israel.

Vanunu spent the entire trip locked in the small cabin. He did not see Cindy anymore. He was worried about her and did not know what had happened to her. He did not realize that she was a member of the Mossad team; she had left him at the threshold of the safe house and probably left Italy that same night. The woman who accompanied Vanunu aboard the ship was the doctor that kept shooting him with anesthetics during the trip.

The ship dropped anchor not far from the Israeli shore, and Vanunu was transferred to an Israeli Navy missile boat. He was met there by police officers and Shabak agents, who formally booked him and took him to the Shikma prison in Ashkelon.

During his first interrogation, Vanunu learned that while he was on his way to Israel, the *Sunday Times* had started publishing the series based on his revelations. The articles, enhanced by photographs and drawings, were reproduced in scores of papers all over the world. The *Sunday Times* revealed that all the previous assessments of Israel's nuclear strength had been mistaken. So far, the experts believed that Israel possessed between 10 and 20 primitive atomic bombs. But the information brought by Vanunu proved that Israel had become a nuclear power, and its arsenal contained at least 150 to 200 sophisticated bombs; it also had the capability of producing hydrogen and neutron weapons. Vanunu got scared by the sensational revelations. He feared that the Israelis would kill him; he also feared for Cindy, and could not believe that she was a part of the plot against him.

For about forty days, the world did not know what had happened to Vanunu. The press published sensational reports that had nothing to do with the truth. The British papers described in full detail how he had been kidnapped in London and smuggled to Israel inside a "diplomatic crate." Others quoted "witnesses" who had seen him with a young woman boarding a yacht that had taken him to Israel. Members of Parliament in London demanded an investigation and severe measures against Israel.

Vanunu was officially indicted in mid-November, and appeared in court several more times. He decided to outwit his jailers. He knew exactly where the reporters were waiting when he was brought to court. In one of the trips to the courthouse, Vanunu sat in the backseat of the police car and waited for it to stop in front of the crowd of reporters and photographers. Then, suddenly, he stuck the palm of his hand to the car window. And the reporters and photographers of the world press could read the phrase he had written on his palm:

> vanunu m was hijacked in rome, itl, 30.9.86. 21:00. came to rome by fly ba 504.

That revelation did not harm Jerusalem's relations with London, as it made clear that Vanunu had left Britain of his own free will, on a regular commercial flight. In Rome, however, the chiefs of the secret services were angry and frustrated, but after a while the Israelis repaired the damage.

Vanunu was charged with espionage and treason. He was sentenced to eighteen years in prison. But overseas, he was not considered a spy or a traitor. Associations and leagues in his name appeared in Europe and America almost overnight, and he was depicted as a bold fighter for peace, a martyr who risked his life to stop Israel's nuclear project.

Vanunu, of course, was nothing of the kind. The heroic, ideological slogans were used only to cover the confused actions of the frustrated Institute 2 operator. He did not try to rise against the Israeli nuclear project while he worked at Dimona. If he had not been laid off, he might be working there this very day. Even when he left the country, he did not hurry to start his holy war, he traveled the world, toured Nepal and Thailand, got baptized in Australia; had he not met Guerrero, he might have kept the photos of "Golda's balcony" and the bomb-assembly labs at the bottom of his rucksack.

But good and naive people throughout the world saw him as a fighter against the Israeli atomic danger. A sweet American couple adopted him as a son—even though his family was still alive—and other good Christians keep nominating him as a candidate for the Nobel Peace Prize.

When he was released from jail, after eighteen years, Vanunu chose to live in a Jerusalem church. Today he keeps displaying his hatred for Israel, refuses to live there, refuses to speak Hebrew, calls himself John Crossman, and publishes ads in the Arab newspapers, looking for an Arab or Palestinian bride ("Non-Israeli Only").

And Cindy? It turned out that because of the urgency of the operation in London, the Mossad had no time to build a solid cover for her; she used her sister's name, Cindy Hanin, and her passport, and that helped British and Israeli reporters to discover her real identity. They found out that her real name was Cheryl Ben-Tov, née Hanin, the daughter of an American millionaire who had made his fortune in the tire business. She was a devout Zionist, and immigrated to Israel at the age of seventeen. She served in the IDF and married a former Aman officer. A Mossad agent recruited her to the organization. Her IQ was high, her motivation intense, and her American passport helpful. She went through an exhausting two-year training course before being urgently flown to London with the other members of Operation Kaniuk. After Vanunu's abduction and the burst of publicity surrounding her, she had to resign from operational activity.

Today Cheryl Hanin Ben-Tov lives in Orlando, Florida. She and her husband are in the real estate business, and lead the life of a model Jewish-American family. The Vanunu affair burned Cheryl as a Mossad agent, and her colleagues sincerely regret that the smart, pretty, and resourceful woman is no longer one of them. It is because of her that Israel got Vanunu out of England without breaking any laws.

Margaret Thatcher easily reined in her tumultuous members of Parliament once it was clear that no illegal act had been committed on British soil.

But it did not take long for the Mossad to get up to its old tricks again. Two years later, Mossad agents Arie Regev and Yaacov Barad planted a Palestinian as a double agent in London. The Palestinian was caught and arrested, but Thatcher closed the Mossad station in London and expelled Regev and Barad.

The Mossad again promised to behave. And they did—until the Mahmoud Al-Mabhouh affair . . .

CHAPTER SIXTEEN

SADDAM'S SUPERGUN

On March 23, 1918, at the height of World War I, a huge artillery shell exploded in the center of Place de la Republique in Paris. An hour later, another shell hit the center of Paris, killing eight people. The explosions terrified the Parisians, since the city, far away from the front lines, was supposed to be safe. The commander of the Paris district immediately sent several squads to scan the forests around the capital, where a German artillery unit must have been hiding. But the search turned up nothing. The French surmised that the shells had been fired from an airship, even though no Zeppelin had been sighted. Six days later, on Good Friday, another shell exploded in Paris; this time it was a direct hit at the Saint Gervais church in the Fourth arrondisement. The explosion killed ninety-one people and wounded a hundred.

Panic spread throughout the city. Army patrols fanned out from the capital and didn't find anything. No one had ever heard of a cannon that could hit Paris from such a fantastic distance anyway. The newspapers compared the monster that bombarded them from afar to the huge cannon that writer Jules Verne had described in his book *From the Earth to the Moon.* Jules Verne's fictional cannon could fire a whole spaceship to the moon.

The French were in luck. The war ended that same year with the victory of the Allies over imperial Germany. Slowly, information started trickling about the horrible cannon that had spread death and panic in the French capital. Some called it the "Paris gun," others named it the "Wilhelm gun," after Wilhelm II, Germany's emperor. It turned out that it had been developed by the Krupp heavy weapons industry, which had produced three of the mysterious cannons. The cannon had an unheard-of range of 128 kilometers; its shells were three feet long, with a charge of gunpowder that was twelve feet long. The shells soared to a height of 42 kilometers, a record that was broken only by the German V-2 rockets in World War II. Krupp assembled the three superguns in utmost secrecy. The guns were pulled by special trains that moved from one position to the other almost daily. Each was manned by eighty artillery soldiers, who were forbidden to speak to anybody. It was imperative to shroud the monstrous weapons in complete secrecy.

As the war approached its end, the maneuvering capacities of the superguns quickly deteriorated. British aircraft discovered the huge guns, hounded them along the rails, and kept bombing them. The French, too, fired at them from positions close to the front lines. Yet none of the attacks were successful. The only gun that was neutralized was one that exploded while firing; five soldiers were killed. The other two vanished without a trace at the war's end. What happened to them remains a mystery. They may have been dismantled, or concealed in some deep cave or an abandoned mine.

The superguns turned into a legend, and many thought their secret would never be solved. But in 1965, an elderly German woman arrived in Canada and met a thirty-seven-year-old scientist, Dr. Gerald Bull, who was in charge of the High Altitude Research Program (HARP) at McGill University in Montreal. The woman was a relative of Fritz Rausenberger, the deceased director of design at Krupp Industries. She brought Bull a lost manuscript that she had discovered in the family archives, which described in detail the big gun and the way it was operated.

The manuscript fired up Bull's imagination. He was reputed to be a genius who had received his Ph.D. at the age of twenty-three, the youngest Ph.D. to graduate from a Canadian university. Bull dreamed of building superguns that would fire shells at targets hundreds of miles away, and even launch satellites to outer space. Using the manuscript, he wrote a book about the Wilhelm guns and the possibilities they offered to the scientists of the future.

But the book was not enough. Bull obtained funding from the U.S. and Canadian governments, as well as from his university. On a testing ground in Barbados, he tested his own huge gun—the longest gun ever built in the world. It was 36 meters long, with a caliber of 424 millimeters. Hundreds of workers, technicians and engineers, many of them local, participated in the building and testing of the formidable firearm.

Bull's cannon excelled in the test-firing and dispatched heavy loads to record altitudes. He claimed that if, instead of shells, he armed his gun with missiles propelled by solid fuel, he could fire a 200-pound missile to a distance of 4,000 kilometers or to an altitude of 250 kilometers.

Bull's gun was a great achievement, but the U.S. and Canadian governments decided, for various reasons, to stop funding the project. In 1968, Bull was forced to leave Barbados. His frustration knew no limits. With spite and hatred, he attacked the "bureaucrats" who had aborted his project.

For a while he produced artillery shells, and even exported fifty thousand shells to Israel for use with American-made guns. He was even rewarded with honorary American citizenship. But he had a very short fuse, was not always able to control his mouth, and clashed with most senior officers and officials he met. The humiliation he had felt at the closure of the test range in Barbados kept burning in him, and he was ready to do anything in order to continue building his big guns. It became his obsession, and nothing could stop him.

First he built the GC-45 gun, the most advanced gun of his time that had a range of forty kilometers. Bull sold the gun to anybody who wanted to buy it. In spite of the United Nations embargo on weapons sales to South Africa, Bull sold his guns to its army, which needed them for the war against neighboring Angola. Bull also sold South Africa a license to build the guns on its territory.

Some say the CIA secretly supported Bull's illegal activity. But as soon as the matter became public, Bull's CIA friends vanished into thin air, and he remained alone, exposed to the UN's accusations of having become a cynical, heartless arms trafficker. He was forced to return to the United States, where an unpleasant surprise awaited him: an American court found him guilty of illegal weapons trade, and sentenced him to six months in jail. When he was released and returned to Canada, he was fined $55,000. Angry and bitter, he moved to Belgium, where he founded a new company, in association with the United Gunpowder Works (Poudreries Réunies de Belgique).

But his obsession did not subside. He kept dreaming of building a huge supergun, worthy of Jules Verne's imagination. Like Goethe's Faust, he was ready to sell his soul to the devil for realizing his dream. And indeed, he found the devil: Iraq's megalomaniac dictator, Saddam Hussein.

In the eighties, Iraq was fighting a ruthless war against Iran. Bull sold the Iraqis two hundred GC-45 guns, made in Austria and smuggled via the port of Akaba, in neighboring Jordan. But that was only the beginning.

Saddam Hussein, like Bull, was deeply frustrated after Israel had bombed the Tamuz nuclear reactor and shattered his dream to make Iraq a nuclear power. He was also utterly jealous that Israel was on the verge of launching satellites into space.

Bull offered to build Saddam the biggest and the longest supergun in the world. With this gun, Bull promised, Saddam would be able to launch satellites into space and fire shells to a distance of more than a thousand kilometers. Saddam realized that he would be able to hit the population centers of Israel and gladly accepted Bull's offier. Bull called his enterprise "Project Babylon."

Bull drew up the plans for Babylon: a gun 150 meters long, weighing 2,100 tons, with a caliber of 1 meter! But before building his mammoth gun, Bull decided to assemble a smaller prototype, for testing purposes. He called the smaller gun "Baby Babylon," even though this baby was bigger than all its ancestors. The gun was 45 meters long, and Saddam's artillery commander was awed by its performance. But this was nothing compared to the real thing that was emerging from the Iraqi desert.

Bull chose to place his giant gun on a bare hill, positioning the components of the longest and the fattest gun in the world on the rising slope. After choosing the location, he ordered the parts of his cannon from various European steel plants. The main component, of course, was the barrel that Bull intended to assemble, using scores of huge steel tubes. He ordered the tubes in England, Spain, Holland, and Switzerland. The orders were camouflaged as "parts of a large oil pipeline." Because Iraq was subject to draconian international restrictions on importation of strategic materials, once again the orders were filed in the name of neighboring Jordan.

The pipes began arriving. The amazing aspect of the entire operation was that most of the states and the companies involved in the production of the pipes understood perfectly well that the pipes were nothing but parts of a giant lethal weapon; but their cynicism and greed, as well as their indifference to the wars in the Middle East, meant that they had no problem cooperating. The huge pipes were given export licenses, loaded on freighters, and sent on their way. Many of them reached Iraq without any trouble.

Bull's private army of technicians and engineers started assembling the gun pieces, pointing them west, toward Israel. But Bull was still not satisfied. He built the Iraqis two self-propelled guns, Al-Majnoon and Al-Fao. Al-Majnoon (The Crazy One) was immediately integrated into Iraq's artillery.

Bull also agreed to improve the Scud missiles in Saddam's arsenal, and modify their warheads. He extended the Scud's range and their performances; these missiles would be used against Israel during the first Gulf War.

Here, though, Bull crossed a line. According to Bull's son's testimony, Israeli agents warned Bull to stop his dangerous activities. Bull refused to listen. Israel was not alone in its desire to stop the scientist. The CIA and MI6 were also worried; the Iranians, too, had unfinished business with Bull. During the Iran-Iraq War, the Iraqis had used the guns built by Gerald Bull against them. Apparently, Bull did not suffer from a lack of enemies; and they were determined to put an end to his projects.

As he ignored the warnings, the foreign agents stepped up their activities. Several times during the winter of 1990, unknown persons broke into Bull's apartment at the Uccle neighborhood in Brussels. They took nothing, just overturned the furniture and emptied cupboards and chest drawers, leaving clear indications of their visit. That was another warning for Bull: We are here. We can get into your home as we please, and may go even further than that.

Once again, Bull ignored the warnings. The gun parts kept arriving, and were placed, one after the other, on the barren hill in Iraq. It seemed that no action could stop Project Babylon. Except one.

On March 22, 1990, Bull returned to his Brussels apartment. While he was fumbling in his pocket for the apartment keys, a man emerged from the dark corridor, a silenced gun in his hand, and fired five bullets in the back of Bull's head. The father of the great gun collapsed, and died on the spot.

The world press plunged in speculations about the identity of the killers. Some said the assassins had been sent by the CIA, others pointed at MI6, Angola, Iran . . . but most of the observers agreed on Israel. The Belgian police started an investigation but did not find a thing. The murderers of Gerald Bull have yet to be found.

With Bull's death, work on the big gun immediately stopped. His assistants, engineers, researchers, buyers scattered throughout the world. They were familiar with parts of the project but the master plan was locked in Bull's head, and only he knew how to proceed. Bull's death was also the death of Babylon.

Two weeks after Bull's death, the British authorities emerged from their long slumber. They finally dispatched a customs unit to the port of Teesport, where they seized eight huge Sheffield steel pipes, listed in the export manifest as "oil pipes." It was a nice try, but too late: the British had missed forty-four other "oil pipes" that were already in service in Iraq. In the following weeks, more components of the giant gun were seized in five other European countries. An official investigation in England tried to establish how respectable companies like Sheffield Forge Masters could ignore Saddam Hussein's devious goals and supply steel pipes for the big gun.

When the U.S. army conquered Iraq in 2003, they found piles of the huge pipes, slowly gathering rust in Al-Iskanderiya junkyard, about thirty miles south of Baghdad. The rusty pipes were all that was left of the grandiose plans of Dr. Gerald Bull.

Gerald Bull's assassination came at a time of profound change in the Mossad character. The new *ramsad*, veteran Mossad agent Shabtai Shavit, found a very different service from what the Mossad used to be when he assumed his duties in 1989. A former Sayeret Matkal fighter and head of Caesarea, he seemed the right man for the job. But starting in the early seventies, with the systematic elimination of the leaders of Black September, and much more so in the eighties and nineties, the emphasis in the Mossad activity shifted from intelligence to special operations. The Mossad gradually had to assume most of the operations against the nonmilitary and nonconventional dangers threatening the State of Israel. The formal state organs were unable to efficiently defeat terrorism. The terrorist leaders lived abroad in relative safety, planned their attacks, and dispatched their men against Israeli bodies or citizens throughout the world. Even when Israel knew who they were and what they were doing, they could not arrest them and bring them to justice. The only way left to the Mossad was to find them and kill them. These were brutal, utterly trying actions for those like David Molad, who carried them out; but they achieved their goals when the killing of the terrorist leaders wiped out or immobilized their organizations for many years. The hunt for the Black September leaders was the best example. The Gerald Bull case had similar results. Even though his assassins were never officially identified, his death was also the death of his evil projects. It was the same with Wadie Haddad.

It all started with a box of chocolates.

Dr. Wadie Haddad, the head of the Popular Front for the Liberation of Palestine, was one of the most dangerous enemies of Israel. His most notorious operation had been the hijacking of an Air France plane on its way from Tel Aviv to Paris on June 27, 1976. Several terrorists, Arabs, Germans, and South Americans, forced the pilot to land in Entebbe, the capital of Uganda, and demanded the exchange of the Jewish and Israeli hostages for the world's most dangerous terrorists. In a heroic rescue operation, Israeli commandos flew thousands of miles, landed in Entebbe, killed the terrorists, and liberated the hostages. After Entebbe, Haddad realized that his life was in danger and moved his headquarters to Baghdad, where he felt safe. From Iraq, he continued to launch terrorist operations against Israel.

The Mossad was determined to kill the arch-terrorist. But how? A painstaking operation was launched, with the goal of discovering everything about Haddad, mostly his weaknesses and vices.

A year after the Entebbe rescue, the Mossad agents found out that Haddad adored chocolate, especially fine, Belgian chocolate. The information on Haddad's secret vice came from a reliable Palestinian, who had infiltrated Haddad's Popular Front.

The *ramsad*, Yitzhak Hofi, presented the information to Israel's new prime minister, Menachem Begin, who immediately approved the operation. Mossad agents then recruited one of Haddad's trusted aides, who was on a mission in Europe; on his return, he brought his boss a big box of mouthwatering Godiva chocolates. Mossad experts injected a deadly biological poison into the chocolates filled with sweet cream. They assumed that Haddad, who craved Godiva, would gobble all the chocolates himself and would not even think of sharing them with anybody.

The agent brought the gift-wrapped box to Haddad, who, once alone, wolfed down the chocolates, each and every one of them. In a few weeks, the plump Haddad started losing his appetite and losing weight. The blood tests performed by his doctors indicated a severe immune deficiency. Nobody in Baghdad understood what was happening to the leader of the Popular Front.

Haddad's health worsened. He became weak, skeletal, and was confined to his bed. As his state became critical, he was urgently transferred to an East German clinic. Like most countries of the Soviet bloc, East Germany offered generous support, training, weapons, and refuge to the Palestinian terrorists. But their otherwise top-notch expertise did not help this time.

The East German doctors could not save Haddad, and on March 30, 1978, he died "of unknown causes." The forty-eight-year-old terrorist leader left his sister millions of dollars he had personally hoarded while leading his patriotic war for Palestine.

The German doctors' diagnosis was that Haddad had died of a terminal disease that had attacked his immune system. Nobody suspected the Mossad. Some of Haddad's closest aides accused the Iraqi authorities of poisoning him because he had embarrassed the regime. Only after many years were Israeli writers allowed to publish the truth about the Mossad's involvement in Haddad's untimely death. When Yasser Arafat died thirty years later, his aides accused Israel of causing his death. This accusation was never proven, despite the thorough examination and tests run by Arafat's French doctors.

With Haddad's death, his lethal organization collapsed. The attacks by Haddad's group against Israel ceased almost completely, and the long battle with one of Israel's vilest enemies was definitely over.

After Bull and Haddad, it was Shaqaqi's turn.

In the middle of the nineteenth century, the sultan of the Ottoman Empire sent the commander of the Imperial Navy, a famous and admired admiral, to conquer the Mediterranean island of Malta. The admiral set sail and wandered for many months in the Mediterranean.

But he did not find Malta.

The admiral returned to Istanbul, reported to the sultan, and announced: "*Malta Yok!*" (In Turkish, There is no Malta.)

But in our times, there were some who found Malta, and not only found the island but also found a man there who arrived in disguise, under an assumed identity, traveling in total secrecy. This was Dr. Fathi Shaqaqi, the head of the Islamic Jihad.

On October 26, 1995, in the late morning, Fathi Shaqaqi came out of the Diplomat Hotel in the town of Selma, in Malta. He was on his way to do some shopping before returning to Damascus, where he had been living for the last few years. Shaqaqi was wearing a wig and carrying a Libyan passport in the name of Ibrahim Shawush. He felt quite safe in the serene Maltese town. He did not know that several Mossad agents had been shadowing him since he flew, a week before, from Malta to Libya, to participate in a conference of underground Palestinian organizations.

Nine months before that, on January 22, two suicide bombers, members of Shaqaqi's Islamic Jihad, killed themselves close to a bus station at the Beit Lid Junction, not far from the city of Netanya. Twenty-one people were killed, most of them soldiers, and sixty-eight were wounded. It was one of the bloodiest terrorist attacks in Israeli history. Prime Minister Yitzhak Rabin, who rushed to Beit Lid, was deeply shocked by the carnage; his wrath peaked when he read Shaqaqi's boasts in a *Time* magazine interview that "This was the biggest military attack ever inside Palestine [outside the Arab-Israeli wars].

"*Time*: It seems to give you satisfaction?"

"*Shaqaqi*: It gives satisfaction to our people."

The furious Rabin ordered *ramsad* Shabtai Shavit, a career Mossad officer, to kill the head of the Islamic Jihad.

Shavit had been stalking Shaqaqi for a long time.

According to the *Der Spiegel* weekly, the Mossad proposed to hit Shaqaqi in his Damascus headquarters. But Rabin refused. He was secretly engaged in peace talks with Syria's president Hafez Al-Assad and did not want to jeopardize the slim chances of ending the conflict with Israel's northern neighbor. Rabin asked the Mossad to propose alternative plans for the operation. It was a very complicated mission, Shavit explained, because Shaqaqi knew he was in the Mossad's crosshairs. That was why he rarely left Syria. Nevertheless, Rabin refused to authorize a hit in Damascus and ordered Mossad to carry out the operation outside of Syria's borders.

But where? For a while, the Mossad leaders were at a loss. But, finally, as luck would have it, Shaqaqi was invited to a conference of Palestinian terrorist organizations in Libya. At first, he replied that he would not come; but then he was told that his archrival, Said Mussa, the head of the hated Abu Mussa organization, intended to participate in the conference. The Mossad experts assumed that Shaqaqi would not cede the floor to his adversary, and would come to the conference, at all costs. And indeed, a secret report from Damascus confirmed: Shaqaqi was going to Libya. In Jerusalem, Rabin gave the go-ahead.

European sources claim that the preparations for the hit started when the Mossad terrorist experts checked the records of Shaqaqi's former flights to Libya. It turned out that he always chose to fly to Tripoli via Malta. The *ramsad* decided to operate in Malta, not in Libya. Malta was a more convenient and quiet location. Mossad agents waited at Valletta Airport for Shaqaqi, who was supposed to make a short stopover there on his way to Libya. Shaqaqi almost fooled his followers by landing in Malta only on the third daily flight from Damascus, in an elaborate disguise. He spent a short while in the transit lounge and took the connecting flight to Libya.

On October 26, in the early morning, he came back to Malta and checked into the Diplomat Hotel, where he had stayed previously. He got room 616, and left the hotel immediately. Two Mossad agents riding a blue motorcycle followed him wherever he went. He spent a couple of hours visiting shops and markets. He was on his way back to the hotel when the blue motorcycle stopped beside him. One of the agents, later described as a man with Middle Eastern features, approached and fired six bullets at him from close range, with a silenced gun. Shaqaqi collapsed on the sidewalk while his killer ran to a nearby alley, where his partner was waiting on the motorcycle, engine running. They darted toward the nearby beach and jumped aboard a speedboat that took them to a freighter waiting in the high seas. The boat officially carried cement from Haifa to Italy; but beside the cement it carried another load: Shabtai Shavit himself, who monitored the operation from an improvised command post on board. The getaway route had been well planned. Nobody followed the two agents and they reached the mother ship safe and sound.

After Shaqaqi's death, his aides at the Islamic Jihad tried to unravel a major mystery: who was the traitor that had leaked the details about his trip to the Mossad? The killers knew everything: the date of his departure for Malta, the flight number, the false identity, the date of his return to Malta and Damascus . . . After a five-month investigation, the Islamic Jihad leaders arrested a Palestinian student, who was a close assistant to Shaqaqi, and accused him of treason. The student broke under interrogation and confessed: he had been recruited by the Mossad while studying in Bulgaria; his handlers instructed him to move to Damascus and join Shaqaqi's group. During the next four years, he had gained Shaqaqi's confidence and even became one of the few in the know about Shaqaqi's activities.

Unlike the Hamas and the Hezbollah, which invested a large part of their resources in social activities, the Islamic Jihad had a sole purpose: terror. It was based on a very small and very compartmentalized number of cells, composed of Palestinians who had no other purpose but to fight Israel. Shaqaqi himself was considered by the Palestinian diaspora to be the ideological father of suicide terrorism. He was the first to find in Islam's holy teachings a legitimization for suicide bombings and killings.

Shaqaqi's organization was responsible for a long list of bloody terrorist attacks: sixteen dead in the attack on a 405 bus on the road from Tel Aviv to Jerusalem on July 6, 1989; nine dead in the attack on a bus of Israeli tourists close to Cairo, on February 4, 1990; eight dead in the bombing of a bus by Kfar Darom, in Southern Israel on November 20, 2000; three soldiers killed at the suicide attack on the Netzarim roadblock in the Gaza strip on November 11, 1994; and the terrible bombing in Beit Lid, where twenty-one people died on January 22, 1995. He had rightfully earned the death sentence that the Mossad carried out in a Malta street. After Shaqaqi's death, the Islamic Jihad almost collapsed, and it took years for the organization to recover from the death of its leader.

Israel never assumed responsibility for the assassination. Prime Minister Yitzhak Rabin said: "I did not know about the assassination—but if it is true I shall not be sorry."

A short while afterward, Yitzhak Rabin himself was assassinated, not by a Palestinian terrorist but by a Jewish fanatic.

CHAPTER SEVENTEEN

FIASCO IN AMMAN

"*Baba! Baba!*" (Father! Father!) the little girl cried, jumped out of the black jeep, and ran after her father into a tall office building in central Amman, Jordan.

"*Baba!*" she called, and triggered one of the worst mishaps in the history of the Mossad.

The operation had been masterly planned. Even though it seemed somewhat clumsy, it had every chance of success. Its goal was to kill Khaled Mash'al, the newly appointed head of the Hamas Political Bureau. Mash'al, a forty-one-year-old computer engineer, was a handsome man, sporting a well-groomed black beard. He was a rising leader of Hamas, which, in the previous few years, had become Israel's worst enemy. This terrorist organization, fueled by Islamic fanaticism, had replaced the PLO in the ruthless fight against Israel after Yasser Arafat and Yitzhak Rabin had made a move toward peace by signing the Oslo agreements together in September 1993. The senior officers of Mossad had proposed Mash'al as a target for assassination after a deadly suicide bombing in Jerusalem on July 30, 1997. Two terrorists blew themselves up in the crowded Mahane-Yehuda market, killing 16 Israelis and wounding 169 others. Prime Minister Benjamin (Bibi) Netanyahu called an emergency meeting of the cabinet that decided to kill one of the Hamas leaders. The *ramsad*, General Danny Yatom, who had been appointed to his post in 1996, was tasked by Netanyahu with designating which man should die.

Yatom had a long military career behind him. A muscular, bald man with a ready smile, he had been a fighter and a deputy commander at Sayeret Matkal, then an Armor Corps officer, and the head of the Israeli Central Command with the rank of major general. Devoted heart and soul to Prime Minister Yitzhak Rabin, he had been his military secretary. After Rabin's death, he was, to the surprise of many, appointed head of the Mossad. All those who knew him appreciated his efficiency and his military record, but he seemed to lack all of the qualities needed in a man at the helm of a secret organization. His appointment seemed to be more of a tribute to the dead Rabin than a choice of the best man for the job.

After his meeting with Netanyahu, in early August 1997, Yatom called an urgent meeting at Mossad headquarters in Tel Aviv. The heads of the Mossad's major departments were summoned to the conference room. These were Aliza Magen, Yatom's deputy; B., the head of Caesarea, the special operations department; Yitzhak Barzilai, the head of Tevel—department in charge of cooperation with foreign intelligence services; Ilan Mizrahi, head of Tzomet, the intelligence-gathering department; D., head of Neviot, which specialized in penetrating enemy targets; and the heads of the research and terrorism departments (persons designed by a letter instead of a name are still on active duty).

At first, the discussion reached a dead end. The Mossad did not have a full list of the Hamas leaders. The most prominent Hamas chief was Mousa Mohammed Abu Marzook, but the man carried an American passport and any attack on him could create complications with the United States. Khaled Mash'al, on the other hand, was unanimously regarded as a suitable target; but his office was in Amman. After signing a peace agree-

ment with Jordan, in October 1994, Prime Minister Rabin had prohib-
ited all Mossad operations in that country. As long as General Yatom was
Rabin's military secretary, he followed Rabin's order to the letter; but after
he was appointed *ramsad*, Yatom decided to ignore the late Rabin's instructions and proposed Mash'al's name to Prime Minister Netanyahu. His suggestion was backed by the head of Caesarea and his intelligence officer,
Mishka Ben-David.

Netanyahu agreed; yet, determined to avoid a crisis with Jordan, he
ordered a "quiet" operation, not a showy hit. Yatom charged the Kidon
group—the elite unit of Caesarea—with executing the operation. A doctor
of biochemistry, employed at the Mossad research department, suggested
using a lethal poison that had been developed in the Biology Institute in
Ness Ziona. A few drops of this poison, sprinkled on a person's skin, would
cause his death. This poison did not leave any traces and could not be
detected even in an autopsy. A similar poison was used in the past, in the
Godiva Affair against Wadie Haddad, the head of the Popular Front for the
Liberation of Palestine (see chapter 16).

"The poison thing didn't bother you?" Israeli journalist Ronen Bergman asked Mishka Ben-David years later. "Such a disgusting way to die . . ."

"Tell me," Ben-David answered, "a bullet in the head or a missile fired
at the car is more humane than poison? . . . It would have been better, of
course, if there was no need to kill people, but in the war against terror this
is unavoidable. The prime minister's decision to carry out a 'quiet' operation in order not to harm our relations with Jordan was a logical one."

In the summer of 1997, some passersby in a Tel Aviv street saw two young
men shaking cans of Coca-Cola, then pulling their tabs and opening
them. The bubbly drink squirted out with a sizzling noise. For a moment,
the people on the street cast annoyed looks at the two young men, and
then kept moving. They could not guess that the two were Mossad agents,
rehearsing Mash'al's killing: one of them would open a Coke can in his
vicinity to divert his attention, while the other would squirt a few drops
of poison at the back of his neck.

Six weeks before the operation, in August 1997, the first agents arrived in Jordan. They carried foreign passports and followed Mash'al's daily routine: when does he leave his home, who rides with him in his car in the morning, what is the route he takes and where does he go, how is the road traffic when he travels? They measured the time between his getting out of his car and entering this or that building, checked if he stopped on his way to talk with other people entering the same building, and collected any other bits of information that could influence the operational plans.

The advance team's report to Kidon headquarters summed up the results of the preliminary mission: Every morning, Mash'al came out of his house without bodyguards. He got into a black SUV driven by his assistant, and headed for the Palestinian Relief Bureau at the Shamia Center building in Amman. After Mash'al got out, the driver departed with the vehicle. Mash'al walked the short distance to the building and entered. The Palestinian Relief Bureau was a cover name for the Hamas headquarters in the Jordanian capital.

The surveillance report by the advance team also suggested the best way to hit Mash'al: in the morning, on the sidewalk, after he got out of the SUV and walked to the office building.

The preparations continued through the summer: surveillance, dispatch of other auxiliary teams to Amman, renting safe houses and vehicles. Suddenly, on September 4, another terrorist attack shook Jerusalem: three Hamas members blew themselves up on Ben-Yehuda Street, killing 5 Israelis, wounding 181. Israel could not wait any longer, it was time to act.

September 24, 1997, a day before the operation. A couple of tourists linger by the pool of a big Amman hotel. The man is wearing a white bathrobe. He tells the hotel employees that he is recovering from a heart attack; his slow, cautious walk proves that he still suffers from the side effects of his illness. The young woman with him is a doctor. Every once in a while, she checks his pulse and his blood pressure. Most of the time, they lie on the chaises by the pool. The "heart patient" is Mishka Ben-David, in charge of the communication between the Mossad headquarters and the agents on the ground. The woman, a Mossad agent as well, is a real doctor who carries an injection of antidote to the poison destined to kill Mash'al. The antidote is capable of neutralizing the effect of the poison. It would be used if one or more Kidon agents are accidentally exposed to some drops of the poison during the operation. An immediate shot of the antidote would be the only way to save them from certain death.

While the phony patient and the doctor are waiting by the pool, the hit team is making the last preparations. In the last few days, several agents have arrived to Amman; they will drive the escape vehicles and fill secondary roles. After them, the hit team itself has arrived: two Kidon agents, posing as Canadian tourists by the names of Shawn Kendall and Barry Beads. The two of them have checked into the Intercontinental Hotel. In retrospect, disturbing questions arise concerning these two: Why were they chosen, even though they had never operated in an Arab country? And why did they get Canadian passports, when even the most superficial inspection would prove that they were not Canadians? Their English was stilted, their accent Israeli, and their cover certain to be pulverized by a serious investigation. But all this paled in comparison with the surveillance team's error, exposed only after the operation was launched.

The hit was to take place at the entrance to the Shamia Center building, where Mash'al's office was located. The encounter between the Kidon agents and Mash'al was supposed to be quick and deadly. "Shawn" and "Barry" had to approach Mash'al, spray the liquid poison on the back of his neck, and escape aboard a vehicle that was waiting nearby. The two "Canadians" were well prepared after their training in the streets of Tel Aviv. Shawn was to hold the Coke can; when facing Mash'al, he had to pull the tab and "accidentally" spray the Coke in his direction. But the Coke, of course, was not the story. Barry, who held the small container of poison, was the main figure in the operation; in a matter of seconds, he had to spray the poison from his container toward Mash'al. The Coke can was supposed to divert his attention from the poison spray; the liquid would spread on his skin and make him die of a "heart attack."

Two other "tourists," a man and a woman, were to wait inside the building lobby in case the hit team needed help. For instance, Mash'al might walk too fast toward the building, and the two Canadians may not be able to get to him. In such case, the "tourists" were supposed to get out of the building and bump into Mash'al, delaying him until the hit men reached him.

That way, the Mossad planners believed, there would be no confrontation with the Jordanians.

The key to success was the situation on the ground: target area clean of bodyguards, family members, acquaintances, police officers, Hamas militants, and others who could thwart the hit. And indeed, the instructions to the eight agents sent to Jordan were clear: carry out the operations only if all the above conditions are fulfilled. Danny Yatom maintains that he had told the agents: "If the conditions differ from the original planning, we can always execute at a later date." As far as we know, that was what really happened. The agents came several times to the target area but aborted the hit because of unexpected problems—the presence of Jordanian police officers in the area, bodyguards who escorted Mash'al, or Mash'al's last-minute decision not to go to the office that day.

September 25, 1997, D-Day.

The operation commander takes position across the street, in front of the office building. It has been decided not to use cell phones or electronic communication instruments in the target area, and the agents would communicate by manual and body signs. In case they needed to abort the operation, the commander would notify the two agents by removing his visor cap.

Behind the building, the getaway car is waiting for the two hit men.

Shawn and Barry are in place, and so is the couple in the lobby of the building.

Everything is ready.

In Mash'al's home, it is almost a perfectly routine morning; but for a small, last-minute change. Mash'al's wife asks him to take the two children to school today. Usually she takes care of that. The children get in the SUV with their father, but the Mossad surveillance team does not notice them, and reports to the Kidon people that Mash'al is on his way, alone in the car with the driver. The agents fail to notice the two kids who are sitting in the back. The car windows are tinted and the children cannot be seen from the outside.

Mash'al arrives to the Shamia Center, gets out of the car, crosses the sidewalk, and starts climbing the stairs leading to the building entrance. The two hit men approach him—ten meters, five, three . . . Suddenly Mash'al's little girl emerges from the SUV. *"Baba! Baba!"* she calls and starts running toward her father. The driver jumps out of the car and follows the child. The operation commander, who is positioned across the street, notices the child. He removes his hat and tries to signal to his men to abort. But in these critical seconds, the two agents are getting around one of the concrete pillars at the building entrance and for a moment they lose contact with their commander. And even worse—they don't see the little girl and the driver who runs after her.

The hit men proceed with their mission. They reach Mash'al, and Shawn shakes the Coke can and pulls the tab. But today, for the first time, the tab tears but the can does not open. The diversion fails. Barry nonetheless raises his hand, to spray the poison on Mash'al's neck. But Mash'al's driver, who runs after the child, sees the stranger's raised hand and thinks he is trying to stab his boss. He starts to shout, darts toward Barry, and tries to strike him with a folded newspaper. Mash'al hears his driver's shouts and turns back. At this moment, Barry sprays the poison and a few drops fall on Mash'al's ear. He feels only a light prick, but realizes that something is wrong, and runs away as fast as he can. Shawn and Barry rush toward the getaway car.

At this point, another character enters the scene: Muhammad Abu Seif, a Hamas militant who is on his way to deliver some documents to Mash'al. He hears the shouts and sees the confrontation between his leader and the two agents. While Mash'al is running for his life, Abu Seif tries to stop Shawn and Barry, who are about to get into the getaway car, a third snag in the ill-fated mission. He struggles with Shawn, who hits him with the unopened Coke can. Shawn and Barry manage to jump into the car. It darts off.

But then they make the most critical mistake in the operation. The driver tells Shawn and Barry that he has seen Abu Seif writing down the car's license plate number. The two hit men decide on the spot to abandon the car. They fear that Abu Seif would alert the police, and if they get to the hotel with that car, as planned, they will be arrested there. They have no address of a safe house, no other escape route. Barry and Shawn get out of the car after a few blocks, and the driver speeds away to get rid of the car.

But it turns out that Abu Seif, a veteran of the mujahideen, who had fought in Afghanistan against the Russians, has not given up. The stubborn and agile man has been running after the Israelis' car. Shawn and Barry, who have left the car and are now walking on both sides of the street, have not noticed him till he jumps Barry, grabs his shirt, and starts yelling that this man has tried to hurt Mash'al. Shawn, who is on the other sidewalk, across the street, rushes to his partner's aid. He slams into Abu Seif, wounding him slightly in the head, and throws him into a roadside ditch. The struggle continues; a crowd quickly assembles around them and converges on the two foreigners who seem to be beating a fellow Arab. A police officer appears on the scene, disperses the crowd, stops a taxi, and makes the two strangers and the badly beaten Abu Seif get in. The taxi heads for the police station.

At the police station, the officers at first thought that Abu Seif had attacked the two foreigners; but after he recovered from the beating, he accused them of assaulting Mash'al. The Jordanian investigators checked the passports of the two men, and when they realized they were Canadians, they alerted the Canadian consul. The diplomat spoke for a short while with Shawn and Barry, and told the Jordanians: "I don't know who these guys are, but of one thing I am sure—Canadians they're not!"

The Jordanians, still unaware of the treasure that had fallen into their hands, decided to keep the two foreigners in custody and allowed them to make one phone call. The agents reached Mossad operational headquarters in Europe and reported their arrest. Simultaneously, a female agent, who had taken part in the operation and watched the scene in front of Shamia Center, understood that a serious failure had occurred, and decided to alert "the heart patient," Mishka Ben-David, the senior Mossad officer in the Jordanian capital. She rushed to his hotel. Seeing her, he immediately understood that the worst had happened. The standing orders for the operation were that no one was to come near him, with one exception: if the operation had misfired and all agents had to be pulled out of the country at once.

Ben-David discarded his robe, dressed quickly, and hurried to the secret meeting place that had been prepared beforehand. Soon after, the operation commander arrived as well. He, too, was aware of the failure. Yet none of them could imagine the chaos that was about to unfold.

Mishka sent an immediate report to Mossad headquarters. *Ramsad* Danny Yatom discussed the situation with the department heads, and decided to order the agents to seek refuge at the Israeli embassy in Amman—and not use the escape route they had rehearsed beforehand. Back in Jordan, everyone left the meeting place and headed for the embassy. Only the doctor remained in the hotel.

In the meantime, in a different Amman neighborhood, the poison had begun its deadly work on Mash'al. He collapsed and was taken to a hospital. The Israelis realized that if he did not get the antidote, he was going to die in a few hours.

Netanyahu received the bad news in his car, while on his way to a Jewish New Year's party at . . . Mossad headquarters—an amazing coincidence. Yatom briefed the prime minister. Netanyahu was appalled. He decided that the *ramsad* should fly to Amman immediately, meet with King Hussein, and tell him everything, without any diversion or lies. From Mossad headquarters, the prime minister called King Hussein and told him he was sending over the *ramsad* on a very important matter. The king agreed right away, even though he had no idea what the meeting was about.

Netanyahu's aides, who were at his side at that time, maintain that he was overwhelmed with anxiety and instructed Yatom to agree to any demand of the king in exchange for the return of the agents to Israel. He also ordered Yatom to offer the antidote to the Jordanians and save Mash'al from certain death. Sharon would say later: "I saw Netanyahu in the Mash'al affair. He went to pieces completely and we had to assemble him again . . . He was under pressure and was ready to give up everything . . ."

King Hussein, distraught, listened to Yatom's report and ordered his people to find out what Mash'al's condition was. The accurate diagnosis arrived right away: the man's condition was quickly deteriorating. The king ordered him transferred immediately to the royal hospital, and accepted Yatom's offer of the antidote that could save him. In an absurd twist in this harrowing affair, the Israelis and the Jordanians engaged in a race against time to save the life of their enemy, an arch-terrorist.

Mishka Ben-David returned to the hotel. The ampoule of the antidote was in his pocket. "I was moving around with the antidote in my possession," he said in a later interview with Ronen Bergman, "knowing that it is of no use anymore, as none of our men had been affected by the poison. Only our target was in critical condition. I decided to destroy the antidote, as I feared I might be caught with it. But then I got a call from the unit commander in Israel. He asked me if I still had the antidote, and when I said yes, he asked me to go down to the hotel lobby. A captain of the Jordanian Army was waiting there for me, he said, and he had to take the antidote to the hospital right away."

But at that moment, another unexpected problem arose: the doctor who was supposed to administer the antidote to the dying Mash'al refused to do it unless the *ramsad* ordered her to do so in person. Danny Yatom, who had left the royal palace and was on his way to the embassy, called her and ordered her to go with Mishka. But upon their arrival at the hospital, the Jordanians flatly refused to have an Israeli doctor inject the antidote. Perhaps they feared she would only try to finish the job . . .

Complicating things further, the king's physician, who was charged with saving Mash'al, refused to administer the antidote without knowing the chemical formulas of the poison and of the antidote. He did not want to assume responsibility for Mash'al's life, lest the Israelis outsmart him and kill the man. A new crisis broke out. Both sides entrenched themselves in their positions, the Jordanians demanding the formulas and the Israelis refusing.

Mash'al's condition worsened rapidly. He stopped breathing and was connected to a respirator in the intensive-care unit of the royal hospital. It was clear to everybody involved that if Mash'al died, it would be disastrous for the fragile relations of the two countries. The king, who felt deeply hurt by the Israelis, even threatened to order his army to break into the embassy and arrest the four Mossad agents, who had found refuge there. He also said that he would put an end to any political and military cooperation with Israel.

The hours ticked by and the tension kept growing. The king announced that if Mash'al died, he would sentence his killers—the two agents kept in custody by the Jordanian police—to death. He also placed an urgent call to U.S. president Bill Clinton.

The Americans immediately started pressuring Israel to deliver the formula to the Jordanians. Netanyahu plunged into a marathon of meetings with various groups of advisers and cabinet ministers. He finally yielded and gave the formula to the Jordanians.

The Jordanian doctor administered the antidote to Mash'al. The reaction was immediate. Mash'al opened his eyes.

When the news about Mash'al's recovery reached Israel, everybody let out a sigh of relief, as if their long-lost brother in Jordan was saved, thank God!

Mishka Ben-David and the doctor were able to leave Jordan. Six Mossad agents remained in Amman—four at the embassy, and two held by the Jordanian police.

In the intensive-care unit, Mash'al's condition kept improving. Israel sent a high-level delegation to Amman, which included Prime Minister Benjamin Netanyahu, Minister of Foreign Affairs Ariel Sharon, and Minister of Defense Yitzhak Mordechai. King Hussein, however, refused to receive the delegation and sent his brother Hassan to meet them.

The cabinet also summoned Efraim Halevy, a former deputy *ramsad* and King Hussein's personal friend. Halevy was now Israel's ambassador to the

European Union in Brussels. He traveled to Amman immediately, and offered the king a deal. In exchange for the four agents at the embassy, Israel would release from prison the charismatic founder and leader of Hamas, the Sheikh Ahmed Yassin. The king agreed, and the four agents returned to Israel with Halevy.

The final negotiation was entrusted to Ariel Sharon, who maintained close relations with the king.

Sharon demanded the release of the two Kidon agents who were still in custody. In exchange, the Jordanians demanded the release of twenty Jordanian prisoners held by Israel. Sharon agreed. But at the last moment, the Jordanians changed their mind, and demanded more concessions from Israel. Sharon lost his cool in the presence of the king. "If you continue like this," he angrily said, "our people will remain in your hands, we'll cut your water (which Israel was supplying to Jordan), and we'll kill Mash'al one more time."

Sharon's outburst turned out to be very effective, and the deal was closed. Two Israeli helicopters landed in Jordan. One of them took the two Kidon agents back to Israel, the other one brought over Sheikh Yassin, who had been released from prison.

The Israeli and world media criticized and ridiculed the Mossad operation in Jordan. Netanyahu was also harshly attacked for his handling of the affair; he had no choice but to establish a board of inquiry, to investigate "the operational failure in Jordan."

The board completely cleared the prime minister, but blamed the *ramsad* for "faults in his performance" and for launching an operation that was bound to fail from the start. Yet they did not ask for Yatom's resignation.

Following the fiasco in Amman, Jordan's relations with Israel reached a new low. Khaled Mash'al, who was still a minor figure in Hamas, gained stature in the organization and became one of its major leaders. After Sheikh Yassin's death, Mash'al rose to the overall leadership of Hamas. The prestige of the Mossad in Israel and the world—and even in the eyes of its leaders and agents—was badly scarred. Danny Yatom, who had failed all throughout the operation, was openly criticized by many of the Mossad senior officers. Aliza Magen, Yatom's deputy, bluntly said that he was not qualified to be a *ramsad*.

In spite of the criticism, Yatom wouldn't resign. The only one who assumed responsibility for the mishap was the head of Caesarea, who immediately submitted his resignation. It took five more months—till February 1998, when a Mossad agent was arrested in Switzerland while trying to tap the phone line of a Hezbollah member—for Yatom to finally give in. "I assumed a commander's responsibility," he said in an interview with the *Haaretz* newspaper, "and decided to resign because of the mishaps in Jordan and Switzerland."

He was replaced by Efraim Halevy, the former deputy *ramsad* who had successfully negotiated with King Hussein the release of the four agents involved in the Mash'al fiasco.

CHAPTER EIGHTEEN

FROM NORTH KOREA
WITH LOVE

On a pleasant London evening in July 2007, a guest left his room in a Kensington hotel. He took the elevator to the lobby and went out to a car waiting for him by the entrance. He was a senior Syrian official who had arrived from Damascus that very afternoon. Now he was on his way to a meeting.

As soon as he exited through the revolving doors, two men got up from armchairs in a far corner of the lobby. They knew exactly where to go. Reaching the Syrian's room, they gained access with a special electronic device. They were ready to search the room methodically, but this time, their task was easy. A laptop computer was on the desk. The two men turned it on and, within moments, expertly installed a sophisticated version of a Trojan horse software. The program allowed them to monitor and copy from afar all the files stored in the computer's memory. The job done, the two men left the hotel undetected.

Mossad analysts in Tel Aviv studied the computer files and were stunned. At an urgent meeting of department heads, they described the priceless information that had fallen into their hands: a collection of files, photographs, drawings, and documents that exposed, for the first time, Syria's top-secret nuclear program. The material was of supreme importance and included the construction plans for a nuclear reactor in a remote desert area; correspondence between the Syrian government and high-level officials in the North Korean administration; and photographs showing the reactor encased in concrete. Another photograph showed two men—one of them turned out to be a senior official in the North Korean atomic project and the other was Ibrahim Othman, the head of the Syrian Atomic Energy Commission.

The findings confirmed several fragmentary reports that had reached the Israel intelligence community in 2006 and 2007. The reports indicated that the Syrian government was building, in utmost secrecy, a nuclear reactor at the desert site of Dir Al-Zur, in the far northeast of the country. The isolated site was adjacent to the Turkish border, and some hundred miles from Iraqi territory. Perhaps the most surprising revelation in the reports was the fact that the Syrian facility was being planned and supervised by North Korean nuclear experts and financed by Iran.

The close cooperation between Syria and North Korea had started with the 1990 visit to Damascus of North Korea's president, Kim Il-sung. During that visit, at the instigation of Syrian president Hafez Al-Assad, the two countries had signed an agreement on military and technological cooperation. Even though the nuclear issue was discussed in talks between the two heads of state, Assad decided to give it only secondary priority at that time and concerned himself mostly with the development of chemical and biological weapons. Moreover, he canceled plans to buy nuclear reactors from Russia. In February 1991, during Operation Desert Storm, a first shipment of Scud missiles from North Korea was unloaded in Syria. Reports on the existence of the missiles reached Moshe Arens, Israel's minister of defense. Several army generals recommended a military strike be initiated to destroy the Scuds before they became operational. Arens dismissed the idea, wishing to avoid another conflagration in the region.

At Hafez Al-Assad's funeral in June 2000, his son and successor, Bashar Al-Assad, met with another North Korean delegation. The two parties secretly discussed the construction of a nuclear facility in Syria, to be overseen by the Syrian Scientific Research Agency. In July 2002, another secret meeting was held in Damascus, with the participation of senior officials from Syria, Iran, and North Korea, at which a tripartite agreement was reached. North Korea would construct a nuclear reactor in Syria, to be financed by Iran. The cost of the entire project, from the drawing board to the production of weapons-grade plutonium, was estimated at $2 billion.

For the next five years, despite small scraps of information that trickled from Damascus, neither the CIA nor the Mossad were aware of the Syrian project. Several warning lights had flashed sporadically, but had been ignored. The American intelligence services failed to grasp the meaning of the information that had accumulated, while the Mossad and Aman were misled by their own estimates that Syria had neither the capability nor the desire to obtain nuclear weapons. And no one sought to challenge that misconception, although evidence was there: in 2005, the cargo ship *Andorra*, a ship carrying cement from North Korea to Syria, sank close to the Israeli coastal town of Nahariya; in 2006, a second North Korean cargo vessel, sailing under a Panamanian flag, was detained in Cyprus with another cargo of cement and a portable radar station; in both cases, the "cement" was evidently equipment for the nuclear reactor. Finally, in late 2006, Iranian nuclear experts visited Damascus to inspect the progress of the construction of the facility. The Israeli and American intelligence services knew of this visit but failed to realize that it was linked to the Dir Al-Zur project.

The Syrians took extreme precautions to protect the secrecy of the project. They imposed a total communications blackout on all the staff working at the site. Possession of cell phones and satellite devices was strictly forbidden; all communications were taken out by messengers, who carried letters and messages and delivered them by hand. The activity at the site could not be identified from space, even though American and Israeli satellites kept passing overhead.

And then, suddenly, on February 7, 2007, a passenger alighted from a plane at Damascus Airport. He was Ali Reza Asgari, an Iranian general and a former deputy minister of defense, who had been one of the leaders of the Revolutionary Guards (see chapter 2). He stayed at the airport until he received confirmation that his family had left Iran. He then flew on to Turkey. Soon after landing in Istanbul, he vanished.

A month later, it was learned that Asgari had defected to the West in an operation masterminded by the CIA and the Mossad. He was interrogated and debriefed at an American base in Germany, where he revealed the existence of the Syrian-Iranian nuclear plans and the agreement between North Korea, Iran, and Syria. He told his interlocutors that Iran was not only financing the Dir Al-Zur project but was exerting strong pressure on Syria to complete it as soon as possible. He supplied the CIA and the Mossad with a wealth of detail about the progress of the project, and identified the key officials in both Syria and Iran, who were involved in it.

This new information shocked the Mossad into action and it immediately switched into an operational mode. Since 2002, the *ramsad* was Meir Dagan, who had replaced Efraim Halevy (see chapter 1). According to foreign sources, Dagan assigned units and agents to verify the Asgari report. Prime Minister Ehud Olmert convened a meeting of the army chiefs of staff, the Ministry of Defense, and the intelligence services. They unanimously agreed that an urgent operation was called for, so as to obtain solid and irrefutable information about the Dir Al-Zur facility. Israel could not accept the transformation of Syria, its most implacable and aggressive foe, into a power with the potential to manufacture nuclear weapons.

It was just five months after Asgari's defection that the Mossad agents achieved their major breakthrough—the laptop of the Syrian official. The heads of the Mossad and Aman could now present Prime Minister Olmert with the definitive evidence the government needed.

Soon after, Dagan allegedly pulled off another coup. In a bold and creative operation, a Mossad case officer managed to recruit one of the scientists employed at the reactor itself. He photographed the reactor extensively, both inside and out, and even made a video of the structures and equipment inside them. These were the first images the Mossad had received of the reactor, taken at ground level. They revealed a large cylindrical structure with thin but solid fortified walls. Other pictures showed an external scaffold designed to strengthen the reactor's outer walls. There were also photos of a second, smaller building equipped with oil pumps, and several trucks could be seen parked around it. A third structure was apparently a tower that supplied water for the reactor.

The Mossad kept the Americans fully briefed at every step and furnished them with copies of all reports and photos, including satellite pictures and transcripts of phone calls between Syria and North Korea. Under relentless pressure from Israel, the United States put its own satellites on the case. Both the satellite pictures and electronic tracking of the exchange of phone calls indicated that the Syrians were constructing at breakneck speed.

In June 2007, Prime Minister Olmert flew to Washington with all the material Israel had collected. He met with President Bush and told him Israel had decided that the Syrian reactor had to be destroyed. Olmert suggested that the United States carry out an air strike against the reactor, but the American president refused. According to American sources, the White House responded that "the U.S. chooses not to attack [the reactor]." Secretary of State Condoleezza Rice and Defense Secretary Robert Gates tried to persuade Israel "to confront [the Syrians] but not attack." Bush and National Security Adviser Steve Hadley expressed their support for military action in principle, but asked that any operation be delayed until more clearly threatening intelligence could be obtained.

In July 2007, Israel carried out high-altitude air sorties and programmed its Ofek-7 spy satellite to take detailed photographs of the reactor. These photos, when analyzed by American and Israeli experts, established clearly that Syria was building a reactor identical to North Korea's nuclear facility at Yongbyon. A video that Israel shared with the United States showed that the cores of both reactors were identical, including the way in which the uranium rods were placed inside the structure. Other videos even showed the faces of North Korean engineers working inside the reactor. Additionally, the Aman intercept department, Unit 8200, produced full transcripts of hectic exchanges between Damascus and Pyongyang.

All this evidence was relayed to Washington, but the United States still demanded irrefutable proof that the facility was indeed a nuclear reactor and that radioactive materials were actually in place. Israel felt it had no choice but to obtain this information as well.

In August 2007, Israel came up with the ultimate proof that the facility at Dir Al-Zur was a nuclear reactor. It was obtained by an elite commando unit, Sayeret Matkal, in an operation that risked the lives of scores of Israeli soldiers. Sayeret Matkal commandos flew to Syria by night in two helicopters. They were wearing Syrian Army uniforms. Bypassing populated areas, military bases, and radar stations, they landed undetected close to Dir Al-Zur, then approached the reactor site and collected soil samples from the earth surrounding the reactor. Upon analysis back in Israel, these samples were found to be highly radioactive, proving irrefutably that radioactive substances were indeed on site.

This new evidence was presented to Steve Hadley. Once his experts had checked the soil samples, he realized that the matter was deadly serious. He summoned his closest aides, and their conclusions were brought before President Bush at Hadley's daily briefing at the Oval Office. Hadley then held talks with Dagan, and concluded that the reactor indeed posed a clear and present danger. The United States now accepted that the Syrian reactor had to be eliminated, and code-named the Dir Al-Zur operation "The Orchard." In his memoirs, George W. Bush wrote that he considered for a while attacking the reactor, but after discussing the options with his national security team, he finally decided against it. He felt that "bombing a sovereign country with no warning or announced justification would create severe blowback." He also ruled out a covert raid by U.S. soldiers.

Nevertheless, Olmert phoned President Bush and asked him to destroy the reactor. During the phone conversation, Bush was in the Oval Office, surrounded by his closest aides: Secretary of State Condoleezza Rice, Vice President Dick Cheney, Steve Hadley and his deputy Elliott Abrams, and others. In the preliminary consultations, Rice had convinced them to reject Israel's demand.

"George, I'm asking you to bomb the compound," Olmert said.

"I cannot justify an attack on a sovereign nation," Bush replied, "unless my intelligence agencies stand up and say it's a weapons program." Bush recommended "using diplomacy."

"Your strategy is very disturbing to me," Olmert bluntly said. "I'll do what I believe necessary to protect Israel."

"This guy has balls," Bush later said. "That's why I like him."

According to London's *Sunday Times*, Prime Minister Olmert met with Minister of Defense Ehud Barak and Minister of Foreign Affairs Tzippi Livni. The three of them, together with the heads of the defense and intelligence communities, discussed the new evidence, as well as the possible repercussions of a military strike. Finally the die was cast: the Syrian reactor would be eliminated. The prime minister briefed opposition leader Benjamin Netanyahu and received his wholehearted support.

The date for the attack was set for the night of September 5, 2007.

The previous day, according to a later report in the *Sunday Times*, another elite commando unit, Shaldag (Kingfisher) had reached the Dir Al-Zur area. The men spent almost a day in hiding close to the reactor. Their mission was to illuminate the reactor with laser beams the following night so the air force jets could home in directly on the target. At eleven P.M. on September 5, ten F-15 aircraft took off from the Ramat David Air Force Base and headed west, over the Mediterranean. Thirty minutes later, three of the planes were ordered to return to base. The other seven were instructed to head for the Turkish-Syrian border, and turn south toward Dir Al-Zur. On the way, they bombed a radar station, crippling the Syrian air defense's ability to identify the approach of foreign aircraft. Minutes later, they reached Dir Al-Zur; and from a carefully calculated distance, they launched Maverick air-to-surface missiles and half-ton bombs, hitting their target with precision. The Syrian reactor, intended to build atomic bombs for Israel's destruction, was obliterated in seconds.

Prime Minister Olmert, anxious to avoid a Syrian military reaction, established urgent contact with the prime minister of Turkey, Tayyip Erdogan, and asked him to convey a message to President Assad. Israel had no intention of going to war with Syria, Olmert emphasized, but could not accept a nuclear Syria on its doorstep. But Olmert's reassurance proved unnecessary. On the morning after the bombing, the reaction from Damascus was total silence. Not a word was uttered by government spokesmen. Only at three o'clock that afternoon was an official statement issued by the Syrian news agency. It stated that Israeli aircraft had penetrated Syrian air space at one A.M. "Our air force forced them to retreat, after [they had] dropped ammunition over a deserted area. There was no damage to people or equipment."

The world media was desperate to learn how the Mossad had managed to obtain photos and even videos from the interior of the Syrian reactor. ABC Television reported that Israel either had planted an agent inside the Syrian reactor or the Mossad had recruited one of the engineers who had supplied it with the pictures of the facility.

In April 2008, some seven months after the destruction of the reactor, the American administration finally announced that the Syrian facility had been a nuclear reactor built with North Korean support and that "it was not designed for peaceful uses." George W. Bush thought Olmert's "execution of the strike" against the Syrian reactor had restored the confidence he had lost in the Israelis during their 2006 war against Lebanon, which Bush felt was bungled.

Officials in the U.S. intelligence community showed amazed congressmen and senators slides that made clear the similarity between the Syrian reactor and the North Korean Yongbyon reactor; a slide show with the satellite photos, drawings, and plans—as well as the videos—established the provenance of these materials.

* * *

Israel succeeded in keeping the secret for just two weeks, during which it
denied it had attacked the reactor. But then opposition leader Benjamin
Netanyahu, interviewed on a live newscast, declared: "When the cabinet
takes action for Israel's security, I give it my full backing . . . and here,
too, I was a partner in this affair from the first moment and I gave it my
full support."

A final episode in the Syrian nuclear project took place eleven months
later, on August 2, 2008. That evening, a convivial dinner party
was taking place on the spacious veranda of a beach house at Rimal El-
Zahabiya, north of the Syrian port of Tartus. The house, close to the
water, had a spectacular view of the Mediterranean. The veranda, facing
the dark waves, was a welcome refuge from the humidity of the Syrian
coast. A soft sea breeze cooled the stifling midsummer heat. The guests,
seated at an oblong table, were close friends of the villa's owner, General
Muhammad Suleiman, who had invited them for a relaxing weekend.

Suleiman was President Assad's closest adviser on military and defense
matters. He had supervised the building of the reactor and managed its
security. In the highest circles of power in Syria he was regarded as Assad's
shadow. His office was in the palace, adjacent to that of the president, yet he
was known only to a select few both inside and outside the country.

His name was never mentioned in the Syrian media, but the Mossad
knew of him and had followed his activities closely. The forty-seven-year-
old Suleiman had studied engineering at Damascus University, where he
had met and befriended another student, Bassel Al-Assad, the favorite son
and heir apparent of President Hafez Al-Assad. When Bassel was killed in
a road accident in 1994, Assad introduced Suleiman to his younger son,
Bashar. Assad died of cancer in 2000 and Bashar replaced him as president,
and then appointed Suleiman his confidant and trusted aide.

Suleiman soon became one of the most powerful men in Syria. President Assad charged him with supervision of all sensitive military mat-

ters. He became the senior liaison between the president and the Iranian intelligence services, especially on matters concerning their secret cooperation with terrorist organizations in the Middle East. He was also the primary Syrian contact with Hezbollah and maintained a close relationship with that organization's military chief, Imad Mughniyeh. After Israel had withdrawn from the security zone in South Lebanon, in May 2000, Suleiman took charge of the transfer of weapons from Iran and Syria to Hezbollah, especially the delivery of long-range rockets. During the Second Lebanon War in 2006, one such rocket scored a direct hit on the Israeli railway workshops in Haifa, killing eight workers. Later on, Suleiman supplied Hezbollah with Syrian-manufactured surface-to-air missiles, thus jeopardizing Israel's air activities in Lebanon.

And Suleiman held another, unique and top-secret position: he was a senior member of the Syrian Research Committee that dealt with the development of long-range rockets, chemical and biological weapons, and nuclear research. He had overseen the liaison with North Korea, coordinated the shipment of reactor parts to Syria, and directed the security measures isolating the North Korean technicians and engineers working on the construction of the reactor.

Israel's destruction of the reactor was a heavy blow for Suleiman. After recovering from the initial shock, he started planning another reactor, the location of which was yet to be decided. But Suleiman's life had become more difficult. He knew now that he was wanted by both the American and Israeli secret services. So, before embarking on plans for his next stage, he took a few days leave at his home in Rimal El-Zahabiya. A quiet weekend with good friends and excellent food seemed the best way to alleviate his stress.

From the center of his large table, Suleiman watched the waves rolling toward the beach. But he failed to notice two motionless figures crouching in the water some 150 yards away. They had swum in from the sea, where a boat had dropped them off about a mile from Suleiman's home. Israeli naval commandos and expert sharpshooters, they carried scuba equipment and had made their way under water to the beach opposite the house. As their feet touched bottom, they stood and picked out Suleiman's home. They studied the house and the veranda, looked at all the people seated at the table, and focused on their target: the general sitting between his guests.

At nine P.M., the sharpshooters calibrated their sights and adjusted the range. The veranda was crowded, and the two uninvited guests in their black diving suits wanted to make sure they could fire at the general without harming anybody else. They emerged from the water and took a few steps, then aimed their weapons equipped with silencers at Suleiman's head. An electronic signal beeped in their earphones and they fired simultaneously. The shots were fatal. Suleiman's head flew back and he collapsed forward, onto the food-laden table. The guests at first did not grasp what had happened. Only when they noticed the blood oozing from Suleiman's head did they understand he had been shot. All hell broke loose on the veranda; some trying to come to their host's aid, others crouching in fear or aimlessly running around, shouting and yelling. In the uproar, the two sharpshooters disappeared.

The *Sunday Times* published a slightly different version of the event. It said that the sharpshooters were members of the Israeli naval commando, Flotilla 13, who had arrived on the Syrian coast aboard a yacht belonging to an Israeli businessman, and had sailed back immediately after fulfilling their mission.

When the news reached Damascus, it caused a tremendous shock, but the government kept silent and did not respond to the media coverage. The military and security establishments were confused. How did the hit team reach Tartus, which was 140 miles away from Damascus? How did they escape? Was there no place in Syria where its leaders were safe?

Only after a few days a laconic communiqué was issued, announcing that "Syria is undertaking an investigation to find the perpetrators of this crime." But the press in other Arab countries had not waited for this official reaction. From the outset, it had published extensive coverage, with detailed reports and speculation about the identity of the assassins. The Arab media focused on who had an interest in eliminating this general and pointed an accusing finger at Israel, claiming that Israel had carried out the assassination because of Suleiman's role in the Dir Al-Zur reactor.

The reaction of the Western secret services was different. None shed a tear over Suleiman's death. In June 2010, Flotilla 13 was decorated by the commander in chief of the Israel Defense Forces for "several feats of arms," the nature of which was not revealed.

One may wonder if the honors bestowed on the naval commando unit are not, at least in part, in recognition of the Suleiman operation.

CHAPTER NINETEEN

LOVE AND DEATH IN THE AFTERNOON

On February 12, 2008, several men surreptitiously fanned out around an apartment building in an exclusive Damascus neighborhood. In the late afternoon they saw a silver Mitsubishi Pajero SUV parked by the building. A man in a black suit, with a smartly trimmed beard, got out of the vehicle and entered the house. He was not accompanied by bodyguards. The agents posted on the street whispered in their miniature transmitters that "the man" had arrived in Damascus and he was on his way to the apartment. They knew that the man in black was about to meet his secret lover, Nihad Haidar, a Syrian woman, who was waiting for him in the apartment. The man was carrying a present for gorgeous Nihad, who celebrated her thirtieth birthday that week.

The lovers spent a few hours in the luxurious apartment that was left at their disposal by Rami Makhlouf, a successful businessman and the cousin of Syrian president Bashar Al-Assad.

Shortly before ten P.M., the man in black left the building and got into the silver Pajero. He was on his way to a meeting in a discreet safe house, in the Kafr Soussa neighborhood, where he met with Iranian, Syrian, and Palestinian envoys.

According to the London *Sunday Express*, the agents following him checked an updated photo of the man on the screens of their mobile phones to make sure there would be no identification mistake. They kept open lines of transmission and reported every move of the "mark" to the Mossad command post.

When he left the building, where he had spent a few hours with Nihad, the agents had a good opportunity to check his face against the photos on their screens. They confirmed the identification to their colleagues in Damascus and to headquarters in Tel Aviv. An overwhelming tension swept the Mossad. The department heads gathered in Meir Dagan's office, where all the necessary equipment was set up for monitoring the operation in real time.

The man started the silver Pajero.

"He's on his way," whispered one of the agents into his miniature mike.

The man in the silver Pajero was Imad Mughniyeh, who had left a bloody trail, years-long, behind him.

November 15, 2001.

Following the attack on the Twin Towers, the FBI publishes a large poster containing the list of the most-wanted terrorists in the world.

The poster is stamped with the logos of the FBI, the State Department, and the Department of Justice.

The list shows twenty-two names and twenty-two pictures.

The first name is the most dangerous of them all.

The award for his capture is $5 million.

Until the attack on the Twin Towers, he had been considered as responsible for the deaths of more Americans than any other living terrorist.

Imad Mughniyeh.

April 18, 1983—bombing of the American embassy in Beirut, Lebanon —63 dead.

October 23, 1983—bombing of the U.S. Marines headquarters in Beirut —241 dead.

October 23, 1983 (same day)—bombing of the French paratrooper headquarters in Beirut—58 dead.

And the abduction and murder of CIA official William Buckley; several attacks on the American embassy in Kuwait; hijacking of a TWA airliner and two planes of the Kuwait airline; the murder of Colonel W. R. Higgins of the UN observer force in South Lebanon; massacre of twenty American soldiers in Saudi Arabia . . .

When the above list is sent to Israel, the Mossad adds its own data:

November 4, 1983—bombing of the IDF headquarters in Tyre, Lebanon —60 dead.

March 10, 1985—attack on an IDF convoy by Metullah, on the Israeli-Lebanese border—8 dead.

March 17, 1992—bombing of the Israeli embassy in Argentina—29 dead.

July 18, 1994—bombing of the Jewish community center in Buenos Aires—86 dead.

And the abduction and murder of three Israeli soldiers at the Har Dov border sector, the abduction of Israeli businessman Elhanan Tannenbaum, a bombing near kibbutz Matzuba, and the most destructive of them all: the abduction and murder of the soldiers Regev and Goldwasser on the Israeli-Lebanese border, which triggered the Second Lebanon War.

Imad Mughniyeh, the arch-terrorist behind all those crimes, was a ghost, who moved constantly between the Middle East capitals. He evaded photographers and refused to be interviewed. The Western secret services knew a lot about his activities, but almost nothing about his outward appearance, his habits, and his hideouts. They knew he was born in 1962, in a South Lebanon village. According to the fragmentary reports, his parents were devoted Shiites; while in his teens, he had moved to Beirut and grown up in a poor neighborhood mostly populated by Palestinians, supporters of the PLO. He had dropped out of high school and joined the Fatah, the terrorist branch of the PLO. Later he had become the body-guard of Abu Ayad, Arafat's deputy, and became a member of Force 17, the special security unit of the Fatah organization that was formed in the mid-seventies and commanded by Ali Hassan Salameh, the Red Prince (see chapter 12). But in 1982, Israel launched the Lebanon war, called Operation Peace for Galilee, invaded Lebanon, and crushed the PLO. Its surviving members, headed by Yasser Arafat, were exiled to Tunisia. Mughniyeh, though, decided to stay behind and joined the first group of Hezbollah founders.

The Hezbollah—literally, the Party of God—was a Shiite terrorist organization created in 1982 in response to the Israeli invasion of Lebanon. Inspired by the Ayatollah Khomeini, trained and supplied by the Iranian Revolutionary Guards, the Hezbollah became Israel's vile enemy, defining its main goal as "Israel's final departure from Lebanon as a prelude to its final obliteration." From the first day of its existence, Hezbollah engaged in violent acts of terrorism against Israel. And Mughniyeh was an ideal recruit for the nascent group.

As a real man of shadows, he chose to operate in secret and refrained from appearing in public. The reports about him became fragmentary and often contradictory. One source described him as the bodyguard of Sheikh Fadlallah, the Hezbollah spiritual leader—while another claimed he had become the operations chief of the organization, the brain behind Hezbollah's most risky actions, which ended in bloodbaths. Unlike the present Hezbollah leader, the Sheikh Nasrallah, Mughniyeh never appeared on television and never made hateful speeches; but in reality he was far more dangerous than the loquacious sheikh. He soon rose to the position of the most efficient and most elusive terrorist in the world, like Carlos in his time, and like his colleague and great admirer Osama bin Laden.

Mughniyeh was a cruel and creative terrorist. He emerged suddenly, when he planned and commanded several mass massacres in Lebanon, at the end of Operation Peace for Galilee. He was only twenty-one years old on this day in October 1983, when he sent explosive-laden trucks, driven by suicide bombers, to the compounds of the American Marines and the French paratroopers in Beirut; a few days later, he repeated the same scenario against the IDF headquarters in Tyre. At twenty-two, he led a group of terrorists on an attack against the fortified American embassy in Kuwait and afterward hijacked his first plane there. After each of his operations, he vanished into thin air. At twenty-three, Mughniyeh hijacked a TWA plane on its way from Athens to Rome and forced its pilot to land in Beirut airport. During the hijacking, he murdered navy diver Robert Dean Stethem and threw his body out the cockpit door. Mughniyeh escaped after the hijacking operation that lasted seventeen days, but this time he left behind a memento: his fingerprint in the aircraft restroom.

Almost nothing was known about his private life, except for his marriage to his cousin, who gave him a son and a daughter. At a very early age, he knew he was in the crosshairs of several Western secret services, and tried to conceal his identity. He went through a rudimentary plastic surgery in Libya, grew a beard, and stayed out of the limelight. Only a single confirmed photo of Mughniyeh—fat, bearded, wearing glasses and a visor cap—made its way to the Western services. His description was flawed as well—the FBI portrayed him as "born in Lebanon, speaking Arabic, brown hair and beard, height 5'8" (170 centimeters), weight 120 pounds (about 60 kilograms)." It is hard to imagine how Mughniyeh's generous dimensions managed to shrink into a 120-pound model body . . . But the description only reconfirmed that Mughniyeh protected himself well and succeeded in misleading all his enemies.

After all the attacks, bombings, and hijackings he carried out, he became an admired hero of the Hezbollah. He was lauded for his sophistication, his bravery, and his operational talents that made the Hezbollah's military arm feared by the world's intelligence services. As his power increased, he became a major target for assassination by Israel and the West. Mughniyeh realized this, and became a paranoid who lived a life of eternal flight, suspected everybody, including his closest confidants, changed his bodyguards very often, and slept every night in another place; his trips between Beirut, Damascus, and Tehran took place under a thick veil of secrecy.

According to the profile prepared by Israel and other secret services, Mughniyeh was a loner, very charismatic, very impulsive, and very knowledgeable about the newest electronic instruments and gadgets. He had an uncanny capacity for changing identities and appearances, which enabled him to fool his enemies; Israeli secret agents used to call him "the terrorist with nine lives."

Aman officer David Barkai, a former major in the secret intelligence Unit 504 that assembled the profile file on Mughniyeh, said in an interview to the British *Sunday Times:* "We tried to knock him down several times in the late 1980s. We accumulated intelligence on him, but the closer we got, the less information we gleaned—no weak points, no women, money, drugs—nothing."

The hunt for Mughniyeh lasted for many years. In 1988, he was almost captured by the French authorities when his plane made a stopover in Paris. The CIA had supplied the French with information about Mughniyeh, including his photograph and some details about the false passport he was using. But the French feared that his arrest might cause the murder of the French hostages that were held in Lebanon at that time, so they chose to ignore his presence and let him go away. The American services tried to capture him in Europe in 1986 and in Saudi Arabia in 1995. But he disappeared, as always.

In those years, Mughniyeh was deeply involved in planning and executing attacks on Israelis and Jews in Argentina. In 1992, he organized the bombing of the Israeli embassy in Buenos Aires by a truck stuffed with explosives, driven by a suicide bomber. Twenty-nine people were killed. Some of the heads of the Mossad saw in the operation an act of revenge for the killing of Hezbollah's leader Sheikh Abbas Al-Musawi, in a helicopter attack in South Lebanon.

Two years later, another bombing shook Buenos Aires, this time at the Jewish community center, leaving eighty-six dead. Once again, some experts thought Hezbollah was avenging the abduction by Israel of one of its leaders, Mustafa Dirani, in Lebanon.

Intelligence crews from the United States and Israel, who flew to Buenos Aires to investigate the two bombings, concluded that they were connected.

The modus operandi was identical—loading a truck with explosives and sending it to its target with a suicide bomber behind the wheel. Mughniyeh had used exactly the same method in Beirut and in Tyre at the outset of his career. The investigators established that the Iranian secret services and their local collaborators were involved in the bombings as well. At least one of the trucks, the one that had served for the embassy bombing, had been sold to the terrorists by a Buenos Aires Shiite car dealer, Carlos Alberto Taladin. The trail clearly led to Imad Mughniyeh.

In those years, Mughniyeh spent long stretches of time in Iran. After the assassination of Sheikh Al-Musawi, he feared that Israel would try to kill him, too. In Tehran, he created an operational team, composed of Hezbollah fighters and Iranian intelligence officers. His partners in setting up that unit were the Commander in Chief of the Revolutionary Guards Mohsen Rezaee, and the Minister of Intelligence Ali Fallahian. Apparently, that unit carried out the two deadly attacks in Buenos Aires. These attacks had one result: Mughniyeh became Israel's most wanted man. By his acts, he sentenced himself to death. But long years would pass by before his death sentence would be carried out.

In December 1994, Mughniyeh was seen in Beirut; shortly after, he escaped an assassination attempt by a booby-trapped car in a southern neighborhood. The Lebanese police quickly published its findings: an explosive charge had been placed underneath a car parked near the mosque where Sheikh Fadlallah read his sermon. The explosion destroyed the store of Fuad Mughniyeh, Imad's brother, and his body was found in the rubble. But Imad, who was supposed to be there, changed his mind at the last moment, decided not to come, and survived. His nine lives saved him again.

A few weeks after the bombing, the security services, acting jointly with the Hezbollah, arrested several civilians suspected of being involved in the attack, as Mossad collaborators. The main suspect was a man named Ahmed Halek.

According to the official police statement, "Halek and his wife had parked their car close to Fuad Mughniyeh's store. Halek entered the store to make sure that Fuad was there, shook his hand, returned to the car, and activated the bomb." The Lebanese newspaper *As-Safir*, quoting reliable sources, said that Halek had participated in a meeting with a senior Mossad official in Cyprus; the Mossad officer had instructed him how to use the bomb and paid him about $100,000. Halek was subsequently executed.

This time Mughniyeh escaped, but the Mossad agents did not give up. They painstakingly collected every small detail they could find, compiled reports from foreign intelligence services, and studied Mughniyeh's personal methods. In 2002, the Mossad received another report about Mughniyeh, linking him to the shipping of fifty tons of weapons to Palestinian terrorists. But then he vanished again, although rumors had it that he had become the commander in chief of the Hezbollah and the likely successor of Sheikh Nasrallah. His main connection was with Iranian intelligence, and he was said to act jointly with the Al-Quds (the Arab name of Jerusalem) Brigades, charged with the cooperation with Shiite communities throughout the world and with Iranian-controlled terrorist organizations. Mughniyeh's high position made it imperative for him to beef up his security measures. Persistent rumors affirmed that he once again had changed his outward appearance, possibly by another plastic surgery.

According to European sources, at the end of the Second Lebanon War, the Mossad recruited quite a few Palestinians living in Lebanon, those strongly opposed to the Hezbollah. One of them had a cousin in Mughniyeh's village. She told the newly recruited agent that Mughniyeh had traveled to Europe and returned to Lebanon with a totally different face.

The Mossad now had a new challenge—spying in plastic surgery clinics throughout Europe.

The unexpected breakthrough occured in Berlin. According to the British writer Gordon Thomas, the Mossad resident agent in Berlin, Reuven, met a German informer who maintained discreet connections with people in the former East Berlin. The informer reported that Imad Mughniyeh had recently gone through several plastic surgeries that completely changed his facial features. The treatment had taken place in a clinic that in the past had belonged to the Stasi, the former East German secret service. The Stasi had used the clinic for remodeling the faces of agents and terrorists sent on covert missions to the West.

After a tough negotiation, Reuven agreed to pay his German collaborator a substantial fee, and received from him a file containing thirty-four updated photos of Mughniyeh.

The analysis of the photos by Meir Dagan's experts showed that Mughniyeh had undergone jaw surgeries: the lower jaws had been cut, and bone taken from him had been grafted in them in order to achieve a more narrow chin line, which made him look skinny and emaciated. Several front teeth had been replaced by artificial teeth of a different shape. The eyes, too, had been treated by a tightening of the skin around them. The treatment was completed by dying his hair gray and replacing his eyeglasses with contact lenses. Mughniyeh bore no resemblance to the "original" anymore, and the old pictures collected by Western services since the eighties had become irrelevant.

According to foreign sources, the Mossad now started to plan Mughniyeh's killing. Meir Dagan summoned his best people, including the head of Caesarea, the commander of the Kidon team, and several other senior officers dealing with the Mughniyeh file. It soon became clear that there was no way to hit Mughniyeh in a non-Muslim country. He very rarely traveled to the West, and felt safe only in Iran and Syria. The Israelis knew any action on their territory would mean great risks. True, Israel had operated in Arab countries in the past and carried out coups in Beirut during its Operation Wrath of God; its commandos had even gone as far as Tunis, where they allegedly killed the terrorist leader Abu Jihad. But Tehran and Damascus were more suspicious, more heavily armed and dangerous than Beirut or Tunis. On the other hand, Meir Dagan knew the tremendous impact a successful operation would have. The killing of the most lethal terrorist leader in Damascus would prove that nobody can escape the long arm of the Mossad. The refuge and fortress of Israel's enemies would spread confusion, fear, and insecurity among the rest of the terrorist leaders.

According to the London *Independent* daily, the plan that emerged from the discussions at Mossad headquarters was based on the probability of

Mughniyeh coming to Damascus on February 12, 2008. On that day, he was supposed to meet Iranian and Syrian officials who were to participate in the celebration of the anniversary of the Iranian revolution.

After the possibilities had been studied, it was decided that the operation would be carried out by placing a rigged vehicle directly beside Mughniyeh's car.

The Mossad now plunged into frantic activity to get detailed intelligence from all its sources, including foreign services: Would Mughniyeh indeed come to Damascus? And if he did—what identity would he choose? In what car would he come? Where would he stay? Who would accompany him? At what time would he arrive at the planned meeting with the Syrian and Iranian representatives? Would the Syrian authorities be informed of his arrival? Would the Hezbollah leaders know about his planned trip?

The report that tipped the scales in favor of the assassination project came from a very reliable source. It confirmed Mughniyeh's intention to travel to Damascus. That information was corroborated, according to the Lebanese *El-Balad* newspaper, by agents who planted tracking devices in the cars of Mughniyeh and the Hezbollah leaders.

The well-oiled machine of Caesarea came in at this point. By labyrinthine routes, the various Kidon teams arrived in Damascus. A special team smuggled the explosives into the Syrian capital.

At the last moment, new, crucial information was reported by a veteran Mossad informer. Whenever he came to Damascus, the report stated, Mughniyeh would meet his mistress. For the first time, the Mossad spymasters learned that Mughniyeh was having a secret affair. The pretty woman, Nihad Haidar, expected Mughniyeh in a discreet apartment in the city. Nihad knew the dates of Mughniyeh's arrival in Damascus in advance, from Beirut or from Tehran. He used to visit their love nest by himself, dismissing his bodyguards and his driver beforehand.

Urgent messages alerted the watchers who were already in place. Will Mughniyeh visit his lover this time as well? Does the owner of the apartment know that he is coming?

On the eve of the operation, the members of the hit team arrived in

Damascus. They flew to the Syrian capital from various European cities. According to the *Independent*, the team numbered three agents: one came from Paris on an Air France flight; the second took off from Milan with Alitalia, and the third used a short flight from Amman with Royal Jordanian. The three agents' false papers indicated that they were businessmen, two of them in the car trade and the third a travel agent. They declared on arrival that they had come to spend a short vacation in Syria, and passed through immigration without any problems. They drove to the city separately and got together only after making sure that they were not followed. They later met with some auxiliaries, who had arrived from Beirut, and were taken to a concealed garage, where a rented car was waiting and, beside it, a load of explosives that included plastic charges and tiny metal balls.

The three hit men locked themselves in the garage, prepared the explosive charge, and placed it in the rented car. The charge was not placed—as certain newspapers would later claim—in the headrest of Mughniyeh's car, but in the radio compartment of the rented vehicle.

Another team of Mossad watchers waited for Mughniyeh's arrival from Beirut. Their role was to stick to him, hang close to the apartment building where he would meet his mistress, and report about his departure. They had to follow him and make sure he arrived at the meeting in Kfar Sousa. Among the people he was to meet there were the new Iranian ambassador to Damascus and the most secretive man in Syria, General Muhammad Suleiman. Suleiman was, among others, in charge of transferring arms from Iran and Syria to the Hezbollah, and he maintained close relations with Imad Mughniyeh. (Suleiman, who had been involved in the secret Syrian nuclear project, had only six months to live; he would be mysteriously assassinated on August 2, during a dinner with friends at his beach house. See chapter 18.)

That same evening, the Iranian embassy had scheduled a celebration of the anniversary of the revolution at the Iranian cultural center at Kfar Sousa, quite close to the safe house where Mughniyeh was to meet the Iranian and Syrian officials. He decided, though, not to participate in the festivities, only to confer with his partners and leave Damascus.

On February 12, in the morning, the Mossad teams were in place. The watchers took position around the apartment building, Mughniyeh's first destination. In the late afternoon, they reported that Mughniyeh had arrived in Nihad's apartment—and in the evening they informed their superiors that he had set out on his way to his second destination. They hoped it would be his last.

The Pajero crossed Damascus and arrived in Kfar Sousa. The watchers followed Mughniyeh, continuously reporting his moves. The rigged car had been brought to the area where Mughniyeh would park. The activation signal was going to be given from a great distance by means of electronic equipment. The agents who had rigged the car had left the place long ago and were on their way to the airport.

The electronic sensors followed the silver SUV. It stopped. An auxiliary parked the rigged car close to the silver Pajero.

Shortly before ten P.M., a thunderous explosion shook the Kfar Sousa neighborhood, not far from an Iranian school (empty at this hour) and by a public park. Exactly at the moment when Mughniyeh got out of his SUV, the car beside him exploded.

Mughniyeh was dead.

His death shook the Hezbollah to the core; it was a terrible blow to the Syrian government, only a few months after its secret nuclear reactor had been pulverized.

Six months after Mughniyeh's death, in November 2008, the Lebanese authorities announced the discovery of a spy ring working for the Mossad. One of the people arrested, fifty-year-old Ali Jarrah from the Bekaa Valley, had worked for the Mossad for the last twenty years for a monthly salary of $7,000. He was accused of traveling to Syria frequently, on missions for the Mossad. In February 2008, a few days before the operation, he had traveled to Kfar Sousa. The Lebanese services that arrested Jarrah discovered a cache of sophisticated photography equipment, a video camera, and a GPS, expertly concealed in his car. Jarrah broke under interrogation and confessed that his Mossad handlers had instructed him to watch, photograph, and collect information about the neighborhoods Mughniyeh was about to visit, including the love nest where he met with Nihad.

Israel denied any connection to the assassination, but the Hezbollah spokesmen repeatedly accused "the Israeli Zionists" of the murder of "the Jihad hero, who died as a *shahid* (martyr)."

The U.S. State Department spokesman Sean McCormack did not share that view. He described Mughniyeh as "a cold-blooded killer, a mass murderer, and a terrorist responsible for ending countless lives."

"The world," McCormack concluded, "is a better place without him."

CHAPTER TWENTY

THE CAMERAS WERE ROLLING

In early January 2010, two black Audi A-6 cars sailed through the fortified gate of a gray building perched on a hill in North Tel Aviv. The building, called "the College," was actually Mossad headquarters. Prime Minister Benjamin Netanyahu was welcomed by the *ramsad*, Meir Dagan, when he came out of the second car. A short while earlier, Netanyahu had extended Dagan's appointment by another year.

Dagan and the Mossad heads felt upbeat and confident after the success of their last operations: the destruction of the Syrian reactor, the killings of Mughniyeh and Suleiman. What was urgent now was to sever another link between Iran and the terrorists, and that link had a name: Al-Mabhouh. According to the journalist Ronen Bergman, the Mossad code name for getting Al-Mabhouh was "Plasma Screen."

In the briefing room, Dagan and his senior aides presented their plan for the killing of Mahmoud Abdel Rauf Al-Mabhouh, a leader of Hamas and the linchpin in the system of smuggling weapons from Iran via Sudan, Egypt, and the Sinai Peninsula into the Gaza strip. Al-Mabhouh,

Dagan's men said, would be killed in Dubai, one of the United Arab Emirates on the Persian Gulf.

Netanyahu approved the execution of Plasma Screen, and the preparations started right away. The plan was to kill Al-Mabhouh in a hotel room in Dubai. The London *Sunday Times* reported that the members of the Mossad hit team rehearsed the killing in a Tel Aviv hotel without notifying hotel management.

Mahmoud Al-Mabhouh, a.k.a. "Abu Abed," was born in 1960 in the Jabalia refugee camp, in the north of the Gaza strip. In the late seventies, he joined the Muslim Brotherhood and, as a fervent Muslim, took part in sabotaging Arab cafés where gambling was practiced. In 1986, he was arrested by the Israeli Army for possession of an AK-47 assault rifle, but was released after less than a year and joined the Izz Ad-Din Al-Qassam Brigade, the military arm of Hamas.

Al-Mabhouh's commander, Salah Shehadeh, tasked him and several other Hamas terrorists with a special mission: kidnapping and killing Israeli soldiers. On February 16, 1989, Al-Mabhouh and another Hamas member stole a car, dressed as ultra-Orthodox Jews, and offered a lift to a soldier, Avi Sasportas, who was standing at a crossroads, trying to hitch a ride home. As Sasportas entered their car, Al-Mabhouh turned back and shot him in the face. The soldier was buried by Al-Mabhouh and his acolytes, after they photographed themselves with the body. Three months after murdering Sasportas, Al-Mabhouh and other Hamas members abducted another soldier, Ilan Saadon, at the Re'em crossroads and murdered him as well. Later, in an Al-Jazeera interview, Al-Mabhouh admitted his part in the assassinations and in burying the dead soldiers.

After the second murder, Al-Mabhouh escaped to Egypt, then to Jordan, and continued his terrorist activities, mostly by smuggling weapons and explosives into Gaza. Back in Cairo, he was arrested by the Egyptians, spent most of 2003 in an Egyptian jail, and later escaped to Syria. He now was labeled a dangerous terrorist, wanted by the police of Israel, Egypt, and Jordan. He was regarded by his superiors as a gifted organizer and climbed the Hamas hierarchy, focusing most of his efforts in smuggling weapons from Iran to the Gaza strip.

Al-Mabhouh realized that he was wanted by the Mossad because of his functions; he also knew that Israel would not forgive and forget the murder of its two soldiers. He took strict precautions, changed identities often, and posed as a businessman traveling between Middle East cities for his legitimate dealings. He told a friend that, when staying in a hotel, he used to barricade his room door with armchairs "to prevent bad surprises."

In a rare interview he gave to the Al-Jazeera network, Al-Mabhouh appeared with his head covered with a black cloth. "They tried to hit me three times," he said, "and they almost succeeded. Once in Dubai, once in Lebanon—six months ago—and a third time in Syria, two months ago, after the assassination of Imad Mughniyeh. That's the price to be paid by all those who fight the Israelis."

Al-Mabhouh actually gave the interview against his will; he thought it was an unnecessary risk but had to obey the explicit orders of the Hamas leadership. Some were to assert later that the interview helped the Mossad to find him. Al-Mabhouh had agreed to appear in front of the cameras on one condition: that his face would be completely blurred. After the recording of the interview, the videotape was sent to Gaza for inspection. It turned out that the distorting of his face failed, and he was instructed to record the interview again. The broadcast of the new interview was postponed (it would be aired only after Al-Mabhouh's death). Al-Mabhouh asked what happened to the first recording, and was told that the videotape was kept in the Hamas archives. Some believe that this tape made its way into the hands of the agents who were trying to find him.

A few weeks after the recording, a senior member of Hamas got a phone call from an Arab who claimed to be connected with a group that specialized in arms-smuggling and money-laundering. He made weapons-hungry Hamas some offers they could not refuse, and asked to meet Al-Mabhouh in Dubai. It was strange that he had chosen Dubai as a meeting place; the bustling city was actually the place where Al-Mabhouh was meeting his Iranian counterparts. Perhaps this mysterious phone call was Al-Mabhouh's death sentence.

And then, an unprecedented episode in the history of the spook wars: the elimination of Plasma Screen was filmed, recorded, and immortalized by closed-circuit security cameras, installed all over Dubai, from the airport counters all the way down to the hotel lobbies, hallways, and elevators.

These tapes are a unique document of the unfolding of the operation and its subsequent stages: they allowed hundreds of millions of spectators throughout the world, comfortably sprawled in their armchairs, to follow a secret, deadly operation of a hit team.

Monday, January 18, 2010.

Several Mossad agents land in Dubai. They are the precursors of a large team of twenty-seven agents that would trickle into Dubai in the next twenty-four hours. Twelve of them would carry British passports, four French, four Australian, one German, and six Irish.

The agents check into different hotels in the city.

Tuesday, January 19, 2010.

12:09 A.M.—two Mossad agents, balding, forty-three-year-old Michael Bodenheimer, carrying a German passport, and his friend James Leonard, carrying a British passport, land in Dubai. The two of them, according to the local police, are the advance team of the group charged with killing Al-Mabhouh.

12:30 A.M.—the operation commander, Kevin Daveron, sporting a goatee and spectacles, arrives in Dubai aboard a direct flight from Paris. He is accompanied by his deputy, Gail Folliard, a vivacious redhead. Both are carrying Irish passports.

01:21 A.M.—Gail Folliard checks into the exclusive hotel Jumeriah and gets a room on the eleventh floor. When asked by the reception clerk for her home address, she answers without batting an eye: 78 Memmier Road, Dublin, Ireland. It would later be established that this address was nonexistent.

01:31 A.M.—Kevin Daveron, the commander, joins his deputy and checks into the Jumeriah. He gets room 3308.

02:29 A.M.—Peter Elvinger, the operation logistics coordinator, arrives in Dubai with a French passport. He is slim, bearded, wearing stylish glasses. According to the police, he carries a "suspicious" case.

02:36 A.M.—at the airport, Peter meets another member of the team and they leave together for a hotel in the city.

10:15 A.M.—Mahmoud Al-Mabhouh departs from Damascus to Dubai, on a direct Emirates airline flight. In Dubai, he is supposed to coordinate with an Iranian envoy the smuggling of another weapons shipment to Gaza.

10:30 A.M.—Peter, the operation coordinator, leaves the hotel and meets the hit team at a big shopping center.

10:50 A.M.—Kevin and Gail, the commander and his deputy, join the meeting at the shopping center. Kevin is not wearing his glasses, and his small mustache has vanished.

12:18 P.M.—the meeting is over, and the team disperses. Kevin returns to the Jumeriah Hotel and checks out. The security cameras show him entering another hotel, where he puts on a wig, eyeglasses, and a false mustache.

02:12 P.M.—two agents dressed in tennis outfits enter the luxurious Al-Bustan Rotana Hotel. They are watchers, waiting for Al-Mabhouh, who is supposed to arrive in the next hour.

03:12 P.M.—Gail also leaves the Jumeriah Hotel. For the night spent in the hotel, she pays the sum of $400.

03:15 P.M.—Mahmoud Al-Mabhouh lands in Dubai. At the immigration booth, he shows a false Iraqi passport and declares he is in the textile import business.

03:25 P.M.—Gail moves to another hotel, where she changes clothes, makes up her face, and puts on a wig.

03:28 P.M.—Al-Mabhouh arrives at the Al-Bustan Rotana Hotel. At check-in, he asks for a room with sealed windows and no terrace. He is given room 230 on the second floor. He takes the elevator to the second floor, unaware of the two Mossad watchers dressed as tennis players, who ride the elevator with him.

03:30 P.M.—the watchers report, by a special transmission device, that Al-Mabhouh has entered his room and the room facing his has the number 237.

03:53 P.M.—Peter, the coordinator, arrives in Al-Mabhouh's hotel and walks into the business center. He calls reception and reserves room 237.

04:03 P.M.—a new watchers team relieves the first and waits for Al-Mabhouh to leave his room.

04:14 P.M.—all the members of the hit team are now in the Al-Bustan Rotana Hotel.

04:23 P.M.—Al-Mabhouh leaves his room, surveys the lobby to make sure that the place is "clean," and leaves the hotel. The watchers follow him.

04:24 P.M.—the watchers transmit to the team commander details about the car that has taken Al-Mabhouh downtown.

04:27 P.M.—Peter, the coordinator, enters the lobby and gives Kevin Daveron his case, which probably contains the objects needed for Al-Mabhouh's assassination.

04:33 P.M.—Peter goes to the reception desk, checks in, and receives the key for room 237, facing Al-Mabhouh's room.

04:40 P.M.—Peter gives the room key to Kevin, and leaves the hotel for an unknown destination.

04:44 P.M.—Kevin enters room 237. He checks the window and the door peephole, by which he would be able to watch Al-Mabhouh enter his room.

05:06 P.M.—Gail goes into room 237. She and Kevin go over the timetables and keep receiving reports about Al-Mabhouh's moves in the city.

05:36 P.M.—one of the watchers enters the hotel wearing a visor cap. At a corner of an empty hallway, he replaces the cap with a wig.

06:21 P.M.—Gail leaves room 237, carrying the case previously delivered to Kevin by Peter. She goes to the hotel parking lot and gives the case to one of the hit team members.

06:32 P.M.—the first detail of the hit team leaves the parking lot and enters the hotel lobby.

06:34 P.M.—the second detail of the hit team enters the hotel and settles on the armchairs and sofas in the far corner of the luxurious lobby, as far as possible from the first detail.

06:43 P.M.—the first watchers detail, the agents wearing tennis clothes, leaves the hotel.

07:30 P.M.—Peter, the logistics coordinator, leaves Dubai on a flight to Munich, Germany.

08:00 P.M.—a hotel employee who cleaned the second floor leaves the place. The hit team detail tries to enter Al-Mabhouh's room.

08:04 P.M.—Kevin, who is posted by the elevators, signals to the members of the hit team to get into the room, because an elevator stops at the second floor and a hotel guest gets out of it. The electronic control system registers an attempt to break into room 230, the room of Al-Mabhouh.

08:20 P.M.—Al-Mabhouh returns to the hotel. The watchers inform Kevin that he is walking toward the elevator.

08:27 P.M.—Al-Mabhouh enters his room. Kevin and Gail are on guard at the second-floor corridor, by the elevators. In room 230, the assassination takes place.

08:46 P.M.—four members of the hit team leave the hotel.

08:47 P.M.—Gail and another member of the hit team leave the hotel.

08:51 P.M.—Kevin enters Al-Mabhouh's room after the killing and places the DO NOT DISTURB sign on the door handle.

08:52 P.M.—the watchers detail leaves the hotel.

10:30 P.M.—Kevin and Gail leave Dubai on a direct flight to Paris. Approximately at the same time, all the team members depart to different destinations.

At 10:00 P.M., Al-Mabhouh's wife called his cell phone. The phone rang and went to voice mail. She called over and over again but with no results. A close friend also tried to reach Al-Mabhouh, but failed. Text messages sent to Al-Mabhouh remained unanswered. Time passed by and there was no sign of life from Al-Mabhouh. The distraught wife called several Hamas senior officials, who decided to send the Hamas resident in Dubai to the Al-Bustan Rotana Hotel. The man went to the reception desk and called room 230; there was no answer.

After midnight, the hotel employees finally went up to Al-Mabhouh's room, unlocked the door, and found his body. A doctor rushed to the room examined the corpse and concluded that the cause of death was cardiac arrest.

The Hamas published an official statement attributing Al-Mabhouh's death to "medical reasons." But Al-Mabhouh's family rejected the medical diagnosis and insisted that Al-Mabhouh had been murdered by the Mossad. His body was sent to the Dubai medical examiner, while a sample of his blood was flown to a laboratory in France. The lab report came back nine days later. The Hamas now announced that Mossad agents had assassinated Al-Mabhouh, first stunning him with an electronic shocker and then suffocating him with a pillow. Simultaneously, the Dubai police announced that no traces of poison were found in Al-Mabhouh's blood. Nevertheless, they quickly reached the conclusion that the Mossad had killed Al-Mabhouh on their territory. On January 31, twelve days after Al-Mabhouh's death, the London *Sunday Times* published a piece about his poisoning by the Mossad. Its reporters claim that Israeli hit men had entered Al-Mabhouh's room and injected him with a poison that simulated a heart attack; the agents then photographed all the documents he carried and exited the room, leaving behind the DO NOT DISTURB sign.

On February 28, the deputy chief of the Dubai police informed the press that the French lab had found in Al-Mabhouh's blood traces of a strong hydrochloride painkiller, used for anesthesia before surgery. This substance, he said, causes a muscular relaxation followed by a loss of consciousness. He assumed that the killers injected their victim with the anesthetic and then suffocated him so that his death would look natural.

The journalist Gordon Thomas published an article in the London *Telegraph* about "the Mossad's license to kill." Thomas asserted that the modus operandi in Al-Mabhouh's death was similar to other assassinations car-

ried out by the Mossad in the past. He added that the eleven members
of the hit team, six of them women, had been chosen out of forty-eight
members of the Kidon operational unit. Yossi Melman of *Haaretz* daily
also stressed that the killers' moves, as reflected by the security cameras
and other findings, were identical to past Mossad operations: arrival by
separate flights from different parts of the world, stays in different hotels,
phone calls placed through international operators, clothes that make
identification difficult, and an effort to pose as genuine tourists or businessmen trying to mix business with pleasure. But other experts dismissed
that theory, saying that these were exactly the methods used by most Western secret services, therefore it was impossible to establish clearly who had
carried out the assassination.

The German weekly *Der Spiegel* revealed that the German intelligence
agency, the BND, had informed the members of the German parliament
that Al-Mabhouh had been killed by Mossad agents. *Der Spiegel* also described how Michael Bodenheimer, born in Israel, had applied in 2009 for
a German passport because his parents had been born in Germany. With
his new passport, he had flown, on November 8, 2009, from Frankfurt to
Dubai and then to Hong Kong, an itinerary identical to his flights before
and after the assassination. According to *Der Spiegel*, nine other agents had
flown to Dubai on the same day in November 2009 from different airports
in Europe. That seemed to be a dress rehearsal for the real operation carried
out in January 2010.

In an interview with the *Al-Arabiya* newspaper, the chief of the Dubai
police, Dhahi Khalfan Tamim, explained why he was certain that the
Mossad had killed Al-Mabhouh: "First, we have some DNA samples and
fingerprints. Second, all of [the hit team members] carried genuine foreign
passports whose details were false, and when it turned out that some of
the owners [of the passports] were from Israel—so what do you think, that
'Peace Now' murdered Al-Mabhouh? . . . It is the Mossad, one hundred
percent!"

The chief of the Dubai police soon became a media star, spending hours
in front of the world televisions, giving interviews to anyone who was ready

to listen. He became the favorite of the television reporters, mostly thanks to Dubai's security cameras. He showed to the press a video film, actually assembled from the tapes of security cameras spread all over Dubai. Tamim cleverly explained and showed how the hit team members moved throughout the emirate, and how they entered and exited hotels, shopping centers, and the airport, in their effort to shadow Al-Mabhouh, often changing clothes and disguises.

According to Tamim, the core of the hit team was composed of eleven members: three Irish citizens, six Britons, one Frenchman, and one German. They arrived in Dubai aboard several flights from various European airports, some of them the night before the operations, others at the same time as Al-Mabhouh, and a few of them a mere couple of hours before the operation. Six hundred forty-eight hours of tape from the security cameras helped the Dubai police to reconstruct the events culminating with Al-Mabhouh's death.

The tapes and the photos taken by immigration authorities of all the passengers entering and exiting Dubai drove the Dubai police chief to the conclusion that not eleven but more than a score of Mossad agents participated in the operation. The official number he mentioned was twenty-seven, but Tamim later added a few more names to his list of suspects.

Yet his conclusions raised several questions: Didn't the Mossad know that a network of security cameras was spread all over Dubai? According to Tamim, Israeli agents had visited Dubai several times, to prepare the operation. Didn't they see the security cameras? And if they did, then perhaps a large part of the getting in and out of hotels, the change of clothes, wigs, and mustaches were nothing but a show for the cameras; and quite a few of the participants were not a part of the operation but were used only to mislead those who would examine the tapes later.

And another point: the chief of police boasted that all the members of the hit team were photographed as they went through immigration. Didn't the Mossad know that was the procedure in Dubai? Didn't it make sure that the faces of its agents would be made up and disguised so that it would be impossible to recognize them afterward?

A third question: How come the security cameras recorded every frame and every second of the secret agents' moves, except for two—the entering and exiting of the hit detail in and out of Al-Mabhouh's room?

Chief Tamim revealed to the press that the members of the hit team used a phone number in Austria for some of their communications; by checking telephone records, Tamim could establish the identities of the foreigners who had used that number and were, apparently, members of the Mossad team. He also pointed out that several of the agents had paid their expenses in Dubai with Payoneer—MasterCard rechargeable credit cards, an Iowa-based company that had a research and development center in Israel.

The most intriguing revelation in the investigation was that most of the hit team members had used real passports of Israeli citizens with dual nationality—and only very few used forged passports. Apparently, this was for a reason—the hit team was operating in an Arab country that is considered enemy territory. If the hit team members were captured, they could ask for the protection of the consuls of Great Britain, Germany, France, and Australia . . . If the consuls checked their computers, they would have found out that these people really existed, and they would have agreed to assist them. If, on the contrary, the hit team had used forged passports, the deception would have been exposed right away, and the agents would have been left without protection.

After all this became known, Israel was harshly criticized by the nations whose passports had been used in Dubai. Great Britain, Australia, and Ireland expelled the Mossad representatives from their soil. Poland arrested a man called Uri Brodsky at Warsaw's airport and extradited him to Germany. Brodsky was suspected of helping the agent Michael Bodenheimer to obtain a German passport under false pretenses. (Brodsky was finally released by Germany after paying a fine of 60,000 euros. Bodenheimer was not found.) Other countries expressed their indignation and fury. These reactions seemed laced with hypocrisy, as the use of forged or doctored passports is the standard rule of secret service activity; the nations now accusing Israel were and are using forged passports exactly the same way as the Mossad. Yet when a Russian spy network was uncovered in the United States in late 2010, nobody accused its members of using forged British and American papers.

The reports in the world press created the impression that the Dubai operation was successful but had suffered from a grave mistake, the result of Israel's gross underestimation of Dubai and the Western nations they involved. That was a blow to Israel's international image, but not to its secret activity. The expelled Mossad envoys were soon replaced by others. The promises of the Dubai chief of police that the hit team members would be apprehended, because their identities were known all over the world, went unanswered. Not one Mossad agent of the Dubai team was identified by any police and arrested.

Yet Dubai became a symbol of the new challenges facing any secret service in a changing world. The cloak-and-dagger era is definitely over. Security cameras, photographs and thumbprints at immigration, rapid checks of passports, DNA . . . all those require much more sophisticated means and methods from the spooks of this world when they set off on their dark, sinister missions.

On April 7, 2011, an unidentified aircraft fired a missile on a passenger car, on a road fifteen kilometers south of Port Sudan, in the African state of Sudan. According to Israeli sources, the car was attacked by a Shoval drone that can fly four thousand kilometers without refueling and carry a load of a ton. The Shoval is of a new generation of drones that Israel now uses in risky over-the-border missions, replacing aircraft piloted by men. The Israeli drones, some of the best in the world, carry out intelligence and attack missions all over the Middle East.

One of the two people killed in the car attack in Sudan was said to be a Hamas leader. The Hamas used the Sudan trail for smuggling weapons from Iran to Gaza. The weapons came by boat, were unloaded in Port Sudan, and proceeded in a convoy of vehicles via Egypt and the Sinai to Gaza, their drivers bribing their way through borders and check posts.

The Sudanese government immediately accused Israel of the coup.

Israel had been designated as the culprit for another mysterious attack on a weapons convoy in January 2009; the trucks carrying weapons, missiles, and explosives had been destroyed, and forty people manning the convoy had been killed.

One of the men allegedly killed was the Hamas leader in charge of smuggling weapons from Iran to Gaza.

CHAPTER TWENTY-ONE

FROM THE LAND OF THE QUEEN OF SHEBA

A group of Ethiopian children, black-skinned and clothed in white, entered the stage of the huge audience hall in Jerusalem. The children, blessed with a unique kind of beauty, watched the public with big, black eyes, filled with curiosity and pride. The famous Israeli composer Shlomo Gronich, sat by the piano. Its first notes smoothly sailed over the hushed crowd, and a beautiful, yet chilling song surged from the children's choir:

> *The moon is watching from above*
> *On my back is a small bag of food*
> *The desert beneath us has no end ahead*
> *And my mother promises my little brothers:*
> *"A little more, a little more,*
> *Lift up your legs, a last push*
> *Toward Jerusalem."*

This was "The Journey Song" of poet Haim Idissis, describing the epic journey of the Ethiopian Jews to the Promised Land, to Israel. The public cheered and applauded. Perhaps that was not Idissis's intention, and perhaps the enthusiastic crowds did not notice, but the children's song described the most moving—and the most terrible—chapter of the Ethiopian Jews' aliyah to the land of their fathers:

The moonlight stood fast
Our bag of food was lost . . .
And at nights bandits attacked
With a knife and a sharp sword
In the desert, the blood of my mother
The moon is my witness
and I promise my little brothers:
"A little bit more, a little more
The dream will be fulfilled
Soon we will arrive in the Land of Israel."

No other Israeli community ever suffered such appalling woes as the Ethiopian tribe on its way to Israel.

It became a living legend.

Its very existence seemed borrowed from a storybook. A Jewish tribe, cut off from the outside world, entrenched in the heart of Africa, they lived in the mountains and valleys of Ethiopia, the land of the Queen of Sheba. For thousands of years, this tribe stubbornly clung to its faith, a pure and innocent biblical religion.

That quiet and shy tribe had been lost to history. Its leaders, the Kessim, venerable elders dressed in white robes, navigated their flock through the ancient rules of Judaism and the basic customs of modern life. Theirs was a tribe that at times lived in peace and serenity among its neighbors, and at other times was persecuted by cruel rulers. But it also had to face the ugly humiliation by rabbis and Jewish theological experts from the outside world, who had decided that the Ethiopian Jews, commonly called Falasha, were not really Jewish.

Yet the Ethiopian Jews did not give up. And generation after generation, inspired by the tradition passed from father to son and from mother to daughter, they dreamed of the day when they would set off on their way to the Land of Israel.

Very few Ethiopians came to Israel in the first thirty years of its existence. Even during the reign of Emperor Haile Selassie, the "Lion of Judea," who was Israel's close friend and ally, no serious effort was made to bring the Jews of Ethiopia to the Jewish state. Things started to change in 1973, when Israel's chief rabbi Ovadia Yosef published an unequivocal Halacha ruling that the Ethiopian Jews, who called themselves Beta Israel, were full-fledged Jews. Two years later, the government of Israel decided to apply the Law of Return to the Ethiopian Jews. And when Menachem Begin became prime minister, in 1977, he called the director of the Mossad, General Yitzhak (Haka) Hofi.

"Bring me the Jews of Ethiopia!" Begin said to the *ramsad*.

In the Mossad structure, a special unit, Bitzur, was charged with protecting Jews in enemy countries and with organizing immigration from those countries to Israel. Bitzur—later renamed Tzafririm—immediately got to work.

Shortly after Begin's order to Haka, David (Dave) Kimhi landed in Addis Ababa, Ethiopia's capital. Dave was deputy director of the Mossad and the head of the Tevel—department for secret international relations. He came to meet Ethiopia's ruler, Mengistu Haile Mariam. In those days, the exit gates of Ethiopia were locked for Jewish emigration. The nation was torn by a civil war, and Mengistu asked Israel for help against the rebels. Kimhi refused to act against the rebels on Mengistu's behalf, but promised to supply him with weapons. And that on one condition: that Mengistu would allow Jewish emigration. We demand, Kimhi said, that every Israeli Hercules aircraft that lands here, loaded with military equipment, take off loaded with Jews. Mengistu agreed. And the exodus of Jews from Ethiopia started.

This arrangement lasted for six months, till it was destroyed in February 1978 by a "slip of the tongue" of then–minister of foreign affairs Moshe Dayan. Dayan had told a Swiss newspaper that Israel was supplying weapons to Mengistu's army. Some claimed Dayan had leaked that on purpose, being opposed to the arms deal with Mengistu's Marxist and pro-Soviet regime.

Mengistu was furious. He could not publicly admit he maintained secret relations with Israel, and canceled the agreement with the Mossad right away. The direct channel for Jewish immigration was now blocked, but Begin's order to Haka was still in force.

The gates of Ethiopia were locked once again, but a letter that reached Mossad headquarters from Khartoum, the capital of Ethiopia's neighbor Sudan, suddenly offered another escape route for the Ethiopian Jews.

The letter was signed by Fereda Aklum, an Ethiopian Jew, a teacher, who had succeeded in crossing the border into Sudan. From Israel's point of view, Sudan was an enemy country. It was plagued with famine, drought, and tribal and religious wars. Thousands of refugees from various parts of the country—and from neighboring Ethiopia—gathered in squalid tent camps. Aklum posted several letters to Israel, and to relief organizations throughout the world, in a desperate effort to get urgent help for the emigration of the Ethiopian Jews. One of Aklum's letters landed in Mossad headquarters and attracted the attention of a senior official. "I am in Sudan," Aklum wrote, "send me a plane ticket." Instead of a plane ticket, the Mossad sent to Sudan one of its men, Danny Limor, to meet Aklum.

When they met, the two of them agreed that Aklum would try to find Jews in the refugee camps and keep Danny informed. In a few months, he, indeed, located thirty Jews, and the Mossad discreetly organized their immigration to Israel. A month later, Aklum was co-opted by the Mossad and charged with tracing Jews in Khartoum. He did not find any Jews there, though, and the Mossad envoy decided to return to Israel. Before leaving, Limor instructed Aklum to leave for Israel as well. But Aklum wanted to stay and keep looking for Jews in other parts of Sudan. Limor, however, was adamant. He ordered Aklum to put an end to his activities and return to Israel within a week.

But Aklum disobeyed the order and started traveling from one town to another, from one refugee camp to another, hoping to find Jews there. He did not find even one Jew, but he knew well that if he returned to Israel now, this would put an end to the immigration of Ethiopian Jews via Sudan. He therefore composed a mendacious report, mentioning the names of many Jews whom he allegedly found in Sudan, faxed it to the Mossad, and announced that he was staying in Sudan "to take care of them."

The Jews whom Aklum included in his lists existed, indeed, but they were not in Sudan; they still lived in their villages in Ethiopia. Now Aklum started operating in Ethiopia as a lone wolf. He visited the villages and tried to convince the local Jews to immigrate to the Land of Israel. The rumor that a secret route to Jerusalem had been found spread like wildfire. First a few men, then families, finally entire villages packed their meager belongings and set off. Thousands of people, including old men, women, and children, secretly left Ethiopia. They were inspired by a messianic dream, by the biblical promises of return to the land of milk and honey.

They prepared food and water, crossed the border, and started an exhausting and dangerous journey in the desert. They marched at night, and during the day they hid in caves and crannies. Many fell sick and died. Babies died of dehydration in their mothers' arms. A father lost his four children during the terrible journey. Some were bitten by snakes and scorpions, others died of infectious diseases. The water and the food they had taken with them were insufficient. Several groups were attacked by robbers that took all their belongings and often left behind heaps of corpses. Years later, the actress Mehereta Barush, who had participated in the journey, described its terrible toll. Every morning, she said, the travelers counted the corpses of their friends. Sometimes there were ten dead bodies spread in the sand, sometimes fifteen. There was not a family that had not lost at least one of their children.

In the summer of 1981, Danny Limor and his Mossad team were back in Sudan, operating under cover. They called themselves "the Hafis," the initials of "Haka's Force in Sudan." Their goal was to establish contact with the Ethiopian Jews throughout Sudan.

But the surviving Jews met with other difficulties when trying to get in touch with the Mossad envoys; even those who reached the refugee camps around Khartoum were heartbroken. They had to conceal their Jewish religion, and yet avoided eating the nonkosher food that the relief agencies were distributing to the refugees. Women were raped and young girls kidnapped by bullies and criminals who were the real rulers of the camps. A group of one hundred girls was abducted and vanished. Their relatives who looked for them learned that they had been sold to Saudi Arabia, where about 120,000 women were held in bondage. Several Jews were identified as such by their neighbors in the camps; they were arrested and tortured by the Sudanese police. Many stayed in the refugee camps for months and even years till they were able to set off for Israel.

The Ethiopian Jews paid a heavy price for their dream to enter the gates of Jerusalem. More than four thousand Jews died during the various stages of their journey. Henry Gold, a Canadian Jew who worked as a volunteer in the camps in Sudan and Ethiopia, was deeply shocked by the situation of the Jews he found there, and harshly criticized the Israeli envoys for failing to carry out their mission properly.

Yet the Mossad was looking for a secure way to get the Jews to Israel. The exodus from Sudan started by regular commercial flights, with forged passports; but the Mossad soon decided to take the refugees to Israel by sea, sending boats that would take them through the Red Sea and the Straits of Tiran—to the port of Eilat.

As a cover, the Mossad established in Europe a company of tourism and travel. "In order to operate in this area, one needs a cover story," said Mossad agent Yonatan Shefa, one of the operation leaders, "for if you don't have a cover story after a week, they would ask you: What are you doing here? You're a tourist? What is here to see?" The company leased an abandoned beach resort close to Port Sudan, called "Arous," and signed an agreement with the Sudanese government for the development of maritime sports in the Red Sea. All the administrative dealings were entrusted to Yehuda Gil, who was regarded then as one of the best Mossad officers. Gil came to Khartoum, met with the regime officials, and with a lot of savvy explained, convinced, and bribed—till finally he got all the necessary permits and licenses for operating the Arous Resort. The man charged with the setting up and the management of the resort was Yonatan Shefa, who had taken part in many Mossad operations. Arous was actually built as a village, with individual bungalows and a few public buildings. Several Mossad agents, carrying forged passports, were sent from Israel and became the resort's instructors and employees. They stuffed the resort store with diving equipment, scuba apparatus, masks, flippers, and snorkels. In the store was hidden a transceiver that was in permanent contact with Mossad headquarters. Emanuel Allon, who had participated in many operations with Shefa, including the rescue of the Syrian virgins, got a call from Yonatan. "He told me, 'I need you for something special. This time it is an operation without killing; something special; something humane. I am talking to you, and I am getting so emotional. I want to establish a resort village in Sudan.'" The village was open to the public, and its posters soon sprouted on the walls of European travel agencies.

Many tourists spent their vacation in Arous, and at least from their point of view, the resort was a success. During the day, they dived, swam, and enjoyed the Red Sea beach. But they did not know that almost every night the Mossad agents set off from the village to bring over Jews from the refugee camps. The "diving instructors" invented a cover story for the local employees of the resort, who were Sudanese. They told the locals that they were going to spend the night with the Swedish nurses of the Red Cross hospital in the town of Kassala. When the merry departures reached a dubious frequency, the local employees started suspecting that something fishy was going on there; but as long as they got their generous salaries, they preferred to look the other way.

The nightly journeys were carried out with four old trucks. The Mossad agents, under the command of Danny Limor, drove to the vicinity of the camps. The young members of a secret Ethiopian organization, the Committee, would gather groups of Jews and take them to the trucks.

But that was not easy. The Israelis were running many dangers. David Ben-Uziel, one of the operation leaders, deemed the approach to the camps as "the most dangerous part" of the mission. "We were very close to the camps," he said. "We could be caught and had to finish this part as soon as possible."

While the Committee was trying to locate the Jews in the refugee camps, there were many who refrained from identifying themselves, for fear of the Sudanese police. The Jews from the mountain villages in Ethiopia had never seen a white man before; they refused to believe that the Israelis were Jews who came to save them, for they did not know that there were also white Jews. Only when Danny Limor came to pray with them did they start believing he was a Jew—a strange one, praying in an unusual way, but a Jew all the same.

Fearing a leak, the Mossad agents did not warn the Jews beforehand. The Committee people told them to be ready to leave at any moment, and when they were contacted, they had to leave everything and go. And so, night after night, groups of Jews sneaked out of the camps and surreptitiously walked to the meeting point in a small ravine close by, where the Mossad agents were waiting.

The four-truck convoy would travel hundreds of kilometers to the Red Sea coast. En route, they had to go through army and police checkpoints. Danny would bribe the guards, and the trucks would be allowed to continue. At the meeting point on the coast, the Israeli Navy would be waiting.

A navy boat would be moored at some distance, and the naval commandos came to the coast in rubber dinghies to collect the Jews and take them aboard the mother ship. The main boat that came every week to the Sudanese coast was *Bat-Galim*. None of the Mossad agents and the naval commandos would ever forget the emotional meeting with their Ethiopian brethren and their dramatic departure toward Israel. Mossad agent David Ben-Uziel described the transfer of the Jews to the boats in a handheld tape recorder. "The sea is stormy," he said. "We are carrying each one of our brothers in our arms so nobody would drown. The emotions of our men here run very high. Some say the sights remind them of their parents, who came to Israel as illegal immigrants; they were on the verge of bursting into tears when they saw our brothers enter the ship."

"They came in complete silence," added Gadi Kroll, the commander of the naval force. "Old men, women, babies in arms. We immediately sailed on the stormy seas. They sat down and didn't utter a word." The navy boats took them to Eilat.

One day, the Canadian-Jewish volunteer Henry Gold came to the resort village. He was exhausted from the hard work at the refugee camps, and some friends talked him into taking a couple of days off, to sun, swim, and dive. He had no idea of the secret activities taking place in and around Arous. But when he toured the village, he felt something was very strange here: he had the impression he was surrounded by Mossad agents. The staff seemed very weird. "They had a strange accent. One woman introduced herself as Swiss, but she didn't have a Swiss accent, and the Iranian didn't have an Iranian accent. At dinner, they put on the tables a very thinly chopped salad. I have been in many places all over the world, but such a salad is served only in Israel." The following morning, Gold did not hesitate anymore and turned to the diving instructor, to ask in Hebrew: "Tell me, what are you people doing here?" The guy, amazed, blushed and collapsed on a chair. Finally, he asked Gold, also in Hebrew: "Who are you?" The very same day, a senior Mossad officer arrived and took Gold aside. Gold confronted him angrily about the treatment of the Jews in the refugee camps.

In one of the operations, in March 1982, while several boats were carrying the Ethiopians to the ship, in complete darkness, a dinghy with four Mossad agents got stuck among some rocks by the beach. At that moment, a squad of Sudanese soldiers armed with AK-47 rifles suddenly emerged on the beach and aimed their weapons at the tiny boat.

Danny Limor pulled himself together, hurled himself on the soldiers, and yelled in English at their commander: "Are you out of your mind? Are you going to fire on tourists?" He kept shouting about the tourists who came to dive in this resort, about Arous's contribution to the tourist trade in Sudan, then threatened to lodge a complaint against the squad commander in Khartoum. The officer, stunned, apologized and explained he had assumed that the people in the boat were smugglers. He ordered his soldiers to leave the place at once.

The Mossad agents were safe, but the departures by sea apparently could not continue. A new way had to be found to transport the Jews to Israel. One morning, the tourists in Arous woke up to find that the entire foreign staff had vanished, except for some locals who had stayed behind to prepare breakfast for the guests. The previous night, the Mossad agents had left the village. They left letters of apology saying that the resort was closed because of budgetary difficulties. The tourists were to get their money back upon return to their countries. That was done, and all the divers were reimbursed in the coming weeks.

After long discussions at Mossad headquarters, the *ramsad* decided that the next transports would be carried out by air, with Rhinos—Hercules C-130 transport aircraft of the Israeli Air Force. It was a risky gamble, implying the penetration into Sudan's air space and the repeated landing of Israeli soldiers on the territory of an enemy country. But Israel had no choice: the Ethiopian Jews had to be rescued.

In May 1982, the Mossad agents returned to Sudan. Their first mission was to locate possible landing areas south of Port Sudan. They found an abandoned British airfield and repaired its runway, making it suitable for the landing of the heavy Rhinos. The first group of Jews was brought from the meeting point to the airfield. Torches were used to light up the landing strip. But when the enormous Air Force Rhino landed, the Ethiopian Jews were scared to death. The huge metal bird that they saw for the first time in their lives landed in a roar of engines, rising clouds of dust, and seemed to head straight at them. Many ran away and agreed to come back only after exhausting efforts of persuasion by the Mossad people. Others stubbornly refused to enter the belly of the steel monster. The aircraft that was supposed to depart immediately finally took off with an hour delay, carrying 213 Jews.

The agents got a telegram of congratulations from headquarters, but they learned an important lesson. In the future, the trucks would wait until the Rhino landed and extended its ramp, and then they would drive to the very tail of the aircraft, so that the Jews would get right into the gaping belly of the plane.

That was a success—but it did not last long. The Sudanese authorities discovered the strange traffic at the abandoned airstrip, and the Mossad agents had to find another landing area. Soon they found another strip, forty-six kilometers southwest of Port Sudan. This time, the Mossad decided to carry out a large rescue operation of seven Hercules flights, each flight to carry two hundred Jews.

Operation Brothers took place under the personal command of the *ramsad*, Haka, and the commander of the Paratrooper Corps, General Amos Yaron. In the following two years, from mid-1982 to mid-1984, it brought to Israel fifteen hundred Ethiopian Jews.

That successful operation almost ended in failure. An informer of the Sudanese security forces pinpointed the contact man of the Mossad in the refugee camps. Addis Solomon, an Ethiopian Jew, was arrested and tortured for forty-two days by the Sudanese. They wanted to know the names of his handlers, and the location of the meeting places with the Mossad agents. But Solomon did not break down and did not reveal the secret.

At the end of 1984, the situation in the camps worsened. The famine and the infectious diseases caused many deaths among the Ethiopians. A civil war raged in Sudan, and threatened the regime of the nation's dictator, Jaafar Nimeiry. His survival now depended on an urgent grant of financial aid and food supplies by the United States.

Israel asked Washington to help Sudan if it allowed the airlift to Israel to continue. The administration agreed, and the U.S. ambassador in Khartoum was instructed to negotiate along those lines. The result was a compromise: the Jews would not be flown to Israel directly but via a third country; Israel would not be involved in the operation; the compensation to Sudan would be in the form of food and fuel shipments.

The U.S. embassy in Khartoum informed Washington that the Jews can be evacuated from Sudan in five or six weeks.

That's how Operation Moses was born.

In the meantime, Haka had been replaced as *ramsad* by his deputy, Nahum Admoni, who had distinguished himself in the previous years by his energetic efforts to organize the immigration of the Ethiopian Jews.

Admoni now authorized his men to fly the Jews via Belgium. A Jewish businessman who owned a small air-charter company agreed to help the operation with his Boeing airliners.

And so, on November 18, 1984, at one twenty A.M., the first Belgian aircraft landed in Sudan. Two hundred fifty starving, exhausted, and badly scared refugees got on the plane. But the Belgian pilot refused to take off, because the plane was equipped with only two hundred ten oxygen masks, not enough for two hundred fifty passengers. The Mossad agent in charge took him aside and whispered, quietly but firmly: "Please, make the selection yourself and decide who will live and who will die!" He then added, not so quietly: "If you don't get in the cockpit and start the engines, I'll throw you out of the plane and put another pilot in your seat."

That was a very persuasive argument. The pilot got in the cockpit, and at two forty A.M., the first flight of Operation Moses took off for Israel, with a stopover in Brussels. During the next forty-seven days, the Boeings carried out thirty-six secret flights and brought over 7,800 Ethiopian Jews.

In Israel, the military censorship made desperate efforts to prevent any leakage of information about the operation. Their efforts succeeded until the Jewish Agency chairman, Arie Dulzin, published a statement saying that "one of the Jewish tribes is about to return to our homeland." In the wake of this communiqué, the *New York Jewish Press* published the details of the operation, followed by the *Los Angeles Times*.

Three days later, Prime Minister Shimon Peres told the Knesset: "The government of Israel acted, and will keep acting, to the limit of its powers and even beyond, to continue the operation until the last Ethiopian Jew reached his homeland." The very same day, the Sudanese canceled the flights and the operation was stopped. The Sudanese were infuriated, not by the articles in the press but by the speech of the Israeli prime minister, who confirmed the story. "If the Israelis had kept quiet for another month," observed a U.S. official in Washington, "it would have been possible to save all the Jews of Ethiopia."

Vice President George H. W. Bush was deeply impressed by Operation Moses and Israel's efforts to bring over the Ethiopians despite great risks.

He decided to act. A few weeks after the cancellation of Operation Moses, seven Hercules aircraft of the U.S. Air Force landed in the Sudanese airfield at Al-Qadarif. They carried aboard several CIA agents. The American task force launched Operation Queen of Sheba, and flew the five hundred Ethiopian Jews remaining in Sudan directly to the Israeli Air Force base at Mitzpeh Ramon, in the Negev.

Two months later, Jaafar Nimeiry was deposed by a junta of army officers. Libyan intelligence officers rushed to Sudan in order to find the Mossad agents who were still in Khartoum. The last three remaining agents were discovered by the Libyans and at the last moment were able to escape to the home of a CIA agent. The American hid them in his house and later flew them, hidden in crates, to the Kenyan capital, Nairobi. David Molad, who had been one of the senior Mossad officers in Sudan, slipped quietly out of the country. The rescue of the Ethiopian Jews was to be one of his last operations before his retirement from the Mossad.

In Operations Moses and Queen of Sheba, the U.S.-Israeli cooperation had been perfect, almost idyllic. Unfortunately, shortly after these events, the Pollard affair exploded in Washington: a Jewish employee of the U.S. intelligence community, Jonathan Pollard, was arrested for spying on behalf of Israel. The U.S. government was stunned and furious; the heads of the CIA felt betrayed by the ally whom they had helped and who, in return, had spied on them.

The Israeli government profusely apologized and returned the documents stolen by Pollard to the United States. But the intelligence relations between Jerusalem and Washington had suffered a serious blow. One of Pollard's handlers turned out to be none other than Rafi Eitan, the legendary Mossad agent, who now headed an obscure intelligence organization in the Ministry of Defense. The organization, Lakam (the Bureau for Scientific Relations), was disbanded right away, and judicial proceedings against Eitan were initiated in Washington. To this very day, he cannot enter the United States for fear of being arrested.

* * *

peration Moses was severely criticized by many Ethiopian Jews, as it took the lives of about four thousand people. In the Mossad, too, the officers of Caesarea, headed at that time by Shabtai Shavit, strongly disapproved of the planning and execution of the operation by the Bitzur department. Shavit and his men claimed that Bitzur was a marginal department that was not equipped to undertake an operation of such magnitude as Moses. The Bitzur people insisted that the operation succeeded precisely because of its spontaneous and improvised character. They also pointed out that they had recruited some of the best Mossad agents for carrying out the various stages of Moses.

The infighting could not change the fact that thousands of Jews had returned to the Land of Israel. And yet, even after the completion of Operation Moses and Operation Queen of Sheba, thousands of Jews remained in Ethiopia. They also wanted to immigrate to Israel, but the gates were locked. Israel felt it was imperative to bring them over, for ideological and Zionist considerations, but also for a humane reason: many families had been split and torn, children had arrived in Israel without their parents, parents without their children, husbands without their wives . . . This separation caused terrible absorption problems—and many personal tragedies, like suicides of young people who could not cope with the new reality without the support of their families. The Jewish Agency emissaries transferred thousands of Jews to camps around the capital Addis Ababa; and the Ethiopian Jews kept praying for a miracle that would take them to the Land of Israel.

And the miracle happened.

Six years after Operation Moses, in May 1991, Operation Solomon was launched. It took place at the height of the civil war, as the rebels against the reigning military junta approached Addis Ababa from all sides. The operation was made possible by a last-minute agreement, brokered by the United States, between the government of Israel and the beleaguered ruler Mengistu in the last days before his collapse.

The agreement was negotiated thanks to the secret activity of Uri Lubrani, one of Israel's "mystery men," who had been special envoy to Iran and Lebanon; he had undertaken the mission at the request of Prime Minister Yitzhak Shamir. Israel agreed to pay Ethiopia $35 million for the immigration of the Jews, while the United States promised some of the major figures in Mengistu's government political asylum in America. Simultaneously, an understanding was reached with the rebel leaders that they would accept a truce in the fighting for a limited time while Israel carried out its operation. It took thirty-six hours, and the operation was over.

The IDF was charged with executing Operation Solomon. The deputy chief of staff, General Amnon Lipkin-Shahak, took over command of the action. At his orders, Israel sent to Addis Ababa "everything that could fly." The El Al airline sent to Ethiopia thirty airliners; the air force sent many of its aircraft. Elite squads of Shaldag (Kingfisher) commandos were brought to Addis Ababa. At their sides were hundreds of infantry soldiers and paratroopers of Ethiopian origin, who had immigrated to Israel as children a few years ago. They deployed at the confines of the airport and led the Jews into the planes. In thirty-four hours, 14,400 Jews were brought to the airport. With lightning speed, they boarded the aircraft and took off for Israel. A world record was broken during the operation: an El Al Boeing 747 took on board 1,087 immigrants; but when it landed, it carried 1,088 people. A baby had been born during the flight.

At the sight of the young Ethiopian soldiers who had arrived from Israel to rescue their brothers, tremendous emotions swept the immigrants; even the tough Ethiopian paratroopers, in their green IDF uniforms, red berets, and jumping boots, burst into tears.

Today, more than twenty years after Operation Solomon, there still are many Jews in Ethiopia, and efforts are made to bring them over to Israel. But the absorption of the Ethiopians in the Israeli society has not been easy, often because of the gap between a rural African community and a modern Western nation; but also because of blunt discrimination or ugly claims by some religious leaders that the Ethiopians are not real Jews.

As the last stanza of "The Journey Song" says:

In the moon
The image of my mother looks at me
Mother, don't disappear!
If only she were by my side
She would be able to convince them
That I am a Jew.

WAR WITH IRAN?

Entebbe Airport, Uganda, July 4, 1976

In the black of night, four Israeli Hercules aircraft, undetected by Ugandan radar, surreptitiously land at Entebbe Airport. They have flown a distance of 2,500 miles from their base in Israel, carrying the Sayeret Matkal commando and several other elite army units. A week before, Arab and German terrorists hijacked an Air France airliner on its way from Tel-Aviv to Paris, and landed it in Entebbe. Protected and supported by Uganda's dictator, General Iddi Amin, the terrorists hold ninety-five Israeli civilians hostage. Israel decides to launch a daring operation to the heart of Africa, to rescue the hostages.

Minutes after the landing, the Israeli commandos spread throughout the airport. Yoni Netanyahu, commander of Sayeret Matkal, leads his men in an assault on the terminal where the hostages are held. In the intense firefight that erupts, Yoni suddenly collapses, hit by a bullet. Another Sayeret officer, Captain Tamir Pardo, bends over his fallen commander, switches his mike on, and calls his comrades. Yoni has been hit, he says. "Muki, take over!" Yoni's deputy, Muki Betzer, assumes command and pursues the mission. Minutes later, the battle is over. The terrorists are killed, the hostages rescued, and the heavy Hercules planes take off, on their way back to Israel.

The rescue of the hostages, so far away from home, is about to become legend. But it has exacted a price: three of the hostages have died in the firefight. As has one soldier, Lieutenant-Colonel Yoni Netanyahu, brother of future Prime Minister Benjamin Netanyahu. The entire Israeli nation mourns Yoni's death. That night, Tamir Pardo, the Sayeret communications officer, knocks on the door of the Netanyahu family in Jerusalem; he has been sent to inform them about the circumstances of Yoni's death. A warm relationship will sprout between Netanyahu's family and Tamir Pardo, who was at Yoni's side in his last moments.

Thirty-five years later, fifty-seven-year-old Tamir Pardo is appointed *ramsad*, replacing Meir Dagan.

Born in Tel Aviv to a Jewish family of Turkish and Serbian origin, eighteen-year-old Tamir had volunteered for the paratroopers, graduated from the officers academy, and served in the Sayeret Matkal and at Shaldag (Kingfisher) commando units. Four years after Entebbe, he joined the Mossad, took part in several unnamed operations, and was awarded the Israel Security Prize three times. In 1998 he was appointed chairman of the Mossad inquiry board that investigated Khaled Mashal's flawed assassination attempt in Amman. Soon after, he became the head of Nevioth, the Mossad department charged with electronic collection of intelligence in foreign countries. He specialized in new technologies and creative planning. In 2002, when Dagan was appointed *ramsad*, Pardo became one of his two deputies, and for the next four years headed the Mossad Operations Staff; but in 2006 he spent a year with the IDF as an army general, advising the General Staff on special operations. He was said to have planned several daring missions during the Second Lebanon War. Pardo was called back to Dagan's side in 2007. He expected to be appointed *ramsad* when Dagan's tenure came to an end in 2009, but the cabinet, impressed by Dagan's achievements, extended his service for another year. Pardo, disappointed, resigned from the Mossad and went into business with a medical services company. That did not last long. On November 29, 2010, Prime Minister Netanyahu appointed him the next *ramsad*, and he assumed his functions in January 2011.

In many ways, Pardo followed the footsteps of his predecessor. The ruthless covert war against Iran continued. In November and December 2011, several explosions rocked a military base where Shehab missiles were being tested, and a Isfahan suburb where the uranium gas, separated in the centrifuge cascades, was again converted to solid matter. Then another scientist, Dr. Mostafa Ahmadi-Roshan, the deputy director of the Natanz underground facility, was killed while driving his car in the streets of Tehran. The modus operandi was similar to others used in several past assassinations.

Iran accused Israel of the attacks and swore revenge. For the first time, the Iranian secret services tried to carry out several coups against Israeli targets in Asia: a bombing of a car in New Delhi wounded an Israeli diplomat's wife; a similar attempt in Tbilisi, Georgia, failed; several explosions went off in Bangkok, Thailand, one of which wounded the perpetrator, an Iranian national. The Egyptian secret services foiled a plot by Iranian agents to blow up an Israeli ship sailing through the Suez Canal. The covert war between Israel and Iran was now coming into the open. Police investigators in New Delhi, Bangkok, and Cairo pointed a finger at Iran's secret services. The world press described in detail the rather clumsy attempts by Iranian spooks to attack Israeli targets abroad.

Coming into the open were also new details about the Israeli operations inside Iran. Western sources claimed that the Mossad had established operational bases in Azerbaijan and Kurdistan, right on the Iranian border. They served as the training grounds and dispatch for agents inside Iranian territory. The same sources claimed that many of the Mossad agents operating inside Iran were actually members of the M.E.K. opposition, Iranian Muslims who could blend into the local population better than any Israeli officer. Quite a few M.E.K. militants had been trained in secret facilities in Israel, and even rehearsed some of the operations on specially built models—like a Tehran street—where they were to ambush an Iranian nuclear scientist's car or plant a bomb near his home.

In other cases, Iranian dissidents were approached by different means. Several CIA memos even maintained that Mossad officers carried out "False Flag" recruiting missions. The Israelis, allegedly posing as CIA agents, recruited militants of the Pakistani terrorist organization Jundallah and sent them on sabotage and assassination missions inside Iran. According to the CIA memos, the Israelis posed as American intelligence officers in order to overcome the devout Muslims' objection to serving the Jewish state.

In the spring of 2012, worried international observers claimed that the Iranian nuclear project was close to completion and sources in the International Atomic Energy Agency even declared that Iran has produced 109 kilograms of enriched uranium, enough to assemble four atomic bombs. If Israel decided to deal a major blow to the Iranian project by launching an all-out attack against its nuclear centers, the covert war would give way to an open one.

According to the world press and quite a few talkative spokesmen, Israel was not alone in its consideration of a military option. In Jerusalem and Washington, official sources confirmed that Israel and the United States were acting together, but disagreed on a major point: when would Iran have to be stopped by all means necessary—military or other. The American services claimed that this would be the moment when the enrichment of uranium by Iran reached 80 percent, a crucial stage in the development of their nuclear capability. Uranium enriched to that level could be very quickly upgraded to 97 percent, the degree needed for the assembly of an atomic bomb.

Israel's timetable was different, based on reports from the ground and satellite detection. The Mossad had discovered that Iran was engaged in a chaotic race against time, building a large number of underground facilities buried at a depth of eighty meters or more. They were transferring all their fissile materials and their secret labs underground. Intelligence reports obtained by the Mossad, with the help of the M.E.K. resistance organization, claimed that Iran had built a new underground facility close to Fordo. In the huge halls of the new facility the Iranians planned to install three thousand new centrifuges, far faster and more sophisticated than the equipment now in service. In that facility the Iranians could feed the centrifuges uranium enriched up to 3.5 percent and keep enriching it till it was ready for use. Israel was convinced that this doomsday cave, like many other bases and labs, had to be destroyed before the centrifuges were installed, becoming fully protected against an aerial attack. "When they reach the critical stage of enrichment," the Israeli envoys told the Americans, "it will be too late to hit them. They will have entered an 'immune area' where no bombings will be able to destroy their project. The time to act is now, in the spring of 2012."

Washington was not convinced and wanted to try a campaign of harsh sanctions. Israel did not believe the sanctions would stop Iran. At a summit meeting in Washington in early spring 2012, President Obama and Prime Minister Netanyahu praised the firm strategic alliance between the two nations but could not agree on a way forward against the Iranian nuclear project. The Mossad reports still indicated that Tehran was relentlessly pursuing atomic power. At the same time, Iranian leaders relentlessly threatened Israel with total annihilation. The very thought of the danger that a fanatic, nuclear Iran represented for Israel and the world reminded the Israelis of the old Talmudic adage: "If someone comes to kill you—rise up and kill him first."

Israel felt that once again it was standing alone. And, as in 1948, the year of its creation, and in 1967, on the eve of the Six-Day War, Israel again faces the most fateful decision of its existence.

ACKNOWLEDGMENTS

An earlier version of *Mossad* was published in Israel in 2010, where it stayed on the bestseller lists for seventy weeks, and received the gold, platinum, and diamond shields for breaking sales records. We want to thank first of all our Israeli publisher, Dov Eichenwald, director general of Yedioth Ahronoth publishing house, who conceived the idea and then encouraged and supported us all along the way.

We are deeply grateful to the former directors and agents of the intelligence community—we could name only a few of them—who helped us with information and advice.

Our research assistants Oriana Almassi and Nilly Ovnat made a tremendous effort to bring the project to life. Nilly Ovnat also assisted us greatly in preparing the rewritten and updated English version of *Mossad*.

In the U.S., we were happy to collaborate with our publisher, Dan Halpern, at HarperCollins/Ecco, and with our devoted editors, Abigail Holstein and Karen Maine. We also want to thank our copyeditor, Olga Gardner Galvin, for her X-ray eyes and inquisitive pencil.

This book appears almost simultaneously in more than twenty countries all over the world, and we greatly appreciate the efforts of our agents, Writers' House of New York, especially of "Mr. Writers' House," Al Zuckerman, and the indefatigable foreign rights director Maja Nikolic.

Finally we thank our ladies, Galila Bar-Zohar and Amy Korman, for advising, reading, correcting, suggesting, arguing—and still apparently not giving up on us.

Michael Bar-Zohar

Nissim Mishal

BIBLIOGRAPHY AND SOURCES

Mossad is based on a large variety of sources, books, documents, newspaper articles, and interviews. As it deals with exclusively secret materials, the importance of reliable, solid sources is crucial. Most of the sources in Hebrew were unpublished documents and in-depth interviews with many of the major players in that world of shadows. We also used a great number of sources in English, after trying to separate the genuine information from the fantastic inventions of fertile minds. We hope to have succeeded in this endeavor.

As for the Hebrew books and articles mentioned in the references, their titles were translated into English. The sources marked with an (H) are in Hebrew.

Among the many different sources for this book, the authors used the following publications by Dr. Ronen Bergman:

Chapter 1: "King of Shadows" is based on, among other sources:
"In His Majesty's Service," Ronen Bergman, *Yedioth Ahronoth*, 5.2.2010 (H)
"Dagan Raised Chaos," Ronen Bergman, *Yedioth Ahronoth*, 7.10.2005 (H)
"Closed Institution," Ronen Bergman, *Yedioth Ahronoth*, 3.7.2009 (H)

Chapter 2: "Funeral in Tehran" is based on, among other sources:
Bergman Ronen, *Point of No Return* (Kinneret: Zmora-Bitan Dvir, 2007), pp. 32, 454–56, 470–71, 473, 478, 481–82, 491–92 (H)
"A Fantastic Incident," Ronen Bergman, *Yedioth Ahronoth*, 7.12.2007 (H)
"The Spy Who Talked," Ronen Bergman, *Yedioth Ahronoth*, 12.9.2009 (H)
"The Brain," Ronen Bergman, *Yedioth Ahronoth*, 19.3.2010 (H)

Chapter 4: "A Soviet Mole and a Body at Sea" is based on, among other sources:
"That's How the Mossad Killed Father (And Lied to Mother)," Ronen Bergman, *Yedioth Ahronoth*, 26.5.2006 (H)

Chapter 14: "Today We'll Be at War!" is based on, among other sources:
"Their Man in Cairo," Ronen Bergman, *Yedioth Ahronoth*, 6.5.2005 (H)
"Code Name Hatuel," Ronen Bergman, *Yedioth Ahronoth*, 7.9.2007 (H)

Chapter 16: "Saddam's Supergun" is based on, among other sources:
"Cut off His Head, Mossad Version," Ronen Bergman, *Yedioth Ahronoth*, 8.6.2007 (H)

Chapter 17: "Fiasco in Amman" is based on, among other sources:
"Less Luck Than Brain," Ronen Bergman, *Yedioth Ahronoth*, 7.7.2006 (H)

Chapter 18: "From North Korea with Love" is based on, among other sources:
"Assad's Nuclear Plan," Ronen Bergman, *Yedioth Ahronoth*, 4.4.2008 (H)
"The Nuclear General Killed on Shore," Ronen Bergman, *Yedioth Ahronoth*, 4.8.2008
"Wikileaks: The Attack on Syria," Ronen Bergman, *Yedioth Ahronoth*, 24.12.2010 (H)

Chapter 20: "The Cameras Were Rolling" is based on, among other sources:
"Turn off the Plasma," Ronen Bergman, *Yedioth Ahronoth*, 31.12.2010 (H)
"The Anatomy of Mossad's Dubai Operation," Ronen Bergman, Christopher Schult, Alexander Smoltczyk, Holger Stark, and Bernard Zand, Spiegel Online, 17.1.2011

Chapter 21: "From the Land of the Queen of Sheba" is based on, among other sources:
"The Price: 4000 Killed," Ronen Bergman, *Yedioth Ahronoth*, 3.7.1998 (H)

CHAPTER 1: KING OF SHADOWS
MEIR DAGAN

"Meir Dagan, the Mastermind Behind Mossad's Secret War," Uzi Mahanaimi, *Sunday Times*, February 21, 2010
"The Powerful, Shadowy Mossad Chief Meir Dagan Is a Streetfighter," London *Times*, February 18, 2010
"Mossad Chief Meir Dagan Is a 'Streetfighter,' " *Nation* (Pakistan), February 18, 2010
"Vegetarian, Painter . . . Spy Chief," Uzi Mahanaimi, *Sunday Times*, February 21, 2010
"Mossad—The World's Most Efficient Killing Machine," Gordon Thomas, Rense .com, September 12, 2002
"Abu Jabel Gets the Mossad," Yigal Sarna, *Yedioth Ahronoth*, September 13, 2002 (H)

Mike Eldar, Sayeret Shaked Association, The Heritage, synopsis of the book *Unit 424*, the story of Sayeret (Commando) Shaked, published by Shaked Association (H)

"Dagan Who?" Sima Kadmon, *Yedioth Ahronoth*, November 30, 2001 (H)

"Mossad in Deep Freeze," Ron Leshem, *Yedioth Ahronoth*, January 18, 2002 (H)

"The First Liquidations," Yigal Sarna and Guy Leshem, *Yedioth Ahronoth*, September 26, 1997 (H)

"For You, Grandpa," Amos Shavit, *Yedioth Ahronoth*, Day of the Holocaust, April 12, 2010 (H)

"One Could Blow Up," Amir Oren, *Haaretz*, March 28, 2010 (H)

"Even in the Yom Kippur War the Best Generals Were Mistaken," Ron Leshem, *Yedioth Ahronoth*, January 14, 2000 (H)

"Sharon Raised Dagan," Nahum Barnea, *Yedioth Ahronoth*, September 13, 2002 (H)

"The Brave Officer Who Did Not Recoil from Killing," *Yedioth Ahronoth*, September 11, 2002 (H)

"Meir Dagan: Israeli Superman," Smadar Perry, *Yedioth Ahronoth*, January 17, 2010 (H)

"Israel Is Conducting a Liquidation Campaign in the Middle East," Dana Herman, *Haaretz*, February 14, 2010 (H)

"His Life's Job," Yoav Limor and Alon Ben-David, YNET, June 4, 2005 (H)

"In the Dark, It's Not Bad to Be Head of the Mossad Meir Dagan," Amir Oren, *Haaretz*, March 23, 2010 (H)

"Even Nasrallah Fears Dagan's Methods," Aluf Ben, *Haaretz*, September 26, 2008 (H)

"Special Profile—The Man Who Gave Back to Israel Its Deterrent," Alon Ben-David, February 4, 2010, News.nana10.co.il/article (H)

"A Politician Takes Risks (About Meir Dagan)," Stella Korin-Lieber, *Globes*, February 18, 2010 (H)

"Who Will Handle the Iranian Nuclear Project," Aluf Ben, *Haaretz*, August 26, 2003 (H)

"Sharon Delegates to the Mossad Director the Dealing with the Iranian Nuclear Threat," Aluf Ben, *Haaretz*, September 4, 2003 (H)

ATTACKS ON TERROR LEADERS IN SYRIA AND LEBANON

"Islamic Jihad Leader Killed in Lebanon," Bassem Mroue, Associated Press, *Washington Post*, May 26, 2006

"Syria Blast Kills Hamas Militant," BBC News, September 26, 2004

"Report: Mashal's Secretary Was Killed in Syria," Yoav Stern, *Haaretz*, September 9, 2008 (H)

"The Explosion in Beirut Targeted Hamas Official Osama Hamdan," Zvi Yechezkeli, Nana 10, December 27, 2009 (H)

BIBLIOGRAPHY AND SOURCES

"Report: Hezbollah Members Were Killed in the Bombing in Beirut," Roie Nachmias, YNET, December 13, 2009 (H)

"Report: 3 Hurt in the Attempt to Kill Hezbollah Member," Roie Nachmias,
YNET, January 13, 2010; *Haaretz*, June 20, 2010 (H)

"Netanyahu Thanked Dagan in the Name of the Jewish People," Shlomo Zesna,
Israel Hayom, January 3, 2011(H)

"Dear Meir Here Is George," Itamar Eichner, *Yedioth Ahronoth*, January 14, 2011

CHAPTER 2: FUNERAL IN TEHRAN
GENERAL

Sokolski, Henry, and Patrick Clawson, eds., *Getting Ready for a Nuclear-Ready Iran*
(PDF), Strategic Studies Institute, 2005

Cordesman, Anthony H., and Khalid R. Al-Rodhan, *Iranian Nuclear Weapons? The
Uncertain Nature of Iran's Nuclear Programs* (PDF), Center for Strategic and International Studies, 2006

Lewis, Jeffrey, *Briefings on Iran's Weaponization Work*, Lewisarmscontrolwonk.com,
March 12, 2008

Risen, James, *State of War: The Secret History of the CIA and the Bush Administration*
(New York:, Simon and Shuster, 2006)

Cockburn, Andrew and Leslie Cockburn, *Dangerous Liaisons: The Inside Story of the
U.S.-Israeli Covert Relationship* (New York: HarperCollins, 1991)

Cordesman, Anthony, *Peace and War—The Arab-Israeli Military Balance Enters the
21st Century* (New York: Praeger, 2001)

Minashri, David, *Iran: Between Islam and the West* (Ministry of Defense Publishing
House, 1996) (H)

"UN Calls US Data on Iran's Nuclear Aims Unreliable," Bob Drogin and Kim
Murphy, *Los Angeles Times*, February 25, 2007

"Juan Cole Interview: Conversations with History, Iran and Nuclear Technology," Harry
Kreisler, Institute of International Studies, UC Berkeley, Berkeley.edu/people5/cole

"The Enduring Threat—a Brief History: Iranian Nuclear Ambitions and American
Foreign Policy," Terence M. Gatt, Information Clearing House, Information-
clearinghouse.info.article, November 3, 2005

"Iran's Nuclear Program, Recent Developments," Sharon Squassoni, CRS Congressional report, 2003, fpc.state.gov/documents/organization

"Iran Nuclear Milestones 1967–2009," Wisconsin Project on Nuclear Arms Control, *The Risk Report*, vol. 15, no. 6 (November–December 2009)

"The Secret Nuclear Dossier: Intelligence from Tehran Elevates Concern in the West," Dieter Bednarz, Erich Follath, and Holger Stark, *Der Spiegel*, January 25, 2010

Parsi, Trita, *Treacherous Alliance: The Secret Dealings of Israel, Iran, and the U.S.* (New Haven: Yale University Press, 2007)

A Brief History of Iran Missile Technology, Liveleak.com/view, June 9, 2007

Weapons of Mass Destruction, Bushehr Background, Globalsecurity.org/wmd/world/iran/bushehr, October 15, 2008

New Nuclear Revelations, transcript of the press conference of Mohammad Mohadessine, Chairman of the Foreign Affairs Committee of the National Council of the Resistance of Iran, IranWatch.org, September 10, 2004

Iranian Entity: Islamic Revolutionary Guard Corps, IranWatch.org, January 26, 2004–August 27, 2008

Zafrir, Eliezer (Gaizi), *Big Satan, Small Satan: Revolution and Escape in Iran*, Maariv, 2002 (H)

Kam, Ephraim, *From the Terror to the Nuclear: The Meaning of the Iranian Threat* (Defense Ministry Publishing House, 2004) (H)

Nakdimon, Shlomo, *Tammuz in Flames* (Tel Aviv: Yedioth Ahronoth, 2004) (H)

"Iranian Organization: The Nuclear Project Renewed After 2003," Reuters, YNET, December 1, 2007 (H)

"Rajavi Against the Ayatollahs," Kraig Smith, Haaretz.co.il, 2005 (H)

"First Nuclear Explosion," Ronen Salomon, Byclick. Info/rs/news (H)

"How to Build a Nuclear Bomb," Minerva.tau.ac.il/bsc/1/1804 (H)

Report: Iran Will Cross the Technological Threshold in 2010, International Institute for Strategic Studies, YNET, January 28, 2009 (H)

"Head of American Intelligence: Iran May Threaten Europe Within Three Years," AP, YNET, January 17, 2009 (H)

"Analyzing the Enigma: What Will Iran Do If Attacked? The Answer Will Surprise You," Dr. Guy Bechor, Forum Intifada, *Internet News*, December 8, 2008 (H)

"Iran Will Be Able to Produce a Bomb This Year," *Der Spiegel*, Forum Intifada, Topics and News, January 25, 2010, and NRG January 25, 2010 (H)

"How to Stop the Bomb," Yoav Limor, YNET, June 19, 2007 (H)

"War Games (Scenarios)," David Sanger, *New York Times, Haaretz*, April 4, 2010 (H)

"Uri Lubrani: An Interview at His Retirement from the Ministry of Defense," Yossi Yehoshua and Reuven Weiss, *Yedioth Ahronoth*, February 15, 2010 (H)

"Palestine Iran Palestine," Ari Shavit, *Haaretz*, March 25, 2010 (H)

"How the Opportunity to Attack and Destroy the Iranian Nuclear Project Was Missed," Aluf Ben and Amos Harel, *Haaretz*, December 18, 2009 (H)

"Appointment in Iran: The Head of the Nuclear Project Is the Scientist Who Survived the Attempt on His Life," *Yedioth Ahronoth*, February 14, 2011 (H)

"An Analysis of the Virus in the Iranian Nuclear Reactor, Confirms Its Purpose: To Sabotage the Centrifuges," Yossi Melman, *Haaretz*, November 19, 2010 (H)

"Mossad, U.S., U.K. Cooperating to Sabotage Iran Nukes," jpost.com.staff, December 30, 2010

KHOMEINI AND THE "ANTI-ISLAMIC" NUCLEAR WEAPONS

Tahiri, Amir, *Allah's Spirit: Khomeini and the Islamic Revolution* (Tel Aviv: Ofakim-Am-Oved, 1985) (H)

"Will Worldwide Recession Create Totalitarianism Again?" Carol Forsloff, *Digital Journal*, December 14, 2008

"Khamenei Vehemently Rejects Nuclear Allegations," Arabianbusiness.com, June 3, 2008

"Has Iran Been Striving for Nuclear Weapons for Many Years?" Kedma Amirpour Katajun, translated from the *Zud Deutsche Zeitung* with the author's permission, Kedma.co.il (H)

"A Speech by the Ayatollah Khomeini About Nuclear Development and the Negative Influence of the American Technology," Answers Yahoo.com, April 9, 2006 (H)

"Before Starting a New War in the Middle East," Yossi Dahan, *Haoketz*, haokets.didila.com, June 5, 2009 (H)

1977—ISRAEL OFFERS BALLISTIC MISSILES TO IRAN

Minutes of Conversation Between Defense Minister Weizman and General Toffinian, July 18, 1977; see also Top Secret Minutes from Israel's Ministry of Foreign Affairs, July 18, 1977, Digital National Security Archive, George Washington University, Washington, DC

The authors' interviews with former Minister of Defense Ezer Weizman and with former Director General of the Ministry of Defense Dr. Pinhas (Siko) Zusman

"The Israeli Past of the Iranian Nuclear Reactor," Gad Shimron, *Maariv*, August 8, 2007 (H)

DR. KHAN AND IRAN'S SECRET NUCLEAR PROGRAM

Eurenco, profile: Eurenco.com/en/about

Dr. Khan's televised confession, Whitemaps.co.il

"Bin Laden's Operatives Still Use Freewheeling Dubai," *USA Today*, September 2, 2004

Dr. Abdul Qadeer Khan discusses Nuclear Program in TV talk show, Karachi Aaj News television, 31 August, 2009

"Iran Was Offered Nuclear Parts; Secret Meeting in 1987 Might Have Begun Program," Daphna Linzer, *Washington Post*, February 27, 2005

"How America Looked the Other Way as Pakistan Sold Nuclear Technology to Iran," Joseph and Susan Trento, War News, Secret History, Iraqwarnews.org, October 20, 2009

"Are You with Us—or Against Us?" Jonathan Shell, Wagingpeace.org, November 14, 2007

"Non-Proliferation Review and Iran—Why China Owes Us One," William Sweet, Arms control and proliferation, arms control foreign policy.com

"Investigation: Nuclear Scandal—Dr. Abdul Qadeer Khan," Simon Henderson, *Sunday Times*, September 20, 2009

"A. Q. Khan and the Limits of the Nonproliferation Regime," Christopher Clary, Center for Contemporary Conflict, Monterey, CA, articles written between April and June 2004, Unidir.orgpdf/articles

DR. CHAUHDRY'S DEFECTION

"Pakistani Says a Strike Was Planned on India," John Kifner, *New York Times*, July 2, 1998

"That Pakistani Nuclear Expert May Be a Lowly Accountant," John Kifner, *New York Times*, July 3, 1998

"Scientists Say Pakistani Defector Is Not Credible," John Kifner, *New York Times*, July 8, 1998

"Pakistan Was 48 Hours Away from a Preemptive Strike: Scientist," Chidanand Rajghatta, *Indian Express*, July 3, 1998

"More Disclosures After Asylum: Defector," *Tribune* (India), July 5, 1998

"Mystifying Spy," Narayan D. Keshavan, *Outlook India*, July 13, 1998

"Iran Part of Pakistan-China Nexus: Khan," Chidanand Rajghatta, *Indian Express*, July 3, 1998

"Asylum Seeker's Story Still Doubted," Associated Press of Pakistan, July 3, 1998

"Articles About Defection—Pakistani Reveals Details of Nuclear Program, Seeks Asylum," Robin Wright, *Los Angeles Times*, July 2, 1998

"Khan Job: Bush Spiked Probe of Pakistan's Dr. Strangelove, BBC reported in 2001," Greg Palast, Gregpalast.com, September 2, 2004

Various reports of the press conferences held by Dr. Iftikhar Khan Chauhdry on July 1, 1998, in the offices of Wildes & Weinberg, attorneys-at-law, 515 Madison Avenue, New York

ISRAEL AND THE DEFECTION OF ASKARI AND AMIRI FROM IRAN

"Former Iranian Defense Official Talks to Western Intelligence," Daphna Linzer, *Washington Post*, March 8, 2007

"Mossad Implicated in Missing Defector Mystery," Tim Butcher, *Telegraph*, March 9, 2007

"Defector Spied on Iran for Years," Uzi Mahanaymi, *Sunday Times*, March 11, 2007

"Iran Nuclear Scientist Defects to the U.S. in CIA 'Intelligence Coup,'" Matthew Cole, ABC News, April 1, 2010

"Report: The Top Iranian Decided to Leave His Country and Defect to USA," Yoav Stern, *Haaretz*, March 7, 2007 (H)

"Contradicting Reports About the Defection of the Iranian General," Yossi Melman, *Haaretz*, March 12, 2007 (H)

"Report: Two Iranian Nuclear Scientists Defected Lately to the West," Yossi Melman, *Haaretz*, October 7, 2009 (H)

"Iran: The USA Is Involved in the Disappearance of Our Atomic Scientists," Yossi Melman, *Haaretz*, October 8, 2009 (H)

"Report: Uranium Scientist Who Disappeared in Saudi Arabia Defected to USA," Reuters, March 31, 2010 (H)

"The Nuclear Scientist Who Disappeared in Saudi Arabia Assists the CIA," Israel Hayom, April 2, 2010 (H)

DR. MOHSEN FAKHRIZADEH ("THE BRAIN")

Iranian Entity: Mohsen Fakhrizadeh Mahabadi. Full bio and functions, including passport numbers. Assets in US and EU frozen, etc. IranWatch.org, June 18, 2007–August 28, 2008

NCRI—Press conference on Resistance in Iran, by Mohammad Mohadessin, Foreign Affairs Committee Chairman, on Fakhrizadeh: Full functions, address, phone numbers, IranWatch.org, November 17, 2004

"Iran Suspends Enrichment in Return for EU Pressure on Opposition," Irannuclear.org, November 15, 2005

"Verbatim: Iranian Opposition Reveals Secret Nuclear Site in Tehran," Iranfocus.com, November 19, 2004

"Iran Is Ready to Build an N-bomb, It's Just Waiting for the Ayatollah's Order," James Hider, Richard Beeston in Tel Aviv, and Michael Evans, defense editor, *Times* (London), August 3, 2009

"Disclosing a major secret nuclear site under the Ministry of Defense," NCRI, Weapons of Mass Destruction newsletter, November 17, 2004

"Ministry of Defense Continues Secret Work on Laser Enrichment Program," Irannuclear.org, February 12, 2006

"Half Sigma: How Much Does a Nuclear Bomb Have to Weigh?" Half Sigma.com, September 29, 2009

Fakhri Zadeh—Dr. Strangelove, seeker 401, wordpress.com

SECRET OPERATIONS IN IRAN

"U.S. Working to Sabotage Iran's Nuke Program," Scott Conroy, Article written by Sheila MacVicar and Ashley Velie with Amy Guttman, May 23, 2007
Article plus report on the *CBS Evening News*

"Report: Israel Secretly Sabotaging Iran's Nuclear Program (Using Assassins, Sabotage, Double Agents and Front Companies)," *Daily Telegraph*, quoted by YNET, February 17, 2009 (H)

"Western Sabotage Undermines Iran Nuclear Drive: Experts," France 24, International News, AFP, April 13, 2010

"Iranian Nuclear Scientist 'Assassinated by Mossad,'" Sara Baxter, *Times* (London), February 4, 2007

"Bush Authorizes New Covert Action Against Iran," ABC News, May 22, 2007

"Jitters Over Iran Blast Highlight Tensions," *World News on MSNBC*, Associated Press, February 16, 2005

"Massive Explosion in Parchin Missile Site of the Guard Corps," Foreign Affairs Committee of the National Council of Resistance of Iran, November 14, 2007

MPG's Bushehr branch video of Petrochemical plant explosion [in Bushehr Province], MPG, Bushehr Branch, Marzeporgohar.org, August 15, 2009

"U.S. Sabotaged Natanz, Sent Defective Equipment to Islamic Republic (Power System Failed and 50 Centrifuges Exploded)," *Iran Times International*, BNET (CBS Interactive), August 29, 2008

Iranian attack complicates nuclear negotiations (murder of Ali-Mohammadi), Stratfor, Global Intelligence, January 12, 2010

Iran-Israel covert war: the Mossad is said to wage a clandestine campaign of assassination and sabotage against Iran's nuclear programme, but this could backfire on President Obama's efforts to negotiate with Tehran, Ed Blanche, The Middle East, Thefreelibrary.com/_/print, July 1, 2009

"Israel Launches Covert War Against Iran," Philip Sherwell, *Daily Telegraph*, February 18, 2009

"Sources Expose Covert Israel War on Iran," Press TV, Payvand Iran News, payvand.com/news, February 17, 2009

"Iran Nuke Laptop Data Came from Terror Group," Gareth Porter, IPS, ipsnews.net, February 29, 2008

"Report Ties Dubious Iran Nuke Documents to Israel, "Gareth Porter, *Counterpunch*, Counterpunch.org, June 4, 2009

"Mysterious Assassination in Iran—Who Killed Masoud Ali Mohammadi?" Dieter Bednarz, *Der Spiegel*, January 18, 2010

"Iran's VIP Plane Crash: Sabotage or Accident?" Stratfor.com, January 10, 2006

"Swiss Engineers, a Nuclear Black Market and the CIA," William J. Broad and David E. Sanger, *New York Times*, August 25, 2008

"Iran Hangs Convicted Spy for Israel," Thomas Erdbrink, *Washington Post*, November 23, 2008

"British Agent Exposed True Purpose of Qom Reactor," Ron Ben-Ishai, YNET, December 15, 2009 (H)

"How Secrecy Over Iran's Qom Nuclear Facility Was Finally Blown Away," Catherine Philip, Francis Elliot, and Giles Whittell, *Sunday Times*, September 26, 2009

"CIA Knew About Iran's Secret Nuclear Plant Long Before Disclosure," Bobby Ghosh, *Time*, October 7, 2009

"How El-Baradei Misled the World About Iran's Nuclear Program," Yossi Melman, *Haaretz* in English, December 3, 2009

"Mossad: Was This the Chief's Last Hit?" Gordon Thomas, *Telegraph*, December 5, 2010

"Israel Seen Engaged in Covert War Inside Iran," Luke Baker, Reuters (London), February 17, 2009

"West Is Assassinating Scientists as Negotiation Strategy," JPost.com.staff, December 1, 2010

"*Time* Magazine: The Scientist Who Was Attacked in Teheran—the Most Senior in the Nuclear Iranian Plan," Anshil Pepper, *Haaretz*, December 3, 2010 (H)

"Iran Blames Israel for Killing Its Defense Minister," Yossi Melman, *Haaretz*, January 2, 2011 (H)

Thomas, Gordon, *Gideon's Spies* (New York: St. Martin's Griffin, 2009), p. 478

"Report: The Mossad Killed an Iranian Nuclear Scientist," Jerry Lewis, Orly Azulay, Itamar Eichner, *Yedioth Ahronoth*, February 4, 2007 (H)

"Nuclear Sting," Eldad Beck, Yaniv Halili, *Yedioth Ahronoth*, August 26, 2008 (H)

"The Enigma of the Chemical Iranian Cargo," Menachem Ganz, *Yedioth Ahronoth*, September 25, 2008 (H)

"They Sold Them Faulty Equipment," Yossi Melman, *Haaretz*, July 13, 2007 (H)

"Did the Mossad Fail?" Yossi Melman, *Haaretz*, November 25, 2008 (H)

"Straw Companies or the Mossad—How We Screwed Iran," Yossi Melman, *Haaretz*, November 28, 2008 (H)

"Iran Hanged a Mossad Agent (Ali Ashtari)," "Inyan Merkazi," news room, November 22, 2008 (H)

THE RUSSIAN AID TO IRAN

"Nuclear Aid by Russians to Iranians Suspected," *New York Times*, October 10, 2008

"The Russian Handicap to U.S.-Iran Policy," Ariel Cohen, *Jerusalem Center for Public Affairs*, vol. 8, no. 28, April 22, 2009

Statement by Director, DCI Non-Proliferation Center, John Lauder, on Russian Proliferation to Iran's Weapons of Mass Destruction and Missile Programs, to the Senate Foreign Relations Committee, as Prepared for Delivery on October 5, 2000, Documents Home Page, CIA Released Documents, faqs.org

The Collapse of the Russian Scientists and Rogue States, T. P. Gerber, 2005, Massachusetts Institute of Technology

"Russia-Iran Nuclear Deal Signed," BBC News, February 27, 2005

"Arctic Sea Was Carrying Illegal Arms Says General," Shaun Walker, *Independent*, July 24, 2009

"Was Russia's Arctic Sea Carrying Missiles to Iran?" Simon Schuster, *Time*, August 31, 2009

"Report: Netanyahu Transferred to the Kremlin a List of Scientists Who Assist Iran," Zach Yoked, *Maariv*, October 4, 2009 (H)

ISRAEL-UNITED STATES—COLLABORATION AND DISPUTE

"U.S. Rejected Aid for Israeli Raid on Iranian Nuclear Site," David Sanger, *New York Times*, January 10, 2009

"An Israeli Preventive Attack on Iran's Nuclear Sites: Implications for the U.S.," James Phillips, Heritage Foundation, Heritage.org, January 15, 2010

"Facing Iran: Lessons Learned Since Iraq's 1991 Missile Attack on Israel," Moshe Arens, The Jerusalem Center for Public and State Matters, March 8, 2010

Segev, Shmuel, *The Iranian Triangle, the Secret Relationship Between Israel, Iran, and USA*, Maariv, 1981 (H)

STUXNET AND ESPIONAGE

"Computer Virus in Iran Actually Targeted Larger Nuclear Facility," Yossi Melman, *Haaretz*, September 28, 2010 (H)

"The Meaning of Stuxnet," *Economist*, October 2, 2010

"Israel May or May Not Have Been Behind the Stuxnet 'Worm' Attack on Iran—and It Doesn't Matter Whether It Was," Yossi Melman, *Tablet*, October 5, 2010

"Iran Executes 2 Men, Saying One Was Spy for Israel," William Yong, *New York Times*, December 28, 2010

"Iranian Citizen Hanged for Spying for Israel," Yossi Melman, *Haaretz*, December 29, 2010 (H)

"Iran: 'We Hanged an Israeli Spy'—Ali Akbar Siadat Was Hanged for Spying for Israel, Which Paid Him US$60,000," Smadar Perry, *Yedioth Ahronoth*, December 29, 2010 (H)

"Tehran Demands UN Intervention, Accuses Israel of Killing Its Minister of Defense (Ali Riza Askari)," Yossi Melman, *Haaretz*, January 2, 2011(H)

"Iran to the UN: Find Out What Happened to the Missing General," YNET, December 31, 2010 (H)

"Outgoing Mossad Head Delivers Farewell Words," Jpost.com.staff, *Jerusalem Post*, January 7, 2011

"Netanyahu Bids Farewell to Mossad Chief," Gil Ronen, Arutz Sheva, Israel National News.com, March 1, 2011 (H)

"Iran Threat Is Too Much for the Mossad to Handle: Israel's Intelligence Agencies Operate Brilliantly but They Can't Tackle Historic Challenges Singlehandedly," Ari Shavit, Haaretz.com, February 18, 2010 (H)

"The Superman of the Hebrew State," Ashraf Abu Al-Houl, *El-Aharam*, January 16, 2010

CHAPTER 3: A HANGING IN BAGHDAD

Eshed, Hagai, *One-Man Mossad, Reuven Shiloach: Father of the Israeli Intelligence* (Tel Aviv: Idanim, 1988) (H)

Teveth, Shabtai, *Ben-Gurion's Spy, The Story of the Political Scandal that Shaped Modern Israel* (New York: Columbia University Press, 1990)

Strasman, Gavriel, *Back from the Gallows* (Tel Aviv: Yedioth Ahronoth Books, 1992) (H)

Bar-Zohar, Michael, *Spies in the Promised Land* (Boston: Houghton Mifflin, 1972)
Interviews with Shlomo Hillel, Yehuda Taggar, Mordechai Ben-Porat

CHAPTER 4: A SOVIET MOLE AND A BODY AT SEA

THE AVNI AFFAIR

Avni, Ze'ev, *False Flag: The Soviet Spy Who Penetrated the Israeli Secret Intelligence Service* (London: St. Ermin's Press, 2000)
Censored and unpublished chapter about Ze'ev Avni, prepared for Michael Bar-Zohar's book *Spies in the Promised Land,* as told by Isser Harel
Interviews of Ze'ev Avni, former *ramsad* Isser Harel, former head of the Shabak Amos Manor, members of the Mossad and Shabak (anonymously)

A BODY AT SEA

Censored and unpublished chapter about Alexander Israel, "The Traitor," prepared for Michael Bar-Zohar's book *Spies in the Promised Land*
Interviews with Isser Harel, Amos Manor, Rafi Eitan, Raphi Medan, Alexander Israel's family members and friends (anonymously)
Michael Bar-Zohar, "The First Kidnapping by the Mossad," *Anashim* (People Magazine), 19–15, April 1997 (no. 14) (H)

CHAPTER 5: "OH, THAT? IT'S KHRUSHCHEV'S SPEECH ..."

Interviews with Victor Grayevski, Amos Manor, Isser Harel, Yaacov Caroz
Khrushchev, Nikita, *The Secret Speech—on the Cult of Personality*, Fordham University, Modern History Sourcebook
"The Day Khrushchev Denounced Stalin," John Rettie, BBC, February 18, 2006
"Khrushchev's War with Stalin's Ghost," William Henry Chamberlin, *Russian Review*, vol. 21, no. 1, 1962
"Dreams into Lightning: Victor Grayevski," Michael Ledeen, asher813typepad.com/dreams_into_lightning/2007/11/victor-grayevski.html, November 5, 2007
"The Man Who Began the End of the Soviet Empire," Abraham Rabinovich, *Australian*, October 27, 2007
Victor Grayevski, Telegraph.co.uk, November 1, 2007
"The Secret About Khrushchev's Speech," Tom Perfit, *Guardian*, as quoted in *Harretz*, February 27, 2006 (H)

Shimron, Gad, *The Mossad and The Myth* (Jerusalem: Keter, 2002) (H)

"There Is a Speech of Khrushchev from the Congress," Yossi Melman, *Haaretz*, March 10, 2006 (H)

"Our Man in the KGB," Yossi Melman, *Haaretz*, September 22, 2006 (H)

Total change (turnabout) in broadcasting with the entrance of Victor Grayevski, Kol Israel, (H), www.iba.org.il/ kolisrael70

CHAPTER 6: "BRING EICHMANN DEAD OR ALIVE!"

Chapters based on interviews and papers of Isser Harel that were censored and not included in Michael Bar-Zohar's book *Spies in the Promised Land* but released in *Yedioth Ahronoth* in 1970, and in Michael Bar-Zohar's book *Day of Reckoning* (Tepper, 1991) (H)

Harel, Isser, *The House on Garibaldi Street* (Maariv, 1975) (H)

Bascomb, Neal, *Hunting Eichmann* (Tel Aviv: Miskal Books, Yedioth Ahronoth, 2010) (H)

Malkin, Peter Z., *Eichmann in My Hands* (Tel Aviv: Revivim, 1983) (H)

"Myth in Operation, the Capture of Adolf Eichmann," Avner Avrahami, *Haaretz*, May 7, 2010 (H)

"The Man with the Syringe," Dr. Yona Elian, Etty Abramov, *Yedioth Ahronoth*, May 13, 2010 (H)

"The Age and the Trick (Rafi Eitan)," Yael Gvirtz, *Yedioth Ahronoth*, March 31, 2006 (H)

"Zvi Malkin: The Man Who Captured Eichmann," Eli Tavor, *Yedioth Ahronoth*, March 15, 1989 (H)

"Fifty Years After Adolf Eichmann's Capture and Transfer to Israel, His Abductors Dispel Some Myths About the Operation and Tell How They Felt When the Top Nazi Was in Their Hands," Avner Avrahami, *Haaretz*, May 8, 2010 (H)

"Yehudith Nessyahu Is Dina Ron, the Woman Who Kidnapped Eichmann," Uri Blau, *Haaretz*, September 19, 2008 (H)

The operation to capture Adolf Eichmann—Official publication of the Shabak and the Mossad, 1960 (H)

"Peter Zvi Malkin, Israeli Agent Who Captured Adolf Eichmann, Dies," Margalit Fox, *New York Times*, March 3, 2005

"Mother, I Captured Eichmann," Michal Daniel, YNET, May 27, 2003 (H)

"A Prickly Souvenir," Etty Abramov, *Yedioth Ahronoth*, June 24, 2011(H)

CHAPTER 7: "WHERE IS YOSSELE?"

Harel, Isser, *Operation Yossele* (Tel Aviv: Idanim, 1983) (H)

Interviews with Isser Harel, Ya'acov Caroz, Amos Manor

"The Convert from Neturei Karta," Yair Etinger, *Haaretz*, July 9, 2010 (H)

"For Them, He Remained Yossele: 45 Years After the Operation, the Fighters Did Not Forget Those Days," Eyal Levi, Maariv NRG, October 18, 2005 (H)

CHAPTER 8: A NAZI HERO AT THE SERVICE OF THE MOSSAD

Interviews with Haim Israeli, Rafi Eitan, Raphi Medan, Isser Harel, Meir Amit, Amos Manor, Wernher von Braun

Trial of Otto Skorzeny and others, General Military Government Court of the US Zone of Germany, August 18–September 9, 1947, a British intelligence file

"The Liquidation of a German Scientist in the '60s," Shlomo Nakdimon, Moshe Ronen, *Yedioth Ahronoth*, January 13, 2010 (H)

Harel, Isser, *The German Scientists Affair 1962–1963* (Tel Aviv: Maariv, 1982) (H)

Bar-Zohar, Michel, *La Chasse aux Savants Allemands* (Paris: Fayard, 1965)

Bar-Zohar, Michael, *Shimon Peres: The Biography* (New York: Random House, 2007)

CHAPTER 9: OUR MAN IN DAMASCUS

Interviews with Elie Cohen's family; brothers and wife; Jacques Mercier

Segev, Shmuel, *Alone in Damascus: The Life and Death of Eli Cohen* (Jerusalem: Keter, 1986) (H)

"Eli Cohen," a series of articles by Michael Bar-Zohar, *Haaretz*, September 1967 (H)

"The Daughter of the Spy Eli Cohen Opens Up All Her Wounds," Jacky Hugi, *Maariv*, October 14, 2008 (H)

CHAPTER 10: "I WANT A MIG-21!"

Interviews with Meir Amit, Ezer Weizman

Amit, Meir, *Head to Head, Maariv* (Or Yehuda, Hed-Arzi, 1999) (H)

Nakdimon, Shlomo, *The Hope that Collapsed: The Israeli–Kurdish Connection 1963–1975* (Tel Aviv: Miskal, 1966) (H)

The Jewel in the Crown, Yael Bar, Lior Estline, Israel Air-Force Internet site (H)

"Broken Wings," Sara Leibovitz-Dar, NRG, *Maariv*, June 2, 2007 (H)

CHAPTER 11: THOSE WHO'LL NEVER FORGET

Interviews with "Anton Kunzle," Menahem Barabash

"Kunzle, Anton" and Shimron Gad, *The Death of the Butcher of Riga* (Jerusalem: Keter, 1997) (H)

Bar-Zohar Michel, *Les Vengeurs* (Paris: Fayard, 1968)

"Menaham Barabash, a Former Lehi Member and One of the Killers of the Butcher of Riga: An Obituary," Uri Dromi, *Haaretz*, October 18, 2006 (H)

"Still from the Same Village," Mika Adler, *Israel Today*, April 16, 2010 (H)

"Critical Mishap in Paraguay," Aviva Lori, Yossi Melman, *Haaretz*, August 19, 2005 (H)

"The Butcher of Riga Was Kidnapped and Found Dead," news service, *Yedioth Ahronoth*, March 7, 1965 (H)

"A Quick Trial for the Murderers of Cukurs," John Alison, *Yedioth Ahronoth*, March 8, 1965 (H)

"When a Hangman Is Offering You His Gun," Amos Nevo, *Yedioth Ahronoth*, July 25, 1997 (H)

"Grandfather Killed a Nazi," Gad Shimron, *Bamachane*, February 25, 2005 (H)

CHAPTER 12: THE QUEST FOR THE RED PRINCE

Bar-Zohar, Michael, and Eitan Haber, *Massacre in Munich* (Guilford, CT: Lyons Press, 2005), an updated edition of *The Quest for the Red Prince* (London: Weidenfeld and Nicolson, 1983)

Dittel, Wilhelm, *Mossad Agent: Operation Red Prince* (Bitan, 1997) (H)

Tinnin, David B., with Dag Christensen, *Hit Team* (Jerusalem: Edan Books 1977) (H)

Klein, Aharon, *Open Account: Israel's Killing Policy After the Massacre of the Athletes in Munich* (Tel Aviv: Yedioth Ahronoth Books, 2006) (H)

Black, Ian, *Israel's Secrets Wars: A History of Israel's Intelligence Services* (New York: Warner Books, 1991)

Landau, Eli, Uri Dan, and Dennis Eisenberg, *The Mossad* (New York: New American Library, 1977)

Payne, Ronald, *Mossad: Israel's Most Secret Service* (London: Corgi Books, 1991)

"Mike Harari: A Private Citizen or an Israeli Secret Agent?" Nahum Barnea, *Yedioth Ahronoth*, December 13, 1989 (H)

"The Spy Who Loved Me: The Husband of Sylvia Rafael . . . ," Zadok Yechezkeli, *Yedioth Ahronoth*, February 25, 2005 (H)

The Head of the Mossad watched the killing of a terrorist leader in Paris, Washington correspondent, *Yedioth Ahronoth*, July 23, 1976 (H)

"Avner's Liquidation Squad Avenged the Killing of the Athletes in Munich," Yochanan Lahav, *Yedioth Ahronoth*, April 29, 1984 (H)

"Revenge Now," Eitan Haber, *Yedioth Ahronoth*, October 3, 2005 (H)

"The Planner of the Munich Massacre: 'I Do Not Regret It,'" YNET, March 17, 2006 (H)

"Death of Muhamad Uda, One of the Planners of the Munich Massacre," wire services, *Haaretz*, July 3, 2010 (H)

CHAPTER 13: THE SYRIAN VIRGINS

Interviews with Avraham (Zabu) Ben-Zeev, Emanuel Allon, Amnon Gonen, others (anonymously)

"Our Forces in the Heart of Damascus," Gadi Sukenik, *Yedioth Ahronoth*, October 17, 2005 (H)

CHAPTER 14: "TODAY WE'LL BE AT WAR!"

Bar-Joseph, Uri, *The Angel, Ashraf Marwan, The Mossad and the Yom Kippur War* (Or Yehuda, Kinneret-Zmora-Bitan–Dvir, 2010) (H)

Bregman, Aharon, *Israel's Wars 1947–1993* (London: Routledge, 2000)

Bregman, Aharon, *A History of Israel* (London: Palgrave Macmillan, 2002)

Shalev, Arie, *Defeat and Success in Warning: The Intelligence Assessment Before the Yom Kippur War*, Maarachot, Ministry of Defense Publications, 2006 (H)

Bar-Joseph, Uri, *The Watchman Who Fell Asleep: The Yom Kippur Surprise* (Zmora-Bitan, Or Yehuda, 2001) (H)

Haber, Eitan, *Today We'll Be at War!* (Tel Aviv: Yedioth Ahronoth, 1987) (H)

Zeira, Eli, *Myth Against Reality: The Yom Kippur War* (Tel Aviv: Yedioth Ahronoth, 1993, new edition 2004) (H)

Landau, Eli, Eli Tavor, Hezi Carmel, Eitan Haber, Yeshayahu Ben-Porat, Jonathan Gefen, and Uri Dan, *The Mishap*, Special edition, Tel-Aviv 1973 (H)

"Meeting the Mossad—Ira Rosen Meets the Former Head of One of the World's Top Spy Agencies," CBS, *60 Minutes*, May 12, 2009

"Dead 'Mossad Spy' Was Writing Exposé," Uzi Mahanaymi, *Sunday Times*, June 1, 2007

"Who Killed Ashraf Marwan," Howard Blum, *New York Times*, July 13, 2007

"Was the Perfect Spy a Double Agent?" CBS, *60 Minutes*, May 10, 2009

"Thirty Years after the Yom Kippur War, Top Secret Is Exposed by Israeli Historian Aharon Bregman," Yossi Melman, August 19, 2003 www.freedomwriter.com/issue 28

"One Dead Israeli Spy, Two Theories of Double Loyalty, Three Explanations of How He Died, Four Suspects: Too Many Unanswered Questions," *Huffington Post*, Haggai Carmon, July 14, 2010

"Revealing the Source," Abraham Rabinovich, *Jerusalem Post*, May 7, 2007

"Billionaire Spy Death Remains a Mystery," Andrew Hosken, *BBC Today*, July 15, 2010 (about his connections with the British and Italian secret services)

"Elite Detectives Called in to Probe Spy's Fatal Fall," Rajeev Syal, *New Zealand Herald*, October 6, 2008

"Inquest: Egyptian Spy Suspect's Death Unexplained," *New York Times*, Associated Press, July 14, 2010

"Who Caused the Death of the Spy?" Yossi Melman, *Haaretz*, May 28, 2010 (H)

"Shabak Investigation: Did Eli Zeira Reveal State Secrets," Efrat Weiss, YNET, July 17, 2008 (H)

"The Nightingale's Song," Moshe Gorali, *Maariv*, June 13, 2007 (H)

"Low Probability: How a Legend Was Born," Eli Zeira, *Yedioth Ahronoth*, December 11, 2009 (H)

"They Tricked Us," Ron Ben Ishai, *Yedioth Ahronoth*, September 29, 1998 (H)

"Zamir: Zeira Should Take His Words Back or Publish the Recording," Amir Rappaport, *Yedioth Ahronoth*, October 2, 1998 (H)

"In Modest Manner You Carried Out Hard and Daring Operations: Prime Minister to Zvi Zamir on His Retirement," Eitan Haber, *Yedioth Ahronoth*, September 2, 1974 (H)

"Indictment Will Be Issued in Rome Against Former Head of the Mossad Zvi Zamir," Yossi Bar, *Yedioth Ahronoth*, February 26, 1989 (H)

"12 Days Before Yom Kippur Golda Got Personal Information: Egypt and Syria Are Planning War," Shlomo Nakdimon, *Yedioth Ahronoth*, October 8, 1989 (H)

"Former Italian Head of Intelligence: There Is No Proof that the Mossad Blew Up the Aircraft," Yossi Bar, *Yedioth Ahronoth*, February 15, 1989 (H)

"Former Head of the Mossad Was Tried and Acquitted in Italy," Yossi Bar, *Yedioth Ahronoth*, December 19, 1999 (H)

"Transcript of the Conversation Between Eli Zeira and Zvi Zamir," Rami Tal, *Yedioth Ahronoth*, October 23, 1998 (H)

"Aman Was Mistaken in Evaluating the Enemy's Intentions, and I Am Responsible," Eli Zeira, *Yedioth Ahronoth*, October 24, 2003 (H)

"The Mossad Alert About the Imminent Eruption of War Did Not Get to the Chief of Staff," Zvi Zamir, *Yedioth Ahronoth*, November 24, 1989 (H)

"Deep Throat Denies," Yossi Melman, *Haaretz*, January 16, 2003 (H)

"This Is Not the Same State (Zvi Zamir)," Etty Abramov, *Yedioth Ahronoth*, March 29, 2007 (H)

"Suspicion: The Spy Was Thrown from His Apartment's Balcony," Modi Kreitman and Smadar Perry, *Yedioth Ahronoth*, June 28, 2007 (H)

"The Betrayed," Nadav Ze'evi, *Maariv*, December 28, 2007 (H)

"What Do We Know About the Mysterious Death of Dr. Ashraf Marwan, the Agent Who Warned Us," Yossi Melman, *Haaretz*, May 28, 2010 (H)

"Egyptian Double Agent in the Mossad (Excerpts from Aharon Bregman's Book)," Rami Tal, *Yedioth Ahronoth*, May 9, 2000 (H)

"How a Relative of Nasser Deceived Israel," Aharon Bregman, *Yedioth Ahronoth*, September 15, 2002 (H)

CHAPTER 15: A HONEY TRAP FOR THE ATOM SPY

"Vanunu Leaked Information 'to Prevent a Second Holocaust,'" Nana News, April 30, 2004 (H)

"About the Protocols of the Vanunu Trial," Yossi Melman, *Haaretz*, November 25, 1999 (H)

"The Story of Vanunu's Capture Is Published This Morning in Israel," *Yedioth Ahronoth*, March 24, 1995 (H)

"The Life and Times of Cindy, the Mossad Agent Who Tempted Vanunu," Yossi Melman, *Haaretz*, April 7, 1997 (H)

"From Australia to the Temptation by Cindy: How Vanunu Was Kidnapped," Yossi Melman, *Haaretz*, April 21, 2004 (H)

"Friends Speak About Cindy," Zadok Yechezkeli, *Yedioth Ahronoth*, April 8, 1997 (H)

"Machanaymi: She Slammed the Phone on Me Three Times," Naomi Levitzky, *Yedioth Ahronoth*, April 27, 1997 (H)

"The Italian Government Will Continue Investigating the Vanunu Kidnapping," Yochanan Lahav, Yossi Bar, and Roni Shaked, *Yedioth Ahronoth*, January 11, 1987 (H)

"I Was Hijacked in Rome—Wrote Vanunu on His Palm," Zadok Yechezkeli and Gad Lior, *Yedioth Ahronoth*, December 23, 1986 (H)

"Vanunu Was Not the First to Fall in the Trap . . . The Tempting Girls," Ohad Sharav, *Yedioth Ahronoth*, November 17, 1986 (H)

"The Girl Who Tempted Vanunu Is Cheryl Ben-Tov from Nataniya," Yohanan
   Lahav, *Yedioth Ahronoth*, February 21, 1988 (H)
"The Girl Who Tempted Vanunu Lives 18 Years Under His Shadow: Cindy Is
   Afraid," Anat Tal-Shir and Zadok Yechezkeli, *Yedioth Ahronoth*, April 20, 2004 (H)
"The *Sunday Times:* These Are the Atom Secrets of Israel. Under a Neglected Store-
   room, 35 Meters Underground, Atom Bombs Are Being Built," *Yedioth Ahronoth*,
   October 6, 1986 (H)
"He Did It Again," Ron Ben-Ishai, *Yedioth Ahronoth*, November 25, 1999 (H)
"That Is How I Photographed the Nuclear Reactor (Second Part of the Interview
   to the *Sunday Times*)," Modi Kreitman, *Yedioth Ahronoth*, June 6, 2004 (H)
"Mordechai Vanunu: 'There Is No Democracy in Israel,'" Gad Lior, *Yedioth Ahro-
   noth*, June 6, 2004 (H)
"'And Then Entered the Blond Guy Who Kicked and Beat Me.' Vanunu Testifies
   About His Kidnapping in Court," Michal Goldberg, *Yedioth Ahronoth*, Novem-
   ber 24, 1999 (H)
"Cindy from the Vanunu Affair Is Selling Apartments in Florida," *Sunday Times*,
   as quoted in *Yedioth Ahronoth*, April 20, 2004 (H)
"Missing Cindy," Shosh Mula and Wata Awissat, *Yedioth Ahronoth*, September 1,
   2006 (H)
"Mordechai Vanunu: That's How I Was Kidnapped," Shlomo Nakdimon and Tova
   Zimuki, *Yedioth Ahronoth*, January 24, 1997 (H)
"I Told Vanunu: Beware of Cindy," Michal Goldberg, *Yedioth Ahronoth*, November 24,
   1999 (H)

CHAPTER 16: SADDAM'S SUPERGUN
THE RISE AND FALL OF GERALD BULL

"Project Babylon: Gerald Bull's Downfall," Anthony Kendall, www.DamnInter-
   esting, February 16, 2007
"The Man Behind Iraq's Supergun," Kevin Toolis, *New York Times*, August 26, 1990
"The Paris Guns of World War One," Christopher Eger, Military History @ Suite 101,
   July 23, 2006
"Shades of Supergun Evoke Hussein's Thirst for Arms," James Glanz, *New York
   Times*, September 10, 2006
"Murdered by the Mossad," Canadian Broadcasting Corporation, February 2, 1991
"Who Killed Gerald Bull," Barbara Frum, (Video) Canadian Broadcasting Corpo-
   ration, http://archives.cbc.ca, April 5, 1990

THE KILLINGS OF WADIA HADDAD AND FATHI SHAQAQI

"Poisoned Mossad Chocolate Killed PFLP Leader in 1977, Says Book," *Middle East Times*, May 5, 2006

"Interview with a Fanatic," Lara Marlowe, *Time*, February 6, 1995

"Mossad's License to Kill," Gordon Thomas, *Telegraph*, February 17, 2010

"Islamic Jihad Betrayed by Mossad's Spy," Patrick Cockburn, *Independent*, March 21, 1996

Cordesman, Anthony H., *Escalating to Nowhere: The Israeli-Palestinian War—The Palestinian Factions That Challenge Peace and the Palestinian Authority*, Center for Strategic and International Studies, Washington, D.C., April 3, 2005

"Arafat's Murder Was Foiled by Malta Killing," Patrick Cockburn and Safa Haeri, *Independent*, December 7, 1995

"*Der Spiegel*: That's How Shaqaqi Was Killed," Tomer Sharon, *Yedioth Ahronoth*, November 5, 1995 (H)

"The Mossad Liquidated the Leader of the Jihad," Smadar Perry, Roni Shaked, and David Regev, *Yedioth Ahronoth*, October 29, 1995 (H)

"Five Bullets in the Head, from Zero Range in a Crowded Street," Yossi Bar and Smadar Perry, *Yedioth Ahronoth*, October 29, 1995 (H)

"A Search for a Frenchman Who Brought the Motorcycle," Alex Fishman and Yossi Bar, *Yedioth Ahronoth*, October 31, 1995 (H)

"The Head of the Mossad Supervised the Operation from a Boat Near Malta," Israel Tomer, *Yedioth Ahronoth*, November 5, 1995 (H)

"The Assassination in Malta: The Professional Skills of the Agents vis-à-vis the Negligence of Shaqaqi. No Bullets Were Found at the Killing Location. The Motorcycle Was Brought Especially to the Island," Yossi Melman, *Haaretz*, October 30, 1995 (H)

"Sometimes a Small Organization Cannot Recover," Yossi Melman, *Haaretz*, October 30, 1995 (H)

"With a Gun, Explosive, Poison, Without Asking Questions," Yossi Melman, *Haaretz*, March 17, 1998 (H)

"*Der Spiegel*: Rabin Ordered the Killing of Shaqaqi," Akiva Eldar, *Haaretz*, November 5, 1995 (H)

"5 Shots in Malta," Yitzhak Letz, *Globes*, April 15, 2001 (H)

"Despite the Iranian Financing, the Islamic Jihad Is Falling Apart Since the Murder of Shaqaqi," Guy Bechor, *Haaretz*, October 14, 1996

CHAPTER 17: FIASCO IN AMMAN

Yatom, Danny, *Secret Sharer: From Sayeret Matkal to the Mossad* (Tel Aviv: Yedioth Ahronoth, 2009) (H)

"Back to the Scene of the Crime," Yossi Melman, *Haaretz*, September 26, 2007 (10th anniversary of the fiasco) (H)

"The Mossad Affair (Mash'al): A Full Recapture of the Events," Anat Tal-Shir; "Netanyahu Will Bury the Head of the Mossad Slowly but Sophisticatedly," Nahum Barnea; "Breaking News: The Jordanians Threatened to Break into the Embassy in Amman. Israel Was Forced to Hand the Secret Formula of the Chemical Weapon," Shimon Shiffer; "Hussein Demands That the Mossad Fire All the People Involved in the Affair, or No Israeli Intelligence Agents Will Be Allowed into Jordan," Smadar Perry; "Due to Previous Successes, the Mossad Developed the Notion That Such an Operation Is Foolproof," Ron Ben-Ishai; "Danny Yatom Was Left Alone; Now Everybody Is Turning Their Backs on Him," Ariela Ringel Hoffman and Guy Leshem; "The Rivalry Between the Intelligence Agencies Is Oozing to the Lower Levels; Senior Security Official: 'If It Doesn't Stop Immediately We'll Pay Dearly,'" Alex Fishman—*Yedioth Ahronoth*, special edition, October 10, 1997 (H)

CHAPTER 18: FROM NORTH KOREA WITH LOVE

September 6, 2007, airstrike, Globalsecurity.org, October 29, 2007

"The Attack on Syria's Al-Kibar Nuclear Facility," Daveed Gartenstein-Ross and Joshua D. Goodman, Spring 2009, http://www.jewishpolicycenter.org

"Israel Struck Syrian Nuclear Project, Analysts Say," David E. Sanger and Mark Mazzetti, *New York Times*, October 14, 2007

"Report: Iran Financed Syrian Nuke Plans—Tip from Defector Said to Lead to Israeli Strike on Suspected Reactor in '07," Associated Press, March 19, 2009

"Former Iranian Defense Official Talks to Western Intelligence," Daphna Linzer, *Washington Post*, March 8, 2007

"Israelis Blew Apart Syrian Cache," Uzi Mahanaymi, Sarah Baxter, and Michael Sheridan, *Sunday Times*, September 16, 2007

"Snatched: Israeli Commandos Nuclear Raid," Uzi Mahanaymi, Sarah Baxter, and Michael Sheridan, *Sunday Times*, September 23, 2007

"How Israel Destroyed Syria's Al-Kibar Nuclear Reactor," Erich Follath and Holger Stark, Spiegel.de, February 11, 2009

Background Briefing with Senior U.S. Intelligence Officials on Syria's Covert Nuclear Reactor and North Korea's Involvement, Council of Foreign Relations, www.cfr. org, April 24, 2008

"The Mossad Planned to Sink a Syrian Freighter with Missiles from Korea: A Chapter from the Book *The Volunteer: A Biography of a Mossad Agent,*" Michael Ross and Jonathan Kay, *Yedioth Ahronoth,* September 12, 2007 (H)

"Report: Syria and North Korea Are Building Together a Nuclear Site," Yitzhak Ben-Horin, *Yedioth Ahronoth,* September 13, 2007 (H)

"That Is How a Syrian Nuclear Project Grew Under Our Nose," Amir Rappaport, *Maariv,* November 2, 2007 (H)

"The Syrian Nuclear Reactor Was Attacked Weeks Before It Became Operative," Yitzhak Ben-Horin, *Yedioth Ahronoth,* April 24, 2008 (H)

"Report: A Commando Unit Landed in Syria a Month Before the Nuclear Reactor Was Bombed," Yossi Melman, *Haaretz,* March 19, 2009 (H)

"Report: An Iraqi Defector Uncovered the Syrian Nuclear Reactor—Reveals a Swiss Newspaper," Amit Valdman, News 2, Mako, March 19, 2009 (H)

"Bush: The Revelations About the Bombing of the Nuclear Reactor in Syria: A Message to Tehran," *Haaretz,* April 29, 2008 (H)

"Exclusive: YNET's Envoy at the Operation Site in Syria," Ron Ben-Ishai, YNET, September 26, 2007 (H)

"The Syrian Nuclear Plan," Tzava Ubitachon, Dr. Yochai Sela, The Mideast Forum, September 15, 2007 (H)

"North Korea Assists the Syrians in the Nuclear Field," Walla, based on the *Washington Post,* September 13, 2007 (H)

"Sayeret Matkal Operated in Syria Prior to the Attack," *Yedioth Ahronoth,* September 23, 2007 (H)

"North Korean Scientists May Have Been Killed in Syria," Yaniv Halili, *Yedioth Ahronoth,* September 18, 2007 (H)

"That Is How the 'Agriculture Compound' Was Bombed," Gad Shimron, *Maariv,* September 16, 2007 (H)

"Aman Chief: Israel Recovered Its Deterrence Capacity," Yuval Azulay and Barak Ravid, *Yedioth Ahronoth,* September 17, 2007 (H)

"North Korea for the Sake of Assad," Smadar Perry and Orly Azulay, *Yedioth Ahronoth,* September 23, 2007 (H)

"Sayeret Matkal Collected Nuclear Samples in Syria," *Yedioth Ahronoth,* September 23, 2007 (H)

"Israel Had an Agent in the Syrian Nuclear Reactor," Orly Azulay, *Yedioth Ahronoth*, October 21, 2007 (H)

"Who Is Assisting Damascus in Upgrading Its Falling Nuclear Program?" Yossi Melman, *Haaretz*, September 16, 2007 (H)

"Israel Made the U.S. Understand," Yossi Melman, *Haaretz*, April 27, 2008 (H)

"Report: Enriched Uranium in the Nuclear Site That Israel Bombed," Yossi Melman, *Haaretz*, November 11, 2008 (H)

"Report: Israel Had a Mole in the Syrian Reactor," YNET, October 20, 2007 (H)

Report: The Compound Which Was Bombed in Syria Was the Building Site of a Nuclear Reactor. The *New York Times:* The Reactor Was Not in an Advanced Stage and Was Being Built According to a North Korean Design, October 14, 2007

ABC: Israel Sent an Agent to the Syrian Reactor, or Recruited One of Its Workers, October 21, 2007

"Satellite Pictures Show: The Syrian Compound Which Was Bombed Had Been Built Six Years Ago," William Broad and Mark Mazzetti, *New York Times* as quoted in *Haaretz*, October 28, 2007 (H)

"Iran Financed the Building of the Nuclear Reactor That Was Bombed in Syria," Yossi Melman, *Haaretz*, March 20, 2009 (H)

"The Iranian Officer Who Defected to the U.S. Caused the Attack on the Syrian Reactor," News 10, news.nana10.co.il, March 19, 2009 (H)

"Report: The Iranian General Emigrated to the U.S.," Yoni Mendel, Walla, http://news.walla.co.il, February 6, 2007 (H)

"Sayeret Matkal Brought Earth Samples and Bush Authorized the Bombing in the North of Syria," Inyan Merkazi, News-israel.net, May 10, 2010 (H)

"Report: A Commando Unit Landed in Syria a Month Before the Reactor Was Bombed," Yossi Melman, *Haaretz*, March 19, 2009 (H)

"Iran to Assad: We'll Assist as Much as Needed," Yoav Stern, *Haaretz*, September 7, 2007 (H)

"The Airplanes Incident: Embarrassed Damascus," Guy Bechor, Gplanet.co.il, September 15, 2007 (H)

"Between the Lines," Prof. Eyal Zisser, news.nana10. co.il, November 15, 2010 (H)

"Bush: Olmert Asked Me to Bomb the Syrian Reactor," NRG News, November 6, 2010 (H)

"The Attack on the Reactor: That's How It Happened," Eli Brandstein, *Maariv*, November 8, 2010 (H)

"Who's Afraid of Syria," Ben Caspit, NRG Maariv, November 7, 2010 (H)

George W. Bush, *Decision Points* (New York: Crown, 2010)

THE DEATH OF GENERAL SULEIMAN

"Syrian General's Killing Severs Hezbollah Links," Nicholas Blandford and James Hider, TimesOnline.com, August 6, 2008

"General Muhammad Suleiman Buried in Syria," cafe-syria.com/syrianews/2706. aspx, August 10, 2008

"Mystery Shrouds Assassination of Syria's Top Security Adviser," Manal Lutfi and Nazer Majli, *Asharq El-Awsat*, August 5, 2008

"Slain Syrian Aide Supplied Missiles to Hezbollah," Uzi Mahanaymi, *Sunday Times*, August 10, 2008

"Meir Dagan: The Mastermind Behind Mossad's Secret War," Uzi Mahanaymi, *Sunday Times*, February 21, 2010

"The Mystery Behind a Syrian Murder," Nicholas Blanford, *Time*, August 7, 2008

"There Was Total Silence," Lilit Wanger, *Yedioth Ahronoth*, June 7, 2010 (H)

"Commendation of the Long Arm," Yossi Yehoshua, *Yedioth Ahronoth*, June 22, 2010 (H) (*Sunday Times*: "The Naval Commando Liquidated Muhammad Suleiman Two Years Ago")

"The End of the Secret Adviser of the Syrian President," Jacky Huggi, *Maariv*, August 4, 2008 (H)

"The Hezbollah Member Who Was Liquidated Was Nicknamed in Israel 'the Syrian Mughniyeh,'" Barak Rabin and Yoav Stern, *Haaretz*, August 4, 2008 (H)

"Death of the North Korean Builder and Security Officer of the Syrian Reactor," Debka Internet site, August 9, 2008 (H)

"Wikileaks: Syria Believes Israel Killed Top Assad Aide," Lahav Harkov, *Jerusalem Post*, December 24, 2010

"Former CIA Director: The Secrecy Around the Attack on the Syrian Reactor Is Unjustified," Amir Oren, *Haaretz*, July 9, 2010 (H)

CHAPTER 19: LOVE AND DEATH IN THE AFTERNOON

"Profile: Imad Mughniyeh," Ian Black, *Guardian*, February 13, 2008

"US Official: World 'Better Place' with Death of Hezbollah Figure," Associated Press, February 13, 2008

"Mossad Most Wanted: A Deadly Vengeance (Imad Mughniyeh)," Gordon Thomas, *Independent*, February 23, 2010

"Commentary: A Clear Message to Nasrallah and the Hezbollah," Amir Oren, *Haaretz*, February 13, 2010 (H)

Hezbollah's report about the liquidation of Mughniyeh, Debka file, February 28, 2008 (H)

"From Argentina to Saudi Arabia, Everybody Was Looking for Mughniyeh," *Yedioth Ahronoth*, February 13, 2008 (H)

"Syria: The Liquidation of Mughniyeh Is a Terrorist Act," Yoav Stern and Yossi Melman, *Haaretz*, 13.2.2008 (H)

"The Terror Attacks That Put Mughniyeh on the Map," Yossi Melman, *Haaretz*, February 13, 2008 (H)

"The Retaliation for the Killing of Mughniyeh Is a Question of Time," Roy Nachmias, *Yedioth Ahronoth*, June 30, 2008 (H)

"Commentary: He Was Higher on the Wanted List Than Nasrallah," Yossi Melman, *Haaretz*, February 13, 2008 (H)

"Iran—The Killing of Mughniyeh Is an Example of the Israeli Terror," Dudi Cohen and Roy Nachmias, *Yedioth Ahronoth*, February 13, 2008 (H)

CHAPTER 20: THE CAMERAS WERE ROLLING

"Assassins Had Mahmoud al-Mabhouh in Sight as Soon as He Got to Dubai," Hugh Tomlinson, *Times* (UK), February 17, 2010

"Mahmoud al-Mabhouh Was Sedated Before Being Suffocated, Dubai Police Say," *Times* (UK), March 1, 2010

"Report from the *Sunday Times:* PM Authorized Mabhouh Killing," YNET, February 21, 2010

"Inquiry Grows in Dubai Assassinations," Robert F. Worth, *New York Times*, February 24, 2010

"Britain's Prime Minister Ordered the Investigation of the Forged Passports; the Israeli Ambassador Was Summoned for a Clarification," Barak Ravid and Dana Herman, *Haaretz*, February 18, 2010 (H)

"The Result Test: Not a Failure, Great Achievement," Eitan Haber, *Yedioth Ahronoth*, February 18, 2010 (H)

"The Hit Team Visited Dubai 3 Times," Smadar Perry, *Yedioth Ahronoth*, February 19, 2010 (H)

"The Last Liquidation of This Kind; There Will Not Be Many More Like This One," Yossi Melman, *Haaretz*, February 19, 2010 (H)

"Netanyahu to the Hit Team: The People of Israel Trust You, Good Luck," *Yedioth Ahronoth*, February 21, 2010 (H)

"Gail Is Checking Out (from the Hotel)," Noam Barkan and Benjamin Tubias, *Yedioth Ahronoth*, February 22, 2010 (H)

"Dubai Exposed 15 More Agents; Ten of Them Have Names of Israeli Citizens," *Haaretz*, February 25, 2010 (H)

"The Liquidation in Dubai: 8 Israelis Carrying Forged Passports Will Be Called to Testify by British Investigators," Modi Kreitman, Zvi Zinger, and Eitan Glickman, *Yedioth Ahronoth*, February 28, 2010 (H)

"The Israeli Ambassador in Australia Was Summoned for Clarification," Dana Herman and Barak Ravid, *Haaretz*, February 25, 2010 (H)

"London Does Not Await the Mossad," Itamar Eichner, *Yedioth Ahronoth*, May 4, 2010 (H)

"Australian Intelligence Report: The Mossad Is Responsible for the Forgery," *Yedioth Ahronoth*, May 25, 2010 (H)

"Forged Passports: An Israeli Diplomat Was Expelled from Ireland," Modi Kreitman and Itamar Eichner, *Yedioth Ahronoth*, June 16, 2010 (H)

"The Killers of the Hamas High Official Are Listed on the 'Wanted' List of the Interpol," Avi Issacharov and Dana Herman, *Haaretz*, February 19, 2010 (H)

"Did Not Withstand the Temptation—A Foreign Woman Is Suspected to Have Made Him Open the Door," Smadar Perry and Roni Shaked, *Yedioth Ahronoth*, February 1, 2010 (H)

"Dubai Presents the Hit Men, That's How He Was Killed, a Woman Agent at the Door," Smadar Perry, *Yedioth Ahronoth*, February 16, 2010 (H)

"'Thank God I Know to Take Precautions,' Mabhouh in an Interview to Al-Jazeera," Smadar Perry, *Yedioth Ahronoth*, February 12, 2010 (H)

"A Dubai Hug—Portrait of Dhahi Khalfan," Smadar Perry, *Yedioth Ahronoth*, March 5, 2010 (H)

"Report: Germany Issued a Warrant for the Arrest of a Suspect in Assisting the Attack in Dubai," Ofer Aderet and Yossi Melman, *Haaretz*, January 16, 2011 (H)

"The 'Mossad Agent' Fined 60,000 Euros in Germany Is Uri Brodsky, Accused of Involvement in the Liquidation of Mabhouh," Eldad Beck, *Yedioth Ahronoth*, January 16, 2011 (H)

"The Man Killed—'A Hamas High Official,' " Smadar Perry, wire services, *Yedioth Ahronoth*, April 7, 2011 (H)

"Dubai Police Allege Assassination Team in Hamas Commander's Slaying Used Credit Cards Issued by Iowa Bank," John McGlothlen, News Hawk, Statewide News, February 24, 2010

"Dubai Police Release New Suspects in Hit Squad Killing," Simon McGregor-Wood, Vic Walter, and Lara Setrakian, ABC News Dubai, February 10, 2010

Payonneer. Com, Elance case study www.payoneer.com/CS.Elance.aspx

"Israel Attacked in Sudan," Yossi Yehoshua, *Yedioth Ahronoth*, April 6, 2011 (H)

Israel Attacked in Sudan, Smadar Perry, *Yedioth Ahronoth*, April 7, 2011 (H)

"Sudan to File a Complaint Against Israel to the UN Over the Air Strike," Al-jazeera.net, April 7, 2011

"Israel Attacked in Sudan to Prevent Arms Smuggling to Gaza," Nile_tv_international.net, April 20, 2011

CHAPTER 21: FROM THE LAND OF THE QUEEN OF SHEBA

Of the many sources for this chapter, the most helpful has been the book by Shimron, Gad: *Bring Me the Jews of Ethiopia, How the Mossad Brought the Ethiopian Jews from Sudan* (Or Yehuda: *Maariv* (Hed Arzi), 1988) (H)

The History of the Ethiopian Jews, Jewish Virtual Library, jewishvirtuallibrary.org

"Israel to Speed Immigration for Jews in Ethiopia," Greg Myre, *New York Times*, February 1, 2005

"Distant Relations," Uriel Heilman, *Jerusalem Post*, April 8, 2005

Falasha: Exile of the Black Jews of Ethiopia, a documentary film by Simcha Jacobovici, 1983

The Emigration of the Ethiopian Jews, Operation Moses 1984 and Operation Salomon 1991, www.jafi.org.il/ JewishAgency/Hebrew (H)

"Operation Moses," Ainao Freda Sanbato, *Haaretz*, March 11, 2006 (H)

"Then I Said in Hebrew: What Are You Doing Here?" David Shalit, *Haaretz*, May 17, 1996 (the story of Harry Gold) (H)

"The Exodus from Ethiopia," Tudor Perfit, *Yedioth Ahronoth*, October 25, 1985 (H)

"Flotilla 13 on the Sudan Shores," *Yedioth Ahronoth*, March 15, 1994 (H)

"Flotilla 13 Landed in Sudan," Arie Kizel, *Yedioth Ahronoth*, March 18, 1994 (H)

"Last Stop Sudan," Shahar Geinosar, *Yedioth Ahronoth*, June 27, 2003 (H)

"First, Bring Some Samples," Yigal Mosko, *Yedioth Ahronoth*, October 12, 2001 (H)

"Israel Lover," Dani Adino Ababa and Zimbabwe (Mengistu Haile Mariam), *Yedioth Ahronoth*, September 23, 2005 (H)

"Following Me in the Desert," Smadar Shir, *Yedioth Ahronoth*, July 17, 2009 (H)

"In the Prairies of Ethiopia," David Regev, *Yedioth Ahronoth*, March 19, 2010 (the story of David Ben-Uziel) (H)

"Hamasa L'Eretz Israel—The Journey to the Land of Israel": lyrics by Haim Idissis, music by Shlomo Gronich

"25 Years to Operation Moses: Interviews with Emanuel Allon, Gadi Kroll, David Ben-Uziel, and Yonathan Shefa," Nir Dvori, The News, Channel 2, June 15, 2010 (H)

"Operation Solomon—Bring the Ethiopian Jews," Harel and Eran Duvdevani, sky-high.co.il (H)

GENERAL SOURCES
BOOKS IN HEBREW

Edelist, Ran, *The Man Who Rode a Tiger* (Zmora-Bitan, 1995)

Bar-Zohar, Michael, ed., *100 Men and Women of Valor* (Ministry of Defense Publishing House, 2007)

Golan, Aviezer, and Danny Pinkas, *Code Name: The Pearl* (Zmora-Bitan-Modan, 1980)

Golan, Aviezer, *Operation Susanna* (Yedioth Ahronoth, 1990)

Thomas, Gordon, *Gideon's Spies: The Secret History of the Mossad* (Or-Am, 2008)

Gilon, Carmi, *Shin-Beth Between the Schisms* (Tel Aviv: Miskal Yedioth Ahronoth, 2000)

Melman, Yossi, Eitan Haber, *The Spies: Israel's Counter-Espionage Wars* (Tel Aviv: Miskal Yedioth Ahronoth, 2002)

Halevi, Ephraim, *A Man in the Shadows* (Matar, 2006)

Westerby, Gerald, *A Mossad Agent in Hostile Territory* (Matar, 1988)

Melman, Yossi, ed., *Report of the CIA on the Israeli Intelligence Services* (Tel Aviv: Zmora-Bitan, 1982)

Amidror, Yaacov, *Intelligence from Theory to Practice* (Ministry of Defense Publications, 2006)

Fine, Ronald, *The Mossad* (Or-Am, 1991)

Kimche, David, *The Last Option* (Miskal Yedioth Ahronoth, 1991)

Sagi, Uri, and Rami Tal, eds., *Lights in the Fog* (Yedioth Ahronoth, 1998)

Shimron, Gad, *The Mossad and the Myth* (Jerusalem: Keter, 2002)

BOOKS IN ENGLISH

Posner Steve, *Israel Undercover: Secret Warfare and Hidden Diplomacy in the Middle East* (Syracuse, New York: Syracuse University Press, 1987)

Raviv, Dan, and Yossi Melman, *Every Spy a Prince: The Complete History of the Israeli Intelligence Community* (Boston: Houghton Mifflin, 1990)

Landau, Eli, Uri Dan, and Dennis Eisenberg, *The Mossad* (New York: Paddington Press, 1978)

Bar-Zohar, Michael, *Spies in the Promised Land* (Boston: Houghton Mifflin, 1972)

BOOKS IN FRENCH

Dan, Uri, *Mossad: 50 Ans de guerre secrete* (Paris: Presses de la Cite, 1995)

Bar-Zohar, Michel, *Les Vengeurs* (Paris: Fayard, 1968)

INTERVIEWS

Isser Harel, Yaa'cov Caroz, Izzi Dorot, Yitzhak Shamir, Amos Manor, Meir Amit, Anton Kunzle, Menachem Barabash, Victor Grayevski, Yitzhak Rabin, Ezer Weizman, Haim Israeli, Dr. Pinhas (Siko) Zusman, Uri Lubrani, Wernher von Braun, Rafi Eitan, Raphi Medan,Yitzhak Sarid, Eli Landau, Hanoch Saar, Avraham (Zabu) Ben-Zeev, Emanuel Allon, Amnon Gonen, Elie Cohen's family, Alexander Israel's family, Ze'ev Avni, and many others who preferred to remain anonymous.

INDEX

Abd el Hir, Hussein, 196, 197

Abrams, Elliott, 285

Abu Abed. *See* Al-Mabhouh, Mahmoud Abdel Rauf

Abu Al-Haul, Ashraf, 24–25

Abu Mussa organization, 263

Abu Seif, Muhammad, 2, 272–73

Adenauer, Konrad, 117, 124

Admoni, Nahum, 245, 249, 327–28

Adwan, Kamal, 200, 202

Aharoni, Zvi, 64–66, 68, 72, 75, 77, 83, 89

Ahituv, Avraham, 113, 126–27

Ahmadinejad, Mahmoud, 9, 11, 23

Air Force, U.S.: exodus of Ethiopian Jews and, 329

Air France plane: Entebbe hijacking of, 260–61, 333–34

Aklum, Fereda, 320–21

Al-Ahram newspaper, 24–25, 237

Al-Din, Zaher, 146–47, 152, 154

Al-Jazeera, 305, 306

Al-Mabhouh, Mahmoud Abdel Rauf ("Plasma Screen", "Abu Abed"): Al-Jazeera interview of, 306; filming of, 307–11, 314, 315; hunt for and killing of, 304–11, 312, 313; Iran and, 304; personal and professional background of, 305; reputation of, 305–6

Al Qaeda, x

"Al Quds" Brigades, 20–21, 298

Aliya Beth organization, 54

Allon, Emanuel (aka "Claudie"), 217, 219–21, 323

Aman (IDF intelligence service): German-Egyptian projects and, 128–29; Lavon Affair and, 132–33; Marwan intelligence and, 234, 237; reputation of, 42; Syrian nuclear program and, 281, 282, 284; Unit 131 of, 135–36, 148; Unit 8200 of, 225, 284; Yom Kippur War and, 225, 226–27. *See also specific person*

Amana, Ben, 205–7

American diplomats; assassination of, 199, 208

Amin, Iddi, 333

Amit, Meir: appointment as Mossad director of, 129, 158; code name for, 161; Cohen case and, 131, 148, 152; Cukurs case and, 173; Diamond Operation/Redfa and, 161, 163, 164, 165, 166–67, 169; German-Egyptian projects and, 128, 129; *Head On* by, 164; Iraqi Kurds and, 160–61; Lavon Affair prisoners and, 169–70; Little Isser and, 130, 157, 158; MiG–21s and,

Gaza: arms smuggling into, 304, 305, 306, 308, 315–16; Dagan military career in, 3; as Israeli possession following Six-Day War, 222; Mossad accomplishments and, 5; Palestinian-Israeli relations in, 1–3; refugee camps in, 3; suicide bombing in, 265

German terrorists: Entebbe attack and, 333–34

Germany: and German scientists in Egypt, 114–30; Israeli relations with, 117, 124, 125, 129; Munich massacre and, 186–87, 189–90, 208, 213; and statute of limitations on war crimes, 172–73, 185. *See also* BND; *specific person*

Gertner family: Yossele case and, 108–9, 111

Gibli, Benyamin, 132–33, 134

girls, Jewish: rescue of, 214–21

Godiva chocolates: Haddad death and, 261–62, 268

Goerke, Heidi, 123, 126

Goerke, Paul, 115, 122–23

Golan Heights, 222–23, 227, 228

Gold, Henry, 322, 325

Goldstein, Wolf. *See* Avni, Ze'ev

Goren, Shmuel, 231–32

Grayevski, Victor, 50–58

Great Britain: Be'eri accusations against, 27; Hushi case and, 27; Iranian nuclear program and, 15, 16, 19; Iraq supergun project and, 259; Israeli relations with, 249, 251, 253; Jewish Commando Corps and, 29; Mossad expulsion from, 314; withdrawal from Egypt of, 132–33. *See also* London, England; MI6

Guerrero, Oscar, 243, 244, 245, 252

Gulf War (1991), 258, 280

Gur-Arie, Israel, 108–9

Gur-Arie, Ze'ev (aka Wolfgang Lutz) "Champagne Spy," 118, 130, 170

Haaretz, 124, 278, 312

Habash, George, 198, 204

Hadar, Avraham "Pashosh" (Thrush), 106

Haddad, Wadie, 260–62, 268

Hadley, Steve, 283, 284, 285

Hafez, Amin el-, 140, 145–46, 148, 151, 153

Haganah, 2, 27, 45. *See also specific person*

Haidar, Nihad, 291, 300–301, 302, 303

Halek, Ahmed, 297–98

Halevy, Efraim, 7, 276–77, 278, 282

Hamas: Al-Mabhouh death and, 311; arms smuggling and, 304–5, 306, 315–16; Dagan and, 24, 25; functions of, 265; Iran and, 304–5, 315–16; Israeli drone attack on leaders of, 315; as Israeli target, 266–68; Mash'al reputation and, 277; Mossad failures and, 6; Palestinian Relief Bureau as cover for, 269; Shalit kidnapping and, 24. *See also* Al-Mabhouh, Mahmoud Abdel Rauf; Mash'al, Khaled

Hamshari, Mahmoud, 195–96, 197

Hanin, Cindy. *See* Ben-Tov, Cheryl (Hanin) (aka Cindy)

Harari, Mike, 191–92, 196, 205–6, 215

Harel, Isser "Little Isser": Amit compared with, 157; Amit as Mossad successor to, 148; Amit relationship with, 130, 158, 160; appointed head of Mossad and Shabak, 37, 42;